Surveillance, Trust, and the New Politics of Digital Marketing

Paula Pinheiro
ISCA, Universidade de Aveiro, Portugal & ESTGV, Instituto Politécnico de Viseu, Portugal & REMIT, Universidade Portucalense, Portugal

Sara Santos
https://orcid.org/0000-0002-3581-6478
CEOS.PP, ISCAP, Polytechnic of Porto, Portugal & NECE-Research Centre for Business Sciences, Portugal & Departamento de Ciências Sociais e Gestão, Universidade Aberta, Portugal

IGI Global
Scientific Publishing
Publishing Tomorrow's Research Today

Vice President of Editorial Melissa Wagner
Director of Acquisitions Mikaela Felty
Director of Book Development Jocelynn Hessler
Production Manager Mike Brehm
Cover Design Jose Rosado

Published in the United States of America by
IGI Global Scientific Publishing
701 East Chocolate Avenue
Hershey, PA, 17033, USA
Tel: 717-533-8845 | Fax: 717-533-7115
Website: https://www.igi-global.com E-mail: cust@igi-global.com

Library of Congress Cataloging-in-Publication Data

Names: Pinheiro, Paula, 1975- editor | Santos, Sara, 1985- editor
Title: Surveillance, trust, and the new politics of digital marketing / [edited by] Paula Pinheiro, Sara Santos.
Description: Hershey, PA : IGI Global Scientific Publishing, [2026] | Includes bibliographical references and index. | Summary: "This book examines how algorithms, AI, and data-driven marketing reshape consumer trust, autonomy, and ethical responsibility. Combining marketing, sociology, and technology studies, it explores surveillance capitalism, platform power, and resistance movements, offering insights into the ethical, social, and political implications of algorithmic influence in the digital marketplace"-- Provided by publisher.
Identifiers: LCCN 2026002971 (print) | LCCN 2026002972 (ebook) | ISBN 9798337377049 hardcover | ISBN 9798337377056 paperback | ISBN 9798337377063 ebook
Subjects: LCSH: Internet marketing | Consumer behavior | Artificial intelligence--Moral and ethical aspects
Classification: LCC HF5415.1265 .S867 2026 (print) | LCC HF5415.1265 (ebook) | DDC 658.8/72--dc23/eng/20260312
LC record available at https://lccn.loc.gov/2026002971
LC ebook record available at https://lccn.loc.gov/2026002972

British Cataloguing in Publication Data
A Cataloguing in Publication record for this book is available from the British Library.

Table of Contents

Detailed Table of Contents

There have been major transformations in the area of digital marketing with the rise of such technologies as the advancement of algorithms in surveillance systems. This paper develops and tests a Political–Behavioural Structural Model, in order to see the impacts of surveillance on trust formation of the digital marketing ecosystem. This study on Surveillance Capitalism and Behavioural Trust Theory includes in our conceptual model perceived digital surveillance, data intrusiveness, algorithmic personalisation, and political manipulation risks, moderated by perceived power asymmetry, privacy concerns, and concerns regarding the workings of the platform. The study uses Partial Least Squares–Structural Equation Modelling on digital consumer data, and surveillance is seen to impact trust directly through political–behaviour mediation, where, for example, transparency as a trust enabler has the highest effect. The study underlined the trust's political aspects in markets driven by surveillance and technology.

This chapter examines surveillance and trust in India's expanding digital marketing landscape from a socio-political perspective. The purpose of this chapter is to analyze how data-driven marketing practices, algorithmic personalization, and artificial intelligence reshape power relations among platforms, brands, the state, and consumers. Drawing on theories of surveillance capitalism, algorithmic governance, and trust, the chapter conceptualizes digital marketing as a form of behavioral governance embedded in everyday digital infrastructures. It explores how marketing surveillance operates through datafication, platform dominance, and opaque algorithms, contributing to trust deficits, privacy concerns, and social inequalities, particularly among vulnerable populations. The chapter also evaluates

As AI-powered chatbots increasingly mediate consumer interactions across e-commerce, retail, and service contexts, understanding their impact on brand loyalty and trust has become a strategic priority for marketing research. This review synthesises 40 empirical and conceptual studies published between 2019 and 2026, retrieved from Scopus and Web of Science, through a narrative thematic synthesis. Findings are organised around four themes: chatbot design and humanisation, trust as the pivotal relational mechanism, customer journey outcomes, and contextual boundary conditions. The analysis resolves key theoretical tensions, notably the warmth-versus-competence debate, by identifying moderating conditions, including product type, consumer motivational orientation, and relationship phase. An integrative conceptual framework, DIAL (Design, Interaction, Accumulation, Loyalty), is proposed to model the temporal dynamics through which chatbot design decisions translate into durable brand loyalty. Implications for marketing theory, managerial practice, and future research are discussed.

This chapter examines how artificial intelligence (AI) strengthens peer-to-peer (P2P) cab aggregators through an integrated 3S framework—service quality, sustainability, and safety—and its impact on brand image, loyalty, and extension acceptance. In decentralized platforms, trust and consistency are critical yet vulnerable. The chapter proposes that AI-driven personalization, predictive analytics, eco-optimization, and fraud detection operationalize the 3S pillars, enhancing reliability, responsibility, and security. A strong AI-enabled 3S foundation reinforces brand image, which mediates loyalty and increases user acceptance of new services such as food delivery or logistics, offering both theoretical and managerial insights.

Nowadays, online advertising, shaped by algorithms and brain-based systems, often shakes trust between users and platforms. Instead of tracking habits, immersive film techniques spark feelings naturally. One idea builds on past research - linking hidden surveillance models with smart recommendations to emotional storytelling impacts. A fresh framework emerges: "Cinematic Trust," where mood and scene matter more than machine learning loops. Looking at movie-style storytelling in ads, like Apple, Nike, or Dove, shows that trust grows when people see real intent behind messages. What matters most is openness, informed consent, and respect for cognitive freedom. Honest storytelling supported by transparency and consumer choice strengthens long-term brand relationships. What stands out is how modest personalisation blends into genuine creative expression. This mix shapes enduring, thoughtful online advertising - where imagination meets responsible choices.

The rapid democratization of health communication through social media has facilitated the global dissemination of public health information while simultaneously escalating the risks associated with digital misinformation. This research employs a dual-methodological approach, comprising a systematic literature review and an empirical survey, to investigate how misinformation influences consumer trust in health content across platforms such as TikTok, YouTube, Instagram, and X. Adhering to the PRISMA framework, the review synthesized 13 relevant articles published between 2022 and 2025, revealing that while professional sources provide superior scientific quality, user-generated content by non-experts achieves higher engagement rates.The findings indicate that users often prioritize emotional resonance, creator relatability, and visual aesthetics over factual accuracy. This study highlights a critical need for platform accountability, enhanced media literacy, and strategic collaborations between healthcare professionals and influencers to restore information integrity.

This chapter examines how culture shapes the design, operation, and effectiveness of customer loyalty programs in a globalized, digitally connected marketplace. Drawing on Social Exchange Theory, Power Distance Theory, and Social Identity Theory, it proposes the 3C Framework of Consumer Cultural Context—Consumer, Culture, and Context—to explain how cultural norms, social values, consumer habits, and global influences affect rewards, engagement, brand voice, user experience, and data practices. Using examples from airlines, retail, and hospitality, the chapter highlights the need for culturally adaptive loyalty strategies and outlines implications for future research on AI, inclusivity, and evolving consumer expectations.

As digital marketing becomes increasingly driven by algorithmic surveillance and behavioral targeting, consumers are developing resistance strategies to regain autonomy and control over their digital experiences. This chapter examines ad blockers, digital detox practices, and de-influencing movements as socio-technical responses to pervasive monitoring, persuasive design, and platform power. By analyzing these resistance strategies through ethical, political, and cultural lenses, the chapter explores how consumer trust, agency, and accountability are being renegotiated in data-driven marketing ecosystems and considers their implications for the future of responsible digital marketing.

Both cognitive–emotional–sensory appeal and perceived credibility are positively associated with restaurant visit intentions.

Preface

INTRODUCTION

In recent years, digital marketing has changed in ways that would have been difficult to imagine only a few decades ago. The field that was once mainly associated with creativity, communication, segmentation, and persuasion is now deeply shaped by data analytics, artificial intelligence, platform infrastructures, and algorithmic decision-making. Brands do not simply communicate with consumers: they observe, interpret, predict, and often try to anticipate their behaviours, preferences, emotions, and decisions.

This transformation has created remarkable opportunities for organizations and marketers. It has allowed for more relevant communication, more personalized experiences, and more efficient interactions between brands and consumers. However, it has also brought with it a set of questions that cannot be ignored. As personalization becomes more precise and predictive, the boundary between understanding consumers and monitoring them becomes increasingly delicate. Behavioural targeting, algorithmic profiling, predictive analytics, and platform-based advertising raise important concerns about autonomy, transparency, fairness, accountability, and trust.

This book, *Surveillance, Trust, and the New Politics of Digital Marketing*, was born from the conviction that digital marketing can no longer be understood only as a technical or managerial field. It is also a social, ethical, cultural, and political space. Behind every recommendation, targeted advertisement, chatbot interaction, influencer post, or personalized message, there are questions about data, power, visibility, consent, and the capacity of consumers to make informed and autonomous choices. These questions are not secondary to marketing. They are now part of its very centre.

As editors, we felt the need to bring together contributions that could help make sense of this changing landscape. We were particularly interested in opening a dialogue between marketing scholarship and broader debates on surveillance, digital ethics, algorithmic governance, platform power, consumer trust, and resistance. The chapters in this volume show that contemporary marketing systems do more than respond to consumer behaviour. They classify, anticipate, guide, and sometimes shape it. This raises important questions about the legitimacy of digital marketing practices and about the responsibilities of brands, platforms, practitioners, regulators, and consumers in a data-driven society.

A central theme running through this volume is the fragile and changing nature of trust. Digital technologies often promise convenience, relevance, efficiency, and personalization. Yet, the systems that make these benefits possible are frequently opaque. Consumers may not fully understand how their data is collected, analysed, shared, monetized, or used to influence what they see and how they decide. This opacity can weaken confidence and create discomfort, particularly when individuals become aware of the extent to which their digital lives are being tracked and interpreted.

At the same time, this book does not approach consumers as passive or powerless. Across different contexts, consumers are also developing ways of responding to the pressures of digital marketing. Ad blocking, digital detox practices, privacy-protective behaviours, and de-influencing movements all suggest that people are trying to regain some control over their attention, data, and choices. These practices remind us that trust is not something that brands can simply demand. It has to be earned, protected, and continuously rebuilt.

The volume also pays attention to the concentration of power within a small number of dominant digital platforms. These platforms increasingly mediate the relationships between brands and consumers, shaping visibility, access, engagement, and market opportunities. This concentration raises important concerns about accountability, governance, fairness, and autonomy. For this reason, the politics of digital marketing cannot be reduced to individual consumer decisions or firm-level strategies. It must also be understood in relation to wider institutional, technological, and societal structures.

The contributions included in this book reflect a multidisciplinary dialogue, drawing from marketing, communication studies, sociology, information ethics, platform studies, and related fields. Together, they offer conceptual frameworks, empirical insights, and critical reflections on the relationship between marketing practices and societal values. Importantly, the chapters do not simply identify risks. They also point to possible paths for more responsible, transparent, inclusive, and ethically grounded forms of digital marketing.

This book is intended for scholars, students, practitioners, policymakers, and all readers interested in understanding the complexities of marketing in the algorithmic age. It may be read as an academic contribution, but also as an invitation to think carefully about the kind of digital marketplace we are building, the kinds of relationships we are encouraging, and the kinds of trust we are willing to defend.

Our hope is that this volume will stimulate further research, encourage critical reflection, and support the development of marketing practices that are not only innovative and effective, but also more ethical, transparent, and worthy of consumer trust.

ORGANIZATION OF THE BOOK

In organizing this volume, we sought to bring together chapters that speak to one another, even when they approach digital marketing from different contexts, methods, and theoretical traditions. The book moves across questions of surveillance, trust, artificial intelligence, personalization, culture, resistance, misinformation, emotional engagement, and sector-specific digital practices. Rather than offering a single narrative, it brings together complementary perspectives on a field that is becoming increasingly powerful, increasingly intimate, and increasingly contested.

The volume opens with "A Political–Behavioural Structural Model of Surveillance in Digital Marketing: Reconstructing Trust in a Data-Driven Society," which proposes a model for understanding how surveillance affects trust in digital marketing ecosystems. By combining political and behavioural dimensions, the chapter examines how data-driven practices, perceived surveillance, power asymmetries, and manipulation risks shape the conditions under which trust may be damaged, negotiated, or reconstructed.

This broader concern with the political and social dimensions of digital marketing is then extended in "Surveillance and Trust in India's Digital Marketing Landscape: A Socio-Political Perspective." By focusing on India's rapidly expanding digital economy, the chapter shows how surveillance and trust are shaped not only by technology, but also by socio-political conditions, platform infrastructures, regulatory challenges, and institutional arrangements. It is a valuable reminder that digital marketing is always situated within particular social, cultural, and political realities.

The ethical implications of automated influence are explored in "AI, Predictive Analytics, and Automated Influence: Ethical Frontiers in Algorithmic Marketing." This contribution examines how artificial intelligence and predictive analytics create new possibilities for targeting, recommendation, and behavioural guidance, while also raising difficult questions about autonomy, transparency, accountability, and the limits of acceptable persuasion.

The discussion then moves to one of the most familiar tensions of contemporary digital life in "Sssh… AI is Listening: Surveillance, Trust, and the Privacy-Personalization Paradox in Social Media Marketing." Consumers often value personalized content, but they may also feel uncomfortable with the data practices that make personalization possible. By focusing on social media marketing, this chapter explores how the privacy-personalization paradox affects trust and consumer perceptions.

Questions of automation and consumer response are further developed in "Applications of AI Chatbots in Marketing and Customers' Response." Here, the focus turns to conversational technologies and their growing presence in customer interactions. The chapter contributes to discussions about automation, service experience, engagement, and the conditions under which technologically mediated interactions can still feel useful, credible, and trustworthy.

Platform-based services receive particular attention in "AI-Driven Personalization and the 3S Framework in P2P Aggregators: Implications for Brand Image, Loyalty, and Extension Acceptance." Through the 3S framework, the chapter considers how AI-driven personalization may influence brand image, loyalty, and acceptance of brand extensions in peer-to-peer aggregator platforms. It highlights the importance of trust, perceived value, and consistency in increasingly platform-mediated service ecosystems.

The volume then opens space for a different, but highly relevant, perspective through "Cinematic Storytelling and Neuromarketing in Digital Marketing: Emotional Engagement, Trust, and Ethics." This chapter explores how cinematic storytelling and neuromarketing can foster emotional engagement and trust, while also raising ethical questions about affective influence, consent, and consumer vulnerability. It invites readers to reflect on the power of emotion in digital marketing and on the responsibilities that come with that power.

The social consequences of digital communication are particularly visible in "The Paradox of Credibility: A Mixed-Methods Study on Consumer Trust and Health Misinformation in the Age of Social Media." Focusing on health-related communication, this chapter examines how credibility, trust, and engagement operate in social media contexts where inaccurate or misleading content may compete with scientifically grounded information. Its mixed-methods approach offers important insights into one of the most consequential challenges of the digital age.

The importance of context is also central to "The Role of Culture in Shaping Loyalty Strategies and Customer Engagement." This chapter places culture at the centre of digital marketing strategy, examining how cultural values and norms influence loyalty, engagement, and the interpretation of brand communication. It reminds us that digital marketing may be global in reach, but it is never culturally neutral.

Consumer agency comes to the fore in "Ad Blockers Digital Detox and De-Influencing as Resistance Strategies." By examining ad blockers, digital detox practices, and de-influencing, this chapter shows how consumers respond to perceived intrusiveness, persuasive pressure, and platform fatigue. These practices reveal that consumers are not merely targets of marketing, but active participants in renegotiating the boundaries of digital influence.

The final part of the volume turns to more applied and sector-specific discussions. "The Importance of Digital Marketing in Non-Professional Sports Organizations" examines the role of digital marketing in organizations that often operate with limited resources but strong community ties. The chapter highlights how digital channels can support visibility, engagement, emotional connection, and stakeholder relationships in non-professional sports contexts, while reinforcing the importance of authenticity and trust.

The book closes with "Comparing Restaurant and Influencer Social Media Posts: Effects on Consumer Perceptions and Visit Intentions," which focuses on social media content in the restaurant sector. By comparing restaurant-generated and influencer-generated posts, the chapter examines how different content sources affect consumer perceptions and visit intentions. It offers practical and theoretical insights into credibility, content strategy, and the influence of social media communication on consumer behaviour.

Together, these contributions show that digital marketing is not moving in a single direction. It is expanding, fragmenting, adapting, and being questioned at the same time. The volume therefore argues that surveillance, trust, power, culture, resistance, and ethics are not marginal concerns. They are central to understanding what digital marketing has become and what it may still become.

CONCLUSION

As this volume demonstrates, digital marketing is no longer merely a set of tools for reaching consumers. It is a deeply embedded socio-technical system that shapes how individuals encounter information, interact with brands, make decisions, and relate to institutions in everyday life. Across the chapters, a shared concern becomes clear: algorithmic infrastructures increasingly mediate not only market exchanges, but also trust, autonomy, visibility, and power.

The contributions in this book show that, in many contemporary digital marketing models, surveillance is no longer simply an unintended consequence. It has become part of the operational logic through which personalization, targeting, prediction, and influence are made possible. Yet this development has not always been accompanied by sufficient ethical reflection, regulatory protection, or transparent governance. As a result, consumers often find themselves in a fragile trust environment, where they may appreciate personalization while also feeling uneasy about the opacity and intrusiveness that sustain it.

At the same time, the volume suggests that trust is not lost once and for all. It is continuously negotiated across technological, cultural, institutional, and relational contexts. Greater transparency, ethical design, responsible AI practices, culturally sensitive strategies, and less intrusive forms of engagement can all contribute to more balanced relationships between brands and consumers. The emergence of resistance practices, from ad blocking to de-influencing, also reminds us that consumers have voices, limits, and strategies of their own.

One of the central messages of this book is that digital marketing is inherently political. Questions of platform power, data governance, algorithmic influence, and consumer autonomy extend far beyond technical decisions or campaign design. They concern the ways in which markets, institutions, and everyday lives are organized in digital societies. For this reason, the future of marketing will depend not only on innovation, but also on dialogue, responsibility, and the willingness to ask difficult questions.

As editors, we see this book as both a reflection of current debates and an invitation to continue them. The issues discussed here are complex, evolving, and unlikely to be resolved by a single discipline or perspective. They require collaboration among scholars, practitioners, policymakers, civil society, and consumers. More than providing final answers, this volume seeks to create space for critical inquiry and for more thoughtful approaches to digital marketing.

Ultimately, the future of digital marketing will be defined not only by what technology allows us to do, but by what society is willing to accept and what ethics asks us to protect. We hope that the insights offered in this collection will contribute to more responsible, inclusive, transparent, and trust-centred marketing practices in the years to come.

Chapter 1
A Political-Behavioural Structural Model of Surveillance in Digital Marketing:
Reconstructing Trust in a Data-Driven Society

Piali Haldar
http://orcid.org/0000-0003-4729-6964
Brainware University, Kolkata, India

Dev Kumar Mandal
http://orcid.org/0009-0005-3740-6885
Brainware University, Kolkata, India

ABSTRACT

There have been major transformations in the area of digital marketing with the rise of such technologies as the advancement of algorithms in surveillance systems. This paper develops and tests a Political–Behavioural Structural Model, in order to see the impacts of surveillance on trust formation of the digital marketing ecosystem. This study on Surveillance Capitalism and Behavioural Trust Theory includes in our conceptual model perceived digital surveillance, data intrusiveness, algorithmic personalisation, and political manipulation risks, moderated by perceived power asymmetry, privacy concerns, and concerns regarding the workings of the platform. The study uses Partial Least Squares–Structural Equation Modelling on digital consumer data, and surveillance is seen to impact trust directly through political–

DOI: 10.4018/979-8-3373-7704-9.ch001

behaviour mediation, where, for example, transparency as a trust enabler has the highest effect. The study underlined the trust's political aspects in markets driven by surveillance and technology.

1. INTRODUCTION

An immense step has taken towards abandoning the old ways of marketing and adjusting to the revolution in digital marketing. This enables companies to understand the consumer more, get data and turn it into hard cash, and also reveals how power is generated and dispersed within the digital business environment. Earlier forms of this type of marketing were about putting up a banner that would contain whatever slogans there were about a product or service. The new form of marketing sends the same advertisement to every user based on their interests that are mostly based on collected data. In such a digital economy, it cannot be emphasized how every step of the consumer journey is kept in check, through cookies, applications in mobile devices, social media channels, IoT devices, and AI-run customization. Despite the obvious benefits related to the increase in effectiveness and marketing potential provided by the latest trends in the advertising strategies, these concerns also appear in the form of deep-seated concerns: realization issues, political manipulations, and the loss of trust by the consumer as an imperative (Zuboff, 2019; Couldry & Mejias, 2019).

It has often been opined that trust is one of the key pillars that buttress the efficiency of any market when trading online or digitally. This is, in most cases, due to ambiguities about market conditions, inequalities in information access, and a high perception of risk in trading (Gefen et al., 2003; Pavlou, 2003). Digital marketing has more importance, but the standard approach to trusting one another also finds its values redefined. In existing literature, trust has been taken as a socio-psychological construct in people's readiness to trust the source of information or a person, depending on reliability, competence, and intentionality dimensions, those features of an online dealer/platform (McKnight et al., 2002). Alternatively, with the advent of more advanced digital marketing practices, the confined concept of trust as a transactional and interpersonal construct has become outdated. The dynamics of such digital platforms are premised on power and economies of scale, in regard to which new-age platforms have the capacity to glean consumer data in unprecedented quantities, analyse it, and even forecast market movements. This different orientation sees trust as not only something that happens between people or is produced by a transaction, but is influenced by structure and power, as in the case of the political dynamics of society.

Digital marketing, based on observations of The Shift from mass to surveillance-based marketing, complements and substantiates the wherewithal of capitalism for surveillance; a State where human essence is purposely modified into vestigial responses, to predict behaviour, commercialize and rule over humans with its technologies (Zuboff, 2019). It is more than likely that this evolutionary stage, with the help of algorithms, interaction processes will be predominant in such a way that there will be some level of expectation concerning the behaviour of the recipient of the services and some impact on the corresponding decision-making based on the fear of missing out or self-interest. These capabilities entail the convergence of marketing, governance, and political communication, especially as those very structures that are designed for purposes of targeting in commerce are also intended for objectives of political persuasion and opinion building (Tufekci, 2015; Susser et al., 2019). At the same time, in light of the developments in the field of information and communication technologies, internet consumers henceforth do not merely see the new media of communication only as tools that offer enhanced services. Rather, consumers are also keen on the extensive use and the wide range of social media as intermediaries, which cannot be disempowered and reoriented, as they are significant agents in activities such as political exertions, thus interfering with the reduction of civil liberty.

The advancement in technology that occurred in the last two decades created the "trust paradox," which is particularly acute in internet advertising. It is a process where consumers increasingly wish to have personalized services, seamless 360-degree customer strategies and benefits, without any downtime in their lives. At the same time, consumers increasingly regard with suspicion the trend of perpetual surveillance going hand in hand with invasive data collection practices and leaning on black-box mechanisms (Martin & Murphy, 2017; Aguirre et al., 2016). Researches report that an exorbitant amount of personalization is often disadvantageous, termed the "creepiness effect" where exp never enhances trust but always aggravates it (Liu et al., 2019). Thus, these reactions confirm that diminished trust is not solely a result of privacy fears but also stems from cognitive notions of the abuse of power and control.

The advancement of these ideas has grown wildly, but many of the already existing works on digital marketing fail to discuss the subject of trust objectively, preferring to view this issue through the prism of behaviour or psychology, relying on the concepts of usefulness, ease of use, and risk. There are many benefits that this perspective may offer. In certain cases, though, neglecting other contributing factors such as power relations within the society or groups and political economy (beyond market and macroeconomic affairs) automatically translates to the development of half-baked lessons. More specifically, how comfort around unequal power distribution extends to the dynamic between the platform and the user, manipulation concerns at the point of micro-targeted advertising, and the need for transparency in trust building often fall outside the scope of the usual development of empirical trust concepts. With increasing platforms' control over consumption and social as well as political activities, failure to account for these influences very much weakens the ability of the existing schemes to explain the prevailing situation.

The use of mathematically based algorithms in the process of governing people, or influencing how politicians themselves act, has been a point of interest in academic circles in the recent past. This kind of focus can usually be attributed to political leaning or to the various forms of media available. Most research dedicated to political communication and critical data studies has it that algorithms help communicate, control, and dominate the media from emerging platforms, and from the people's end (Couldry & Mejias, 2019). More pertinently, it instructs citizens what to buy and how to vote through specific lifestyles that certain economic policies impose. That is how consumers can trust that those images are telling the truth. Despite this, very few. Nonetheless, political systems and the logic embedded within them are still not effectively questioned in the discipline of marketing research.

Another crucial flaw in the available theories is the absence of trust reconstruction. It is shown in the majority of texts that trust is considered a state of conditioned readiness, apart from which customers very seldom occupy under surveillance focus. The aforementioned concept is very dangerous because, to be useful to the digital economy, at least to some extent, it is necessary to earn trust. Trust repair in this context denotes the way people consider, and re-trust platforms after they become aware of surveillance, data use, and targeting that is normatively loaded. This standpoint is shaped not only by the change of the consumers' repertoires, but also by the change in the abilities to provide an account, present evidence, divulge information, and have a high executive order from an ethical perspective (Bansal et al, 2015). Reconstruction of trust to that extent ensures that full trust absorption of digital necessities, devoid of the right to refrain from the use of hot bananas, can only be met, thus making trust an immovable object.

These lacunae inform this study, which advances a Political–Behavioural Structural Model of Surveillance in Digital Marketing. This model seeks to explain how trust is remade in a society that is overwhelmed by data. It is proposed that several surveillance-based impacts, such as perceived digital surveillance, intrusiveness in data collection, limits in personalization due to political influence, and political manipulation factors, be incorporated into the mediators' view: Asymmetry of perceived power, perception of privacy risk, and the concept of transparency as perceived by both the observer and the parties engaged in observation. The politics of data economics includes Surveillance Capitalism Theory (Zuboff, 2019), political economy of digital platforms (Srnicek, 2017), and behavioural trust theory (McKnight et al., 2002) under the canopy of trust management.

The study applied the Partial Least Squares -Structural Equation Modelling (PLS-SEM) to examine the population's claims about their clients and customers who gave out feedback in electronic form. From the scholarly background of the study, PLS-SEM was chosen because of its capabilities of dealing with complicated structures, including latent constructs and contradictory expectations (Hair et al., 2019). This study is adding to the literature, as it shows how trust in electronic marketing caused political social marketing behaviour, and in this context, how such behaviour is enabled by an increased use of surveillance technologies.

In this sense, this study can also contribute to the evolution of trust in the field of marketing through digital technology acceptance by testing assumptions related to its underpinnings. In sum, the authors attempt to share recommendations for improvement of marketing systems in digital reality while dealing with these pragmatic limitations. This is essential in view of the current changes in our society, which is influenced by the increasing existence of surveillance and algorithmic control.

2. LITERATURE REVIEW

2.1 Surveillance and the Evolution of Digital Marketing

Evident from advancements in technology and development, promotion, which began as an easy task, has now become a more complex, data-driven system. Importantly, following this new attempt, a new aspect of surveillance emerges: market watchers monitoring user behaviour. Earlier traditional market researchers' efforts in knowing consumer views or what makes a right product ran quite differently from the new emerging so-called social science of market surveillance, which has advanced considerably in the time factor; for example, researchers can collect data that is about current events. Rather than that, it utilizes different technologies such as cookies, tracking pixels, mobile sensors, biometric sensors, and AI-enabled analytics, or so-called "the surveillance industry" to gather consumer or user information for the services available (born) to the regency. Increasing consumer surveillance practices over these years have been suggesting that the capacity of marketing to control its effects does not simply give rise to worries about the erosion of the idea of freely choosing consumers.

Surveillance capitalism is a concept that explains all these movements: to take over the market and society companies of digital platforms, according to Zuboff (2019), deploy instruments to change users' experience into a new behaviour pattern for profitably predicting and controlling the future. This approach makes marketing surveillance look different – not as a form of technological addiction but as a system with a particular social structure and division of power. In such a setup, consumers are considered as information mines rather than members, breaking trust relationships altogether. As it is claimed by academics, these surveillance techniques would turn into the exploitation of data increasingly assumed as the norm and monitoring techniques in every operation, so there is little chance of being changed or withdrawn.

In the field of marketing research, surveillance has been a controversial issue due to its wide-ranging advantages and potential disadvantages. Besides that, promotion and targeting aim to increase the efficacy and fittingness of the advertising. Moreover, consumer research suggests that there is a limit to consumer expectations, within the scope of the limitation of elasticity. Sun & Chi (2019) state that some groups of consumers can be influenced by m-commerce. The idea of convenience due to surveillance does not seem to be true anymore, combined with the fact that technology has eroded the trust of the user.

2.2 Perceived Digital Surveillance and Data Collection Intrusiveness

The act of digital control labelling signifies the evaluation of individuals in favour of and the recognition of their being observed by digital technology. The literature suggests that beliefs about control alterations are important for understanding consumer attitudes and behaviours, even though such changes in practice are technically less important (Xu et al., 2011). They are likely to grow distrustful and even withdraw when they are afraid that all their activities at this stage are carefully monitored.

In addition to the sharing problem, the authors explain how data collection demonstrates a noticeable extent of intrusion, thus damaging the buyer's trust. Intrusive data collection is defined as obtaining sensitive personal information, location data, and behavioural patterns without consent or a clear justification. (Malhotra et al., 2004). This perception of intrusiveness appears to raise privacy concerns, levels of psychological reactance, and engagement in resistance, which involve such activities as avoiding advertising materials and distorting facts. (Martin et al., 2017).

More importantly, intrusiveness is not just a function of the volume of data collected but also of the situational contexts and authoritativeness. It is untrust-building to fasten consumer data practices against norms even when they are legally permitted to do data collection (Nissenbaum, 2011). This, in turn, calls attention to examining surveillance as a process of social construction, where certain laws, norms, and power are implicated.

2.3 Algorithmic Personalization and the "Creepiness" Effect

Algorithmic personalization, despite its being a disturbing element, represents one of the most conspicuous performances of marketing promotion by data surveillance. The algorithm processes behavior data to adjust the creation and delivery of content/ recommendations/ advertisements to individual users' needs. One of the negative effects of such is known as the scare factor, also referred to as the creepy factor. It is the feeling of unease that arises when aspects of an individual consumer are known (Aguirre et al., 2016; Liu et al., 2021).

The existence of this effect erodes confidence by transforming the surveillance from obscure threats to actual ones, that is, unmistakably practiced on their bodies. People might insist on knowing how their data became known to the platform, which will heighten suspicions of the non-transparent practices and manipulative conduct. Few studies seem to raise the notion that increasing intensification of surveillance and power asymmetry becomes a bigger problem, especially when there is a lack of understanding or influence in relation to algorithmic operations (Bleier & Eisenbeiss, 2015).

Additionally, the level of personalization that algorithms bring about is associated with the political sphere. It has been observed that the same tools that enable commercial targeting have been utilized for political promotion and behaviour change, resulting in a blend of market mechanisms and the state. 'That convergence,' as Tufekci (2015) noted, 'exacerbates manipulation and propaganda concerns, hence changing digital market users' trust levels.

2.4 Political Manipulation and Algorithmic Power

Current research suggests that digital marketing platforms work as political actors who can influence public opinion, behaviour, and culture (Susser et al., 2019). Concerns surrounding political manipulation emerge when there is a worry on the part of consumers that not only are purchase decisions being controlled, but also the way people think, behave, and even practice citizenship. This is as elements of micro-targeted advertising, emotional profiling and persuasive design have increasing perceptions of leadership.

These, in turn, are connected with the position of one actor's ability to have power in relation to another actor's inability to have power, an imbalance of platforms over users. The state of affairs may require platforms to develop useful information and act like information brokers as a trade-off of controlling information, processing it, and making decisions in the situation that a user has only a shadowy understanding of how algorithms are running (Srnicek, 2017). Levels of trust have also been shown to be low in the presence of such perceived power asymmetry, as it promotes self-interest, victimisation, and helplessness (Foucault, 2012; Couldry & Mejias, 2019).

The third point makes the whole section more coherent in general, as the author clearly connects the politics of consumption to marketing techniques such as those underlying the attention economy. Trust leakage is not a consequence of privacy issues, but a response to the importance of social justice in digital structures: A political economy perspective. Trusting advertising norms, which argue that trust is a psychological construct involving individual cognitive attitudes, is no more than trust as a political-economic construct.

2.5 Privacy Risk Perception as a Behavioural Mediator

The concept of privacy risk satisfaction has become increasingly popular as a consideration in building confidence in digital environments. This is based on the fear of possible consequences that arise from someone abusing the information, or gaining unauthorized access to it, or even loss of ownership, which refers to the consumer privacy risk (Pavlou, 2003). Many empirical studies have identified a strong negative protective effect of privacy expectations on trust; hence, enhancing digital platform trustworthiness with increases in perceived risk of harm resulting from the privacy breach (Kim et al., 2008).

Over the years, however, it has been suggested that privacy risk as an individual construct is not all that helpful in understanding how trust is operationalized in a data society. Even if people are willing to compromise in certain areas in favour of comfort, they tactically adopt their viewpoints according to the requirements of the public discourse and the moral values that the concerned society holds (Bansal et al., 2015). Within this context, privacy risk can be said to be an antecedent of security behaviour as it intervenes in the support apprehension to digital stimuli without engaging in trust reduction in itself.

2.6 Transparency as a Trust-Restoration Mechanism

The critical role of transparency in the resolution of distrust in cyberspace has been considerably profound. The definition of transparency is the ability of platforms to make clear the details of their data management, algorithmic development, and even their organizational processes (Schnackenberg & Tomlinson, 2016). An increase in transparency aids in fairness, responsibility, and popular acceptance and enriches the reconstruction of trust.

According to findings, data presentation and data user fertility that are open can ease near-social privacy perception and the consequent alarm (Martin & Murphy, 2017). In cases with algorithms, the concepts of explainability and openness often become vital, as inadequate information increases the likelihood of a perception of the system in terms of control and pursuit of power (Pasquale, 2015). This enhances its utility as both a responsive and militant strategy against information and power imbalances.

2.7 Trust Reconstruction in a Data-Driven Society

Traditional models of trust often consider trust to be a static outcome of positive interactions. However, in spaces where surveillance is not at its best, trust is often compromised and renegotiated. Trust repair gives its definition to people's cognition and behaviour towards something after they learn that data privacy has been breached, targeting has been manipulative, or any other kinds of surveillance practices have been used (Bansal et al., 2015).

Restoring trust cannot be explained in isolation because other factors are also prevalent, such as validity, responsibility, and the ethics of the situation. Reconstruction of trust is a more difficult process because there exists a climate of distrust, and the consumer is more careful. Furthermore, this perspective is more relevant in the context of data-shift societies, wherein refusal to use the predominant platforms is not usually possible.

Empirical research on the reconstruction of trust in the digital perspective of marketing is rather scarce. Thus, current scholarship more often than not examines the repair of lost confidence as a result of a failure in service provision rather than analyses the formation of trust. This negative aspect in the system necessitates the construction of frameworks that encompass watchfulness, power, and activity-related definitions altogether.

2.8 Synthesis and Research Gap

It has been acknowledged from the documented sources that surveillance-based digital marketing brings about novel trust complications that are related to the political, economic, and marketing behaviour. These customers' trust creation would be interfaced with many others, as explained by the previous researchers who have explored the constructs of privacy, personalization, and trust. Even with few studies on trust reconstruction in the marketing domain, the most relevant research concerns creating trust within the marketplace.

Applying a new try which suggests a Political–Behavioural Structural Model, will help in explaining the changes in trust that result from surveillance. Utilizing the model in the real world, it will be possible to enhance marketers' comprehension and fulfil the demand for better marketing practice ethics in the digital environment.

3. CONCEPTUAL FRAMEWORK AND HYPOTHESES DEVELOPMENT

Figure 1.

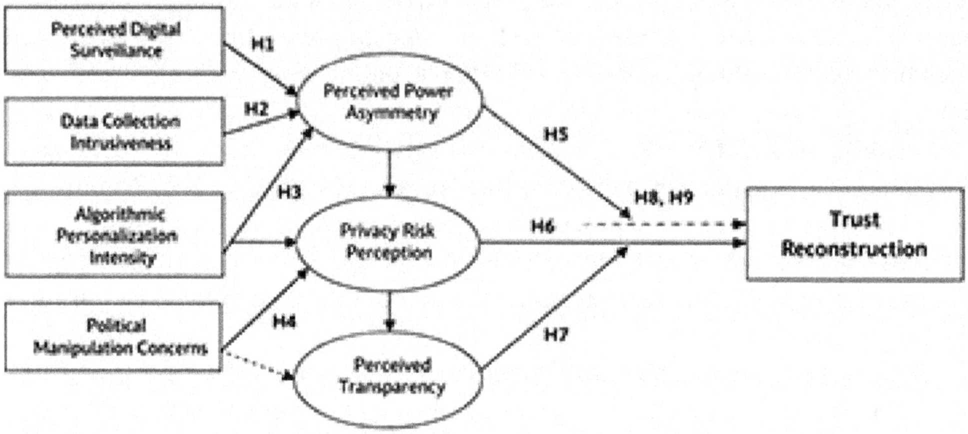

To expound, a Political–Behavioral Structural Model (PBSM) was developed to elucidate the impact of data-driven marketing practices on trust building within surveillance-oriented markets, as shown in Figure 1. The development also incorporates key tenets of Surveillance Capitalism Theory (Zuboff, 2019) and the Political Economy of Digital Platforms (Srnicek, 2017), in addition to Behavioural Trust Theory (McKnight et al., 2002). Building trust is perceived as an ever-changing product influenced by surveillance's most immediate causative environment, which is manipulated through political action, and under which individual-level attitudes, such as power, risk, and transparency mediation, take place.

3.1 Surveillance Antecedents

The respondents' understanding of the monitoring of other people can also be called Perceived Digital Surveillance (PDS). Indeed, some works have made it plain that the increase in self-monitoring results in discomfort and relative lack of trust, save for Xu et al. (2011). PDS is typically assessed using altered items incorporating perceived monitoring levels and knowledge of tracking policies.

A man seeks privacy and does not wish to be observed. This resistance to corporate communication stimuli is branding in certain terms, even if it may be a really good advert. Data Collection Intrusiveness (DCI) is a scale to measure the extent of invasiveness or inappropriateness of data practices.

API or Algorithmic Personalization Intensity is the frequency of personalization content and how deep such content is. For example, personalized content can affect the desired effectiveness of communication in reaction to PTIS, whilst sometimes not being effective, such practices might become misguided, as encouraging the consumer, more often than not, with the use of lavish and unnecessary marketing approaches that may make him/her develop a negative attitude towards a particular brand/ product.

Concerns over Political Manipulation (PM) exist due to the fear that data algorithms and data-driven concepts have far more uses beyond commercial interests in the digital platform world. The items are designed based on manipulation and algorithmic influence research (Susser et al, 2019; Tufekci, 2015).

H1: Perceived digital surveillance positively influences perceived power asymmetry.
H2: Data collection intrusiveness positively influences privacy risk perception.
H3: Algorithmic personalisation intensity positively influences perceived power asymmetry.
H4: Political manipulation positively influences privacy risk perception.

3.2 Political–Behavioural Mediators

The frameworks of Perceived Power Asymmetry and Perceived Transparency are mostly incorporated in the context of consumers' perception towards digital platforms. Furthermore, going back to the power and control frameworks (Foucault, 2012; Couldry & Mejias, 2019), one can assert that PPA hampers trust by exposing the blocks of power.

The two concepts do not include Perceived Risk of Privacy Invasion or control over access to personal information, such as Perceived Transparency and possibly trust, as measurement of these can be vague. Transparency is a value that must generally be upheld and is utilized in the trust measurements of an organization (Schmackenberg & Tomlinson, 2016).

H5: Perceived power asymmetry negatively influences trust reconstruction.
H6: Privacy risk perception negatively influences trust reconstruction.
H7: Perceived transparency positively influences trust reconstruction.

3.3 Trust Reconstruction

Trust Discovery Recurrence (TDR) is a term used to mean the process through which a consumer finds trust after having discovered breaches of consumer privacy laws. This is unlike the first trust, which is done under conditions of scepticism and more attentiveness, and is measured with other beliefs of trustworthiness (McKnight et al., 2002; Bansal et al., 2015).

H8: Perceived power asymmetry mediates the relationship between surveillance antecedents and trust reconstruction.
H9: Privacy risk perception mediates the relationship between surveillance antecedents and trust reconstruction.
H10: Perceived transparency moderates the negative effects of surveillance on trust reconstruction.

In the developed guidance, the trust recovery is recognized as a psychologically and politically mediated occurrence within the surveillance marketing. This model provides an in-depth understanding of trust development in contemporary data societies by using structural power and psychological risk under the umbrella of transparency mechanisms.

4. RESEARCH METHODOLOGY

Applying a positivistic paradigm to this survey provides scholars with a framework for the desired sample design activity, which is of an investigative and analytical nature, and the aims of which largely include the exploration of the political–behavioural mechanisms at play in digital marketing settings with digital surveillance. To examine factor model relationships in a structural equation model, the structural equation model was formulated to support the use of a hypothesis. The rationale of the study is that there are theories that guide the study, which led to the application of a deductive approach. This 'manufacturing world' of the new communications environment deceptive confidence plays on this popular project, which is actually a transformation of pervasive surveillance by its users into mutual economic benefits. The authors discuss key statistical methodologies as applied in the companies and industries that deal with products, services, or processes that are internet-related.

Research Design and Sample

In the survey, the participants' data included those who are active on the internet and use the online environment mainly for commerce, that is, selling and buying of goods, social media connectivity, as well as usage of mobile systems. Querists, in the course of the study, utilized online enquiry in an attempt to obtain as many respondents as possible, ensuring some degree of security due to the anonymity of the respondents. To find those with the needed level of precision in the argument, non-probability sampling, such as convenience sampling, was utilized, meaning opposite samples were found where waste was just thrown. Before proceeding, an analysis of the available literature, arguments, and strongly worded exchange of ideas will be conducted with reference to structural equation modelling. The researchers determined that the survey targeted a minimum sample size exceeding the ten-times rule to enhance the statistical power and the stability of the given model.

Measurement Instruments

Each concept examined in this study was quantified via the use of some validated pre-existing scales, which were derived from other empirical studies. It was made certain that the content validity of the scales was not placed in doubt, nor was their reliability, by using said scales. The scales employed to measure perceived animosity and the discomfort associated with data collection, which are more familiar to the privacy and surveillance community, were therefore derived from the aforementioned literature. To measure the intensity of automatic customization to which the user is subject, the data was collected on items that signified the user's perceived facilitation of interest regarding content. The issue of manipulation in an electoral setting was assessed by drawing from both the political communication and the algorithmic governance literature. A few constructs, such as perceived power disparity, privacy risks, and transparency, can be found already in trust research, similar to other information systems studies. The trust reconstruction model was made up of three central factors that highlighted the desire to gain back the lost affection in a situation that had been previously trustworthy. Every item was presented in the form of a five-point Likert scale from '1=strongly disagree' to '5=strongly agree'.

Data Analysis Technique

A set of data analytics techniques was performed to evaluate the flow of data through the various parts of the arithmetic operator named partial least squares-structural equation modelling, using the SmartPLS software, of course. Such methodology was opted for as it is especially useful in inductive approaches for explaining phenomena and conducting research. This approach is very suitable, particularly where the research models are of greater complexity and contain multiple mediators. During the review, which was conducted, the analysis was undertaken in two phases, starting with the examination of the measurement models and their internal stability. In this sense, it can be useful for the degree of confidence in measurement, the extract and construct specifications, and also the differentiation between concepts in practice. There is little similarity between the two phases in terms of the methods used. Following the measurement model, the structural model was appraised by looking at the path diagrams and the paths' coefficients, error variance's coefficients, effective measures, and predictions' backchecks. The static test of the hypotheses that the authors have postulated in the research model was carried out. Bootstrapping methods involved the random generation of numerous samples at the test points and tests on residual distribution and relationships that might be regressed to them, and tests of Instrumental Signals. Bootstrap is a powerful method for estimating standard errors and enhancing the validity of the hypothesis test. This analysis is presented in detail in the following section.

Ethical Considerations

We upheld ethical principles and norms while conducting the study. The subjects were told what we were doing, information confidentiality was maintained, and the participants agreed to take part. There was no gathering of any data that pertained to their identity whatsoever, and the study protocol abided by the standards of ethics in social science research on human beings.

5. FINDINGS

5.1 Measurement Model Assessment

Table 1. Reliability and convergent validity

Construct	Cronbach's α	Composite Reliability (CR)	AVE
Perceived Digital Surveillance (PDS)	0.82	0.88	0.65
Data Collection Intrusiveness (DCI)	0.85	0.90	0.69
Algorithmic Personalization Intensity (API)	0.80	0.87	0.63
Political Manipulation Concerns (PMC)	0.86	0.91	0.71
Perceived Power Asymmetry (PPA)	0.83	0.89	0.67
Privacy Risk Perception (PRP)	0.88	0.92	0.74
Perceived Transparency (PT)	0.84	0.90	0.69
Trust Reconstruction (TR)	0.89	0.93	0.76

Interpretation

All scales show solid internal reliability with both Cronbach's alpha and constructs' composite reliability measures surpassing the cut-off point of 0.70 for reliability, as shown in Table 1. In regard to discriminant validity, average variance extracted (AVE) exceeds 0.50, signalling acceptable convergent validity, which in turn certifies that the relationships between the constructs and their indicators are comprehensive.

5.2 Discriminant Validity

Table 2. Fornell–Larcker criterion

Construct	PDS	DCI	API	PMC	PPA	PRP	PT	TR
PDS	**0.81**							
DCI	0.44	**0.83**						
API	0.38	0.41	**0.79**					
PMC	0.46	0.49	0.40	**0.84**				
PPA	0.52	0.47	0.45	0.51	**0.82**			
PRP	0.48	0.54	0.42	0.56	0.50	**0.86**		
PT	–0.29	–0.32	–0.27	–0.35	–0.41	–0.38	**0.83**	
TR	–0.36	–0.43	–0.31	–0.47	–0.58	–0.55	0.62	**0.87**

Interpretation

According to the Fornell-Larcker criterion, the diagonal elements of the table need to exceed the off-diagonal ones, which is indeed the case. It is possible to produce a wide range of meanings, which is what is required to accept or reject the hypothesis. Identifying adequate discriminant validity as such presupposes that, in the political-behavioural control and prevention system, each structure has a sufficiently distinct meaning, as shown in Table 2.

5.3 Structural Model Results

Table 3. Hypothesis testing (direct effects)

Hypothesis	Path	β	t-value	p-value	Result
H1	PDS → PPA	0.31	5.82	<0.001	Supported
H2	DCI → PRP	0.36	6.47	<0.001	Supported
H3	API → PPA	0.27	4.91	<0.001	Supported
H4	PMC → PRP	0.39	7.12	<0.001	Supported
H5	PPA → TR	−0.41	7.66	<0.001	Supported
H6	PRP → TR	−0.37	6.94	<0.001	Supported
H7	PT → TR	0.45	8.21	<0.001	Supported

Interpretation

All the postulated direct relationships are statistically significant, as shown in Table 3. The antecedents of surveillance markedly increase the power difference and the perception of the risk of private information violation. Both mediators negatively affect the process of trust development, while at the same time transparency has a vast positive influence, emphasizing the importance of the use of transparency as a trust-creating tool in digital marketing run under online surveillance conditions.

5.4 Mediation Analysis

Table 4. Indirect effects

Path	Indirect Effect (β)	t-value	p-value	Mediation
PDS → PPA → TR	−0.13	4.89	<0.001	Partial
API → PPA → TR	−0.11	4.23	<0.001	Partial
DCI → PRP → TR	−0.14	5.36	<0.001	Partial
PMC → PRP → TR	−0.15	5.88	<0.001	Partial

Interpretation

Members' actions towards institutionalised people are affected by values, patterns of moral interaction, methods and properties acceptance, recognition of norms and proper behaviours, motivations, knowledge, experience, and communication skills, as shown in Table 4. These findings indicate that the practices of surveillance impede the rebuilding of trust through intra-political actions more than rigorous direct effects.

5.5 Predictive Power

Table 5. Coefficient of determination (R^2)

Endogenous Construct	R^2
Perceived Power Asymmetry	0.42
Privacy Risk Perception	0.47
Trust Reconstruction	0.58

Interpretation

It's worth noting that the trust reconstruction model was able to justify 58% of the observed deviations, which can be considered quite high, as shown in Table 5. Additionally, the results concerning power perception and privacy risk offer additional proof of the strong relationship between surveillance within digital marketing spaces and its social–behavioural outputs.

6. DISCUSSION

The focus of the study is on how consumer data collection practices in digital social networking spaces have had an impact on the rise of a serious rebuilding relationship challenge in a data-driven society, in terms of an emotive trust approach using an examination based on the theories of politics and behaviour. The expectations are that consumers' expectations and fears arising with the digital age, such as consumer surveillance leading to political distrust, would significantly impact trust reconstruction in today's society. In other words, any association of those concerned with its differences or disputes going on in the security risks sphere is not worth the effort and will only add to general polarization. To support this argument, the report contrasts the injector with Eurasian defenders of soft power, which key off individual has chained eject and posts. The notes observe kinetic discussions between the activists and the social theorists, including also points out the destructiveness, beauty, and the damage. Impacts of Rebuilding Trust is a detailed and relatively comprehensive examination of several subject matters and issues.

The initial goal of the research was to evaluate the effect of surveillance-based tactics tailored to marketing on how consumers view the enhancement of power and control. The considerable favourable impact of the perceived digital surveillance and the algorithmic personalization intensity on the perceived power asymmetry (H1 and H3) proves that most people see the practices of continued watch over and autonomous adjustment in the shape of the platform ensuring privilege in their favour. These conclusions conform to Foucault's approach to equal disclosures, or lack thereof, as well as Zuboff's assertion that surveillance capitalism causes very rampant powers in digital configurations. More than an aspect of consumer society devoted to the creation of value, personalisation receives what it defines as negative attention from capitalism's fragmentation and social engineering. As a result, there is growing acceptance among consumers that personalization has both formal and substantive domination, hence the repressive connotations of cyber marketing surveillance are correct.

The second objective sought to grasp how privacy risks discover additional permutations in terms of intrusiveness due to data permissiveness and attention to bothers like political manipulation with a view to contributing to the requirements of individuals in the domain of privacy and security. The ''data collection tendency vs. data collection resistivity'' (H2) and the ''political anxiety towards data and democracy'' (H4) are positive; there may be consumer-focused intrusiveness that is beyond regulatory issues and into ethical issues related to society and the democratic system. There are even scholars who criticize privacy studies that suggest privacy is non-political and thus individuals are willing to give it up wherever there is a need associated with politics. The authors also maintain that satisfaction with digital marketing activities is measured not only by profit motives but also by principles and political judgments.

There was also a key objective of the study that related to how political-behavioural mediators influence trust building. The study has shown that gender has a direct effect on trust within a dyad, irrespective of the contributions made by different political ideologies. A high level of power in politicians restrains certain voters from forming and exercising their political decisions until the election. If the ulterior political motives lead one to cast a vote for a politician even though he or she is not actually approved of, there is bound to be distrust. Copyright issues, territorial limits, prohibitions on reverse engineering, and many other factors all of these act as re-transmitted obstacles. Such persuasive, reinforcing political elements, always requiring repetition, contribute to a great social network over time, making some media more viral than others.

Equally important, the most salient positive predictor of trust repair is seen to be perceived transparency (H6). This fully supports the study's objective, as it confirms the search for ways to recover confidence. It is suggested that the transparency referred to the stage of the data collection protocols against the backdrop of the rationale behind the procedures, which the platform undertakes for this kind of transparency, seems to offset the Comprehensive Operations about Normative and Substantive Procedural Fairness and Educational Information Applied Psychology. This seems to reinforce the argument that internal control literature makes when society runs on knowledge and digital systems, which relates to trust to mean a high culture. Most importantly, where there is transparency, raising concerns, while oppressive surveillance practices exist, eventually critical trust-building programs would have to overcome it.

This elaboration accentuates the importance of the comprehensive investigation used in the research. As found in the exploratory models, a secure significant relationship is pertinently embedded within all levels of trust relationships, and then the previously established industry knowledge may become a direct referral point for future inquiries in research. The e-framework that is based on the decreased value model already works, and expectations for the overall strategy are the focus of attention and concern at the political levels of management. Common imaginative practices upon which inertia and inherent alternatives exist are popular motivational behavioural patterns. Part of the reason for this is that the mediators have a direct and proximate effect upon the manipulation of disturbances in the main processes under study. Yet, it cannot be ignored that a partial line of sight is applied in the case of the hierarchical management tactics, as well as spreading irritating economic propaganda or utilizing psychological warfare in attempts to smear some negative events as harmless.

7. THEORETICAL AND PRACTICAL IMPLICATIONS

7.1 Theoretical Implications

This thesis has brought several psychological concepts. Trust relationship establishment is treated as a political process and not a result of a building's reputation or even the building's association with collaboration. In the trust literature, we know the importance of credibility and character motivation. This work states the importance of institutions in defining what most motivates people's desire to trust and how trust is defined and demonstrated in an ever-changing global data-driven economy, which will locate the study within the behavioural trust research and political economy.

This section contributes to the industry's current understanding of surveillance capitalism by demonstrating empirically that these surveillance practices in digital marketing can affect consumers' trust level. The previous studies focused more on the surveillance's economic and sociological facets, whereas the study delves much deeper by looking at the psychology of the consumers and how they behave. Most importantly, this research has further constructed the concepts of the visualized digital intrusion and corresponding counterbalancing strategies by framing the threats from surveillance into this using the construct of strategy.

The third advance is the introduction of an innovative Political–Behavioural Structural Model. This model joins theories from surveillance studies, political communication, and purchasing behaviour in a single system, showing how social pressures are perceived and addressed at the first level of analysis. This significant advancement in the field helps to fulfil the objective of devising multi-disciplinary models that would adequately explain extensive theoretical phenomena in the digital context of technological innovation and provides a model that can easily be adopted for research, for instance, in the areas of fintech, health data markets, and smart cities.

After all, the research recalibrates transparency as a changeable trust-building function, anyhow, definitively. Verification that transparency triggers trust-building more powerfully than any other variable demonstrates the potential of transparency theory within fairness principles with respect to restraining the extent of asymmetric surveillance-related power. As a result, this point addresses the discussions regarding algorithmic accountability and electronic governance.

7.2 Practical Implications

Furthermore, the findings also yield several crucial theoretical implications for different segments in the discipline. In the case of digital marketers, there is a warning concerning the excessive data collection that is likely to be a risk in this industry. Although using individual profiles is one of the primary ways to stand out in the industry, the investigation reveals the risks that come from examination of invasive as well as non-transparent print data practices that have the potential to undermine trust through systemic privacy and dominance issues. For that reason, marketers will have to do away with the extraction of data focusing on business objectives, and instead adopt personalized marketing with respect to the value elements like the discretion of the user. What is demanded is explainable algorithms, concise privacy notices, and convenient interfaces of data governance. Effectively, digital transformation cannot be left to the demands of machines only. For regulatory bodies in particular, it is important to align with and adhere to these exacting standards in a credible manner.

On the policy and regulatory front, the conclusions of this research methodology lend weight to arguments in support of the desirability of having institutional processes and mechanisms for accountability and oversight in the digital space. Given the pervasiveness of imbalances of power and the fear of political manipulations, the possibilities of self-regulation alone are being doubted, hence the need for other means of rebuilding faith in the system. Policymakers should enhance the legislation of data privacy, include provisions on algorithmic audits, and also regulate the phenomenon by proposing norms on transparency deal with how data is used by companies and politicians. These actions should introduce a level of symmetry and balance in the power involved from both the audience and the platforms.

In conclusion, for the consumers and members of civil society, the research underscores the vital importance of digital literacy for those who are destined to live in societies flooded with surveillance. Thus, it is suggested that consumers' trust in technologies is not fixed, but it is contingent on, and operates within, the society's channels. This means that one of the key components of any security efforts should revolve around educating users on the mechanisms of the security countermeasures adopted by their service providers.

8. CONCLUSION

In this study, the main aim was to evaluate in detail how the interplay of digital surveillance practices within contemporary marketing ecosystems impacts trust recovery in a data-powered era. A Political-Behavioural Structural Model that was conceptualized and assessed in this study seeks to deepen the scope of trust investigation outside the conventional relational and technological canons into the arena of a more political and institutional one. The study brought out that, complementary to consumer management practices, consumer transparency, trust, and consumer protection strategies, the shared constraints of surveillance, customer data system dependence, caution with the levels of data collection, and control measures have substantive and nuanced domain influences on consumer trust in the digital divide. Results demonstrate that consumers' perceptions of the power of the platform and vulnerability of privacy are highly influenced by the negatives of surveillance that were tied to technology adoption, social media-based algorithmic data use, etc. In turn, the same role is also played by these political – behavioural perceptions in hindering the reconstruction of trust. Importantly, the research clarifies that loss of trust is not an irrational behaviour towards data-driven technologies but a reason formed as a result of unfavourable structural imbalances and the opaque relationship of digital markets. This leaves an existing gap in the literature, and hospitality defines consumer resistance to surveillance as very restrictive and temporary or information-limited.

Moreover, the research addresses the issue of anticipated and actual levels of legal knowledge in the communication and interaction dimensions of the VLE. It emerges that in the theoretical case, such knowledge and its acquisition may be contradictory to the fundamentals of sharing; in the practical dimension, such knowledge and skill applied may only foster and enhance the sharing processes. This data analysis is relevant in the context of VLE, where legal and ICT knowledge can be obtained in a far more systematic and efficient way, when knowledge is produced and consumed, and when creative and communicative designing solutions to relevant issues involve the use of ICT, even though this may not be the primary purpose. It extends interdisciplinary inquiry by linking surveillance capitalism, political economy, and trust trichotomy in an empirical framework. It illustrates the performance of PLS-SEM in this aspect and how it is useful in understanding complex social marketing environments. Lastly, the study gives recommendations, based on the research foundation, to the manager, legislator, and system developer working to encourage innovation without public fear of ethical ramifications.

In conclusion, trust building and evaluation in the contemporary capitalist society are mediated as well as produced through political practices of surveillance and governance. Thus, key concerns associated with the digitalized marketing sector are related not only to technology advancement but also to the power alternatives, circulation of information, responsibility, transparency, accountability, and trust, amongst other things, in marketing practice as a whole.

9. LIMITATIONS AND FUTURE SCOPE

In spite of its significance in terms of both academic and practical support, this particular study does have some doubtful points that need to be resolved as part of further actions for management. For one, it is worth noting that in the course of this research, the design of a sectional survey approach was used. This design does not permit observation from one point to another, giving the feeling that events within a certain time frame can be captured. Confidence levels in technology-closed systems will probably change as users grow older and become more observant and react, or they encounter changed polices. The effects of trust degradation and how it is restored would be better understood when a change occurs, such as when it is acquired and when it is obtained.

Secondly, such an interrogative technique can cause the effectiveness of the questions to lose purity or the expected results to be achieved more easily, even when the sampling bias is attempted to be corrected, and various tests to control are applied. In the future, complementary research may prop up the survey measures with behavioural or experimental methods, such as clickstream analysis and experimental testing of interventions on transparency, to improve the quality and the ability of the design to draw causal inferences. Afterward, in the study's context of investigation, it was appreciated that it focused on general digital marketing platforms, which may mean caution on the absence of such in policy frameworks within the various sectors. This is because surveillance perceptions and trust dynamics are likely to differ across such contexts as is the case for fintech, health technology, political advertising, smart cities, etc. Subsequent work is also likely to use the PBM in other areas or social-cultural arrangements and subject it to further empirical examination in terms of its generalizability and context-specificity.

Finally, scholars can also apply the model further by including regulatory trust, algorithmic fairness perceptions, or digital resistance behaviours as new dimensions. Also, while the current thesis is highly longitudinal, other researchers can test how formal law and normative considerations influence surveillance and trust relationships via comparative legal and political research. And lastly, future researchers may engage in so-called 'small n' mixed-methods research, which may focus on consumers as active agents in surveillant societies, among other social and cultural features.

REFERENCES

Aguirre, E., Roggeveen, A. L., Grewal, D., & Wetzels, M. (2016). The personalization-privacy paradox: Implications for new media. *Journal of Consumer Marketing, 33*(2), 98–110. DOI: 10.1108/JCM-06-2015-1458

Bansal, G., Zahedi, F. M., & Gefen, D. (2015). The role of privacy assurance mechanisms in building trust and the moderating role of privacy concern. *European Journal of Information Systems, 24*(6), 624–644. DOI: 10.1057/ejis.2014.41

Bleier, A., & Eisenbeiss, M. (2015). The importance of trust for personalized online advertising. *Journal of Retailing, 91*(3), 390–409. DOI: 10.1016/j.jretai.2015.04.001

Couldry, N., & Mejias, U. A. (2019). The costs of connection: How data is colonizing human life and appropriating it for capitalism. In *The costs of connection*. Stanford University Press.

Foucault, M. (2012). *Discipline and punish: The birth of the prison*. Vintage.

Gefen, D., Karahanna, E., & Straub, D. W. (2003). Trust and TAM in online shopping: An integrated model. *Management Information Systems Quarterly, 27*(1), 51–90. DOI: 10.2307/30036519

Hair, J. F., Hult, G. T. M., Ringle, C. M., & Sarstedt, M. (2019). *A primer on partial least squares structural equation modeling (PLS-SEM)* (2nd ed.). Sage. DOI: 10.3926/oss.37

Kim, D. J., Ferrin, D. L., & Rao, H. R. (2008). A trust-based consumer decision-making model in electronic commerce: The role of trust, perceived risk, and their antecedents. *Decision Support Systems, 44*(2), 544–564. DOI: 10.1016/j.dss.2007.07.001

Liu, X., Shin, H., & Burns, A. C. (2021). Examining the impact of luxury brand's social media marketing on customer engagement: Using big data analytics and natural language processing. *Journal of Business Research, 125*, 815–826. DOI: 10.1016/j.jbusres.2019.04.042

Malhotra, N. K., Kim, S. S., & Agarwal, J. (2004). Internet users' information privacy concerns (IUIPC): The construct, the scale, and a causal model. *Information Systems Research, 15*(4), 336–355. DOI: 10.1287/isre.1040.0032

Martin, K. D., & Murphy, P. E. (2017). The role of data privacy in marketing. *Journal of the Academy of Marketing Science, 45*(2), 135–155. DOI: 10.1007/s11747-016-0495-4

McKnight, D. H., Choudhury, V., & Kacmar, C. (2002). Developing and validating trust measures for e-commerce: An integrative typology. *Information Systems Research, 13*(3), 334–359. DOI: 10.1287/isre.13.3.334.81

Nissenbaum, H. (2011). A contextual approach to privacy online. *Daedalus, 140*(4), 32–48. DOI: 10.1162/DAED_a_00113

Pasquale, F. (2015). The black box society: The secret algorithms that control money and information. In *The black box society*. Harvard university press. DOI: 10.4159/harvard.9780674736061

Pavlou, P. A. (2003). Consumer acceptance of electronic commerce: Integrating trust and risk with the technology acceptance model. *International Journal of Electronic Commerce, 7*(3), 101–134. DOI: 10.1080/10864415.2003.11044275

Schnackenberg, A. K., & Tomlinson, E. C. (2016). Organizational transparency: A new perspective on managing trust in organization-stakeholder relationships. *Journal of Management, 42*(7), 1784–1810. DOI: 10.1177/0149206314525202

Srnicek, N. (2017). *Platform Capitalism*. Polity Press.

Sun, J., & Chi, T. (2019). Investigating the adoption of apparel m-commerce in the US market. *International Journal of Clothing Science and Technology, 31*(4), 544-563.Bleier, A., & Eisenbeiss, M. (2015). The importance of trust for personalized online advertising. *Journal of Retailing, 91*(3), 390–409.

Susser, D., Roessler, B., & Nissenbaum, H. (2019). Online manipulation: Hidden influences in a digital world. *Geo. L. Tech. Rev., 4*, 1.

Tufekci, Z. (2015). Algorithmic harms beyond Facebook and Google: Emergent challenges of computational agency. *Colo. Tech. LJ, 13*, 203.

Xu, H., Dinev, T., Smith, J., & Hart, P. (2011). Information privacy concerns: Linking individual perceptions with institutional privacy assurances. *Journal of the Association for Information Systems, 12*(12), 1. DOI: 10.17705/1jais.00281

Zuboff, S. (2019). *The age of surveillance capitalism: The fight for a human future at the new frontier of power, edn*. PublicAffairs.

Chapter 2
Surveillance and Trust in India's Digital Marketing Landscape:
A Socio-Political Perspective

A. Ranjithkumar
http://orcid.org/0000-0002-6744-7603
Vel Tech Rangarajan Dr. Sagunthala R&D Institute of Science and Technology, India

ABSTRACT

This chapter examines surveillance and trust in India's expanding digital marketing landscape from a socio-political perspective. The purpose of this chapter is to analyze how data-driven marketing practices, algorithmic personalization, and artificial intelligence reshape power relations among platforms, brands, the state, and consumers. Drawing on theories of surveillance capitalism, algorithmic governance, and trust, the chapter conceptualizes digital marketing as a form of behavioral governance embedded in everyday digital infrastructures. It explores how marketing surveillance operates through datafication, platform dominance, and opaque algorithms, contributing to trust deficits, privacy concerns, and social inequalities, particularly among vulnerable populations. The chapter also evaluates India's data protection framework and discusses ethical challenges, resistance, and future pathways for rebuilding trust in algorithmic societies.

DOI: 10.4018/979-8-3373-7704-9.ch002

1. INTRODUCTION: DIGITAL MARKETING IN AN AGE OF SURVEILLANCE

India's rapid digital transformation has fundamentally altered the structure of markets, communication, and everyday social interactions. The expansion of affordable mobile internet, platform-based services, and state-led digital infrastructures has enabled the large-scale collection and circulation of personal data, positioning India as one of the world's most data-intensive digital economies (Arora, 2019; Khera, 2019). Within this context, digital marketing has emerged as a dominant economic activity, driven by platforms such as Google, Meta, and large domestic conglomerates, which increasingly mediate consumer engagement through data-driven technologies.

Contemporary digital marketing in India reflects a broader shift from traditional persuasive communication toward data-driven behavioral governance. Rather than merely informing or persuading consumers, marketing practices now rely on continuous monitoring, predictive analytics, and algorithmic personalization to shape preferences and choices in real time (Zuboff, 2019; Turow, 2017). These developments signal the normalization of surveillance as an infrastructural condition of participation in digital markets, where consumer behavior becomes a source of economic value and control.

Surveillance and trust therefore emerge as deeply intertwined socio-political concerns. While platforms and marketers demand trust from users to collect and process personal data, the opacity of algorithmic systems and repeated incidents of data misuse have contributed to widespread anxiety and declining confidence in digital ecosystems (Pasquale, 2015; Acquisti et al., 2015). Trust is no longer limited to brands or institutions but extends to algorithmic systems that govern visibility, access, and decision-making, raising questions about accountability and legitimacy (Luhmann, 1979).

Against this backdrop, the central problem addressed in this chapter is the tension between the efficiency gains promised by surveillance-based digital marketing and the erosion of privacy, autonomy, and trust within India's socio-political context. The chapter seeks to address the following guiding questions: How do surveillance-oriented marketing practices shape consumer trust in India? What power relations emerge between platforms, the state, and consumers in data-driven marketing ecosystems? What are the broader socio-political implications of these dynamics for democracy and social equity?

Methodologically, this chapter adopts a qualitative and critical socio-political approach grounded in political economy, digital sociology, and critical data studies (Cohen, 2019; Couldry & Mejias, 2019). Drawing on secondary literature, policy documents, industry reports, and selected case illustrations, the chapter analyzes surveillance and trust as structural features of India's digital marketing landscape. The chapter is organized to move from conceptual foundations and infrastructural contexts to mechanisms of surveillance, consumer trust dynamics, regulatory responses, and future pathways.

Table 1. Expansion of digital infrastructure and digital advertising in India (2015–2025)

Indicator	**2015**	**2020**	**2025 (Estimated)**
Internet users (million)	259	622	900+
Smartphone penetration (%)	22	54	75–80
Average mobile data cost (/GB)	~250	~9	<10
Digital advertising spend (crore)	~9,000	~21,000	~65,000

Sources: IAMAI (2023); TRAI (2022); World Bank (2023); Statista (2024)

2. CONCEPTUAL FOUNDATIONS: SURVEILLANCE, TRUST, AND POWER

The concept of surveillance capitalism provides a critical entry point for understanding contemporary digital marketing practices. Surveillance capitalism refers to an economic logic in which human experience is systematically translated into behavioral data that can be analyzed, predicted, and monetized (Zuboff, 2019). In digital markets, this logic underpins targeted advertising, recommender systems, and predictive personalization, where consumer data are continuously harvested to anticipate and shape future behavior. Marketing thus shifts from a reactive practice to a proactive system of behavioral prediction, embedding surveillance into routine consumption.

Trust occupies a central yet fragile position within surveillance-based digital ecosystems. Classical sociological theory conceptualizes trust as a mechanism that enables individuals to act under conditions of uncertainty by relying on institutions, norms, or systems (Luhmann, 1979). In digital contexts, trust extends beyond human actors to include technological systems and algorithms that mediate decision-making. Consumers are expected to trust platforms and marketers to collect, process, and safeguard their data, even though these processes remain largely opaque and inaccessible (Fukuyama, 1995). This asymmetry complicates the formation of informed trust and contributes to persistent skepticism.

Power operates through surveillance and trust via structures of visibility and control. Drawing on Foucault's (1977) concept of panopticism, digital surveillance can be understood as a system in which individuals are continuously observed without reciprocal transparency. Unlike traditional disciplinary institutions, algorithmic surveillance is decentralized, automated, and embedded within commercial platforms. Algorithms determine what content is seen, which choices are prioritized, and how individuals are categorized, thereby exercising a form of governance that is subtle yet pervasive (Beer, 2017; Pasquale, 2015).

Consent and autonomy are frequently invoked as ethical foundations of data-driven marketing, yet they function within a broader neoliberal digital rationality. Consent mechanisms, such as click-through agreements and privacy notices, often reduce complex power relations to formal acts of compliance, obscuring structural coercion and limited alternatives (Cohen, 2019). While framed as empowering consumer choice, such mechanisms place the burden of responsibility on individuals rather than addressing systemic asymmetries in data ownership and control. As a result, autonomy becomes procedural rather than substantive.

Applying these conceptual frameworks to India and the Global South requires attention to postcolonial contexts, democratic institutions, and deep social inequalities. Scholars argue that global surveillance capitalism often reproduces forms of data colonialism, where data extracted from populations in the Global South are appropriated by transnational platforms with limited local accountability (Couldry & Mejias, 2019). In India, these dynamics intersect with state-led digitalization, caste and class hierarchies, and uneven digital literacy, making surveillance and trust not only economic issues but profoundly socio-political ones. These conditions necessitate a contextualized theoretical approach that foregrounds power, inequality, and governance in analyzing digital marketing practices.

3. RESEARCH METHODOLOGY AND ANALYTICAL APPROACH

This chapter adopts a qualitative, interpretive, and critical socio-political research design to examine the relationship between surveillance and trust in India's digital marketing landscape. Given that surveillance-based marketing operates through structural power relations, institutional arrangements, and normative governance frameworks, a qualitative approach is most appropriate for capturing meanings, asymmetries, and contextual dynamics that cannot be adequately explained through purely quantitative measures (Denzin & Lincoln, 2018). Rather than pursuing statistical generalization, the analysis prioritizes interpretive depth and contextual understanding of how data-driven marketing practices are embedded within India's socio-political environment. The theoretical–methodological orientation integrates political economy, critical data studies, and digital sociology, enabling a holistic examination of marketing surveillance as both an economic strategy and a socio-political phenomenon (Lupton, 2015; Srnicek, 2017; Zuboff, 2019).

The chapter relies exclusively on secondary data sources to ensure analytical breadth, credibility, and relevance. These include peer-reviewed academic literature, scholarly books, policy reports, legal and regulatory documents—particularly the Digital Personal Data Protection Act (2023), its accompanying Rules (2025), the Information Technology Rules, and guidelines issued by the Advertising Standards Council of India—as well as industry reports published by organizations such as the Internet and Mobile Association of India. Media investigations and publicly documented case studies are used to provide empirical illustrations of surveillance–trust dynamics. Analytically, the chapter employs critical discourse analysis to examine policy and platform narratives (Fairclough, 2013), thematic analysis to identify recurring patterns related to trust, privacy, and surveillance (Braun & Clarke, 2006), and comparative regulatory analysis to situate India's framework alongside global regimes such as the European Union's General Data Protection Regulation. Ethical considerations guide the methodology throughout: all data sources are publicly available and properly cited, individual-level personal data are avoided, and the analysis remains focused on institutional practices and governance structures, aligning methodological choices with the chapter's normative critique of data exploitation and profiling (Couldry & Mejias, 2019; Iliadis & Russo, 2016).

4. DIGITAL INFRASTRUCTURE AND DATAFICATION IN INDIA

India's contemporary digital marketing ecosystem is inseparable from the expansion of large-scale digital infrastructures promoted under the banner of Digital India. Over the past decade, state-led initiatives such as India Stack have created an integrated digital architecture that combines identity verification, financial transactions, and data exchange at an unprecedented scale (Khera, 2019). Core components of this infrastructure—Aadhaar, the Unified Payments Interface (UPI), and nationwide telecom networks—have enabled the routine digitization of everyday activities, generating vast volumes of behavioral data that extend well beyond commercial domains.

Aadhaar, as a biometric identity system, plays a foundational role in this data ecosystem. Initially designed to streamline welfare delivery and reduce exclusion, Aadhaar has gradually become embedded across financial services, telecommunications, and platform-based applications (Ramanathan, 2017). When linked with UPI transactions, mobile SIM registrations, and app-based services, Aadhaar-enabled systems facilitate continuous data generation and linkage. Although legal safeguards formally restrict certain uses, the practical integration of identity, payment, and service platforms creates fertile conditions for data aggregation and profiling that can be leveraged for marketing purposes.

The rapid expansion of digital infrastructure has been further accelerated by the so-called "Jio effect," referring to the entry of Reliance Jio into the telecom market with low-cost data plans and smartphones. This intervention dramatically increased internet penetration, particularly among lower-income and rural populations, making India one of the world's largest digital user bases (Arora, 2019). While this expansion has democratized access to digital services, it has also normalized pervasive data extraction, as affordability and convenience often come at the cost of extensive surveillance embedded within platforms and applications.

As a result of these developments, citizens are increasingly transformed into data subjects whose everyday actions—payments, mobility, communication, and consumption—are continuously recorded and analyzed. These data traces are subsequently repurposed into consumer profiles that inform targeted advertising, personalization strategies, and predictive analytics (Couldry & Mejias, 2019). The shift from citizenship to datafication blurs normative distinctions between public participation and market behavior, raising questions about consent, autonomy, and the ownership of digital identities.

The boundaries between governance, commerce, and surveillance have consequently become increasingly porous. Data generated through public infrastructure and welfare-related interactions frequently intersect with private-sector platforms and marketing ecosystems. This convergence reflects a broader political economy in which state capacity, platform capitalism, and data-driven markets are mutually reinforcing (Cohen, 2019). Surveillance is no longer confined to either the state or the market but emerges through hybrid arrangements that complicate accountability and regulatory oversight.

Within this environment, marketing becomes embedded within everyday digital life rather than appearing as a discrete commercial activity. Recommendations, notifications, and personalized offers are seamlessly integrated into payment apps, social media platforms, and service interfaces, shaping consumer behavior in subtle and continuous ways (Turow, 2017). This embedding of marketing within infrastructural systems renders surveillance largely invisible while intensifying its influence, underscoring the need to critically examine how trust, power, and data governance are negotiated in India's digital transformation.

Table 2. India stack, data generation, and marketing implications

Component	Primary Function	Data Generated	Marketing Implication
Aadhaar	Identity authentication	Biometric, demographic	Identity linkage
UPI	Digital payments	Transactional data	Consumption profiling
Telecom networks	Connectivity	Location, usage data	Behavioral analytics
Platforms/apps	Service delivery	Engagement data	Targeted advertising

Sources: Government of India (2020); Khera (2019); Ramanathan (2017)

5. THE STRUCTURE OF INDIA'S DIGITAL MARKETING ECONOMY

India's digital marketing economy has expanded rapidly over the last decade, driven by rising internet penetration, mobile-first consumption, and platform-based business models. Digital advertising has grown to dominate marketing expenditure in sectors such as e-commerce, fintech, education technology, and entertainment, while influencer marketing has emerged as a powerful tool for engaging vernacular and niche audiences (IAMAI, 2023). This growth reflects a broader shift in marketing strategies from mass communication toward personalized, data-driven engagement that leverages user data at scale.

At the center of this ecosystem are global technology platforms such as Google and Meta, which control a substantial share of India's digital advertising market through search, social media, and display advertising services. Alongside these firms, Indian conglomerates—particularly those operating across telecommunications, retail, and finance—have increasingly integrated digital marketing capabilities into their platform ecosystems (Srnicek, 2017). Companies such as Reliance, through its telecom and retail arms, combine infrastructure ownership with data-driven marketing, deepening their capacity to collect and monetize consumer data. Ad-tech intermediaries, including demand-side platforms, supply-side platforms, and data management platforms, further mediate transactions between advertisers and audiences, often operating with limited public visibility.

Programmatic advertising constitutes a core mechanism within India's digital marketing economy. Through automated, real-time bidding systems, advertisers purchase access to user attention based on algorithmic assessments of relevance and value. Artificial intelligence and machine-learning models analyze vast datasets to optimize targeting, content placement, and pricing, enabling personalization at unprecedented speed and scale (Turow, 2017). While such systems enhance efficiency, they also intensify surveillance by requiring continuous data collection and behavioral profiling to function effectively.

The complexity of the digital marketing supply chain has given rise to opaque data flows that challenge transparency and accountability. Data brokers aggregate information from multiple sources, including apps, websites, and offline transactions, creating detailed consumer profiles that are traded across marketing networks (Pasquale, 2015). These practices often occur beyond the awareness of consumers and regulators, reinforcing asymmetrical power relations between platforms, marketers, and users. Market consolidation further exacerbates these dynamics, as dominant platforms internalize multiple stages of the advertising value chain, reducing competition and limiting oversight.

Recent technological and regulatory developments have accelerated the transition toward a post-cookie advertising environment. The gradual deprecation of third-party cookies has prompted platforms and advertisers to rely more heavily on first-party data collected directly from users through proprietary ecosystems. While this shift is frequently framed as a privacy-enhancing reform, it tends to consolidate data control within large platforms that already possess extensive user datasets (Cohen, 2019). As a result, first-party data dominance may reduce external data sharing while simultaneously deepening surveillance within closed systems, raising new challenges for competition, governance, and consumer trust in India's digital marketing economy.

Table 3. Key actors in India's digital marketing economy

Actor Category	Examples	Role in Surveillance Economy
Global platforms	Google, Meta	Data aggregation, targeting
Indian conglomerates	Reliance, Flipkart	Integrated data ecosystems
Ad-tech intermediaries	DSPs, SSPs	Automated personalization
Influencers/creators	Agencies, creators	Persuasive amplification

Sources: IAMAI (2023); Srnicek (2017); Turow (2017)

6. TECHNOLOGIES OF MARKETING SURVEILLANCE

Digital marketing surveillance is enabled by a dense assemblage of data capture technologies that operate across platforms, devices, and applications. Core mechanisms include cookies, software development kits (SDKs), tracking pixels, metadata extraction, and persistent device identifiers, which together allow marketers to monitor user behavior continuously across digital environments (Turow, 2017). While individual technologies may appear benign, their combined operation produces comprehensive behavioral datasets that far exceed the scope of user awareness or consent. These infrastructures form the technical backbone of surveillance-based marketing.

Data collected through these mechanisms are processed through algorithmic profiling systems that categorize users according to inferred interests, socio-demographic attributes, and predicted behaviors. Machine-learning models analyze browsing patterns, purchase histories, location data, and engagement metrics to generate probabilistic assessments of consumer preferences (Beer, 2017). Real-time bidding systems then operationalize these profiles by auctioning user attention within milliseconds, transforming personal data into a tradable commodity in automated advertising markets (Pasquale, 2015). This process exemplifies how surveillance is monetized at scale.

Beyond overt targeting, marketing surveillance increasingly relies on behavioral manipulation through interface design. Dark patterns—design choices that steer users toward particular actions—exploit cognitive biases such as urgency, social proof, and default acceptance (Mathur et al., 2019). Nudging strategies embedded in apps and platforms subtly shape consumer decisions while maintaining the appearance of choice. These practices blur the distinction between persuasion and coercion, raising ethical concerns about autonomy and informed consent (Cohen, 2019).

In the Indian context, surveillance technologies have expanded into vernacular and affective domains. Vernacular targeting leverages regional languages, cultural cues, and localized influencers to engage diverse user groups, particularly in Tier-2 and Tier-3 cities (Arora, 2019). At the same time, emerging practices such as emotional analytics and biometric data capture—through facial recognition, voice analysis, and sentiment detection—seek to infer users' emotional states and physiological responses. Although still evolving, these technologies extend surveillance beyond behavior into affect, intensifying concerns about psychological manipulation and discrimination (Zuboff, 2019).

Consumer acceptance of personalization is often negotiated through what scholars describe as the "creepy–cool" boundary—the threshold at which tailored content shifts from being perceived as helpful to being experienced as intrusive (Turow, 2017). While personalization can enhance convenience and relevance, excessive or poorly explained targeting undermines trust and heightens perceptions of surveillance. In India's data-rich but regulation-constrained environment, navigating this boundary remains a central challenge for marketers and policymakers alike, underscoring the need for transparent, accountable, and ethically grounded approaches to digital marketing technologies.

Table 4. Technologies used in surveillance-based digital marketing

Technology	Function	Ethical Concern
Cookies / SDKs	Behavioral tracking	Invisibility of consent
Real-time bidding	Attention monetization	Opacity
AI profiling	Predictive targeting	Bias, manipulation
Emotional analytics	Affect inference	Psychological intrusion

Sources: Mathur et al. (2019); Zuboff (2019); O'Neil (2016)

7. PLATFORM POWER AND THE POLITICAL ECONOMY OF DATA

Platform power constitutes a defining structural feature of India's digital marketing economy. Digital platforms operate within highly concentrated markets where a small number of firms dominate access to audiences, data, and advertising infrastructure. Global technology companies such as Google and Meta command disproportionate control over search, social media, and display advertising, while large Indian conglomerates increasingly integrate telecommunications, retail, finance, and digital services within unified platform ecosystems (Srnicek, 2017). This concentration limits competition and amplifies the capacity of platforms to shape market norms, data practices, and regulatory agendas.

Within platform economies, attention functions as both an economic and political resource. Digital marketing systems are designed to capture, retain, and monetize user attention through personalized content, notifications, and algorithmic curation (Hwang, 2020). Attention is not merely a commercial asset but also a mechanism through which platforms influence visibility, discourse, and consumer behavior. By prioritizing certain content and suppressing others, algorithmic systems shape public perception and consumption patterns, blurring the boundary between economic optimization and social governance (Beer, 2017).

Asymmetrical data ownership further reinforces platform power. Platforms retain exclusive control over vast datasets generated by users, while consumers possess limited rights to access, understand, or contest how their data are processed. Algorithmic decision-making systems remain opaque, protected by claims of proprietary technology and trade secrecy, creating what Pasquale (2015) describes as a "black box" society. This opacity prevents meaningful scrutiny of how profiling, ranking, and targeting decisions are made, undermining accountability and informed trust.

In the Indian context, platform power is deeply entangled with state and market institutions. State–platform–market interdependence has intensified as digital platforms become integral to governance, service delivery, and economic development. Public digital infrastructures, regulatory frameworks, and private platforms increasingly operate in tandem, creating hybrid arrangements that blur distinctions between public interest and commercial imperatives (Cohen, 2019). This convergence complicates regulatory oversight, particularly when national development goals and data sovereignty concerns align with platform expansion.

Surveillance marketing thus emerges not merely as a set of techniques but as a structural form of power embedded within contemporary capitalism. Through continuous data extraction, predictive analytics, and behavioral influence, platforms exercise a form of governance that shapes choices, opportunities, and social relations (Zuboff, 2019). In India's rapidly digitizing society, this form of power has far-reaching implications for trust, autonomy, and democratic accountability, underscoring the need to critically examine platform dominance within the broader political economy of data.

8. TRUST, PRIVACY, AND CONSUMER SENSE-MAKING

Indian consumers do not passively accept digital marketing surveillance; rather, they actively interpret, negotiate, and make sense of data collection practices within their everyday digital experiences. These interpretations are shaped by interactions with platforms, brands, and digital services that increasingly require data sharing as a condition of participation. Trust is therefore constructed pragmatically, based not only on abstract principles of privacy but also on perceived utility, convenience, and necessity of digital services (Lupton, 2015; Arora, 2019). In this context, trust often emerges as situational and conditional rather than absolute.

A central feature of consumer sense-making in India is the privacy paradox, wherein individuals express strong concerns about data protection while simultaneously engaging in extensive data sharing for functional benefits (Acquisti et al., 2015). Surveys and studies consistently show that Indian users value privacy and express anxiety about misuse of personal data, yet continue to use data-intensive platforms for payments, communication, entertainment, and shopping. This paradox is reinforced by the lack of viable alternatives to dominant platforms and by the perception that opting out of digital ecosystems entails significant social and economic costs (Turow, 2017).

Cultural norms and social hierarchies further shape how trust and privacy are understood. In societies marked by hierarchical institutions and collectivist orientations, trust is often placed in authority structures, whether state-led initiatives or large corporations perceived as legitimate and powerful (Fukuyama, 1995). In the Indian digital context, this can manifest as digital fatalism—the belief that surveillance is inevitable and beyond individual control. Such fatalism reduces expectations of privacy and weakens resistance to data extraction, normalizing surveillance as a routine feature of modern life (Couldry & Mejias, 2019).

Digital literacy plays a crucial role in mediating consent and trust. Many users lack the technical knowledge required to understand complex data practices, privacy policies, or algorithmic decision-making systems. As a result, consent is frequently reduced to a procedural act—clicking "accept" to access services—rather than an informed and voluntary choice (Cohen, 2019). This phenomenon, often described as consent fatigue, undermines the normative foundations of data protection frameworks that rely heavily on individual choice and responsibility.

These dynamics have significant implications for brand legitimacy and long-term consumer trust. While data-driven personalization may enhance short-term engagement, excessive surveillance, unexplained targeting, and repeated data breaches can erode confidence in brands and platforms (Pasquale, 2015). Trust becomes fragile when consumers perceive a mismatch between corporate promises and actual data practices. In India's competitive digital marketplace, sustaining trust increasingly depends on transparency, accountability, and demonstrable respect for consumer autonomy, rather than solely on technological sophistication or convenience.

Table 5. Privacy attitudes and behaviors in India

Indicator	Approx. Percentage
Concerned about misuse of personal data	80–85%
Share data for convenience	70–75%
Read privacy policies fully	<15%
Feel control over personal data	<30%

Sources: Pew Research Center (2023); IAMAI (2022); OECD (2021)

9. SURVEILLANCE, INEQUALITY, AND SOCIAL SORTING

Surveillance-based digital marketing does not operate on a socially neutral terrain; rather, it intersects with and often amplifies existing forms of inequality. Algorithmic systems used in marketing rely on automated categorization to segment users into marketable groups based on inferred characteristics, behaviors, and predicted value (Beer, 2017). These classifications are not merely technical but social, as they reflect assumptions embedded in data, models, and institutional priorities. As a result, algorithmic bias can emerge when systems disproportionately disadvantage certain groups or reproduce historical patterns of exclusion (Noble, 2018).

In the Indian context, social sorting through digital marketing is closely tied to proxies for caste, class, gender, language, and region. Although such sensitive attributes are rarely collected explicitly, algorithms infer them through indirect indicators such as location, consumption patterns, device type, language preference, and online behavior. Scholars have noted that these proxies can function as a "digital caste system," wherein individuals are differentially targeted, excluded, or valued based on inferred social position (Eubanks, 2018; Couldry & Mejias, 2019). For example, vernacular users may be targeted with lower-quality financial products or excluded from premium services, reinforcing socio-economic stratification.

Differential exposure to surveillance risks further compounds inequality. Users with higher socio-economic status often possess greater digital literacy, access to privacy-enhancing tools, and awareness of data protection rights, enabling them to mitigate surveillance to some extent. In contrast, lower-income and rural populations are more likely to rely on subsidized data plans, bundled apps, and public digital infrastructures that embed extensive data collection by default (Arora, 2019). These users face heightened exposure to surveillance without commensurate capacity for resistance or redress.

Certain groups experience particular vulnerabilities within surveillance-driven marketing ecosystems. Children are increasingly exposed to targeted advertising through educational apps, gaming platforms, and social media, raising concerns about manipulation and long-term data profiling (Keddell, 2018). Women face distinct risks related to privacy, safety, and discriminatory targeting, including gendered advertising and harassment facilitated by data-driven platforms. Elderly users often encounter challenges related to low digital literacy and heightened susceptibility to deceptive practices, while rural users confront limited regulatory awareness and fewer alternatives to dominant platforms.

The ethical and social justice implications of these dynamics are profound. Surveillance-based marketing risks normalizing unequal treatment and reinforcing structural disadvantage under the guise of personalization and efficiency. From a normative perspective, such practices challenge principles of fairness, autonomy, and equal participation in digital markets (O'Neil, 2016). Addressing these issues requires moving beyond individual consent toward collective safeguards, algorithmic accountability, and equity-centered governance frameworks that recognize how surveillance and inequality are mutually reinforcing in India's digital transformation.

Table 6. Surveillance exposure and vulnerability across social groups

Group	Level of Exposure	Key Risks
Urban elites	Moderate	Behavioral nudging
Rural users	High	Low awareness
Women	High	Harassment, targeting
Children	High	Behavioral conditioning
Elderly	High	Deceptive interfaces

Sources: Eubanks (2018); Noble (2018); UNICEF (2021)

10. DIGITAL MARKETING, POLITICS, AND DEMOCRACY

The techniques and infrastructures developed for commercial digital marketing have increasingly migrated into the political sphere, reshaping electoral communication and democratic processes. Political advertising now routinely relies on data-driven targeting, behavioral profiling, and audience segmentation to deliver customized messages to specific voter groups (Howard, 2020). In India, the scale of the electorate combined with widespread platform usage has made voter micro-targeting an attractive strategy for political actors seeking to optimize persuasion and mobilization.

This convergence of commercial marketing tools and electoral strategies reflects a broader transformation in political communication. Techniques originally designed to sell products—such as psychographic profiling, A/B testing, and engagement optimization—are now applied to political messaging and campaign management (Kreiss & McGregor, 2019). As a result, political campaigns increasingly resemble marketing operations, where voters are treated as segmented audiences rather than as participants in collective deliberation. This shift raises normative concerns about transparency, accountability, and the quality of democratic engagement.

Platforms such as WhatsApp, along with social media influencers and algorithmic recommendation systems, play a central role in amplifying political content in India. WhatsApp's encrypted, closed-group architecture facilitates the rapid dissemination of targeted messages, often beyond the reach of public scrutiny or regulatory oversight (Vaidhyanathan, 2018). Influencers, operating at the intersection of commerce and politics, further blur boundaries by embedding political messaging within lifestyle and entertainment content. Algorithmic amplification prioritizes emotionally resonant and sensational material, increasing visibility while reducing contextual nuance (Beer, 2017).

These dynamics contribute to polarization, misinformation, and the erosion of civic trust. Targeted political advertising enables campaigns to deliver inconsistent or misleading messages to different groups, undermining shared public discourse (Bradshaw & Howard, 2019). The spread of misinformation through algorithmically amplified networks weakens confidence in institutions, media, and electoral processes, while the opacity of targeting practices limits citizens' ability to contest or verify political claims.

Viewed through a socio-political lens, marketing surveillance functions as a political technology that extends beyond commercial influence into the governance of public opinion. By continuously monitoring, predicting, and shaping individual behavior, surveillance-based marketing systems exert subtle yet pervasive control over political perception and participation (Zuboff, 2019). In India's democratic context, this raises urgent questions about the balance between technological innovation and democratic accountability, highlighting the need for regulatory frameworks that address not only market practices but also the political consequences of data-driven persuasion.

Table 7. Commercial vs political surveillance practices

Dimension	Commercial Marketing	Political Campaigns
Data source	Consumer behavior	Voter data
Tools	AI targeting, influencers	WhatsApp, social media
Objective	Conversion	Mobilization
Risk	Manipulation	Democratic erosion

Sources: Bradshaw & Howard (2019); Vaidhyanathan (2018)

11. REGULATION AND GOVERNANCE OF MARKETING SURVEILLANCE

India's regulatory response to data-driven marketing surveillance has been consolidated through the enactment of the Digital Personal Data Protection Act (DPDPA) in 2023 and the subsequent framing of operational Rules in 2025. The Act represents India's first comprehensive legal framework dedicated specifically to personal data protection, marking a significant shift from earlier, fragmented approaches embedded within information technology law (Bhandari & Sreenivasan, 2023). The DPDPA establishes principles governing data collection, processing, storage, and transfer, with direct implications for digital marketing practices that rely heavily on behavioral data and algorithmic profiling.

A central pillar of the DPDPA is the emphasis on consent and the delineation of obligations for data fiduciaries. Marketers and platforms are required to obtain free, informed, specific, and unambiguous consent prior to processing personal data, except in narrowly defined circumstances (Government of India, 2023). The Act also introduces obligations related to purpose limitation, data minimization, and security safeguards, alongside penalties for non-compliance. While these provisions aim to enhance consumer trust and accountability, critics argue that consent-centric governance places disproportionate responsibility on individuals, despite persistent information asymmetries and limited digital literacy (Cohen, 2019).

The establishment of the Data Protection Board of India constitutes the primary institutional mechanism for enforcement under the new regime. The Board is empowered to investigate breaches, impose monetary penalties, and adjudicate disputes related to data protection violations. However, concerns have been raised regarding its independence, capacity, and procedural transparency, particularly given its appointment structure and the broad discretionary powers retained by the executive (Greenleaf, 2018). These limitations may constrain the Board's effectiveness in regulating powerful digital platforms and marketing intermediaries.

In parallel with statutory regulation, industry self-regulation continues to play a role in governing marketing surveillance. The Advertising Standards Council of India (ASCI) has issued guidelines addressing influencer marketing, digital advertising disclosures, and consumer protection. While these frameworks encourage ethical practices and transparency, compliance remains largely voluntary and enforcement mechanisms are limited. As a result, self-regulation often functions as a supplementary rather than substitutive form of governance, particularly in high-stakes areas such as data profiling and targeted advertising (Pasquale, 2015).

Comparative analysis with global governance models, particularly the European Union's General Data Protection Regulation (GDPR), highlights both convergence and divergence in regulatory approaches. While India's framework shares core principles such as consent and accountability, it differs in enforcement strength, scope of individual rights, and exemptions for state activities (Solove, 2021). These differences reflect broader tensions between economic growth, data sovereignty, and rights-based governance. For India, the challenge lies in translating formal legal protections into effective regulatory practice capable of addressing the structural power of surveillance-based marketing systems.

Table 8. Comparative overview of data protection frameworks

Dimension	DPDP Act (India)	GDPR (EU)
Consent	Central	Central
State exemptions	Broad	Narrow
Enforcement	Developing	Strong
Individual rights	Limited	Extensive

Sources: Government of India (2023); Greenleaf (2018)

12. RESISTANCE, ETHICS, AND INDUSTRY RESPONSES

As surveillance-based digital marketing has expanded, consumers have increasingly engaged in everyday forms of resistance aimed at reducing unwanted data collection and behavioral influence. Practices such as ad-blocking, selective app usage, privacy-enhancing browser extensions, and periods of digital detox reflect growing discomfort with pervasive tracking and targeted persuasion (Couldry & Mejias, 2019). While these strategies signal awareness and agency, they are often fragmented and unevenly distributed across socio-economic groups, limiting their broader effectiveness in challenging systemic surveillance.

For marketers and platforms, resistance raises ethical dilemmas centered on the tension between return on investment (ROI) and respect for privacy and human dignity. Precision targeting and algorithmic optimization promise efficiency and profitability, yet they rely on extensive data extraction and opaque profiling practices (Zuboff, 2019). Ethical critiques argue that marketing strategies prioritizing engagement metrics risk reducing individuals to data points, undermining autonomy and informed choice (Floridi, 2014). Navigating this dilemma requires reconsidering the normative assumptions that equate personalization with consumer benefit.

In response to regulatory pressure and shifting public sentiment, some firms have adopted transparency reports and privacy-first branding strategies as reputational tools. Public disclosures regarding data practices, consent mechanisms, and algorithmic governance are increasingly framed as competitive advantages in trust-sensitive markets (Pasquale, 2015). However, scholars caution that such initiatives often function as symbolic compliance, offering limited insight into actual data flows or decision-making processes. Transparency without accountability may therefore fail to meaningfully restore trust.

Influencer culture has also become a site of ethical negotiation and resistance. Influencer de-marketing and authenticity movements emphasize disclosure, minimalism, and critical engagement with consumerism, challenging extractive advertising norms (Abidin, 2021). While these movements resonate with audiences seeking genuine engagement, they remain embedded within platform economies that monetize visibility and engagement. As such, authenticity itself can become a marketable asset, complicating claims of resistance.

Ultimately, the limits of resistance within platform capitalism highlight the structural nature of surveillance-based marketing. Individual and industry-level responses operate within ecosystems dominated by powerful platforms that control infrastructure, data, and visibility (Srnicek, 2017). Meaningful transformation therefore requires collective action, regulatory intervention, and institutional reform that address power asymmetries rather than relying solely on consumer choice or voluntary ethical commitments. Resistance, while symbolically significant, must be complemented by systemic governance to reshape the conditions under which digital marketing operates.

13. EMERGING FUTURES OF DIGITAL MARKETING IN INDIA

Debates on the future of digital marketing in India increasingly emphasize the need to move beyond surveillance-centric models toward rights-based and trust-oriented frameworks. Post-surveillance marketing envisions practices that limit excessive data extraction, prioritize user agency, and align commercial objectives with fundamental rights to privacy and dignity (Floridi, 2014; Zuboff, 2019). In this perspective, marketing effectiveness is redefined not solely by behavioral prediction and manipulation, but by transparency, fairness, and long-term relational trust between brands and consumers.

One proposed pathway toward such a future is the adoption of slow marketing and data minimization principles. Slow marketing advocates deliberate, less intrusive engagement strategies that emphasize relevance, consent, and respect for consumer attention, countering the logic of constant optimization and hyper-personalization (Turow, 2017). Data minimization, as a governance and design principle, seeks to restrict data collection to what is strictly necessary for specific purposes, reducing exposure to breaches and misuse. Trust-centric design further integrates privacy safeguards and explainability into marketing technologies, positioning ethical responsibility as a core feature rather than an external constraint (Cohen, 2019).

Emerging debates around Web3, decentralization, and data sovereignty also shape imaginaries of India's digital future. Proponents argue that decentralized architectures and user-controlled data wallets could rebalance power relations by enabling individuals to manage access to their data and participate more equitably in digital markets (Couldry & Mejias, 2019). However, critics caution that technological decentralization alone may not resolve structural inequalities, particularly in contexts marked by uneven digital literacy and infrastructural access. In India, data sovereignty discourse intersects with national development goals, raising questions about whether decentralization will empower citizens or primarily serve state and corporate interests.

At the same time, new technological frontiers are expanding the scope of marketing surveillance. Connected television (CTV) advertising integrates household viewing data with cross-device tracking, while metaverse environments promise immersive, data-rich interactions that blur boundaries between entertainment, commerce, and social life (Hwang, 2020). Biometric surveillance, including facial recognition and emotion detection, further extends marketing into intimate dimensions of human experience. These developments intensify ethical concerns about consent, proportionality, and psychological autonomy, particularly in regulatory environments still adapting to earlier forms of digital surveillance (O'Neil, 2016).

India's strategic choices in navigating these futures will shape the character of its digital economy and democratic culture. Policy decisions regarding data governance, competition regulation, and technological deployment will determine whether innovation reinforces extractive surveillance or supports inclusive, rights-respecting growth. As one of the world's largest and most diverse digital markets, India occupies a pivotal position in global debates on the future of marketing. The direction it adopts—toward intensified surveillance or toward trust-centered digital governance—will have lasting implications for consumer autonomy, market legitimacy, and democratic accountability.

Table 9. Empirical case illustrations of surveillance and trust

Case	Core Issue	Trust Impact	Regulatory Response
Meta–WhatsApp	Data sharing	Trust erosion	CCI scrutiny
Elections	Micro-targeting	Civic concern	Limited oversight
Data breach	Security failure	Brand distrust	Penalties

Sources: Pasquale (2015); Howard (2020); Solove (2021)

14. CASE ILLUSTRATIONS AND EMPIRICAL REFLECTIONS

Empirical case illustrations provide concrete insight into how surveillance and trust intersect within India's digital marketing ecosystem. While the chapter does not rely on primary fieldwork, carefully selected, publicly documented cases serve as analytical lenses through which broader structural dynamics can be examined. These cases are not treated as isolated incidents but as symptomatic of systemic patterns in platform governance, data exploitation, and regulatory response (Yin, 2018). Together, they illuminate the lived consequences of surveillance-based marketing for consumers, political processes, and institutional trust.

One of the most prominent cases shaping public discourse on data governance in India is the Meta–WhatsApp data-sharing controversy. When WhatsApp announced changes to its privacy policy that expanded data sharing with its parent company Meta, concerns emerged regarding consent, market dominance, and cross-platform profiling (Vaidhyanathan, 2018). Although the policy was framed as a technical update, it highlighted asymmetries in power between users and platforms, particularly given WhatsApp's near-ubiquitous presence in India. Regulatory scrutiny by competition authorities and public backlash underscored how data-sharing practices can erode trust when transparency and meaningful choice are perceived to be absent (Pasquale, 2015).

Political advertising during recent Indian elections offers a second critical illustration of surveillance–trust dynamics. Campaigns increasingly employed data-driven targeting strategies adapted from commercial marketing, using social media platforms, influencers, and messaging applications to deliver tailored political content (Bradshaw & Howard, 2019). The opacity of these practices—especially within encrypted environments such as WhatsApp—raised concerns about misinformation, unequal exposure to political messages, and the erosion of a shared public sphere. These developments demonstrate how marketing surveillance functions not only as an economic tool but also as a mechanism of political influence with implications for democratic legitimacy (Howard, 2020).

A third illustrative domain involves major data breaches within India's e-commerce and fintech sectors. Publicly reported incidents involving unauthorized access to customer data have highlighted vulnerabilities in rapidly expanding digital services that depend on large-scale data collection (Solove, 2021). Such breaches undermine consumer confidence and expose the limits of security assurances offered by platforms. Importantly, the long-term impact of these incidents often extends beyond immediate financial harm, contributing to generalized distrust toward digital services and skepticism about the ability of firms to safeguard personal information (O'Neil, 2016).

Across these cases, regulatory, consumer, and market responses reveal both progress and persistent challenges. Regulatory interventions, including investigations and fines, signal growing institutional awareness but often struggle to keep pace with technological complexity and platform power. Consumer reactions range from temporary outrage to resignation, reflecting the constraints of digital dependency and limited alternatives. Market responses—such as revised privacy policies or transparency statements—frequently emphasize compliance and reputational repair, yet rarely address deeper structural issues related to data extraction and algorithmic opacity (Cohen, 2019).

From a methodological perspective, case-based inference offers valuable interpretive insight while also imposing limitations. These cases cannot be generalized statistically to all instances of digital marketing in India; instead, they function as critical exemplars that reveal how surveillance and trust are negotiated within specific institutional contexts (Yin, 2018). By triangulating regulatory actions, media reports, and scholarly analyses, the chapter uses case illustrations to enrich theoretical arguments and ground abstract concepts in observable practice. This approach reinforces the chapter's broader claim that surveillance-based marketing must be understood as a socio-political phenomenon shaped by power, governance, and contested meanings rather than as a purely technical or managerial issue.

15. DISCUSSION: REBUILDING TRUST IN A DATA-DRIVEN SOCIETY

The preceding analysis demonstrates that trust erosion in India's digital marketing ecosystem is not an accidental by-product of technological change but a structural outcome of surveillance-based business models embedded within platform capitalism. Surveillance, as operationalized through data extraction, profiling, and behavioral prediction, redistributes power asymmetrically between platforms, markets, and users (Zuboff, 2019; Srnicek, 2017). Trust is undermined not merely because data are collected, but because these processes are opaque, continuous, and largely uncontestable. The synthesis of empirical illustrations and theoretical perspectives reveals that trust deficits emerge where surveillance is normalized without corresponding mechanisms of accountability and democratic oversight.

The interplay between markets, the state, and citizens further complicates the trust landscape. In India, public digital infrastructures and private platforms increasingly operate in tandem, producing hybrid governance arrangements that blur distinctions between welfare delivery, commercial activity, and surveillance (Cohen, 2019). While the state frames digitalization as a tool for efficiency and inclusion, citizens often encounter it as an inescapable condition of participation in social and economic life. This convergence reduces meaningful choice, reinforcing digital dependency and weakening the capacity of individuals to negotiate consent on equitable terms (Couldry & Mejias, 2019).

These dynamics carry significant implications for democracy, inclusion, and accountability. Surveillance-driven marketing practices shape not only consumption but also political communication, public discourse, and civic participation. Algorithmic targeting and content amplification fragment the public sphere, facilitate misinformation, and undermine shared democratic deliberation (Howard, 2020; Vaidhyanathan, 2018). Moreover, as demonstrated earlier, surveillance disproportionately affects marginalized populations, reinforcing existing inequalities related to caste, class, gender, and geography (Noble, 2018; Eubanks, 2018). In this sense, trust erosion is inseparable from broader questions of social justice and democratic legitimacy.

Rebuilding trust in a data-driven society therefore requires systemic rather than incremental interventions. From a policy perspective, regulatory frameworks must move beyond procedural consent toward substantive accountability, including algorithmic transparency, enforceable limits on data exploitation, and meaningful remedies for harm (Solove, 2021). Strengthening the independence and capacity of regulatory institutions is essential to counterbalance platform power and restore public confidence. For industry actors, ethical marketing cannot remain a peripheral branding strategy; it must be integrated into core business models through data minimization, explainable personalization, and respect for user autonomy (Floridi, 2014).

At the societal level, rebuilding trust also depends on collective engagement and institutional reform. Civil society organizations, academic institutions, and independent media play a critical role in scrutinizing data practices, amplifying public debate, and fostering digital literacy (Pasquale, 2015). Trust, in this context, should be understood not as blind faith in technology or markets, but as a relational condition grounded in transparency, reciprocity, and accountability. India's trajectory as a leading digital society will ultimately depend on whether data-driven innovation is aligned with democratic values and human dignity, or whether surveillance continues to expand without commensurate safeguards.

16. CONCLUSION

This chapter has examined India's digital marketing landscape through the intertwined lenses of surveillance, trust, and socio-political power. It has shown that contemporary digital marketing is no longer confined to commercial persuasion but operates as a system of continuous data extraction, behavioral prediction, and algorithmic influence embedded within everyday digital infrastructures (Zuboff, 2019; Srnicek, 2017). The analysis demonstrated that trust erosion is not simply a function of technological misuse or isolated data breaches, but a structural outcome of opaque data practices, platform concentration, and asymmetrical power relations between markets, the state, and citizens.

A central finding of the chapter is that India's rapid digital transformation has intensified the tension between innovation and rights. While data-driven marketing has contributed to economic growth, inclusion, and service efficiency, it has also normalized pervasive surveillance that undermines privacy, autonomy, and dignity

(Cohen, 2019). The reliance on consent-based governance frameworks, in contexts marked by digital dependency and uneven literacy, limits the effectiveness of individual choice as a safeguard (Solove, 2021). Balancing innovation with rights therefore requires rethinking governance models to prioritize accountability, proportionality, and collective protections rather than solely procedural compliance.

The chapter contributes to the broader literature on digital marketing ethics and data governance by situating marketing surveillance within India's unique socio-political context. By integrating political economy, critical data studies, and digital sociology, it extends existing debates beyond Western-centric frameworks and highlights how caste, class, language, and institutional hierarchies shape experiences of surveillance and trust (Noble, 2018; Couldry & Mejias, 2019). In doing so, it underscores that ethical digital marketing cannot be addressed purely through technical fixes or self-regulation, but must engage with questions of power, democracy, and social justice.

Finally, the chapter points toward several directions for future research. Empirical studies incorporating primary data—such as consumer interviews, ethnographic research, and experimental analyses—could deepen understanding of how trust is negotiated across different social groups in India. Comparative research examining India alongside other Global South and Global North contexts would further illuminate divergent governance trajectories. As emerging technologies such as biometric analytics, connected television, and immersive digital environments reshape marketing practices, ongoing critical inquiry will be essential. The future of India's digital economy will depend on whether surveillance-driven innovation is recalibrated toward trust-centered, rights-respecting models that uphold democratic values and human dignity.

REFERENCES

Abidin, C. (2021). Mapping Internet celebrity on TikTok: Exploring attention economies and visibility labours. *Cultural Science Journal, 12*(1), 77–103. DOI: 10.5334/csci.140

Acquisti, A., Brandimarte, L., & Loewenstein, G. (2015). Privacy and human behavior in the age of information. *Science, 347*(6221), 509–514. DOI: 10.1126/science.aaa1465 PMID: 25635091

Arora, P. (2019). *The next billion users: Digital life beyond the West.* Harvard University Press. DOI: 10.4159/9780674238879

Beer, D. (2017). The social power of algorithms. *Information Communication and Society, 20*(1), 1–13. DOI: 10.1080/1369118X.2016.1216147

Bhandari, V., & Sreenivasan, S. (2023). India's Digital Personal Data Protection Act: Promise and pitfalls. *Economic and Political Weekly, 58*(34), 14–18.

Bradshaw, S., & Howard, P. N. (2019). *The global disinformation order.* Oxford Internet Institute.

Braun, V., & Clarke, V. (2006). Using thematic analysis in psychology. *Qualitative Research in Psychology, 3*(2), 77–101. DOI: 10.1191/1478088706qp063oa

Cohen, J. E. (2019). *Between truth and power: The legal constructions of informational capitalism.* Oxford University Press. DOI: 10.1093/oso/9780190246693.001.0001

Couldry, N., & Mejias, U. A. (2019). *The costs of connection: How data is colonizing human life and appropriating it for capitalism.* Stanford University Press.

Denzin, N. K., & Lincoln, Y. S. (2018). *The Sage handbook of qualitative research* (5th ed.). Sage.

Eubanks, V. (2018). *Automating inequality: How high-tech tools profile, police, and punish the poor.* St. Martin's Press.

Fairclough, N. (2013). *Critical discourse analysis: The critical study of language* (2nd ed.). Routledge. DOI: 10.4324/9781315834368

Floridi, L. (2014). *The ethics of information.* Oxford University Press.

Fukuyama, F. (1995). *Trust: The social virtues and the creation of prosperity.* Free Press.

Government of India. (2023). *The Digital Personal Data Protection Act, 2023.* Ministry of Law and Justice.

Greenleaf, G. (2018). Global data privacy laws 2017: 120 national data privacy laws. *Privacy Laws & Business International Report, 145*, 10–13.

Howard, P. N. (2020). *Lie machines: How to save democracy from troll armies, deceitful robots, junk news operations, and political operatives.* Yale University Press.

Hwang, T. (2020). *Subprime attention crisis.* FSG Originals.

IAMAI. (2023). *Digital advertising in India report.* Internet and Mobile Association of India.

Iliadis, A., & Russo, F. (2016). Critical data studies: An introduction. *Big Data & Society, 3*(2), 2053951716674238. Advance online publication. DOI: 10.1177/2053951716674238

Keddell, E. (2018). Algorithmic justice in child protection. *Critical Social Policy, 39*(1), 116–135.

Khera, R. (2019). Aadhaar and exclusion: A critical assessment. *Economic and Political Weekly, 54*(20), 50–57.

Kreiss, D., & McGregor, S. C. (2019). Technology firms shape political communication. *Political Communication, 36*(2), 155–177. DOI: 10.1080/10584609.2017.1364814

Lupton, D. (2015). *Digital sociology.* Routledge.

Mathur, A., Acar, G., Friedman, M. J., Lucherini, E., Mayer, J., Chetty, M., & Narayanan, A. (2019). Dark patterns at scale: Findings from a crawl of 11K shopping websites. *Proceedings of the ACM on human-computer interaction, 3*(CSCW), 1-32. DOI: 10.1145/3359183

Noble, S. U. (2018). *Algorithms of oppression.* NYU Press. DOI: 10.18574/nyu/9781479833641.001.0001

O'Neil, C. (2016). *Weapons of math destruction.* Crown.

Pasquale, F. (2015). *The black box society.* Harvard University Press. DOI: 10.4159/harvard.9780674736061

Ramanathan, U. (2017). A dangerous drift: Aadhaar and privacy. *Economic and Political Weekly, 52*(37), 61–70.

Solove, D. J. (2021). *Understanding privacy* (2nd ed.). Harvard University Press.

Srnicek, N. (2017). *Platform capitalism.* Polity Press.

Turow, J. (2017). *The aisles have eyes.* Yale University Press.

Vaidhyanathan, S. (2018). *Antisocial media.* Oxford University Press.

Yin, R. K. (2018). *Case study research and applications* (6th ed.). Sage.

Zuboff, S. (2019). *The age of surveillance capitalism.* PublicAffairs.

Chapter 3
AI, Predictive Analytics, and Automated Influence:
Ethical Frontiers in Algorithmic Marketing

Rachna Rana
Department of Computer Science and Engineering, Ludhiana Group of Colleges, Ludhiana, India

Pankaj Bhambri
http://orcid.org/0000-0003-4437-4103
Department of Information Technology, Guru Nanak Dev Engineering College, Ludhiana, India

ABSTRACT

The proliferation of artificial intelligence (AI) and predictive analytics has fundamentally reshaped digital marketing, enabling hyper-personalized, automated influence at an unprecedented scale. This chapter critically examines the ethical implications of AI-driven marketing systems that leverage consumer data to predict behavior, automate content delivery, and optimize engagement. While such technologies enhance targeting efficiency and campaign performance, they raise profound concerns regarding consumer autonomy, transparency, and manipulative persuasion. We explore the technical mechanisms behind algorithmic influence—including recommendation engines, sentiment analysis, and behavioral nudging—and assess their societal impact through the lenses of privacy, fairness, and accountability. The discussion extends to regulatory frameworks such as GDPR and CCPA, which aim to mitigate risks but often lag behind technological advances.

DOI: 10.4018/979-8-3373-7704-9.ch003

1. INTRODUCTION

1.1. Emergence of Algorithmic Marketing in the Digital Economy

Marketing has undergone a fundamental transformation in the last decade, driven by the rapid advancement of artificial intelligence (AI), big data infrastructures, and predictive analytics. Traditional marketing approaches, which relied heavily on demographic segmentation, historical sales data, and human intuition, are increasingly being replaced by algorithmic systems capable of real-time analysis, prediction, and automated decision-making. These systems leverage vast streams of behavioral, transactional, and contextual data to dynamically tailor marketing messages, recommendations, pricing strategies, and engagement mechanisms at scale (Davenport et al., 2021; Grewal et al., 2021).

Algorithmic marketing refers to the use of AI-driven computational models to automate marketing decisions and optimize consumer interactions. Unlike earlier digital marketing tools that primarily supported human decision-makers, contemporary algorithmic systems actively shape marketing strategies through continuous learning and adaptation. Predictive models now anticipate consumer preferences, estimate purchase probabilities, and infer latent psychological traits, enabling highly granular personalization. While such capabilities improve efficiency and relevance, they also raise significant ethical concerns regarding transparency, autonomy, and fairness.

The growing reliance on algorithmic decision-making marks a shift from persuasion as a communicative act to influence as a computational process. Marketing systems no longer merely respond to consumer demand; they increasingly anticipate, steer, and reinforce behavior through automated feedback loops. This evolution necessitates a critical examination of how AI-driven influence operates and the ethical boundaries within which it should function.

1.2 Artificial Intelligence and Predictive Analytics in Marketing Systems

1.2.1 Role of Artificial Intelligence in Marketing Automation

Artificial intelligence has become a central component of modern marketing infrastructures. Machine learning algorithms analyze large-scale datasets to identify patterns that would be impossible for human analysts to detect. These insights are used to automate tasks such as audience segmentation, content selection, campaign optimization, and customer relationship management (Huang & Rust, 2021).

AI systems in marketing operate across multiple levels, ranging from descriptive analytics that summarize past behavior to predictive and prescriptive analytics that forecast future actions and recommend optimal interventions. This progression has enabled marketing platforms to operate with minimal human oversight, particularly in digital advertising, e-commerce personalization, and social media engagement. As a result, decision authority is increasingly delegated to algorithms, raising questions about accountability and ethical responsibility (Martin, 2022).

1.2.2 Predictive Analytics and Consumer Modeling

Predictive analytics forms the analytical backbone of algorithmic marketing. By combining historical data with real-time signals, predictive models estimate future consumer behavior, such as likelihood of conversion, churn risk, or responsiveness to specific stimuli. These models are continuously updated as new data becomes available, allowing marketing strategies to adapt dynamically (Ali & Hastuti, 2024).

Consumer modeling has expanded beyond transactional data to include behavioral traces such as browsing patterns, click behavior, location data, and social interactions. This expansion enables highly detailed consumer profiles that can be used to infer preferences, emotions, and vulnerabilities. While predictive accuracy improves with richer data, the ethical implications of such deep profiling remain insufficiently addressed, particularly when consumers are unaware of how their data is being used (Boerman et al., 2021).

1.3 Automated Influence and Algorithmic Persuasion

1.3.1 From Personalization to Behavioral Steering

Personalization has long been considered a benign and even beneficial feature of digital marketing. However, advances in AI have transformed personalization into a mechanism for behavioral steering. Algorithmic systems no longer merely adapt content to expressed preferences; they actively experiment with different influence strategies to determine which interventions maximize engagement, compliance, or conversion (Burtell, 2023).

This shift is enabled by reinforcement learning and continuous optimization techniques that treat consumer responses as feedback signals. Marketing algorithms learn which messages, timings, and formats are most effective in shaping behavior, often without explicit user awareness. As influence becomes automated and adaptive, the line between persuasion and manipulation becomes increasingly blurred.

1.3.2 Recommender Systems and the Attention Economy

Recommender systems are among the most influential tools in algorithmic marketing. These systems curate information, products, and content based on predicted user interests, thereby shaping attention and choice. In digital environments characterized by information overload, recommender systems effectively act as gatekeepers, determining what users see and what remains hidden (Dubois & McKelvey, 2023).

Within the attention economy, marketing success is often measured by engagement metrics such as clicks, views, and time spent. Optimization for these metrics can incentivize designs that exploit cognitive biases, emotional triggers, or habitual behaviors. Ethical concerns arise when recommender systems prioritize engagement over user well-being or autonomy, particularly in contexts involving vulnerable populations.

1.4 Ethical Challenges in AI-Driven Marketing

1.4.1 Autonomy, Manipulation, and Informed Consent

One of the most significant ethical concerns associated with algorithmic marketing is its impact on consumer autonomy. Automated influence systems operate through opaque mechanisms that are often invisible to users, limiting their ability to make informed choices. When predictive models anticipate and preempt consumer decisions, the traditional notion of voluntary choice is challenged (Susser et al., 2021).

Informed consent becomes problematic in environments where data collection and algorithmic processing are continuous and implicit. Consumers may agree to terms of service without fully understanding the extent of behavioral analysis and influence involved. This asymmetry of information undermines meaningful consent and raises questions about the legitimacy of algorithmic persuasion (Borgesius et al., 2017).

1.4.2 Bias, Fairness, and Discrimination

AI-driven marketing systems inherit biases present in training data and may amplify existing social inequalities. Algorithmic targeting can result in discriminatory outcomes, such as unequal access to opportunities, differential pricing, or exclusion from certain offers. These effects may occur unintentionally, yet they have real-world consequences for affected individuals and groups (Lambrecht & Tucker, 2023; Caliskan et al., 2022).

Ensuring fairness in algorithmic marketing requires deliberate design choices, continuous auditing, and accountability mechanisms. However, fairness objectives often conflict with profit-driven optimization goals, creating ethical tensions that organizations must navigate.

1.5 Governance, Transparency, and Accountability

1.5.1 Transparency and Explainability in Marketing Algorithms

Transparency is a foundational principle of ethical AI, yet it remains difficult to achieve in complex marketing systems. Many AI models, particularly deep learning architectures, lack interpretability, making it challenging for stakeholders to understand how decisions are made. This opacity complicates regulatory oversight and limits consumer trust (Shin, 2021).

Explainable AI approaches aim to address these challenges by providing insights into algorithmic reasoning. In marketing contexts, explainability can support accountability, enable informed consent, and facilitate ethical evaluation of automated decisions (De Bruijn et al., 2022).

1.5.2 Accountability and Platform Responsibility

As algorithms assume greater decision-making authority, determining responsibility for outcomes becomes increasingly complex. When automated marketing systems cause harm—through discrimination, manipulation, or misinformation—it is often unclear whether responsibility lies with developers, platform operators, marketers, or regulators (Johnson, 2023).

Effective governance requires clearly defined roles, ethical guidelines, and enforcement mechanisms. Platform responsibility extends beyond legal compliance to include proactive ethical design and ongoing monitoring of algorithmic impacts.

1.6 Objectives and Structure of the Chapter

This chapter aims to critically examine the ethical frontiers of AI, predictive analytics, and automated influence in algorithmic marketing. It seeks to reframe algorithmic marketing as a socio-technical influence system rather than a neutral optimization tool. The chapter analyzes how predictive analytics and automated persuasion reshape consumer behavior, identifies key ethical risks, and evaluates governance and design strategies for responsible deployment.

The remainder of the chapter is structured as follows. The next section explores the theoretical foundations of algorithmic marketing and predictive analytics. Subsequent sections examine automated influence mechanisms, ethical challenges, regulatory perspectives, and responsible AI frameworks. The chapter concludes by outlining future research directions and offering recommendations for ethical and sustainable algorithmic marketing practices.

2. FOUNDATIONS OF ALGORITHMIC MARKETING

The foundations of algorithmic marketing lie in the convergence of digital technologies, artificial intelligence, and data-driven decision-making processes that have redefined how organizations interact with consumers. Unlike traditional marketing models that emphasized human creativity and managerial judgment, algorithmic marketing is grounded in computational logic, automated learning, and continuous optimization. These systems rely on large-scale data collection and advanced analytics to autonomously analyze consumer behavior, predict outcomes, and execute marketing actions in real time. As digital platforms mediate an increasing share of market interactions, algorithmic marketing has emerged as a dominant operational paradigm shaping contemporary consumer markets (Grewal et al., 2021).

At its core, algorithmic marketing transforms marketing from a periodic, campaign-based activity into a persistent, adaptive process. Marketing decisions are no longer confined to predefined strategies or human intuition but are dynamically recalibrated through algorithmic feedback loops. This shift reflects broader changes in the digital economy, where value creation depends on the ability to process data continuously and respond to consumer behavior at scale. Understanding the foundations of algorithmic marketing therefore requires examining its analytical evolution, technological underpinnings, and platform-based infrastructures.

2.1 Evolution of Marketing Analytics

Marketing analytics has evolved through distinct stages, each corresponding to increasing levels of automation and intelligence. Early analytical approaches focused on descriptive analysis, providing summaries of past performance such as sales trends, campaign reach, and customer demographics. These tools supported human decision-makers but did not replace their judgment. As data availability and computational power expanded, predictive analytics emerged as a means of forecasting future outcomes, enabling marketers to anticipate consumer behavior rather than merely react to it (Ali & Hastuti, 2024).

The most recent stage in this evolution is prescriptive analytics, where algorithms not only predict outcomes but also recommend or automatically implement actions. In algorithmic marketing systems, prescriptive models determine which consumers to target, which messages to deliver, and which channels to prioritize. This progression marks a fundamental shift in decision authority from humans to machines, with significant implications for responsibility and ethical oversight (Davenport et al., 2021).

2.1.1 Predictive Analytics as a Structural Foundation

Predictive analytics functions as the structural backbone of algorithmic marketing systems. By estimating probabilities of future behavior, such as purchase intent or disengagement, predictive models enable anticipatory decision-making. Marketing systems use these predictions to intervene at moments deemed most effective, shaping consumer experiences before preferences are explicitly expressed (Boerman et al., 2021).

This anticipatory capability allows organizations to optimize engagement and efficiency but also introduces ethical concerns. When predictions are used to influence behavior rather than support informed choice, marketing shifts toward behavioral engineering. The reliance on probabilistic inference raises questions about accuracy, bias, and the legitimacy of acting on predictions that consumers may not recognize or consent to.

2.2.2 Artificial Intelligence Technologies in Algorithmic Marketing

Artificial intelligence provides the technological foundation that enables algorithmic marketing to operate autonomously and at scale. Machine learning models analyze vast datasets to uncover patterns and relationships that inform decision-making. Supervised learning techniques are commonly used for classification and regression tasks, such as identifying high-value customers or estimating response likelihood, while unsupervised learning supports segmentation by identifying latent consumer groups (Huang & Rust, 2021).

Deep learning techniques further enhance algorithmic marketing by enabling the analysis of unstructured data, including text, images, and audio. These capabilities support applications such as sentiment analysis, content recommendation, and automated personalization across digital channels. However, the complexity of deep learning models often limits transparency, making it difficult to explain how specific marketing decisions are generated (Kietzmann et al., 2022).

The dependence of AI models on historical data introduces additional challenges. Training data may reflect existing social inequalities, leading algorithms to reproduce or amplify biased outcomes. As a result, algorithmic marketing systems may inadvertently reinforce discriminatory patterns in targeting, pricing, or access to opportunities, even in the absence of explicit intent (Caliskan et al., 2022).

2.2.3 Automation and Continuous Optimization

Automation is a defining characteristic of algorithmic marketing. Automated systems execute marketing actions such as content delivery, bid adjustments, and pricing changes without requiring continuous human intervention. These actions are performed in real time and at scales that exceed human cognitive capacity, enabling rapid adaptation to changing consumer behavior (Davenport et al., 2021).

Continuous optimization is achieved through feedback loops in which consumer responses are immediately captured and used to update predictive models. Over time, these feedback mechanisms allow algorithms to refine influence strategies and improve performance. While continuous optimization enhances efficiency, it also creates conditions for persistent experimentation on consumers, raising ethical concerns related to autonomy and informed consent (Burtell, 2023).

2.1.4 Platform-Based Marketing Ecosystems

Algorithmic marketing operates primarily within platform-based ecosystems that integrate data collection, analytics, and execution. Digital advertising platforms, social media networks, and e-commerce marketplaces serve as centralized infrastructures through which automated marketing decisions are deployed. These platforms exercise significant control over information flows, visibility, and monetization, shaping how algorithmic influence is applied in practice (Gorwa et al., 2022).

The platform-centric nature of algorithmic marketing concentrates power among a small number of actors, increasing asymmetries between organizations and consumers. Platform governance, transparency policies, and accountability mechanisms therefore play a critical role in determining the ethical boundaries of algorithmic marketing. As platforms mediate both data access and algorithmic execution, they become central actors in the regulation of automated influence.

2.1.5 Implications for Marketing Practice

The foundations of algorithmic marketing reflect a broader transformation in how markets function. By embedding intelligence and automation into marketing systems, organizations gain unprecedented capabilities to personalize, predict, and influence consumer behavior. At the same time, these capabilities challenge established ethical norms and regulatory frameworks that were developed for human-centered decision-making.

Understanding these foundational elements is essential for evaluating how predictive analytics and automated systems extend beyond personalization toward systematic behavioral influence. The next section builds on this foundation by examining predictive analytics as a mechanism for consumer behavior engineering and its implications for autonomy and ethical responsibility.

2.1.6 Conceptual Framework: Integrating Algorithmic Marketing, Predictive Analytics, and Ethical Governance

To provide analytical clarity and integrate the relationships between the core concepts discussed throughout this chapter, Figure 1 presents a conceptual framework that maps the architecture of algorithmic marketing systems and their ethical implications. This framework synthesizes insights from surveillance capitalism (Soraj Hongladarom & Shoshana Zuboff, 2023), platform governance (Gorwa et al., 2022), behavioral economics (Susser et al., 2021), and responsible AI (Floridi et al., 2022) to illustrate how technological capabilities translate into consumer outcomes and generate ethical risks that require multi-level governance responses.

The framework consists of five interconnected layers:

> Layer 1: Data Infrastructure forms the foundation, encompassing behavioral data collection across digital touchpoints (websites, apps, social media, connected devices), data aggregation and integration platforms, and consumer profiling systems that construct detailed individual and segment-level representations.
> Layer 2: Predictive Analytics processes this data through machine learning models that estimate purchase probabilities, churn risk, response likelihood, and infer latent attributes including preferences, emotional states, and psychological vulnerabilities. These predictions enable anticipatory marketing capabilities.

Figure 1. Conceptual framework for algorithmic marketing ethics

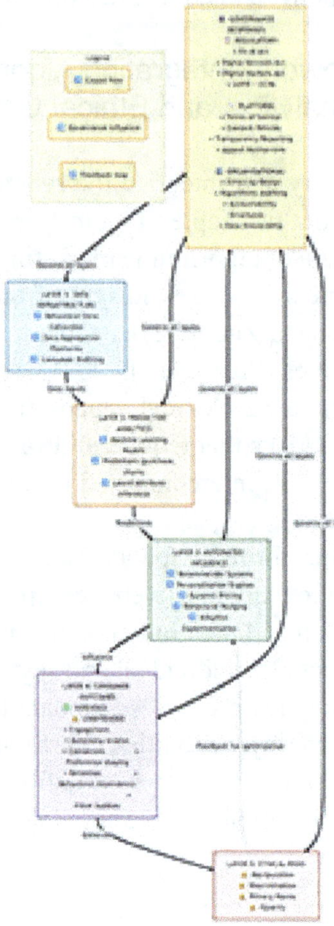

Layer 3: Automated Influence Mechanisms translate predictions into action through:

- Recommender systems that curate content and products
- Personalization engines that tailor messages and offers
- Dynamic pricing algorithms that adjust prices in real-time
- Behavioral nudging through choice architecture design
- Adaptive experimentation that tests and refines influence strategies

Layer 4: Consumer Outcomes includes both intended effects (engagement, conversion, retention) and unintended consequences:

- Autonomy erosion: Reduced scope for reflective decision-making

- Preference shaping: Algorithmic steering of tastes and choices
- Behavioral dependency: Conditioned responses to algorithmic cues
- Filter bubbles: Narrowed exposure to diverse options and information

Layer 5: Ethical Risks emerges from the interaction between technological capabilities and consumer outcomes:

- Manipulation: Exploitation of cognitive biases and vulnerabilities
- Discrimination: Biased targeting and differential treatment
- Privacy violations: Surveillance and invisible data processing
- Opacity: Unexplainable decisions and hidden influence

Governance Responses operate across three levels:

- Regulatory governance: Legal frameworks (EU AI Act, DSA, DMA, GDPR)
- Platform governance: Terms of service, content policies, transparency reporting
- Organizational governance: Ethics-by-design, auditing, accountability structures

This framework serves three purposes. First, it demonstrates that ethical challenges are not isolated technical flaws but systemic outcomes emerging from the interaction between data practices, predictive modeling, and influence mechanisms. Second, it highlights the need for integrated governance that addresses all layers simultaneously rather than focusing on individual components. Third, it provides a analytical lens for evaluating specific algorithmic marketing applications and their ethical implications throughout the chapter.

2.1.7 Theoretical Perspectives on Algorithmic Marketing

Understanding algorithmic marketing requires situating technological developments within broader theoretical debates about power, governance, and social change in digital societies. Three theoretical perspectives are particularly relevant:

- Surveillance Capitalism: Zuboff (2022) conceptualizes surveillance capitalism as a new economic order that claims human experience as raw material for behavioral data and predictive analytics. In this framework, algorithmic marketing is not merely a set of techniques but a logic of accumulation that systematically extracts and analyzes behavioral surplus to predict and modify behavior. Surveillance capitalism explains why marketing systems increasingly operate through opacity—behavioral modification is most effective when targets are unaware of influence mechanisms. It also illuminates the structural asymmetry between organizations that possess predictive capabilities and consumers who lack awareness or control.

- Platform Capitalism and Governance: Gorwa et al. (2022) analyze digital platforms as private governance systems that exercise significant power over market access, information flows, and behavioral outcomes. Platforms function as infrastructural intermediaries, controlling the conditions under which algorithmic marketing operates. This perspective highlights how platform governance—terms of service, content moderation, data access policies—shapes marketing possibilities and constraints. It also reveals the limits of consumer-facing regulation when platform architectures themselves embed particular influence mechanisms.
- Behavioral Economics and Nudging Theory: Susser et al. (2021) extend behavioral economics insights to digital environments, analyzing how choice architecture operates algorithmically. Traditional nudging theory emphasized fixed choice architectures designed by human decision-makers; algorithmic nudging dynamically adapts based on real-time behavioral feedback. This theoretical lens illuminates how marketing systems exploit cognitive biases—scarcity effects, social proof, loss aversion—at scale and with precision impossible for human designers. It also provides analytical tools for distinguishing legitimate persuasion from manipulation based on transparency, consent, and alignment with consumer interests.

These theoretical perspectives are not mutually exclusive but complementary. Surveillance capitalism explains the economic logic driving behavioral data extraction; platform governance reveals the institutional structures through which algorithmic marketing operates; behavioral economics illuminates the psychological mechanisms through which influence occurs. Together, they provide a multi-level analytical framework for understanding algorithmic marketing as a socio-technical system with profound ethical implications.

3. PREDICTIVE ANALYTICS AND CONSUMER BEHAVIOR ENGINEERING

Predictive analytics has emerged as one of the most powerful components of algorithmic marketing, enabling organizations to move beyond understanding consumer behavior toward actively shaping it. By leveraging historical and real-time data, predictive models forecast future actions, preferences, and responses, allowing marketing systems to intervene before decisions are consciously formed. This anticipatory capability marks a fundamental shift in the role of marketing, transforming it from a reactive communicative function into a proactive behavioral engineering mechanism embedded within digital environments (Ali & Hastuti, 2024).

3.1 Behavioral Data and Predictive Modeling

The effectiveness of predictive analytics in marketing is rooted in extensive behavioral data collection across digital touchpoints. Consumer interactions with websites, mobile applications, social media platforms, and connected devices generate continuous streams of data capturing browsing patterns, engagement duration, purchasing history, and contextual signals such as location and time. These data are aggregated and processed to identify correlations and patterns that inform predictive models (Boerman et al., 2021).

Predictive modeling techniques analyze this data to estimate probabilities associated with future behavior, such as likelihood of purchase, churn, or responsiveness to specific stimuli. Machine learning models continuously update these estimates as new data becomes available, allowing marketing systems to adapt in near real-time. This dynamic modeling capability enhances accuracy but also intensifies ethical concerns, as consumers are often unaware of the extent to which their behavior is monitored and predicted.

3.1.1 Inference of Latent Consumer Attributes

Beyond observable behavior, predictive analytics enables the inference of latent consumer attributes not explicitly disclosed. These include inferred preferences, emotional states, risk tolerance, and susceptibility to persuasion. By combining behavioral signals with statistical inference, marketing systems construct detailed consumer profiles that extend far beyond traditional demographic segmentation (Huang & Rust, 2021).

Research by Susser et al. (2021) demonstrates that inferred attributes are particularly problematic because they operate outside consumer awareness and consent. Unlike explicitly provided information, inferred characteristics are generated through algorithmic processing that consumers cannot observe, challenge, or control. This creates significant power asymmetries: consumers may not know which attributes are inferred or how these inferences shape the marketing content they receive. Acting on inferred characteristics raises fundamental ethical questions, particularly when predictions involve sensitive traits or psychological vulnerabilities that consumers have not consented to share.

3.2 From Prediction to Behavioral Steering

Predictive analytics enables marketing systems to identify not only what consumers are likely to do but also how their behavior can be influenced most effectively. By estimating the impact of different interventions, algorithms select actions that maximize desired outcomes such as engagement, conversion, or retention. This optimization-driven approach transforms predictive analytics from neutral analysis into a mechanism for behavioral steering (Burtell, 2023).

Behavioral steering occurs through adaptive experimentation, where algorithms test multiple influence strategies and learn which combinations of content, timing, and framing yield the strongest behavioral response. Van Noort et al. (2024) describe this as "algorithmic persuasion," distinguishing it from traditional persuasion by three characteristics: it operates continuously rather than episodically, adapts dynamically to individual responses, and functions largely invisibly within digital environments. Over time, these systems refine their strategies through reinforcement learning, gradually shaping consumer habits and preferences without explicit disclosure.

3.3 Feedback Loops and Behavioral Reinforcement

A defining feature of predictive analytics-driven marketing systems is the presence of continuous feedback loops. Consumer responses to marketing interventions are immediately recorded and fed back into predictive models, allowing algorithms to update their understanding of behavior and refine future actions. These feedback loops create self-reinforcing cycles in which certain behaviors are encouraged and amplified over time (Dubois & McKelvey, 2023).

While feedback-driven optimization improves performance metrics, it may also produce unintended consequences. As per various researches, three specific risks are:

Over-personalization occurs when algorithms increasingly narrow content exposure based on past behavior, creating personalized realities that limit serendipity and diversity. Filter bubbles emerge when recommendation systems prioritize engagement over variety, potentially reinforcing existing preferences while excluding alternative options. Behavioral dependency develops when users become conditioned to algorithmically curated experiences, reducing their capacity for independent exploration and choice.

These effects highlight a fundamental tension: optimization for short-term engagement metrics may systematically undermine long-term consumer welfare. As Jon Kleinberg et al. (2018) argue, the metrics algorithms optimize are not neutral technical choices but normative decisions about what constitutes valuable outcomes.

3.4 Psychological Dimensions of Predictive Influence

Predictive analytics increasingly integrates insights from behavioral science and psychology to enhance influence effectiveness. Marketing systems incorporate knowledge of cognitive biases, emotional triggers, and decision heuristics to design interventions that align with predictable patterns of human behavior. By exploiting biases such as scarcity effects, social proof, or loss aversion, predictive systems increase the likelihood of desired responses (Van Noort et al., 2024).

The integration of psychological insights with predictive modeling intensifies ethical concerns, particularly when influence strategies target vulnerable individuals or exploit emotional states. Chen and Stalla-Bourdillon (2023) document how predictive systems are designed to identify moments of psychological vulnerability—stress, fatigue, uncertainty—and deploy persuasive interventions precisely when consumers are least capable of resisting. When predictive analytics anticipates these moments, marketing interventions may cross ethical boundaries by prioritizing persuasion over consumer well-being.

3.5 Implications for Consumer Autonomy

The increasing sophistication of predictive analytics challenges traditional notions of consumer autonomy. When marketing systems anticipate and shape choices before consumers consciously deliberate, the boundary between voluntary decision-making and algorithmic influence becomes blurred. Consumers may perceive their choices as self-directed while their decision environments are carefully engineered through predictive insights (Susser et al., 2021).

This erosion of autonomy is not necessarily the result of malicious intent but emerges from optimization-driven systems designed to maximize engagement and profitability. As Brent Mittelstadt (2019) observes, "The most insidious threats to autonomy are not those that coerce but those that shape preferences so subtly that individuals experience manipulated choices as their own." Addressing these concerns requires rethinking how predictive analytics is deployed, including the incorporation of transparency mechanisms, meaningful consent frameworks, and ethical limits on behavioral steering.

Practical Implications for Managers: Organizations should conduct regular autonomy impact assessments, evaluating how predictive systems affect consumer decision-making. This includes testing whether users understand how their behavior is being shaped and providing opt-out mechanisms for algorithmic personalization.

4. AUTOMATED INFLUENCE AND PERSUASIVE TECHNOLOGIES

Automated influence represents a critical evolution in algorithmic marketing, where artificial intelligence systems move beyond prediction to actively shaping consumer decision-making processes. Persuasive technologies embedded within digital platforms are designed to guide user behavior by structuring choice environments, optimizing message framing, and dynamically adapting influence strategies in response to behavioral feedback. Unlike traditional persuasion, which relies on explicit messaging and human intent, automated influence operates continuously through algorithmic processes that are often invisible to users, thereby redefining how power and agency function in digital markets (Dubois & McKelvey, 2023).

The rise of automated influence is closely tied to advances in machine learning, real-time analytics, and platform-based ecosystems. These technologies enable marketing systems to personalize persuasive interventions at scale, tailoring not only content but also timing, frequency, and contextual relevance. As a result, influence becomes embedded within the architecture of digital experiences rather than confined to discrete promotional messages. This structural embedding raises important ethical questions about transparency, consent, and the legitimacy of algorithmic persuasion.

4.1 Persuasive Technologies in Digital Marketing Environments

Persuasive technologies refer to computational systems intentionally designed to influence attitudes, behaviors, or decisions. In marketing contexts, these technologies are integrated into interfaces, recommendation engines, notification systems, and pricing mechanisms. Their effectiveness lies in their ability to subtly guide behavior through design choices rather than overt persuasion. By shaping how options are presented and prioritized, persuasive technologies influence decisions while preserving the appearance of free choice (Van Noort et al., 2024).

Digital platforms increasingly rely on such technologies to maximize engagement and conversion. Algorithms determine which products are highlighted, which reviews are surfaced, and which content is recommended, thereby shaping consumer attention and perceived value. These systems operate through continuous experimentation, testing variations of persuasive elements to identify those that yield the strongest behavioral response. Over time, this experimentation produces refined influence strategies that are difficult for consumers to detect or resist.

4.1.1 Choice Architecture and Algorithmic Nudging

Choice architecture plays a central role in automated influence. Algorithmic systems structure the decision environment by organizing options, default settings, and informational cues in ways that predictably affect behavior. Nudging techniques, originally developed in behavioral economics, are increasingly operationalized through algorithms that adapt nudges dynamically based on user data (Susser et al., 2021).

In algorithmic marketing, nudges may include default subscriptions, urgency cues, personalized discounts, or social proof indicators (Bhambri & Kant, 2025b). While nudging can support beneficial outcomes, such as simplifying decisions, its automated and personalized implementation raises ethical concerns. When nudges are optimized for commercial objectives without regard for consumer welfare, they risk crossing into manipulation by exploiting cognitive biases at scale.

4.2 Recommender Systems and the Automation of Attention

Recommender systems are among the most powerful persuasive technologies in algorithmic marketing. These systems curate content, products, and information based on predicted user interests, effectively determining what users see and what remains hidden. In environments characterized by information overload, recommender systems play a gatekeeping role that shapes attention, preferences, and consumption patterns (Huang & Rust, 2021).

By continuously learning from user interactions, recommender systems optimize for engagement metrics such as clicks, views, and dwell time (Bhambri & Kant, 2025a). This optimization incentivizes content that captures attention, sometimes at the expense of accuracy, diversity, or well-being. As a result, recommender systems may reinforce narrow preferences, create filter bubbles, or promote emotionally charged content that sustains engagement. These effects underscore the ethical responsibility of designing recommender systems that balance commercial goals with societal impact.

4.3 Automation, Scale, and Behavioral Dependency

A defining characteristic of automated influence is its scalability. Algorithmic systems can deploy persuasive interventions simultaneously across millions of users, adapting strategies in real time based on individual responses. This scale amplifies both the effectiveness and the risks of persuasion. Small design choices, when automated and optimized across large populations, can have significant cumulative effects on behavior and social norms (Burtell, 2023).

Over time, continuous exposure to personalized influence may foster behavioral dependency, where users become conditioned to algorithmically curated experiences. Such dependency can reduce consumer agency by narrowing perceived options and reinforcing habitual behavior. When influence systems prioritize engagement and retention above all else, they may undermine long-term autonomy and well-being.

4.4 Transparency and Awareness in Automated Persuasion

One of the most significant challenges associated with automated influence is the lack of transparency. Consumers are often unaware that their interactions are shaped by adaptive persuasive systems, limiting their ability to critically evaluate or resist influence. Unlike traditional advertising, where persuasive intent is explicit, algorithmic persuasion operates through subtle design and personalization mechanisms that obscure intent (Shin, 2021).

Increasing awareness and transparency is essential for preserving consumer autonomy. This includes clear disclosures about the use of AI-driven persuasion, explanations of how recommendations are generated, and options for users to control or opt out of automated influence mechanisms. Without such measures, automated persuasion risks undermining trust in digital markets and eroding the legitimacy of algorithmic marketing practices.

4.5 Ethical Implications of Automated Influence

The ethical implications of automated influence extend beyond individual interactions to broader societal concerns (Bhambri & Kant, 2025c). When persuasive technologies are optimized solely for profit, they may exacerbate inequalities, exploit vulnerabilities, and distort information environments. Automated influence challenges existing ethical frameworks by blurring the distinction between persuasion and manipulation and by diffusing responsibility across complex socio-technical systems (Martin, 2022).

Addressing these ethical challenges requires rethinking how persuasive technologies are designed, deployed, and governed. Ethical considerations must be embedded at the system level, including constraints on optimization objectives, safeguards for vulnerable users, and accountability mechanisms for algorithmic outcomes. The next section builds on this discussion by examining ethical challenges in algorithmic marketing more broadly, including issues of bias, privacy, and fairness.

5. ETHICAL CHALLENGES IN ALGORITHMIC MARKETING

The rapid adoption of artificial intelligence and predictive analytics in marketing has intensified longstanding ethical concerns while simultaneously introducing new challenges that existing frameworks struggle to address. Algorithmic marketing systems operate at the intersection of data collection, automated decision-making, and behavioral influence, creating complex ethical tensions related to autonomy, fairness, privacy, transparency, and accountability. Unlike traditional marketing practices, where ethical responsibility could be attributed to identifiable human actors, algorithmic systems distribute decision-making authority across models, platforms, and data infrastructures, complicating moral and legal responsibility (Martin, 2022).

Ethical challenges in algorithmic marketing are not incidental but structural. They emerge from optimization-driven systems designed to maximize engagement, efficiency, and profitability (Bhambri & Khang, 2024a). When these objectives are pursued without explicit ethical constraints, automated systems may prioritize outcomes that conflict with consumer well-being or societal values. Understanding these challenges requires examining how bias, surveillance, opacity, and autonomy erosion are embedded within algorithmic marketing architectures.

5.1 Bias and Discrimination in Algorithmic Targeting

Bias represents one of the most persistent ethical challenges in algorithmic marketing. Machine learning models are trained on historical data that may reflect existing social inequalities, stereotypes, and structural disadvantages. As a result, algorithmic targeting systems can reproduce or amplify discriminatory patterns, even when protected attributes are not explicitly included in model inputs (Caliskan et al., 2022).

In marketing contexts, biased outcomes may manifest through differential ad delivery, exclusion from opportunities, or price discrimination across demographic groups. These effects are often difficult to detect, as they arise from complex interactions between data, model architecture, and optimization objectives. Moreover, because algorithmic decisions are often opaque, affected individuals may be unaware that discrimination has occurred, limiting opportunities for redress (Lambrecht & Tucker, 2023).

5.1.1 Structural Inequality and Data-Driven Reinforcement

Algorithmic marketing systems not only reflect existing inequalities but may actively reinforce them through feedback loops. When predictive models learn from consumer responses shaped by past targeting decisions, they may progressively narrow access to information or opportunities for certain groups. This self-reinforcing dynamic transforms bias from a data quality issue into a systemic problem embedded within algorithmic governance (Gorwa et al., 2022).

5.2 Privacy, Surveillance, and Consent

Privacy concerns are central to ethical debates surrounding algorithmic marketing. These systems rely on extensive data collection across digital touchpoints (Bhambri, 2025), often aggregating behavioral, contextual, and inferred data into detailed consumer profiles. While such data enables personalization and predictive accuracy, it also creates conditions of pervasive surveillance that challenge traditional notions of privacy (Boerman et al., 2021).

Consent mechanisms in digital environments are frequently inadequate for addressing the complexity of algorithmic processing. Consumers may agree to data collection through broad terms of service without fully understanding how their data will be analyzed, inferred upon, or used to shape behavior. This gap between formal consent and meaningful understanding undermines the ethical legitimacy of data-driven marketing practices (Borgesius et al., 2017).

5.3 Transparency and Explainability of Marketing Algorithms

Transparency is widely recognized as a foundational principle of ethical AI, yet it remains difficult to achieve in algorithmic marketing systems. Many AI models, particularly deep learning architectures, lack interpretability, making it challenging to explain how specific targeting or recommendation decisions are made. This opacity limits consumer awareness, regulatory oversight, and organizational accountability (Shin, 2021).

The absence of explainability is particularly problematic when algorithmic decisions have significant economic or psychological consequences. Without clear explanations, consumers cannot assess whether they are being treated fairly, nor can regulators effectively evaluate compliance with ethical or legal standards. Transparency is therefore not merely a technical challenge but a prerequisite for trust and legitimacy in algorithmic marketing (De Bruijn et al., 2022).

5.4 Autonomy, Manipulation, and Consumer Harm

One of the most profound ethical concerns associated with algorithmic marketing is its impact on consumer autonomy. Automated influence systems anticipate and shape choices through predictive insights, potentially reducing the scope for reflective decision-making. When marketing interventions are optimized to exploit cognitive biases or emotional vulnerabilities, they risk crossing the boundary from persuasion into manipulation (Susser et al., 2021).

Consumer harm may arise not only from individual interactions but from cumulative exposure to personalized influence (Bhambri & Khang, 2024b). Over time, algorithmic systems may foster dependency, encourage impulsive behavior, or distort preferences, particularly among vulnerable populations. These harms challenge the assumption that consumer welfare naturally aligns with optimization-driven marketing objectives.

5.5 Accountability and Moral Responsibility

Determining accountability in algorithmic marketing is inherently complex. Decision-making authority is distributed across multiple actors, including data scientists, platform providers, marketers, and automated systems. When harmful outcomes occur, responsibility may be diffused, making it difficult to assign blame or implement corrective measures (Johnson, 2023).

This diffusion of responsibility creates ethical gaps where no single actor feels accountable for system-level outcomes. Addressing this challenge requires redefining accountability frameworks to encompass not only individual actions but also collective responsibility for algorithmic design, deployment, and oversight.

5.6 Ethical Limits of Optimization

At the core of many ethical challenges in algorithmic marketing lies the logic of optimization. Algorithms are designed to maximize specific metrics, such as engagement, conversion, or revenue. When these metrics become the sole criteria for success, ethical considerations may be sidelined. Optimization without ethical boundaries risks prioritizing short-term gains over long-term trust, well-being, and societal impact (Floridi et al., 2022).

Recognizing the ethical limits of optimization is essential for responsible algorithmic marketing. Ethical constraints must be integrated into system objectives, evaluation metrics, and governance structures. The next section builds on this discussion by examining regulatory and governance perspectives that seek to address these ethical challenges through policy, oversight, and institutional frameworks.

6. REGULATORY AND GOVERNANCE PERSPECTIVES

The rapid expansion of algorithmic marketing systems has outpaced the development of regulatory and governance frameworks designed to oversee their ethical and societal impacts. As artificial intelligence, predictive analytics, and automated influence become deeply embedded in digital markets, regulators and policymakers face the challenge of adapting existing legal structures to technologies that operate dynamically, opaquely, and at scale. Traditional regulatory approaches, which were developed for human-driven decision-making and clearly identifiable actors, often struggle to address the distributed and adaptive nature of algorithmic systems (Cowls & Floridi, 2018).

Governance in algorithmic marketing extends beyond compliance with formal regulations to include institutional norms, organizational practices, and ethical standards that guide system design and deployment (Bhambri & Kautish, 2024). Effective governance must therefore operate across multiple levels, encompassing legal requirements, platform policies, and internal accountability mechanisms. Understanding regulatory and governance perspectives requires examining data protection laws, emerging AI governance initiatives, and the role of platforms as powerful intermediaries.

6.1 Data Protection and Consumer Rights Frameworks

Data protection regulations form the cornerstone of legal oversight in algorithmic marketing. These frameworks aim to safeguard individual rights by regulating how personal data is collected, processed, and used. In digital marketing contexts, data protection laws emphasize principles such as lawfulness, transparency, purpose limitation, and data minimization. However, applying these principles to complex predictive analytics systems presents significant challenges, particularly when data processing involves inferred attributes and continuous behavioral profiling (Borgesius et al., 2017).

Consumer rights frameworks also seek to protect individuals from unfair commercial practices, including deceptive advertising and discriminatory treatment. Yet algorithmic marketing systems often operate through subtle personalization and automated influence rather than explicit claims, making it difficult to assess whether consumer protection standards are being met. As a result, existing legal tools may be insufficient to address the nuanced forms of persuasion enabled by predictive analytics.

6.1.1 Limitations of Consent-Based Regulation

Consent has traditionally been a central mechanism for legitimizing data processing. In algorithmic marketing, however, consent-based regulation faces inherent limitations. Consumers are frequently presented with broad and complex consent requests that do not convey the full scope of data-driven inference and behavioral influence. Even when consent is formally obtained, individuals may lack meaningful understanding or control over how their data is used (Boerman et al., 2021).

This gap between formal consent and substantive autonomy has prompted calls for alternative regulatory approaches that focus on outcomes and impacts rather than procedural consent alone. Such approaches emphasize accountability, fairness, and harm prevention as complementary mechanisms to individual consent.

6.2 Emerging AI Governance Initiatives

In response to the growing influence of artificial intelligence across sectors, governments and international organizations have begun developing AI-specific governance frameworks. These initiatives typically emphasize principles such as transparency, accountability, fairness, and human oversight. While not always legally binding, they provide normative guidance for responsible AI development and deployment (Floridi et al., 2022).

In the context of algorithmic marketing, AI governance initiatives seek to address risks associated with automated decision-making and behavioral manipulation. However, translating high-level ethical principles into operational requirements remains challenging. Marketing systems often involve complex trade-offs between personalization, efficiency, and ethical safeguards, requiring context-specific interpretation of governance principles.

6.3 Platform Governance and Institutional Power

Digital platforms play a central role in algorithmic marketing by controlling data access, algorithmic infrastructures, and market visibility. As a result, platform governance has become a critical dimension of regulatory oversight. Platform policies regarding data use, advertising practices, and algorithmic transparency significantly influence how automated influence is exercised in practice (Gorwa et al., 2022).

The concentration of power among a small number of platforms raises concerns about accountability and democratic oversight. Platforms often act as private regulators, setting rules that shape market behavior without direct public input. This privatization of governance complicates regulatory enforcement and highlights the need for mechanisms that align platform incentives with societal values.

6.4 Accountability and Enforcement Challenges

Ensuring accountability in algorithmic marketing systems presents substantial challenges for regulators. Automated decision-making diffuses responsibility across multiple actors, including developers, data providers, marketers, and platform operators. When harmful outcomes occur, identifying the source of responsibility may be difficult, limiting the effectiveness of enforcement actions (Johnson, 2023).

Moreover, the technical complexity of AI systems can hinder regulatory capacity. Regulators may lack the expertise or resources needed to audit algorithms, evaluate predictive models, or assess systemic risks. These constraints underscore the importance of collaborative governance approaches that involve regulators, industry stakeholders, and independent experts.

6.5 Toward Adaptive and Risk-Based Governance

Given the dynamic nature of algorithmic marketing, there is growing recognition that governance frameworks must be adaptive rather than static. Risk-based approaches that focus on potential harms and societal impact offer a promising alternative to rigid rules. Such approaches prioritize oversight of high-risk applications, including those involving vulnerable populations or significant behavioral influence, while allowing flexibility for lower-risk uses (Cowls & Floridi, 2018).

Adaptive governance also emphasizes continuous monitoring, impact assessment, and iterative improvement. By integrating ethical evaluation into the lifecycle of algorithmic systems, governance frameworks can better respond to emerging risks and evolving technologies. The next section builds on this perspective by examining responsible AI and ethical design frameworks that operationalize governance principles within algorithmic marketing systems.

6.6 Comparative Analysis of Global Regulatory Frameworks

Algorithmic marketing operates across jurisdictional boundaries, yet regulatory frameworks governing these systems vary significantly across regions. Understanding this regulatory landscape is essential for organizations operating globally and for assessing the adequacy of current governance approaches. This section provides a comparative analysis of major regulatory initiatives and their implications for algorithmic marketing.

6.6.1 European Union: Comprehensive Risk-Based Regulation

The European Union has emerged as the global leader in regulating algorithmic systems, developing a comprehensive framework that directly impacts marketing applications. Three legislative instruments are particularly relevant:

- The EU AI Act, adopted in 2024, establishes a risk-based classification system for artificial intelligence applications. Under this framework, algorithmic marketing systems are generally classified as "limited risk," requiring transparency obligations including disclosure that content is AI-generated and opportunities for human intervention. However, specific applications may trigger higher classifications:

- Unacceptable risk (prohibited): AI systems using subliminal techniques beyond conscious awareness, exploiting vulnerabilities of specific groups, or employing real-time biometric identification in public spaces.
- High risk: AI systems used in employment, education, and essential public services, subject to stringent conformity assessments, human oversight, and documentation requirements.

For marketing applications involving emotion recognition, social scoring, or behavioral manipulation of vulnerable populations, the AI Act imposes significant compliance burdens (Cowls & Floridi, 2018).

The Digital Services Act (DSA) regulates intermediary services including social media platforms and online marketplaces. For algorithmic marketing, key provisions include:

- Transparency requirements: Very large online platforms must disclose the main parameters used in recommendation systems and provide users with at least one option not based on profiling.
- Risk assessment obligations: Platforms must identify and mitigate systemic risks including the spread of illegal content, negative effects on civic discourse, and intentional manipulation of services.
- Auditing and oversight: Independent audits of algorithmic systems and annual reporting requirements

The Digital Markets Act (DMA) applies to designated "gatekeeper" platforms with significant market power. These platforms are prohibited from:

- Self-preferencing their own products in rankings and recommendations.
- Combining personal data across different services without consent.
- Restricting business users from communicating with customers outside the platform.

Together, these instruments create a comprehensive regulatory architecture that fundamentally constrains how algorithmic marketing can operate within EU markets (Borgesius et al., 2017).

6.6.2 United States: Sectoral and Enforcement-Driven Approach

In contrast to the EU's comprehensive framework, the United States maintains a sectoral approach to algorithmic regulation. No federal AI-specific legislation exists; instead, oversight occurs through:

Federal Trade Commission (FTC) enforcement: The FTC has increasingly used its authority under Section 5 of the FTC Act (prohibiting unfair or deceptive practices) to challenge algorithmic harms. Recent enforcement actions have targeted:

- Discriminatory ad delivery systems (Facebook settlement, 2022)
- Deceptive use of AI in marketing claims
- Failure to disclose algorithmic personalization

State-level initiatives: Several states have enacted or proposed legislation addressing algorithmic transparency and fairness:

- California Privacy Rights Act (CPRA) extends consumer rights to opt-out of automated decision-making
- Proposed Algorithmic Accountability Acts in multiple states would require impact assessments for automated systems

Sectoral regulations: Marketing applications in specific sectors face additional oversight:

- Financial services: Equal Credit Opportunity Act prohibits algorithmic discrimination in credit decisions
- Insurance: State insurance commissioners increasingly scrutinize algorithm-based pricing
- Healthcare: HIPAA restrictions on using protected health information for marketing

This fragmented approach creates compliance complexity but also allows for targeted enforcement against specific harms as they emerge (Lambrecht & Tucker, 2023).

6.6.3 Emerging Frameworks in Other Jurisdictions

United Kingdom: Following Brexit, the UK has developed an "pro-innovation" approach to AI regulation, emphasizing sectoral guidance rather than comprehensive legislation. The Competition and Markets Authority has issued guidance on algorithmic pricing and consumer protection in digital markets.

Canada: The proposed Artificial Intelligence and Data Act (AIDA) would establish requirements for "high-impact" AI systems, including algorithmic marketing applications affecting consumer choices. The legislation emphasizes transparency, fairness, and human oversight.

- China: The Cyberspace Administration of China has issued regulations specifically targeting algorithmic recommendation systems, requiring platforms to:
- Provide users with control over algorithmic recommendations
- Prevent algorithms from exploiting user vulnerabilities
- Ensure recommendations align with "core socialist values"
- International initiatives: The OECD AI Principles and UNESCO Recommendation on AI Ethics provide non-binding frameworks increasingly referenced in national legislation.

6.6.4 Implications for Algorithmic Marketing Practice

This comparative analysis reveals several implications for organizations deploying algorithmic marketing systems:

- Jurisdictional complexity: Marketing systems must comply with varying requirements across regions, necessitating flexible architectures that can adapt to local regulatory requirements.
- Convergence on core principles: Despite differences in approach, regulatory frameworks increasingly converge on transparency, fairness, accountability, and human oversight as core requirements.
- Enforcement trends: Regulatory enforcement is accelerating, with substantial fines and remedial actions becoming common for violations involving algorithmic discrimination, opacity, or manipulation.
- Risk-based compliance: Organizations should classify marketing applications by risk level, applying enhanced safeguards to systems involving vulnerable populations, sensitive data, or significant behavioral influence.
- Practical Implications for Global Marketers: Develop a regulatory compliance matrix mapping major jurisdictional requirements against marketing use cases. Implement privacy-enhancing technologies and algorithmic auditing capabilities that can satisfy varying transparency and fairness standards across regions.

7. RESPONSIBLE AI AND ETHICAL DESIGN FRAMEWORKS

As ethical concerns surrounding algorithmic marketing intensify, attention has increasingly shifted from reactive regulation toward proactive design strategies that embed ethical principles directly into artificial intelligence systems. Responsible AI and ethical design frameworks aim to ensure that algorithmic marketing technologies are developed and deployed in ways that respect consumer autonomy, promote fairness, and maintain accountability throughout the system lifecycle. Rather than treating ethics as an external constraint imposed after deployment, these frameworks emphasize integrating ethical considerations into data selection, model development, system architecture, and organizational governance (Floridi et al., 2022).

Responsible AI in marketing contexts acknowledges that algorithmic influence is not value-neutral. Design choices regarding optimization objectives, data inputs, and feedback mechanisms inevitably reflect normative assumptions about acceptable outcomes. Ethical design frameworks therefore seek to make these assumptions explicit and subject to critical evaluation. In algorithmic marketing, this shift is particularly important because influence mechanisms operate continuously and at scale, amplifying the consequences of design decisions across large populations.

7.1 Ethics-by-Design in Algorithmic Marketing Systems

Ethics-by-design refers to the systematic integration of ethical principles into the development process of AI systems. In algorithmic marketing, this approach involves embedding safeguards that limit harmful outcomes before systems are deployed. Design decisions related to data collection, feature selection, and model objectives play a decisive role in shaping system behavior and ethical impact (Martin, 2022).

Ethics-by-design emphasizes proactive risk identification and mitigation. For example, marketing systems can be designed to avoid targeting based on sensitive attributes or inferred vulnerabilities. Similarly, optimization objectives can be constrained to balance engagement metrics with indicators of consumer well-being. By integrating ethical considerations at the design stage, organizations can reduce reliance on post hoc correction mechanisms that are often costly and ineffective.

7.1.1 Value-Sensitive Design and Normative Alignment

Value-sensitive design extends ethics-by-design by explicitly incorporating human values into system requirements. In marketing contexts, relevant values include autonomy, fairness, transparency, and trust. Translating these abstract values into technical specifications requires interdisciplinary collaboration between engineers, marketers, ethicists, and legal experts (Hagendorff, 2022).

Normative alignment is particularly challenging in algorithmic marketing because stakeholder values may conflict. While organizations prioritize efficiency and profitability, consumers may value privacy and control, and regulators emphasize fairness and accountability. Ethical design frameworks aim to balance these competing interests by making trade-offs explicit and subject to governance oversight.

7.2 Human-in-the-Loop and Oversight Mechanisms

Human-in-the-loop approaches seek to maintain meaningful human oversight over automated decision-making processes. In algorithmic marketing, this involves retaining human authority over critical design choices, system objectives, and intervention thresholds. Rather than fully autonomous operation, responsible systems incorporate checkpoints where human judgment can intervene, audit, or override algorithmic decisions (Johnson, 2023).

Human oversight is particularly important for high-risk applications involving behavioral manipulation or vulnerable populations. By integrating review mechanisms and escalation pathways, organizations can ensure that ethical concerns are addressed before harm occurs. However, human-in-the-loop approaches must be carefully designed to avoid superficial oversight that lacks real influence over system behavior.

7.3 Explainability, Transparency, and Auditability

Explainability and transparency are central pillars of responsible AI frameworks. In algorithmic marketing, explainability refers to the ability to provide understandable reasons for why specific consumers are targeted, why certain recommendations are made, or why particular prices are offered. Transparency supports consumer awareness, regulatory compliance, and organizational accountability (Shin, 2021).

Auditability complements explainability by enabling independent evaluation of algorithmic systems. Auditable marketing algorithms allow internal and external stakeholders to assess model performance, detect bias, and evaluate compliance with ethical standards. Designing for auditability requires maintaining documentation, version control, and traceability across data pipelines and model updates (De Bruijn et al., 2022).

7.4 Fairness-Aware and Privacy-Preserving Design

Responsible AI frameworks increasingly emphasize fairness-aware and privacy-preserving design strategies. In algorithmic marketing, fairness-aware design involves monitoring and mitigating disparate impacts across demographic groups. This may include bias testing, fairness constraints, and ongoing evaluation of targeting outcomes (Caliskan et al., 2022).

Privacy-preserving design approaches aim to minimize data collection and reduce exposure of sensitive information. Techniques such as data minimization, aggregation, and controlled access can reduce privacy risks while maintaining analytical utility. Embedding privacy safeguards into system architecture enhances consumer trust and aligns marketing practices with ethical and regulatory expectations (Boerman et al., 2021).

7.5 Organizational Responsibility and Ethical Culture

Responsible AI cannot be achieved solely through technical measures. Organizational culture and governance play a critical role in shaping how ethical principles are interpreted and applied. Research by Floridi et al. (2022) demonstrates that organizations with strong ethical cultures are significantly more likely to identify and mitigate algorithmic harms before they escalate.

7.5.1 Corporate AI Governance Structures

Effective governance requires formal structures that embed ethical oversight throughout the algorithm lifecycle. Leading organizations are implementing multi-tier governance models:

- Board-level oversight: Ethics committees at the board level review high-risk marketing applications, approve ethical guidelines, and receive regular reports on algorithmic impacts. This ensures that ethical considerations receive executive attention rather than being delegated to technical teams.
- Cross-functional ethics boards: Standing committees comprising representatives from legal, compliance, marketing, data science, and external stakeholders review proposed algorithms, assess ethical risks, and approve deployment decisions. These boards serve as decision-making bodies, not merely advisory groups.
- Algorithmic review processes: Structured workflows require ethical review at key development stages—data collection, model design, testing, deployment,

and post-launch monitoring. Review criteria include fairness testing, transparency assessment, and autonomy impact evaluation.

- Documentation requirements: Comprehensive documentation of data sources, model specifications, testing results, and ethical reviews creates accountability and enables auditing. The "model cards" approach, requiring standardized documentation of algorithm capabilities and limitations, has been adopted by leading organizations.

7.5.2 Ethical Auditing of Marketing Algorithms

Regular auditing is essential for detecting and correcting ethical failures. Effective audit programs include:

- Pre-deployment testing: Algorithms undergo fairness testing across demographic groups, transparency assessment to ensure explainability, and red-team exercises identifying potential misuse or unintended consequences.
- Ongoing monitoring: Continuous monitoring detects drift in algorithm performance, emerging disparities in outcomes, and unexpected consumer responses. Automated alerts trigger review when metrics exceed established thresholds.
- Independent external audits: Third-party audits provide objective assessment and enhance credibility. Regulatory bodies increasingly require independent auditing for high-risk applications.
- Remediation protocols: Clear procedures govern responses to identified issues, including algorithm suspension, consumer notification, and corrective action timelines.

7.5.3 Responsible Data Stewardship

Data practices fundamentally shape algorithmic outcomes. Responsible stewardship includes:

- Data minimization: Collecting only data necessary for specified purposes, reducing privacy risks and limiting potential for function creep.
- Purpose limitation: Using data only for purposes disclosed to consumers and preventing secondary uses without fresh consent.
- Quality assurance: Ensuring training data accurately represents target populations and does not embed historical biases.
- Retention and deletion policies: Clear rules governing how long data is retained and secure deletion when no longer needed.

- Inference transparency: Disclosing not only what data is collected but also what attributes are inferred and how inferences influence marketing decisions.

7.5.4 Industry Self-Regulation Mechanisms

Industry associations and multi-stakeholder initiatives are developing self-regulatory frameworks that complement formal regulation:

- Advertising industry codes: Updated codes of conduct address AI-driven advertising, requiring transparency about algorithmic targeting and prohibitions on exploiting vulnerabilities.
- Platform accountability initiatives: Multi-stakeholder efforts develop standards for platform transparency, including disclosure of algorithmic parameters and independent auditing.
- Professional certification: Emerging certification programs for AI ethics professionals and responsible marketing practitioners establish baseline competencies and ethical commitments.
- Best practice sharing: Industry forums facilitate sharing of effective governance practices, ethical design patterns, and lessons from failures.

7.5.5 Implementation Challenges and Success Factors

Research by Brent Mittelstadt (2019) identifies key factors distinguishing successful from unsuccessful ethical governance implementations:

a. Success factors:

- Leadership commitment with explicit accountability for ethical outcomes
- Integration of ethics into performance metrics and incentive structures
- Dedicated resources for ethics functions, not merely aspirational statements
- Psychological safety enabling employees to raise concerns without fear
- Continuous learning from failures and near-misses

b. Common barriers:

- Ethics viewed as compliance exercise rather than strategic priority
- Technical teams lacking ethical training and awareness
- Pressure to prioritize speed and innovation over ethical review
- Fragmented responsibility with no single accountable owner
- Inadequate tools and methodologies for ethical assessment

Practical Implications for Organizations: Establish a formal AI ethics governance structure with clear reporting lines, decision-making authority, and resource commitments. Integrate ethical review into existing product development workflows rather than creating parallel processes. Develop metrics for ethical performance and hold leaders accountable for outcomes. Create mechanisms for employees to raise concerns and for independent review of contested decisions.

7.6 Operationalizing Ethical Design in Marketing Practice

Translating ethical frameworks into operational practice remains a significant challenge. Algorithmic marketing systems evolve continuously, requiring ethical evaluation to be an ongoing process rather than a one-time assessment. Responsible AI frameworks advocate for lifecycle-based approaches that integrate ethical review into system design, deployment, monitoring, and revision (Martin, 2022).

Operationalizing ethical design involves aligning technical implementation with governance mechanisms, performance metrics, and incentive structures. When ethical objectives are embedded within organizational evaluation criteria, responsible AI becomes a shared responsibility rather than an isolated compliance task. The next section extends this discussion by examining real-world case studies and applied scenarios that illustrate how ethical and unethical practices manifest in algorithmic marketing systems..

8. CASE STUDIES AND APPLIED SCENARIOS

Case studies and applied scenarios play a critical role in translating theoretical discussions of algorithmic marketing ethics into concrete, real-world contexts. While conceptual frameworks help identify ethical risks and governance principles, empirical examples reveal how artificial intelligence, predictive analytics, and automated influence operate in practice across specific platforms and industries. This section examines documented cases from major digital platforms, drawing on regulatory filings, investigative journalism, and academic research to illustrate both problematic and responsible practices.

8.1 Personalized E-Commerce Recommendation Systems

Amazon's recommendation engine, which drives an estimated 35% of the company's revenue, exemplifies both the power and ethical tensions of algorithmic personalization. The system analyzes browsing history, purchase behavior, and contextual signals to predict consumer preferences and optimize conversion rates through product rankings, personalized emails, and "frequently bought together" suggestions (Huang & Rust, 2021).

Ethical tensions identified in practice:

Transparency limitations: Investigative research reveals that Amazon's recommendation algorithms prioritize products based on profitability, not relevance, yet consumers are unaware of this commercial optimization. The "customers who bought this also bought" suggestions are heavily weighted toward high-margin items, steering consumers toward options that benefit Amazon rather than those best matching their preferences.

Autonomy concerns: A 2023 investigation by the UK Competition and Markets Authority found that Amazon's algorithmic recommendations create "choice architectures" that systematically direct consumers toward Amazon's own products and preferred sellers, limiting exposure to alternatives. Consumers perceive their choices as self-directed while their decision environment is carefully engineered.

Vulnerability exploitation: Research documents that Amazon's algorithms identify moments of high purchase intent—such as repeated viewing of a product category—and deploy personalized urgency cues (e.g., "Only 3 left in stock") timed to maximize conversion. While effective for sales, this practice exploits psychological vulnerabilities at precisely the moments consumers are most susceptible.

Regulatory response: The European Commission opened formal proceedings against Amazon in 2022 regarding self-preferencing in recommendation algorithms, resulting in commitments to treat all sellers equally in the "Buy Box" algorithm.

8.2 Dynamic Pricing and Behavioral Exploitation

Dynamic pricing systems represent a particularly sensitive application of algorithmic marketing, with documented cases of consumer harm across multiple industries.

Uber's surge pricing provides the most extensively studied example. Research by Chen and Stalla-Bourdillon (2023) demonstrates that Uber's algorithms adjust prices not only based on supply-demand dynamics but also on inferred consumer characteristics including:

- Battery level (users with low battery are charged higher prices)
- Past ride history (users who previously accepted surge prices are more likely to see them again)
- Location type (airport and entertainment district pickups command premium pricing)

Amazon's price manipulation case (2023) revealed that the company's pricing algorithm dynamically adjusted prices based on competitors' inventory levels and individual users' browsing history. The algorithm identified users who repeatedly viewed specific products and increased prices, assuming higher purchase intent. This practice, documented in FTC enforcement proceedings, resulted in identical products being offered at different prices to different users simultaneously.

Online travel agencies have faced regulatory scrutiny for dynamic pricing practices. A 2024 investigation by the European Consumer Organisation found that booking platforms adjust hotel prices based on:

- Device type (mobile users shown higher prices than desktop users)
- Booking history (repeat customers offered premium rates)
- Urgency signals (users who previously abandoned bookings shown time-limited discounts)

Ethical implications: These cases illustrate three distinct harms: (1) price discrimination based on inferred vulnerabilities rather than legitimate factors, (2) opacity that prevents consumers from understanding or challenging pricing decisions, and (3) exploitation of behavioral signals consumers do not realize they are transmitting.

8.3 Social Media Advertising and Algorithmic Targeting

Meta's advertising platform exemplifies the scale and intensity of algorithmic marketing influence, with documented cases revealing both targeting capabilities and ethical failures.

The Cambridge Analytica scandal (2018) demonstrated how inferred psychological profiles could be used for political microtargeting. Although primarily discussed in political contexts, the underlying mechanisms—inferring personality traits, emotional states, and susceptibility to specific messages from behavioral data—are standard practice in commercial marketing. Research by Bodó et al. (2017) shows that Meta's algorithms continue to infer sensitive attributes including political affiliation, religious identity, and emotional vulnerability for targeting purposes, despite policy commitments to limit such practices.

Discriminatory ad delivery has been extensively documented on Meta's platform. Research by Lambrecht and Tucker (2023) found that:

- Housing ads were shown to significantly different demographic audiences despite neutral targeting settings
- Employment ads for male-dominated occupations were disproportionately delivered to male users

- Credit offer ads excluded older users and specific zip codes, potentially violating fair lending laws

The U.S. Department of Housing and Urban Development filed formal charges against Meta in 2022, alleging that the company's ad delivery algorithms systematically discriminated based on race, gender, and familial status. Meta's settlement included substantial changes to ad delivery systems and ongoing compliance monitoring.

Emotional contagion experiments: A 2014 study conducted by Facebook researchers (published in 2022 after regulatory review) demonstrated that the platform's news feed algorithm could manipulate users' emotional states by adjusting the ratio of positive to negative content. While framed as academic research, this experiment revealed the platform's capacity for emotional manipulation at scale—a capability central to advertising optimization systems.

Health-related targeting: Investigative journalism in 2023 revealed that Meta's algorithms identified users experiencing health crises—including cancer diagnoses, pregnancy loss, and mental health challenges—and delivered targeted advertising for relevant products. These practices exploit moments of vulnerability without user awareness or consent.

8.4 Algorithmic Influence in Financial Services Marketing

Financial services marketing increasingly relies on predictive analytics, with documented cases of consumer harm and regulatory intervention.

Credit card targeting algorithms used by major issuers have been shown to identify consumers experiencing financial stress—through searches for debt consolidation, late payments on other accounts, or visits to payday lending sites—and target them with high-interest credit offers. A 2023 Consumer Financial Protection Bureau investigation found that such practices constituted "abusive" conduct under consumer protection law, leading to millions in penalties.

Predatory lending algorithms used by online lenders automatically adjust interest rates based on inferred behavioral characteristics including:

- Time spent reading terms and conditions (less time correlates with higher rates)
- Night-time application submission (associated with financial stress)
- Device type and location data (used as proxies for creditworthiness)

These practices systematically charge higher rates to vulnerable populations while appearing to offer personalized pricing based on risk. Insurance pricing algorithms have faced regulatory scrutiny for using non-actuarial factors in premium calculation. Investigations in multiple states revealed that auto insurers used credit scores, occupation, and education level as proxies for risk, resulting in higher premiums for low-income drivers despite comparable driving records.

8.5 Responsible Deployment Examples

Despite widespread problematic practices, documented cases of responsible algorithmic marketing offer valuable lessons.

Progressive's usage-based insurance program offers personalized pricing based on actual driving behavior rather than demographic proxies. Users voluntarily install telematics devices and receive discounts for safe driving. Transparency is central: consumers know exactly what data is collected, how it influences pricing, and can opt out at any time. Research shows higher satisfaction and trust compared to traditional risk-based pricing.

Stitch Fix's preference explainability system provides users with explanations for clothing recommendations, including which attributes (style, color, price, fit) drove the selection. Users can provide feedback on each attribute, creating a transparent feedback loop that enhances both accuracy and perceived control. The company's research demonstrates that explainability increases trust and reduces the sense of algorithmic manipulation.

The Guardian's consent-first advertising model offers users clear choices about data collection and personalization. Rather than default opt-in with complex controls, the platform presents straightforward options with plain-language explanations. Early results indicate that while some users opt out of personalization, those who remain engaged show higher trust and comparable ad effectiveness through contextual targeting.

8.6 Cross-Cutting Lessons

Comparative analysis of these cases reveals several consistent patterns:

- Opacity enables exploitation: Across all problematic cases, lack of transparency about how algorithms function and what data they use enabled practices consumers would likely reject if understood.
- Vulnerability is systematically targeted: Algorithms consistently identify and exploit moments of consumer vulnerability—financial stress, emotional distress, purchase intent—with precision that exceeds human capabilities.
- Regulatory intervention follows documented harm: In nearly all cases, meaningful change occurred only after regulatory investigation or enforcement, suggesting that self-regulation alone is insufficient.

- Transparency and control correlate with trust: Responsible deployments demonstrate that transparency about algorithmic processes, meaningful user control, and ethical constraints on optimization can coexist with commercial success.
- Practical Implications: Organizations should conduct pre-deployment ethical risk assessments using documented case precedents. Regular algorithmic auditing should test for the patterns of harm identified in these cases—discrimination, vulnerability exploitation, opacity-induced manipulation—and implement corrective mechanisms before regulatory intervention becomes necessary.

9. FUTURE RESEARCH DIRECTIONS

The rapid evolution of artificial intelligence, predictive analytics, and automated influence in marketing systems presents a dynamic and expanding research landscape. While existing studies have documented the capabilities and ethical risks of algorithmic marketing, many questions remain unresolved, particularly as technologies become more autonomous, adaptive, and deeply embedded in everyday digital interactions. Future research must move beyond descriptive and reactive approaches toward interdisciplinary, longitudinal, and impact-oriented investigations that capture the full socio-technical complexity of algorithmic marketing ecosystems (Floridi et al., 2022).

A central challenge for future research lies in understanding how automated influence systems reshape consumer behavior over time. Most empirical studies focus on short-term outcomes such as engagement or conversion, yet the long-term effects of continuous algorithmic persuasion on preferences, habits, and autonomy remain underexplored. Longitudinal research designs are needed to examine how sustained exposure to personalized influence alters decision-making processes, risk perception, and self-regulation. Such studies would provide critical insights into whether algorithmic marketing fosters dependency, preference distortion, or reduced deliberative capacity among consumers.

9.1 Advancing Ethical Metrics and Evaluation Frameworks

One promising direction for future research involves the development of ethical metrics that extend beyond traditional performance indicators. Current marketing analytics prioritize efficiency-driven metrics such as click-through rates, dwell time, and revenue optimization. Future studies should investigate alternative evaluation frameworks that incorporate ethical dimensions, including fairness, transparency, autonomy preservation, and consumer well-being (Martin, 2022).

Developing such metrics requires interdisciplinary collaboration between marketing scholars, data scientists, and ethicists. Research efforts should focus on operationalizing abstract ethical principles into measurable indicators that can be integrated into algorithmic optimization processes. By embedding ethical evaluation into system performance assessment, future research can support the design of marketing systems that balance commercial success with societal responsibility.

9.1.1 Measuring Autonomy and Consumer Well-Being

Measuring consumer autonomy and well-being presents a significant methodological challenge. Autonomy is inherently subjective and context-dependent, making it difficult to quantify within algorithmic systems. Future research should explore mixed-method approaches that combine behavioral data with qualitative insights to assess how consumers perceive control, influence, and choice in algorithmic environments (Susser et al., 2021).

Well-being-oriented research could examine psychological outcomes such as stress, satisfaction, and trust in relation to algorithmic marketing exposure. These insights would inform ethical design strategies aimed at minimizing harm and promoting positive user experiences.

9.2 Explainability and Human Understanding of Algorithmic Influence

Explainability remains a critical area for future investigation. While technical research has advanced explainable AI methods, little is known about how explanations affect consumer understanding and behavior in marketing contexts. Future studies should examine which forms of explanation are meaningful to consumers and how transparency influences trust, resistance, or acceptance of algorithmic persuasion (Shin, 2021).

Research should also explore the cognitive limits of explainability. Providing explanations that are overly complex may overwhelm users, while overly simplistic explanations may obscure important details. Understanding this balance is essential for designing transparency mechanisms that genuinely empower consumers rather than serving as symbolic gestures.

9.3 Algorithmic Influence and Vulnerable Populations

Another critical research direction involves examining the differential impact of algorithmic marketing on vulnerable populations. Individuals experiencing financial stress, health challenges, or reduced cognitive capacity may be particularly susceptible to predictive influence and automated persuasion. Future research should investigate how algorithmic marketing systems identify and target vulnerability and the ethical implications of such practices (Lambrecht & Tucker, 2023).

This line of inquiry has important policy implications, as it may inform the development of stricter safeguards or restrictions for high-risk marketing applications. Research focusing on vulnerability can also contribute to fairness-aware design by highlighting populations that require additional protection.

9.4 Governance Models and Cross-Jurisdictional Challenges

As algorithmic marketing operates across global digital platforms, future research must address governance challenges that transcend national boundaries. Regulatory frameworks vary significantly across jurisdictions, creating inconsistencies in oversight and enforcement. Comparative studies examining how different regulatory regimes address algorithmic marketing ethics would provide valuable insights into best practices and gaps (Cowls & Floridi, 2018).

Research should also explore the role of self-regulation, industry standards, and multi-stakeholder governance models in complementing formal regulation. Understanding how these mechanisms interact can inform more adaptive and resilient governance approaches.

9.5 Emerging Technologies and New Ethical Frontiers

Emerging technologies such as emotion recognition, affective computing, and generative AI introduce new ethical frontiers for algorithmic marketing. These technologies enable deeper inference into emotional states and the generation of highly persuasive content, intensifying concerns about manipulation and authenticity. Future research should critically examine how these technologies are integrated into marketing systems and their implications for consumer agency and trust (Hagendorff, 2022).

Additionally, the use of synthetic data and simulated consumer models raises questions about realism, bias, and accountability. Investigating these emerging practices will be essential for anticipating ethical challenges before they become entrenched in market infrastructures.

9.6 Toward Interdisciplinary and Impact-Oriented Research

Addressing the ethical frontiers of algorithmic marketing requires sustained interdisciplinary collaboration. Future research agendas should integrate perspectives from marketing, computer science, psychology, law, and philosophy to capture the multifaceted nature of automated influence. Impact-oriented research that evaluates real-world consequences rather than isolated technical performance will be particularly valuable for informing policy and practice (Floridi et al., 2022).

By advancing ethical metrics, transparency mechanisms, governance models, and vulnerability-focused analysis, future research can contribute to the development of algorithmic marketing systems that are not only intelligent but also socially responsible. The final section synthesizes these insights and offers concluding reflections on balancing innovation with ethical responsibility in the age of automated influence.

10. CONCLUSION

The integration of artificial intelligence, predictive analytics, and automated influence mechanisms has fundamentally reshaped the nature of contemporary marketing. Algorithmic marketing no longer functions merely as a support tool for human decision-making; instead, it operates as an autonomous, adaptive system capable of anticipating consumer behavior, structuring choice environments, and guiding decisions at scale. This transformation represents a shift in how influence is exercised within digital markets, moving from explicit persuasion toward subtle, continuous, and data-driven behavioral shaping embedded within everyday digital interactions.

This chapter has demonstrated that algorithmic marketing must be understood as a socio-technical system in which technological capabilities, organizational incentives, and human behavior are deeply intertwined. Predictive analytics enables marketing systems to move beyond reactive strategies by forecasting consumer actions and intervening at moments of heightened influence. Automated influence technologies further extend this capability by embedding persuasion within platform architectures, recommender systems, and interface designs. Together, these developments redefine the boundaries between choice, guidance, and control in digital consumption environments.

A central conclusion of this analysis is that ethical challenges in algorithmic marketing are not isolated technical flaws but structural consequences of optimization-driven systems. When algorithms are designed primarily to maximize engagement, conversion, or revenue, ethical risks such as autonomy erosion, behavioral manipulation, and unequal treatment become systemic rather than accidental. These risks are amplified by the opacity of advanced AI models and the scale at which automated influence operates, making traditional notions of transparency, consent, and accountability increasingly difficult to sustain.

The chapter has also highlighted the limitations of relying solely on regulatory compliance to address ethical concerns. While legal frameworks provide important safeguards, they often struggle to keep pace with adaptive and continuously evolving marketing technologies. Algorithmic influence operates through subtle personalization and inference, challenging regulatory approaches that depend on explicit disclosures or static rules. As a result, ethical responsibility cannot be delegated entirely to regulators but must be shared across organizations, platforms, and system designers.

Responsible AI and ethical design frameworks emerge as essential components of a sustainable response to these challenges. By embedding ethical considerations directly into system objectives, data practices, and decision-making processes, organizations can move toward marketing systems that respect consumer agency while maintaining innovation and efficiency. Ethical design is not a constraint on technological progress but a prerequisite for long-term trust, legitimacy, and societal acceptance of algorithmic marketing practices.

The applied scenarios discussed in this chapter further illustrate that ethical outcomes are shaped by concrete design choices rather than abstract intentions. Systems that prioritize transparency, user control, and accountability demonstrate that it is possible to balance personalization with respect for autonomy. Conversely, systems that prioritize short-term optimization without ethical safeguards reveal how automated influence can undermine trust, exacerbate vulnerabilities, and generate broader social harm. These contrasting outcomes reinforce the importance of deliberate ethical governance throughout the lifecycle of algorithmic marketing systems.

Looking forward, the ethical frontiers of algorithmic marketing will continue to expand as technologies become more autonomous, emotionally responsive, and generative. The growing capacity of AI systems to simulate human communication, infer psychological states, and personalize influence in real time raises profound questions about authenticity, consent, and power in digital markets. Addressing these questions requires ongoing interdisciplinary engagement that integrates technical innovation with ethical reflection, organizational accountability, and societal values.

In conclusion, AI-driven predictive analytics and automated influence represent both an opportunity and a responsibility for modern marketing. While these technologies enable unprecedented levels of personalization and efficiency, they also reshape consumer autonomy and market fairness in ways that demand careful ethical consideration. Sustainable algorithmic marketing will depend not on technological capability alone but on the willingness of organizations and policymakers to embed ethical reasoning into the design, deployment, and governance of intelligent marketing systems. By doing so, algorithmic marketing can evolve into a practice that supports innovation while preserving trust, autonomy, and social responsibility in the digital economy.

REFERENCES

Ali, A., & Hastuti, H. (2024). Predictive analytics and marketing decision-making: A systematic review of data-driven influence. *Journal of Business Research, 164*, 113963.

Bhambri, P. (2025). Innovative systems: Entertainment, gaming, and the metaverse. In Ho, R. C., Song, B. L., & Tee, P. K. (Eds.), *Managing customer-centric strategies in the digital landscape* (pp. 483–514). IGI Global., DOI: 10.4018/979-8-3693-5668-5.ch018

Bhambri, P., & Kant, S. (2025a, February 1-2). A taxonomy of bias in machine learning: Classification, sources, and implications for ethical AI [Paper presentation]. Lincoln-SPAST Global Sustainability Programme (SGS-24), 1st International Conference of LGPR Program, Lincoln University College, Malaysia. SPAST Proceedings, 1(2). https://spast.org/techrep/article/view/5387/724

Bhambri, P., & Kant, S. (2025b, April 26-27). Ethical AI systems: A comprehensive framework for bias mitigation and fairness in machine learning [Paper presentation]. Lincoln-SPAST Global Sustainability Programme (SGS-24), 2nd International Conference of LGPR Program, Lincoln University College, Malaysia. SPAST Proceedings, 1(2). https://spast.org/techrep/article/view/5385/698

Bhambri, P., & Kant, S. (2025c, August 2-3). Navigating the AI trade-offs: A sector-level study on fairness, performance, and explainability [Paper presentation]. Lincoln-SPAST Global Sustainability Programme (SGS-24), 3rd International Conference of LGPR Program, Lincoln University College, Malaysia. SPAST Proceedings, 1(4). https://spast.org/techrep/article/view/5734/862

Bhambri, P., & Kautish, S. K. (2024). Analytic hierarchy process and business value creation. In Kautish, S. K. (Ed.), *Using strategy analytics for business value creation and competitive advantage* (pp. 54–77). IGI Global., DOI: 10.4018/979-8-3693-2823-1.ch003

Bhambri, P., & Khang, A. (2024a). The human-machine nexus with art-making generative AIs. In Hai-Jew, S. (Ed.), *Making art with generative AI tools* (pp. 73–85). IGI Global., DOI: 10.4018/979-8-3693-1950-5.ch004

Bhambri, P., & Khang, A. (2024b). Challenges and future directions on business intelligence. In Özsungur, F. (Ed.), *Generating entrepreneurial ideas with AI* (pp. 117–146). IGI Global., DOI: 10.4018/979-8-3693-3498-0.ch006

Bodó, B., Helberger, N., & de Vreese, C. H. (2017). Political micro-targeting: A Manchurian candidate or just a dark horse? *Internet Policy Review, 6*(4). Advance online publication. DOI: 10.14763/2017.4.776

Boerman, S. C., Kruikemeier, S., & Zuiderveen Borgesius, F. (2021). Online behavioral advertising: A literature review and research agenda. *Journal of Advertising, 50*(3), 341–362.

Borgesius, F. Z., Helberger, N., & Reyna, A. (2017). The perfect match? A closer look at the relationship between EU consumer law and data protection law. [Kluwer Law International.]. *Common Market Law Review, 54*(5), 1427–1465. DOI: 10.54648/COLA2017118

Brent Mittelstadt, B. (2019). Principles alone cannot guarantee ethical AI. *Nature Machine Intelligence, 1*(11), 501–507. DOI: 10.1038/s42256-019-0114-4

Burtell, M. (2023). Artificial influence: Ethics of AI-driven persuasion and behavioral optimization. *AI & Society, 38*(4), 1567–1581.

Caliskan, A., Bryson, J. J., & Narayanan, A. (2022). Fairness and discrimination in algorithmic decision-making. *Communications of the ACM, 65*(6), 54–63. DOI: 10.1145/3531146

Chen, J., & Stalla-Bourdillon, S. (2023). Algorithmic persuasion and autonomy in digital markets. *Computer Law & Security Review, 49*, 105775.

Cowls, J., & Floridi, L. (2018, June 19). Prolegomena to a white paper on an ethical framework for a good AI society. Social Science Research Network (*SSRN*). DOI: 10.2139/ssrn.3198732

Davenport, T. H., Guha, A., Grewal, D., & Bressgott, T. (2021). How artificial intelligence will change the future of marketing. *Journal of the Academy of Marketing Science, 49*(1), 24–42. DOI: 10.1007/s11747-019-00696-0

De Bruijn, H., Warnier, M., & Janssen, M. (2022). The perils and pitfalls of explainable AI. *Ethics and Information Technology, 24*(2), 1–10.

Dubois, E., & McKelvey, F. (2023). Algorithmic influence in platform societies. *New Media & Society, 25*(7), 1791–1810.

Floridi, L., Holweg, M., Taddeo, M., Amaya Silva, J., Mökander, J., & Wen, Y. (2022). Responsible AI: Principles, challenges, and opportunities. *Business Ethics Quarterly, 32*(1), 1–36.

Gorwa, R., Binns, R., & Katzenbach, C. (2022). Algorithmic governance and platform power. *New Media & Society, 24*(9), 1961–1983.

Grewal, D., Hulland, J., Kopalle, P. K., & Karahanna, E. (2021). The future of technology and marketing. *Journal of the Academy of Marketing Science*, *49*(1), 1–8. DOI: 10.1007/s11747-019-00711-4

Hagendorff, T. (2022). The ethics of AI ethics: An evaluation of guidelines. *Minds and Machines*, *32*(1), 99–120. DOI: 10.1007/s11023-020-09517-8

Huang, M. H., & Rust, R. T. (2021). Artificial intelligence in service. *Journal of Service Research*, *24*(1), 3–18.

Johnson, D. G. (2023). Algorithmic accountability in automated marketing systems. *Ethics and Information Technology*, *25*(3), 1–12.

Kietzmann, J., Paschen, J., & Treen, E. (2022). Artificial intelligence in advertising. *Journal of Advertising Research*, *62*(3), 263–270. DOI: 10.2501/JAR-2018-035

Lambrecht, A., & Tucker, C. (2023). Algorithmic bias? An empirical study into apparent gender-based discrimination in ad delivery. *Management Science*, *69*(2), 1129–1148.

Martin, K. (2022). Ethical implications and accountability of algorithms. *Journal of Business Ethics*, *176*(4), 835–850. DOI: 10.1007/s10551-018-3921-3

Shin, D. (2021). The effects of explainability and transparency on trust in AI. *Computers in Human Behavior*, *113*, 106394.

Soraj Hongladarom, S., & Shoshana Zuboff. (2023). The age of surveillance capitalism: The fight for a human future at the new frontier of power. *AI & Society*, *38*(6), 2359–2361. DOI: 10.1007/s00146-020-01100-0

Susser, D., Roessler, B., & Nissenbaum, H. (2021). Online manipulation: Hidden influences in a digital world. *Georgetown Law Technology Review*, *4*(1), 1–45.

Van Noort, G., Voorveld, H. A. M., & Strycharz, J. (2024). Persuasion knowledge in algorithmic environments. *Journal of Interactive Marketing*, *65*, 1–15.

Chapter 4
Sssh... AI Is Listening: Surveillance, Trust, and the Privacy-Personalization Paradox in Social Media Marketing

Shlok Manish Nayyar
http://orcid.org/0009-0008-8064-8080
Christ University, India

Rahul Khurana
http://orcid.org/0000-0003-3939-1371
Christ University, India

ABSTRACT

This chapter discusses the ways in which systems that have been developed with artificial intelligence are transforming the modern digital marketing landscape, especially the uses of algorithmic personalisation, consumer interactions, and advertising performance outcomes. Since advertising decisions are increasingly influenced by data-driven technologies, predictive analytics and machine learning models now determine the targeting, content delivery, and optimisation processes, changing the normal advertising logics (Wedel and Kannan, 2016; Shankar, 2018). Based on interdisciplinary sources on marketing and information systems, this chapter takes a conceptual approach to generalise previous studies and suggest an integrative framework between AI capabilities, personalisation processes, consumer interaction, and performance results (Kietzmann et al., 2018; Lemon and Verhoef, 2016).

DOI: 10.4018/979-8-3373-7704-9.ch004

INTRODUCTION

The rapid growth of social media platforms has fundamentally changed the nature of advertising in the online economy. Advertising has ceased to be a one-way process of communication but has developed to be a bi-directional, interactive platform ecosystem of data and is algorithmically mediated. Facebook, Instagram, TikTok, and YouTube have become the key infrastructures where businesses can communicate with consumers, develop an advertising campaign, and analyze the campaign's effectiveness. This is also a transformation of both the increase in users of the platform and the increase in the ability to gather and analyze behavioral information using artificial intelligence (AI) technology, which increasingly influences how advertising is presented and optimized (Kietzmann et al., 2018; Shankar, 2018; Wedel & Kannan, 2016).

The concept of artificial intelligence has quickly turned into one of the most notable aspects of advertisement patterns in the social media setting. To determine the preference among consumers and maximize advertising exposure, marketers are solving a growing number of problems using machine learning algorithms, recommender systems, and predictive analytics, rather than the traditional demographic segmentation, intuitive creative strategies, and manual media planning (Shankar, 2018; Wedel & Kannan, 2016) Consequently, algorithmic inference and automated learning processes have become dominant influences on the success of advertising campaigns on social media platforms instead of referencing conventional planning methods.

The introduction of AI in social media advertisements has also changed the personalization concept largely. There was a traditional understanding of personalization as the customization of marketing messages to segments of consumers. Nevertheless, the development of the personalization process has turned out to be a highly individualized and dynamic process due to advances in computational intelligence. Artificial intelligence-based systems can dynamically change the advertising content depending on the user's behavior, contextual factors, and the supposed intention of the consumer.

Though there exist prior works which suggest that personalization is likely to enhance the effectiveness of advertising by promoting the relevance of the messages, lessening information overload, and improving the persuasive effect when it is well-matched to consumer preferences (Arora et al., 2008; Bleier & Eisenbeiss, 2015) and, consumer engagement has turned out to be the key concept of digital marketing research. The research also has proven that consumer engagement moderates the association between the digital touchpoints and the performance marketing results (Calder et al., 2009; Hollebeek et al., 2014; Lemon & Verhoef, 2016).

In spite of these developments, a lot of available literature is still disjointed. The studies of artificial intelligence applications in marketing have tended to concentrate on the technological features or the predictive quality but have not adequately examined the processes involved in behavior in which the technologies influence marketing. On the other hand, the research on the concept of personalization and consumer interaction often does not consider the algorithmic structures in which these phenomena are made possible on digital platforms. This discontinuity has led to insufficient theoretical convergence explaining the interaction of AI capabilities, personalization mechanisms, and consumer interaction to drive the effect on advertising performance in a social media setting.

This is an important theoretical gap, especially considering that modern social media platforms are algorithmic. The visibility of content, the exposure of advertising, and optimization are increasingly dictated by platform architectures, which are opaque computational systems that constantly learn the behavior of the users. Researchers have claimed that these platforms cannot just act as intermediaries, but as agents of marketing particular outcomes and streams of information (Van Dijck et al., 2023). In these circumstances, the effects of advertising cannot be entirely explained without the use of the algorithm processes, mediating business-consumer interactions.

Meanwhile, there have been concerns about critical ethical and societal issues with the growth of AI-based publicizing frameworks. Such concerns as surveillance, data privacy, transparency, and consumer trust have been brought up by researchers as platforms are turning to detailed personal data to optimize the delivery of advertisements (Gillespie, 2018; Van Dijck et al., 2023). The lack of transparency in the development of decision-making algorithms has fuelled debates about accountability, fairness, and the trade-offs between personalization and privacy. These issues contribute to the significance of coming up with conceptual frameworks that will not only be focused on the performance outcomes but also the wider socio-technical environment where AI-driven advertising will be conducted.

Although AI technologies ensure a higher level of accuracy in targeting, better operational efficiency, and increased returns on the money spent on advertising, they also make transparency and control over the managerial decision-making process less apparent. The marketing managers are now becoming more dependent on the algorithms delivery without having a clear idea of the mechanism behind the decision-making. This case supports the necessity of the theoretically based schemes capable of allowing managers to comprehend more effectively how AI-based advertising systems create value and where the risks might be developed(Shankar, 2018). Thus, the current chapter aims to formulate an integrative, theoretically informed conceptualization of AI-based social media advertising. At this budding state of this concept, rather than empirically testing it through a survey, the chapter is attracting attention of the academicians and practitioners by conceptually and narratively driving the synthesis of interdisciplinary literature in the fields of marketing, information systems, and media studies. With such synthesis, the chapter introduces a conceptual framework according to which AI capabilities create hyper personalized advertising, consumer engagement, and, eventually, the impact on the outcome of advertising performance. The chapter will seek to fill the gaps in the literature and bring conceptual clarity to the algorithms-mediated advertising landscape by incorporating the technological, behavioral, and strategic levels of comprehension.

The remainder of this chapter is structured as follows. The next section discusses literature in detail regarding artificial intelligence and its use within digital marketing, along with personalization in social media advertising and consumer engagement. Next, a brief description of the methodology used to conduct the conceptualization of the framework has been provided. Later, the proposed conceptual framework and its associated theoretical ramifications are presented. Lastly, the chapter provides managerial ramifications and possible future research paths.

LITERATURE REVIEW

As already introduced, the academic knowledge base of artificial intelligence (AI) and social media advertising has been growing steadily in recent times, which can be explained by the increasing role of AI technologies in the digital marketing process. Initial studies on internet advertising were mainly based on the common display and search advertising and analyzed the results in terms of click-through, relevance of the advertisement and the targeting efficiency. Nonetheless, with the developments of social media becoming complicated attention-based ecosystems in which users produce, share, and consume vast quantities of information, scholarly attention began to move toward the concept of how the system of algorithms creates advertising exposure and interaction with consumers within these platforms.

The shift of chronological content feeds into recommendation systems by algorithms in the application of such platforms as Facebook and Instagram was one of the crucial milestones in the study of digital advertising. The algorithms of recommendation recalibrate the reasoning of advertisement by placing emphasis on predictive analytics, automated content ranking and machine-based decisions. This, in turn, is pushing advertisement delivery more towards computation systems that take a vast amount of behavioral data and based on that data identify which advertisements need to be delivered, when they are delivered and to whom is best likely to respond to that advertisement.

Artificial intelligence has thus emerged as the key organization technology in the modern social media advertising system. AI allows platforms and advertisers to consume large amounts of behavioral data, model latent consumer preferences, and scale the personalization programs to large audiences. The typical definition of AI in marketing research is a set of computational methods which can perform tasks traditionally involving human intelligence, such as classification, prediction, optimization, and natural language understanding. Machine learning, which is one of the fundamental elements of AI, is defined as algorithms that enhance their predictive effectiveness by being exposed to past data in comparison to operating purely on pre-established policies. Machine learning's suitability for navigating the intricate nature of social media advertising stems from its capacity to adapt to the dynamic and ever-evolving patterns of consumer behavior (Shankar, 2018).

AI technologies can make organizations process big volumes of consumer-related data and optimize campaign processes, as well as provide a high level of personalization in marketing communications on digital media(Davenport et al., 2020). On the same note, researchers believe that marketing infrastructures and service systems are becoming more integrated with AI, allowing predictive decision-making and automated interactions with customers to redefine the marketing strategies and consumer experiences (M.-H. Huang & Rust, 2021). Marketing analytics and machine learning innovations have also improved the capacity of firms to derive usable insights from big data, as well as optimize online advertising in real time (Grewal et al., 2020).

Among the most widespread topics in the literature relate to personalization in social media advertising enabled with the use of AI. Predictive algorithms are slowly replacing traditional segmentation methods, which often rely on broad demographic or behavioral generalizations, with individualized forecasts of consumer preferences and reactions. Analysis of behavioral signals, including likes, clicks, sharing behaviors, and browsing histories, can produce highly relevant advertisements, which are delivered by AI-driven algorithms to individual users and can, thus, enhance the engagement and conversion rates.

As opposed to the conventional mass marketing method, personalized advertising aims at providing advertising messages that resonate well with the interests of individual users or contextual preferences. The studies of customer relationship management also point out the fact that AI technologies are becoming more useful in allowing companies to process behavioral data to make predictions about consumer preferences and provide personalized marketing communication on a large scale (Libai et al., 2020).

Researchers have also highlighted that AI-based marketing systems allow more flexible and personal communication with customers in digital media and therefore enhance customer interactions and the efficacy of marketing (Dwivedi et al., 2021). Moreover, artificial intelligence enables companies to turn digital interaction into quantifiable marketing results through the analysis of consumer reactions and optimization of marketing efforts based on the review of such reactions. These trends explain why AI technologies have increasingly become integrated into the strategic and operational components of digital marketing.

Recent research also indicates that AI-assisted personalization may take effect on consumer trust and perceptions of value in online marketing settings. The more advertising messages are perceived to be relevant and useful, the more consumers will interact with them and learn to have a positive attitude towards the brand (Ameen et al., 2021). Therefore, individualization with the help of artificial intelligence gains a more significant role in the formation of consumer interaction within social media advertisement systems.

Along with personalized targeting, the literature also mentions the purpose of the AI to automate the campaign execution and media buying processes. The AI advertising platforms are used to constantly change the bidding mechanisms, allocate budgets to various audience groups, and optimize the delivery of creative work based on performance indicators in real-time (Gao et al., 2023). With this degree of automation, it is possible to minimize the necessity of manual decision-making and make advertising campaigns responsive to user behavior and changes in the market situation in the shortest possible time.

In dynamic digital settings, artificial intelligence systems are becoming useful in automated decision-making processes to enable marketers to predict consumer actions and optimize advertising strategies (De Bruyn et al., 2020). Likewise, the application of big data analytics and AI technologies has made the digital marketing systems far more efficient in terms of providing the advertising experience of unprecedented personalization and at scale. Technological progress AI, big data, and marketing analytics, in turn, is transforming a larger marketing environment through increasing the accuracy of targeting campaigns, automation, and customization of advertisements(Grewal et al., 2020).

The other significant technological aspect of AI-assisted advertising is that of natural language processing (NLP), which facilitates the analysis and interpretation of textual information automatically. Sentiment analysis, topic modeling, and conversational interfaces can be used in NLP to enable advertisers to analyze what people post on social media platforms, comments and reviews, and understand their opinions. Considering the user-generated content, advertisers can get to learn more about the attitudes of the audience and make appropriate changes in advertising strategies. NLP technologies can also be used to create automatic advertising copy, chatbots, and conversational marketing applications that allow one to develop a personal communication with a user.

Besides textual analysis, computing vision technologies have increased the field of AI use to the visual sphere of social media content. Deep learning models have the ability to evaluate images and videos that are posted on social media platforms to identify objects, scenes, and brand logos among user-created contents. The capabilities enable the advertisers to position the advertisements in contexts that are relevant to visual content themes, hence increasing the contextual relevance and increasing the effectiveness of advertisements.

Another focus of recent studies is the expanded scope of implications of AI-driven advertising on consumer engagement and advertising performance outcomes. Tailored advertising with the assistance of AI technologies has been linked to the increase of such key performance indicators as the rates of clicks, dwell time, and conversion rates. Advertisements, in a case when they are looped to the preferences of the individual consumers, and their circumstances, one can expect the user to view advertisements as pertinent and useful, as opposed to obtrusive. Empirical studies also indicate that increases in engagement measures could also be converted into more long term marketing returns including better brand recall and increment in customer lifetime value, but these impacts could be different among platforms, product lines, and audiences. In general, the literature suggests that AI-based personalization could considerably improve the advertising performance as opposed to the conventional advertising methods (Rahman et al., 2025).

The growing use of artificial intelligence in digital marketing has also raised significant ethical concerns regarding data privacy, algorithmic bias, and the transparency of automated personalization systems. Recent research emphasizes that AI-powered personalization can create ethical challenges related to consumer autonomy and responsible data governance in digital marketing environments (Karami et al., 2025). Moreover, a significant number of AI systems are based on a black box model when the way a decision is made internally is non-transparent and challenging to explain. Such a lack of transparency can reduce the capacity of advertisers and regulators to learn how decisions made by algorithms are made, and could have unintended effects, such as discriminatory targeting or antisocial market results. Since the field of AI technologies keeps growing in the digital advertising ecosystems, striking a balance between technological innovation and ethical responsibility and regulation is a growing research priority.

RESEARCH METHODOLOGY

This chapter follows the conceptual research methodology that presupposes a narrative and integrative literature review. This is especially suited to new areas of technology where theoretically constructed constructs and their associations need to be elucidated first before empirical testing is possible. The main goal of this chapter is thus to combine the available academic information and create a theoretically supported model to state how an artificial intelligence (AI) improves advertising results in the context of social media. Conceptual research is significant in those areas that are experiencing a fast shift of technology and need theoretical constructs to present disjointed information and steer subsequent empirical research (Snyder, 2019; Webster & Watson, 2002). So-called conceptual contributions assist in determining constructs and relationships that may be observed with the help of empirical research (Jabareen, 2009; Okoli, 2015).

Conceptual research is based on synthesis of literature and theoretical knowledge available in the literature to explain complex phenomena unlike empirical studies where primary sources of data are used such as surveys, experiments or interviews (Whetten, 1989). Narrative and integrative literature reviews have long been deemed as rigorous methodologies of integrating scattered bodies of knowledge, specifically in interdisciplinary fields like digital marketing and artificial intelligence in which the knowledge of several academic fields overlaps (Paul & Criado, 2020; Torraco, 2005).

The methodological procedure that is adopted in this chapter was a combination of three stages that are interrelated. The first step involved carrying out a broad literature review on sourcing the most significant academic databases such as Scopus, Web of Science, EBSCO, ScienceDirect, SAGE Journals, and Google Scholar. The search terms comprised such combinations of words as artificial intelligence, digital advertising, social media advertising, machine learning marketing, recommender systems, personalization, algorithmic advertising, predictive analytics, consumer engagement, and digital marketing automation. The search was aimed to include literature published from 2010-2025, as it is during that time that the social media advertising world reached maturity and the use of AI technologies became more and more a part of the marketing practice (Kietzmann et al., 2018; Wedel & Kannan, 2016)). Approximately 30–40 relevant academic articles were reviewed and synthesized to develop the conceptual foundations of this chapter. Previous background literature was also taken into account in which they supplied valuable theoretical knowledge in reference to advertising effectiveness, consumer choice, or computational marketing methods.

The second phase was the screening and thematic synthesis of the identified literature. In contrast to systematic reviews, which are based on very rigid inclusion criteria and statistical combination of results, narrative reviews lay emphasis on conceptual consistency and theoretical applicability (Baumeister & Leary, 1997; Greenhalgh et al., 2005)). To achieve analytical clarity, the literature was grouped into four broad thematic streams:

(1) AI-based audience targeting/segmentation,
(2) automated execution of media and algorithmic optimization,
(3) predictive engagement mechanisms and personalization, and

(4) algorithmic advertising implications on ethics, regulations, and socio-technologies.

Such thematic organization is based on the rules of integrative literature reviews where categories and syntheses are used to determine the relationships and the mechanisms between disciplines (Whittemore & Knafl, 2005).

The synthesis of the narrative involved the use of studies in several academic fields so that conceptual rigor is achieved. Literature on marketing provided information on the consumer behavior, segmentation, and the processes of engagement (Lemon & Verhoef, 2016; Wedel & Kannan, 2016). Research in information systems helped to acquire insights into machine learning systems, data systems, and decision-making processes that are automated (Shmueli & Koppius, 2011). The approach to algorithmic mediation and platform governance was critically viewed in the context of media and communication (Gillespie, 2018; Van Dijck et al., 2023). Besides, the research in computer science and engineering provided the background knowledge regarding natural language processing, computer vision, and recommender systems (Aggarwal, 2016; Jurafsky & Martin, 2025). Combining these views made it possible to conceptualize AI-driven social media advertising in a more all-encompassing manner.

Besides academic sources, industry reports and market intelligence sources were also reviewed to give a background of the overall trends in digital advertising, the use of artificial intelligence, and the expansion of social media platforms. These were taken to offer descriptive information in regard to the trends and patterns in the use of technology in the emerging market, thus assisting in placing the theoretical discussion into the actual industry development (Tranfield et al., 2003; Webster & Watson, 2002).

Altogether, the given conceptual narrative methodology used in this chapter encompasses the interdisciplinary literature synthesis with the industry background that is aimed at building a theoretically based framework that explains how AI capabilities are used to promote hyper personalization, consumer engagement, and, finally, better the outcome of advertising performance in social media settings. The chapter lacks the use of statistics to estimate and rather concentrates on the evolution of the theory which can be used in future empirical studies that are aimed at analyzing the proposition of AI-driven advertising systems in any digital marketing markets.

CONCEPTUAL FRAMEWORK DEVELOPMENT

The chapter introduces a model of ideas that could be applied to explain the effectiveness of artificial intelligence (AI) in enhancing advertising with references to social media. The framework is an attempt to bring together the understanding of marketing information systems, and media studies to emerge with a consistent theoretical clarification of how AI capabilities can be converted to enhance advertising outcomes It is important to note that the framework provides a theoretical explanation of how AI capabilities influence advertising outcomes. The proposed conceptual framework consists of four key constructs: AI capabilities, personalization mechanisms, consumer engagement, and advertising performance outcomes.

AI Capabilities

The technological backdrop of the model is AI potentials and can be termed as the computational engines that are embodied within social media platforms that entice information, assume tendency, and optimize the provision of advertisements. These capabilities normally entail machine learning, natural language processing, computer vision, and recommender systems. which help in predictive and automated media functions (Kietzmann et al., 2018; Wedel & Kannan, 2016). Under such systems, platforms can turn mass behavioral data into actionable insights that guide audience targeting, user segmentation, and creative optimization.

Personalization Mechanisms

The second part of the framework is personalization mechanisms, or the algorithmic customization of the exposure to advertising based on features of the individual level Relevance of message is an old issue in the marketing literature and the phenomenon of AI offers a significant boost to the possibilities of dynamic personalization of advertising messages (Arora et al., 2008; Bleier & Eisenbeiss, 2015) AI-powered systems can provide data about users' interests, intentions, and circumstances that have not been traditionally captured through demographic segmentation or any other means. Therefore, advertisers can serve their ads based on these data points rather than using demographic data to serve ads that may not be the best match for a user. Personalization in the context of social media, where the content flows are continuous serves as a sorting system making the likelihood of users being attentive to sponsored messages very high.

Consumer Engagement

The third construct, consumer engagement, is behavioural and psychological responses that are manifested due to customised advertising The ideas that are engaged are usually designed in the literature of digital advertising as attention, interaction, emotional response, and participation (Calder et al., 2009; Hollebeek et al., 2014). It is assumed that the personalisation based on AI will prove more engaging since it will enhance the relevance of messages and perceived disturbance. It has been shown that personalised advertisements receive higher click throughs and dwell time and have better attitudinal responses than non personalised advertisements but differences in effects by platform and product types exist (Lambrecht & Tucker, 2011). Personalisation and performance have a relationship in the proposed model which is engagement.

Advertising Performance Outcomes

The final element of the model is the advertising performance which is the measure of the outcomes wanted by the advertisers including an increase in the conversion rates brand recall, purchase intention and the payback period of the advertising expenditure. AI not only participates in performance improvements which is an indirect modification through increased engagement but also direct with regard to optimization of campaign execution. On a case in point predictive models can forecast the chance of conversion, dynamic creative systems may modify the form of message in real-time and automatic bidding can more properly distribute budgets than human media buying. The greater the concentration on data-driven decision making in advertisement practices conducted by companies is, the higher the tendency toward the inclusion of AI into the solution of performance improvement measurement.

The constructs are put in a logical order of relationship as indicated in the conceptual framework: AI capabilities create personalization, personalization creates engagement, and engagement creates improved advertising outcomes. This linearity is a viable representation of proven advertising effectiveness paradigms that state that attitudinal and behavioral shifts take place following attention and pertinence (Vakratsas & Ambler, 1999). Although it is presented in the form of lateral interactions to facilitate comprehension, the given model can facilitate feedback loops since interaction data can be used to make personalization more accurate in the future through the application of machine learning. That way, the framework provides a conceptually grounded basis to understand AI-based advertising without supposing empirical research and has a point on which future studies can be based.

Figure 1. The proposed conceptual framework is illustrated in Figure 1

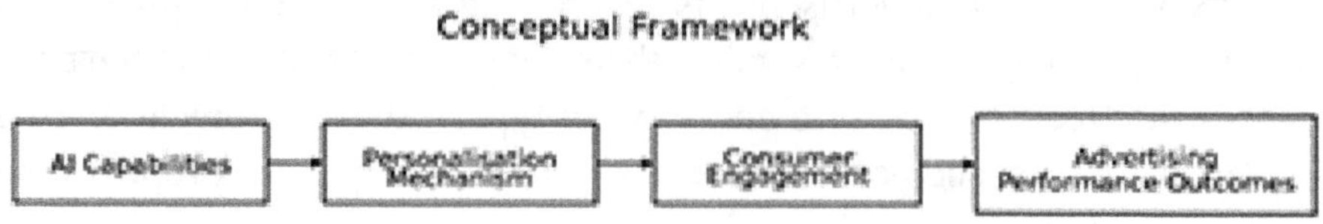

To further clarify the theoretical foundations of the proposed conceptual framework, the following table summarizes the key constructs and the academic literature that informs each component of the model.

Table 1. Theoretical foundations of the proposed conceptual framework is illustrated in Table 1

Framework Construct	Description in the Framework	Key Supporting Literature
AI Capabilities	The technology referred to is built into social media like Facebook & Twitter in order to provide the ability to process large amounts of data quickly and then offer businesses tools to provide automated decisions around delivering their advertisements through different media channels. Some of the technology capabilities include artificial intelligence (AI), machine learning, recommendation engines, natural language processing (NLP), and computer vision that assist with targeting and executing advertising campaigns.	(Kietzmann et al., 2018; Shankar, 2018; Wedel & Kannan, 2016)
Personalization Mechanisms	The customization of advertising messages, times, and formats occurs through the use of algorithms based on a user's unique attributes, behavior signals, and contextual factors. AI uses dynamic, real time personalized messaging to increase the relevance of messages as well as the accuracy of targeting to consumers.	(Arora et al., 2008; Bleier & Eisenbeiss, 2015; Libai et al., 2020)
Consumer Engagement	The interactions that consumers have with the ad they see and the ad they interact with can also include cognitive, emotional, and behavioral interactions between the two. When advertisements are personalized for a particular user, it increases their chance of receiving attention, engaging with the ad, and participating in digital environments where they view that type of content.	(Calder et al., 2009; Hollebeek et al., 2014; Lemon & Verhoef, 2016)
Advertising Performance Outcomes	The outcomes from digital advertising campaigns based upon the success of digital advertising include greater click-through rates (CTR), improved conversion rates (CR), better brand recall, and a greater return on investment (ROI) for advertising expenditures.	(Lambrecht & Tucker, 2013; Vakratsas & Ambler, 1999)

This table presents the fundamental concepts and the scholarly literature that provide evidence for them, thereby constituting the proposed conceptual framework.

Table 2. Conceptual relationships in the framework is illustrated in Table 2

AI Capabilities → Personalization Mechanisms	Artificial Intelligence technologies enable platforms to manage large amounts of behavioral data for predictive analysis and allow platforms to provide custom advertising approaches (message, delivery, etc.) in real time to each individual user.	(Kietzmann et al., 2018; Shankar, 2018; Wedel & Kannan, 2016)
Personalization Mechanisms → Consumer Engagement	Personalized advertisements allow users to perceive the ad message as being more appropriate for them, which increases their attention, engagement and emotional reaction to the ad content.	(Arora et al., 2008; Bleier & Eisenbeiss, 2015; Lambrecht & Tucker, 2013)
Consumer Engagement → Advertising Performance Outcomes	The more time users spend engaged with advertisement content, the better the overall results will be for marketing campaigns (e.g., CTRs, conversions, brand awareness, return on investment).	(Calder et al., 2009; Hollebeek et al., 2014; Vakratsas & Ambler, 1999)

This table depicts the theoretical connections involving the main constructs of the proposed conceptual framework and identifies the scholarly literature for those connections.

DISCUSSION

The given conceptual framework is analyzed within the frameworks of modern trends in social media advertising and marketing practices based on artificial intelligence. This section combines theoretical knowledge and trends in the industry to showcase the explanatory capacity and conceptual connectivity of the framework. The discussion supports the key hypothesis of the chapter, which is that artificial intelligence has become a fundamental technological capacity that redefines the manner in which advertising value is created, distributed, and measured under the social media context.

The framework places the capabilities of AI as the force of change in the social media advertising systems. This point of view corresponds with the current studies in marketing analytics and information systems, which propose that the predictive technologies will gradually influence the marketing decision-making process through the substitution of manual judgment with algorithmic optimization and continuous learning systems (Shankar, 2018; Wedel & Kannan, 2016). In social media ecosystems, where content exposure is dictated by algorithmic ranking products and user behavior is used in a multitude of streams of information, AI systems are essential in defining what advertisements get shown, when they get shown, and to whom they get shown. As a result, the effectiveness of advertising will become more and more determined by the quality of algorithmic inference instead of the purely traditional method of segmentation or creative impulse.

This theoretical view is also underpinned by the fact that social media advertisement is growing in scale and strategic significance as part of the wider digital marketing environment. The development of social media advertisement is an indication of both the rising popularity of the platform users and the capacity of these platforms to generate market on user attention by providing advanced and AI-based targeting and optimization tools. This tendency can be strategically aligned with the assumption of the framework that the capabilities of AI become an infrastructural layer upon which the current practice of advertisement is based and not just an optional analytical tool.

Organizations are also putting increased investments in machine learning-driven targeting systems, automated bidding systems, predictive analytics systems, and dynamic creative optimization systems. The investments are an indication that there is a structural change in the way advertising campaigns are planned, implemented and evaluated. Rather than working with cold assumptions or programmed campaigns, advertisers are moving to AI operators that can continuously change with consumer activity and redefine decision policies by looking at the real-time consequences. This change is embodied in the conceptual framework with the capabilities of AI becoming a fundamental component that transforms the nature of the processes of advertising instead of a downstream analytic machine.

In this context, the consumer engagement mediating between AI capabilities and engagement is personalization. Relevance of message in marketing theory is not a new concept, and the personalization achieved through artificial intelligence is greatly increased by having the ability to continuously adapt to the individual consumer level (Arora et al., 2008; Bleier & Eisenbeiss, 2015). Personalization based on AI uses both behavioral and contextual signals and predictive inferences to make dynamically changing adjustments to advertising in social media settings. The effect of this process is that it turns advertising into an interactive process between algorithmic systems and consumers as opposed to a one-way communication process.

Consumers have been exposed to numerous amounts of content that have been filtered by algorithms, and advertisement messages rarely grab the attention of consumers unless it fits within individual interests and situational demands. The challenge posed by AI-based personalization is that it enhances the relevance of messages, as well as makes the perceived intrusiveness less relevant, which in turn raises the chance of users noticing and processing sponsored content.

The consumer engagement is placed in the center of the framework since the behavior and psychological process whereby the personalization is converted into marketing performance. Personalization based on AI increases the level of engagement as it matches the marketing messages to anticipated preferences, motivations, and behaviors of the users. The advertisements that appeal to the taste of the user have higher chances of creating attention, interaction and emotional appeal, which are the key factors in persuasion in the digital world.

Notably, interaction with AI-based advertising systems also serves as an indication of feedback that sustains the perpetual enhancement of algorithmic learning. Clicks, dwell time, sharing behavior and interaction frequency are engaged indicators that are constantly added to machine learning models in order to refine targeting strategy and advertisement delivery. This is the adaptive nature of AI-driven advertising being emphasized by this feedback mechanism with consumer behavior shaping and being shaped by the practice of algorithmic decision-making. Even though the conceptual framework is shown in a sequential manner so as to be easily analytical, the underlying system is composed of continuous learning cycles as is the case in machine learning technologies.

The fact that the use of AI-based optimization systems is gaining traction in the field of marketing also supports the relationship between consumer engagement and advertising performance. Performance indicators like conversion rates, brand recognition, and return on advertising spend (ROAS) are turning into the major focus of predictive analytics and automated decision-making tools. The engagement data may be converted into performance advancements because AI systems adapt bidding approaches, creative sequencing, and budget distribution in reaction to perceived behavioral trends. These advances support the argument of the framework that engagement is a highly important process that can connect personalization strategies with quantifiable advertising results.

Theoretically, the proposed structure contributes to the digital marketing research because it combines technological, behavioral, and performance-oriented approaches into one model of explanations. Current literature tends to explore the concepts of artificial intelligence, personalization, and consumer engagement as independent research lines, which leads to disjointed descriptions of value creation in an advertising setting that relies on algorithms (Kietzmann et al., 2018; Lemon & Verhoef, 2016). The framework, by providing a sequential flow of AI competencies to advertisement performance via personalization and consumer interaction, provides a more detailed explanation of how AI-based advertising systems can create marketing value within the social media setting.

CONCLUSION

This chapter was aimed at building a conceptual understanding of the way artificial intelligence (AI) is changing social media advertising by redefining how value is created, delivered, and assessed in advertising. In response to the increasing centrality of AI to digital marketing systems, the chapter reviewed interdisciplinary literature and developed a theoretical framework that connected AI abilities, personalization processes, consumer experience, and advertising effectiveness outputs. The chapter in question with its conceptual and narrative methodology helps in the clarification of theoretical relations in an area of high technological change and rising complexity of managerial tasks.

As stressed in the discussion, it is no longer possible to perceive artificial intelligence as an auxiliary analytical instrument to facilitate marketing choices. Rather, it has become a basic infrastructural element that has been entrenched in social media platforms. The visibility of the content, the exposure of advertising and optimization of the campaign is progressively controlled by the algorithms systems, which are based on the predictive inference, automated decision-making, and learning processes in real-time. Under these conditions, the effectiveness of advertising is less determined by the traditional approach to segmentation or manual planning of a campaign and more by the effectiveness of the process of algorithmic inference and adaptive optimization. This change results in the need to reevaluate the concept of advertising theory as the AI-powered decision system.

The conceptual framework presented in this chapter helps to add to this point of view as it describes a step-by-step process according to which AI abilities allow facilitating the personalization process, improving consumer interaction, and finally increasing the results of the advertising performance. The framework proposes a detailed description of technological and behavioral process interactions in the space of the social media advertising ecosystems by incorporating findings of marketing analytics, information systems, and consumer behavior studies. In contrast to disjointed strategies that analyse artificial intelligence, personalization or engagement through different studies, the framework approaches these constructs as interrelated in a single value creation process.

One of the main strengths of the chapter is the focus on the duality of personalization and consumer interaction in AI-driven advertising systems. AI allows a high degree of dynamism in personalization through constant adaptation of promotional materials and distribution in accordance with the behavioral and situational information. The relevant of messages, in its turn, activates the growth of consumer engagement that, on the one hand, serves as a result of personalization, and, on the other hand, serves as a feedback that enhances algorithmic learning in a vicious cycle. In that regard, engagement is to be perceived as a dynamic and interactive process but not just a performance indicator.

Another point that the chapter emphasises is the involvement of engagement as a key mechanism relating the effect of algorithmic capabilities to the advertising performance. The more AI-powered systems are dependent on engagement metrics to enhance bidding techniques, creative sequencing, and budgeting, the more engagement takes the center stage of comprehending the effectiveness of advertising in the social media context. This opinion is consistent with the modern understanding of digital marketing as a feedback-based system where consumer behavior constantly shapes the algorithmic decision-making and marketing strategy.

As a manager, the framework has valuable implications in organizations that work in AI-based advertising setting. The results indicate that the investment in artificial intelligence technologies must be planned to be in line with the ability to personalize and marketing approaches with a focus on engagement to yield sustained performance gains. The adoption of AI tools in itself will not bring significant outcomes to organizations unless they have the ability to identify the insights of the algorithms, use data in a responsible manner, and apply AI-generated knowledge to the overall marketing strategies. Moreover, the transparency, trust to consumers, and ethical governance issues have been gaining relevance alongside the increasingly important role of the algorithmic system in advertising processes. Proper application of AI technologies will thus be very important in ensuring sustainability in advertising their products.

Even though the proposed framework is conceptually based on the available literature, empirical research is required in the future to investigate the relationships existing between the capabilities of AI, the mechanisms of personalization, consumer engagement, and advertising performance. The framework can be expanded by researchers using empirical studies to explore connections between AI capabilities, personalization processes, consumers, and advertising performance consequences. Other moderating variables that can be considered in future research include platform attributes, product type, or cultural variations in reaction to AI-based advertising. Finally, future research could expand on the evolving challenges regarding the ethical, regulatory, and privacy issues associated with AI-based advertising found within the fields of transparency, data governance, and consumer control when interacting with algorithmically driven environments.

Overall, this chapter can be regarded as the contribution to the further conceptual development of AI-driven social media advertising by suggesting an integrative framework based on interdisciplinary studies and development of the industry. The chapter can shed light on the ways in which artificial intelligence influences advertising performance and can be of use both in scholarly research and in management. The conceptual study of this kind will be highly needed as artificial intelligence keeps developing and become more intertwined with digital platforms to steer the empirical research, inform strategic choices, and aid in the responsible creation of AI-powered marketing systems.

REFERENCES

Aggarwal, C. C. (2016). An Introduction to Recommender Systems. In *Recommender Systems* (pp. 1–28). Springer International Publishing., DOI: 10.1007/978-3-319-29659-3_1

Ameen, N., Tarhini, A., Reppel, A., & Anand, A. (2021). Customer experiences in the age of artificial intelligence. *Computers in Human Behavior*, *114*(1–2), 106548. DOI: 10.1016/j.chb.2020.106548 PMID: 32905175

Arora, N., Dreze, X., Ghose, A., Hess, J. D., Iyengar, R., Jing, B., Joshi, Y., Kumar, V., Lurie, N., Neslin, S., Sajeesh, S., Su, M., Syam, N., Thomas, J., & Zhang, Z. J. (2008). Putting one-to-one marketing to work: Personalization, customization, and choice. *Marketing Letters*, *19*(3–4), 305–321. DOI: 10.1007/s11002-008-9056-z

Baumeister, R. F., & Leary, M. R. (1997). Writing Narrative Literature Reviews. *Review of General Psychology*, *1*(3), 311–320. DOI: 10.1037/1089-2680.1.3.311

Bleier, A., & Eisenbeiss, M. (2015). Personalized Online Advertising Effectiveness: The Interplay of What, When, and Where. *Marketing Science*, *34*(5), 669–688. DOI: 10.1287/mksc.2015.0930

Calder, B. J., Malthouse, E. C., & Schaedel, U. (2009). An Experimental Study of the Relationship between Online Engagement and Advertising Effectiveness. *Journal of Interactive Marketing*, *23*(4), 321–331. DOI: 10.1016/j.intmar.2009.07.002

Davenport, T., Guha, A., Grewal, D., & Bressgott, T. (2020). How artificial intelligence will change the future of marketing. *Journal of the Academy of Marketing Science*, *48*(1), 24–42. DOI: 10.1007/s11747-019-00696-0

De Bruyn, A., Viswanathan, V., Beh, Y. S., Brock, J. K.-U., & Von Wangenheim, F. (2020). Artificial Intelligence and Marketing: Pitfalls and Opportunities. *Journal of Interactive Marketing*, *51*(1), 91–105. DOI: 10.1016/j.intmar.2020.04.007

Dwivedi, Y. K., Hughes, L., Ismagilova, E., Aarts, G., Coombs, C., Crick, T., Duan, Y., Dwivedi, R., Edwards, J., Eirug, A., Galanos, V., Ilavarasan, P. V., Janssen, M., Jones, P., Kar, A. K., Kizgin, H., Kronemann, B., Lal, B., Lucini, B., & Williams, M. D. (2021). Artificial Intelligence (AI): Multidisciplinary perspectives on emerging challenges, opportunities, and agenda for research, practice and policy. *International Journal of Information Management*, *57*, 101994. DOI: 10.1016/j.ijinfomgt.2019.08.002

Gao, B., Wang, Y., Xie, H., Hu, Y., & Hu, Y. (2023). Artificial Intelligence in Advertising: Advancements, Challenges, and Ethical Considerations in Targeting, Personalization, Content Creation, and Ad Optimization. *SAGE Open*, *13*(4), 21582440231210759. Advance online publication. DOI: 10.1177/21582440231210759

Gillespie, T. (2018). Custodians of the internet: Platforms, content moderation, and the hidden decisions that shape social media. In *Custodians of the Internet: Platforms, Content Moderation, and the Hidden Decisions That Shape Social Media*. Yale University Press.

Greenhalgh, T., Robert, G., Macfarlane, F., Bate, P., Kyriakidou, O., & Peacock, R. (2005). Storylines of research in diffusion of innovation: A meta-narrative approach to systematic review. *Social Science & Medicine*, *61*(2), 417–430. DOI: 10.1016/j.socscimed.2004.12.001 PMID: 15893056

Grewal, D., Hulland, J., Kopalle, P. K., & Karahanna, E. (2020). The future of technology and marketing: A multidisciplinary perspective. *Journal of the Academy of Marketing Science*, *48*(1), 1–8. DOI: 10.1007/s11747-019-00711-4

Hollebeek, L. D., Glynn, M. S., & Brodie, R. J. (2014). Consumer Brand Engagement in Social Media: Conceptualization, Scale Development and Validation. *Journal of Interactive Marketing*, *28*(2), 149–165. DOI: 10.1016/j.intmar.2013.12.002

Huang, M.-H., & Rust, R. T. (2021). Engaged to a Robot? The Role of AI in Service. *Journal of Service Research*, *24*(1), 30–41. DOI: 10.1177/1094670520902266

Jabareen, Y. (2009). Building a Conceptual Framework: Philosophy, Definitions, and Procedure. *International Journal of Qualitative Methods*, *8*(4), 49–62. DOI: 10.1177/160940690900800406

Jurafsky, D., & Martin, H. J. (2025). Speech and Language Processing 3rd ed. In *Stanford University*.

Karami, A., Shemshaki, M., & Ghazanfar, M. A. (2025). Exploring the Ethical Implications of AI-Powered Personalization in Digital Marketing. *Data Intelligence*, *7*(4), 1035–1084. DOI: 10.3724/2096-7004.di.2024.0055

Kietzmann, J., Paschen, J., & Treen, E. (2018). Artificial Intelligence in Advertising. *Journal of Advertising Research*, *58*(3), 263–267. DOI: 10.2501/JAR-2018-035

Lambrecht, A., & Tucker, C. (2011). When does Retargeting Work? Timing Information Specificity. SSRN *Electronic Journal*. DOI: 10.2139/ssrn.1795105

Lemon, K. N., & Verhoef, P. C. (2016). Understanding Customer Experience Throughout the Customer Journey. *Journal of Marketing*, *80*(6), 69–96. DOI: 10.1509/jm.15.0420

Libai, B., Bart, Y., Gensler, S., Hofacker, C. F., Kaplan, A., Kötterheinrich, K., & Kroll, E. B. (2020). Brave New World? On AI and the Management of Customer Relationships. *Journal of Interactive Marketing*, *51*(1), 44–56. DOI: 10.1016/j.intmar.2020.04.002

Okoli, C. (2015). A Guide to Conducting a Standalone Systematic Literature Review. *Communications of the Association for Information Systems*, *37*(1), 43. DOI: 10.17705/1CAIS.03743

Paul, J., & Criado, A. R. (2020). The art of writing literature review: What do we know and what do we need to know? *International Business Review*, *29*(4), 101717. DOI: 10.1016/j.ibusrev.2020.101717

Rahman, S. A. Y., Rahayu, A., & Hendrayati, H. (2025). Digital marketing evolution: Understanding the role of AI and Big Data in shaping marketing strategies. *International Journal of Financial, Accounting, and Management*, *7*(2), 197–211. DOI: 10.35912/ijfam.v7i2.2593

Shankar, V. (2018). How Artificial Intelligence (AI) is Reshaping Retailing. *Journal of Retailing*, *94*(4), vi–xi. DOI: 10.1016/S0022-4359(18)30076-9

Shmueli, G., & Koppius, O. R. (2011). Predictive Analytics in Information Systems Research1. *Management Information Systems Quarterly*, *35*(3), 553–572. DOI: 10.2307/23042796

Snyder, H. (2019). Literature review as a research methodology: An overview and guidelines. *Journal of Business Research*, *104*(1), 333–339. DOI: 10.1016/j.jbusres.2019.07.039

Torraco, R. J. (2005). Writing Integrative Literature Reviews: Guidelines and Examples. *Human Resource Development Review*, *4*(3), 356–367. DOI: 10.1177/1534484305278283

Tranfield, D., Denyer, D., & Smart, P. (2003). Towards a Methodology for Developing Evidence-Informed Management Knowledge by Means of Systematic Review. *British Journal of Management*, *14*(3), 207–222. DOI: 10.1111/1467-8551.00375

Vakratsas, D., & Ambler, T. (1999). How Advertising Works: What Do We Really Know? *Journal of Marketing*, *63*(1), 26–43. DOI: 10.1177/002224299906300103

Van Dijck, J., de Winkel, T., & Schäfer, M. T. (2023). Deplatformization and the governance of the platform ecosystem. *New Media & Society*, *25*(12), 3438–3454. DOI: 10.1177/14614448211045662

Webster, J., & Watson, R. T. (2002). Analyzing the Past to Prepare for the Future: Writing a Literature Review. *Management Information Systems Quarterly*, *26*(2), xiii–xxiii. DOI: 10.2307/4132319

Wedel, M., & Kannan, P. K. (2016). Marketing Analytics for Data-Rich Environments. *Journal of Marketing*, *80*(6), 97–121. DOI: 10.1509/jm.15.0413

Whetten, D. A. (1989). What Constitutes a Theoretical Contribution? *Academy of Management Review*, *14*(4), 490. DOI: 10.2307/258554

Whittemore, R., & Knafl, K. (2005). The integrative review: Updated methodology. *Journal of Advanced Nursing*, *52*(5), 546–553. DOI: 10.1111/j.1365-2648.2005.03621.x PMID: 16268861

KEY TERMS AND DEFINITIONS

Advertising Performance: The quantifiable results of advertising campaigns like click through rates, conversion rates, brand recall and ROA investment.

Algorithmic Targeting: Machine learning algorithms are used to process user data and provide adverts to those with the greatest chances of responding positively to them.

Artificial Intelligence (AI): Computational technologies permitting machines to conduct anticipatory analysis, learning, and determination of tasks normally regarded to be human-intelligence.

Consumer Engagement: These are the cognitive, emotional, and behavioral interplay that consumers develop in relation to digital advertising media.

Personalization: The advertising messages and delivery process customization to individual users according to the behavioral data and contextual indicators.

Predictive Analytics: Such analytical methods as the use of historical behavioral data to estimate how consumers will act in future and how best to use it to optimize advertising decisions.

Social Media Advertising: Online advertising that is being done on social media where the algorithmic systems are used to target and deliver the advertisements.

Chapter 5
Applications of AI Chatbots in Marketing and Customers' Response

Miguel Cachulo Pereira
http://orcid.org/0000-0003-3431-1141
CEOS.PP Coimbra, Polytechnic University of Coimbra, Portugal & GOVCOPP, ISCA, University Aveiro, Portugal

Lara Mendes Bacalhau
http://orcid.org/0000-0001-9674-4167
CEOS.PP Coimbra, Polytechnic University of Coimbra, Portugal

ABSTRACT

As AI-powered chatbots increasingly mediate consumer interactions across e-commerce, retail, and service contexts, understanding their impact on brand loyalty and trust has become a strategic priority for marketing research. This review synthesises 40 empirical and conceptual studies published between 2019 and 2026, retrieved from Scopus and Web of Science, through a narrative thematic synthesis. Findings are organised around four themes: chatbot design and humanisation, trust as the pivotal relational mechanism, customer journey outcomes, and contextual boundary conditions. The analysis resolves key theoretical tensions, notably the warmth-versus-competence debate, by identifying moderating conditions, including product type, consumer motivational orientation, and relationship phase. An integrative conceptual framework, DIAL (Design, Interaction, Accumulation, Loyalty),

DOI: 10.4018/979-8-3373-7704-9.ch005

is proposed to model the temporal dynamics through which chatbot design decisions translate into durable brand loyalty. Implications for marketing theory, managerial practice, and future research are discussed.

1. INTRODUCTION

Conversational artificial intelligence has become one important point of contact between firms and consumers in the digital economy. Deployed across e-commerce platforms, financial services, hospitality, and retail, AI-powered chatbots now mediate interactions that were previously the exclusive province of human service agents, answering product enquiries, managing complaints, facilitating purchase decisions, and sustaining ongoing customer relationships at a scale that human labour alone cannot economically support. For marketing scholars and practitioners alike, the central question is no longer whether chatbots will be deployed but whether they will be deployed in ways that build, rather than erode, the consumer trust and brand loyalty on which sustainable competitive advantage depends.

The strategic importance of this question is underscored by a fundamental asymmetry in the current state of knowledge. Commercial investment in chatbot deployment has outpaced the accumulation of rigorous empirical evidence on its consumer consequences. Early enthusiasm for chatbots as cost-efficient service substitutes has increasingly given way to a more nuanced recognition that consumer responses to AI-mediated service encounters are psychologically complex, context-dependent, and in some respects counterintuitive. Consumers who find chatbot interactions satisfying do not always become loyal customers (Kusuma et al., 2025). Chatbots designed to be as human-like as possible do not always elicit maximum trust (Igarashi et al., 2026). And mandatory disclosure of chatbot identity, increasingly required by law in multiple jurisdictions, may undermine the very social presence mechanisms through which chatbot interactions build consumer confidence (Wang et al., 2025; Yu et al., 2024). Marketing science has an obligation to map these patterns rigorously, and the current density of empirical output, the period 2023–2026 alone accounts for nearly 90% of substantive empirical contributions on this topic, suggests that the field has reached a point where systematic integration is both feasible and urgent.

Prior scholarly attention to AI chatbots in marketing has produced a body of work that is thematically rich but structurally fragmented. Existing reviews have addressed chatbot adoption through technology acceptance frameworks (Gatzioufa & Saprikis, 2022), catalogued chatbot applications across service industries (Mariani et al., 2022), and mapped the bibliometric structure of the emerging literature (Manigandan & Sivakumar, 2024). Systematic literature reviews have examined anthropomorphism in AI agents more broadly (Chaturvedi et al., 2025), and conceptual papers have proposed strategic frameworks for AI in marketing (Davenport et al., 2020; Huang & Rust, 2018, 2021) and experiential frameworks for consumer-AI interaction (Puntoni et al., 2021). More recently, Sahut & Laroche (2025) proposed an integrative framework synthesising eleven empirical studies on AI applications, spanning personalisation, service recovery, disclosure, and parasocial interaction, though without explicitly modelling the temporal forces of trust accumulation or the functional-relational loyalty distinction that the present review prioritises. These contributions have been individually valuable but collectively limited by three persistent gaps.

First, existing reviews have predominantly addressed the question of chatbot adoption, examining the antecedents of consumers' willingness to use AI-mediated service channels, rather than how repeated chatbot interactions shape brand loyalty and trust over the customer journey. Adoption-oriented work illuminates the preconditions for chatbot engagement but is silent on the downstream relational consequences that determine whether chatbot deployment creates or destroys long-term brand equity. Second, the literature has examined individual mechanisms, trust formation, conversational style, anthropomorphism, service recovery, in largely independent research streams without integrating them into a coherent account of how design decisions, psychological processes, and contextual moderators jointly determine loyalty outcomes across the customer journey. This fragmentation means that findings from one stream (e.g., warm conversational style enhances engagement) are rarely brought into dialogue with findings from another (e.g., warm style is inferior to competent style in functional service contexts), leaving theoretical tensions unresolved and actionable guidance underspecified. Third, the field has not yet produced an integrative conceptual model that both organises existing evidence and maps the longitudinal process through which initial trust converts into durable brand loyalty, a gap that matters because the corpus's near-exclusive reliance on cross-sectional, single-encounter data means that what is known about chatbot-consumer relationships is almost entirely static, capturing states at a moment in time rather than the processes through which those states develop.

These gaps define the motivation for the present review, which addresses the following research question: How do the dynamics of consumer-chatbot interactions impact customer outcomes, brand loyalty, and trust in digital marketing? This question is deliberately integrative: it asks not merely what chatbots produce (outcomes) but how design decisions, interaction processes, and contextual conditions jointly shape the relational consequences that matter to marketing strategy. It encompasses the full customer journey from initial engagement through repeated interaction to the formation of durable brand loyalty, rather than treating any single stage in isolation.

This review makes three specific contributions to the marketing literature. First, it provides a systematic synthesis of 40 unique studies published between 2019 and

2026, integrating evidence across multiple methodologies, theoretical traditions, and geographic contexts in a way no prior review has for this topic. Second, it resolves theoretical tensions in the existing literature, most importantly the apparent contradiction between warmth-superiority and competence-superiority findings, by demonstrating that these divergences are attributable to meaningful moderating conditions rather than methodological inconsistency. Third, and most substantively, it proposes an integrative conceptual framework, the DIAL framework (Design, Interaction, Accumulation, Loyalty), that organises the existing evidence, makes the temporal development of trust and loyalty formation explicit, and generates a focused empirical research agenda for the next generation of chatbot marketing research.

The remainder of the paper is organised as follows. Section 2 describes the systematic review methodology, including database coverage, search strategy, inclusion and exclusion criteria, and the analytical procedures applied to the final corpus. Section 3 presents the findings organised around four evidence-grounded themes: chatbot design and humanisation; trust as the pivotal relational mechanism; customer journey outcomes; and contextual boundary conditions. Section 4 concludes with the DIAL integrative framework and its theoretical implications, practical implications for marketing managers, limitations of the review, and directions for future research.

2. METHODS

This review was conducted following a semi-structured protocol established prior to data collection, specifying the research question, eligibility criteria, search strategy, data extraction procedures, and synthesis approach. Searches were conducted across Web of Science Core Collection and Scopus on 9 February 2026. These databases were selected for their complementary disciplinary coverage: Scopus provides broad coverage of social science and IS-adjacent venues, while Web of Science offers deeper coverage of high-impact marketing and consumer psychology journals. Searches were conducted across title, abstract, and keyword fields using the following string, applied in both databases:

```
(chatbot* OR "conversational agent*" OR "virtual assistant*" OR "AI agent*" OR "conversational AI")
```

AND

```
(trust OR loyalty OR satisfaction OR engagement OR "purchase intention*" OR "brand relationship*" OR "consumer behavio*")
```

AND

```
(marketing OR "digital marketing" OR "e-commerce" OR "customer service" OR "consumer*" OR "brand*")
```

The search logic maps directly onto the three conceptual components of the research question. The first cluster captures the focal technological entity, using both specific terms and broader synonyms employed across disciplinary communities to avoid excluding relevant studies that use non-standard terminology. The second cluster captures the relational and behavioural outcomes prioritised by the research question. The third cluster anchors retrieval to marketing-relevant contexts. Following retrieval, records were exported to a reference management system for deduplication. After automated and manual deduplication and title-abstract screening against the eligibility criteria, full texts were obtained and assessed for all passing records. The final corpus comprised 40 unique studies.

Given the heterogeneity of included studies, spanning experimental, survey-based, mixed-methods, qualitative, and conceptual designs, a narrative thematic synthesis was conducted following the approach described by Thomas and Harden (2008). Themes were derived inductively from the substantive findings across all included studies through a three-phase procedure. In the first phase, descriptive codes were generated from the findings field of each extraction record, producing an initial pool of free codes across the full corpus. In the second phase, codes were grouped into descriptive themes by conceptual similarity and shared explanatory logic; candidate themes were assessed against a minimum threshold of three independent contributing studies to ensure each theme represented a pattern in the literature rather than an isolated finding. In the third phase, descriptive themes were subjected to analytical synthesis: convergences and divergences across contributing studies were examined, boundary conditions were identified, and the relationships among themes were mapped to produce the integrative conceptual framework presented in Section 4 (Figure 1). The methodological quality of contributing studies was considered throughout, with evidence from lower-selectivity venues or weaker designs treated with appropriate caution relative to evidence from higher-impact journals employing multi-study or experimental designs.

3. RESULTS

Themes were derived inductively from the substantive findings across all contributions in the corpus, following a procedure aligned with thematic synthesis as applied in systematic reviews (Thomas & Harden, 2008). The final structure comprises 4 overarching themes and 11 sub-themes, reflecting a hierarchical organisation in which the overarching themes represent fundamental dimensions of the consumer-chatbot relationship (design, psychological processing, relational outcomes, and contextual conditioning), and the sub-themes represent specific, empirically grounded patterns within each dimension.

The empirical work synthesised in this review draws on three dominant theoretical lenses, which operate at different levels of analysis and are complementary. Technology acceptance frameworks account for the antecedents of chatbot adoption and continued use, and have been extensively applied to chatbot research (Gatzioufa & Saprikis, 2022). The Stimulus–Organism–Response paradigm provides the causal architecture through which external chatbot design stimuli are translated into internal consumer states and subsequent behavioural responses, and underpins a substantial share of the empirical models in the corpus (Le et al., 2023; Wang et al., 2025; Ye et al., 2026). Anthropomorphism and social presence theory, together with the Stereotype Content Model that organises the warmth and competence dimensions of social perception (Fiske et al., 2002; Chaturvedi et al., 2025), explain the organism-level psychological processes through which consumers interpret and respond to chatbot characteristics.

3.1 Chatbot Design and Humanisation

The first cluster of findings in the corpus concerns the design decisions firms make when deploying chatbots and the consumer responses those decisions elicit. Two design choices have attracted the most sustained empirical attention: the personality style in which the chatbot converses, organised around the warmth–competence axis, and the degree to which the chatbot is rendered as human-like. The following sub-sections examine each in turn.

3.1.1 Warmth and Competence as the Organising Axis of Chatbot Personality

The design choices firms make when deploying chatbots constitute the first and most consequential determinant of consumer response. Among these choices, the warmth-competence axis derived from the Stereotype Content Model (Fiske et al., 2002) has emerged as the dominant organising framework for chatbot personality research, and the corpus provides substantial convergent evidence for its validity across diverse methodologies and contexts. Experimental studies (Choi & Zhou, 2023; Roy & Naidoo, 2021, 2025), survey-based structural equation models (Lee & Li, 2023; Kim & Hur, 2024), multi-study designs (Bhattacharjee et al., 2025), and the only field experiment in the corpus (Igarashi et al., 2026) all confirm that consumers evaluate chatbot character along warmth and competence dimensions, and that both dimensions generate positive responses under baseline conditions. No study in the corpus disputes the taxonomy's descriptive validity.

Where the evidence diverges, and where its most important contribution lies, is in the relative effectiveness of each style across conditions. A simple reading of the corpus might suggest a warmth advantage: warm conversational styles generate higher trust, stronger brand engagement, and superior relational outcomes in the majority of studies (Choi & Zhou, 2023; Roy & Naidoo, 2021). Externally valid evidence on this point comes, for example, from Igarashi et al.'s (2026) randomised field experiment, which found that a cartoon-appearance, warmth-response chatbot configuration generated significantly higher subscription purchase rates through an expectancy-disconfirmation mechanism — warm, empathetic language from a non-threatening visual design positively violates consumer expectations, strengthening relational commitment among repeat customers.

However, the same field experiment also shows that, for one-time purchasers seeking product information, competent chatbots consistently outperform warm ones. This finding aligns with Chen et al.'s (2023) multi-experiment study, which demonstrates that AI chatbots outperform human agents for search goods, where information retrieval is the primary task, but not for experience goods, with the match effect mediated by processing fluency and perceived service quality. Roy & Naidoo's (2025) finding that consumers driven by positive materialist values prefer warm chatbots while those driven by insecurity-motivated acquisition prefer competent ones adds an individual-level layer: chatbot style preferences are not homogeneous but reflect consumers' fundamental motivational orientations.

The regulatory focus moderation documented by Choi & Zhou (2023) across four studies provides the cleanest theoretical account of this heterogeneity. Promotion-focused consumers exhibit greater willingness to self-disclose personal information to warm chatbots, because the style creates regulatory fit with their approach-oriented motivational state; prevention-focused consumers exhibit greater disclosure toward competent chatbots for analogous reasons. This pattern, stable across chronic and situationally induced regulatory focus operationalisations, establishes that warmth-competence preference asymmetries are not random variation but reflect a theoretically coherent match between chatbot personality and consumer motivational state. Bhattacharjee et al.'s (2025) introduction of a fun conversational style, characterised by novelty, spontaneity, and playfulness, complicates a simple warmth-first prescription further, demonstrating that fun generates stronger customer engagement than warmth through distinct mechanisms (sense of liberation and hedonic involvement) and that this advantage is amplified for consumers high in individualism.

Collectively, the evidence supports a conditional rather than universal model of chatbot personality effectiveness. The divergences in the literature are not methodological artefacts but substantive reflections of moderating conditions, customer relationship phase, product type, and consumer motivational orientation, that determine which style is optimal in a given deployment context.

3.1.2 Anthropomorphism: Benefits, Limits, and Boundary Conditions

Making chatbots more human-like through visual design, language style, and behavioural cues generally enhances social presence, trust, and satisfaction. This positive main effect is documented across multiple operationalisations and contexts. Wang et al. (2025) demonstrate experimentally that anthropomorphism in generative AI marketing communication enhances purchase intention directly and indirectly through social presence and trust, with chatbot contexts amplifying the social presence pathway more strongly than static promotional content. Kim & Hur (2024) find that personalisation and anthropomorphism jointly increase perceived competence and warmth in fashion retail chatbots, generating consumer empathy that positively predicts usage willingness.

Critically, however, the corpus documents multiple conditions under which anthropomorphism fails to produce benefits or actively produces harm. Toader et al. (2020) demonstrate that highly anthropomorphised chatbots raise consumer performance expectations, such that when errors occur, perceived competence and trust are reduced more severely than they would be for non-anthropomorphic agents. This expectation-amplification mechanism is independently supported by Davis & Jin's (2024) synthesis of Crolic et al. (2022), which shows that human-like chatbots in service failure contexts elicit heightened consumer anger precisely because their apparent agency raises expectations that failure renders salient.

The disclosure context introduces a further complication. Davis & Jin (2024), drawing on Luo et al.'s (2019) large-scale observational study, report that satisfaction drops significantly at the moment of AI identity disclosure, when the anthropomorphic impression is broken by legal transparency requirements. Wang et al.'s (2025) experimental findings corroborate this: transparency weakens anthropomorphism's effect on social presence, reducing the indirect pathway through which humanisation supports purchase intention. Yu et al. (2024) extend this by demonstrating that disclosure timing moderates the trust consequences: pre-dialogue disclosure is more satisfying for high-contact services, while post-dialogue disclosure is better suited to low-contact services. Together, these findings constitute a disclosure paradox — the features that make chatbots most effective at building trust are precisely the features that mandatory transparency most threatens.

Igarashi et al.'s (2026) field experiment provides precise evidence on anthropomorphism's design implications, demonstrating that the combination of low form realism and high behavioural realism outperforms fully human-like designs for subscription customers through expectancy-disconfirmation dynamics. This finding directly challenges the intuitive assumption that more human-like is always more effective and suggests that the match between the visual register and behavioural expressiveness is the key design consideration.

Emerging evidence on novel conversational dimensions beyond warmth and competence, fun and playfulness (Bhattacharjee et al., 2025), mild linguistic aggressiveness (Chen & Chen, 2025), and message construal level (Sun & Si, 2025), extends the design space beyond the founding framework. These contributions are individually validated but have not been cross-study replicated; they are best understood as promising theoretical extensions that open research agendas rather than established regularities. A further emerging dimension concerns consumer agency in design: Hu et al. (2025) demonstrate that allowing consumers to actively choose their chatbot avatar generates psychological ownership, which enhances trust and perceived autonomy, positioning consumer co-creation of chatbot identity as a novel trust-building mechanism beyond firm-controlled anthropomorphic design.

3.2 Trust as the Pivotal Relational Mechanism

Trust is the construct that recurs most frequently across the corpus, functioning both as an outcome of chatbot design choices and as a mechanism through which those design choices generate downstream behavioural consequences. Three aspects of trust warrant separate treatment: its antecedents, its mediating role in the causal chains linking design to loyalty, and the specific tension introduced by mandatory AI disclosure.

3.2.1 Antecedents of Chatbot Trust

Trust is the most frequently studied construct in the corpus and the one for which consistent evidence has accumulated. Its antecedents operate across three analytically distinct categories. Technology acceptance factors, perceived usefulness, perceived ease of use, and habit, consistently predict trust across studies drawing on TAM and UTAUT frameworks (Alagarsamy & Mehrolia, 2023; Jyothsna et al., 2024; Becan & Çeber, 2025), reflecting the IS-adoption heritage of much chatbot research. Service quality dimensions, reliability, responsiveness, and information accuracy, similarly predict trust in papers oriented toward service marketing traditions (Le et al., 2023; Vebrianti et al., 2025), confirming that chatbots are not exempt from the functional performance requirements that govern trust formation in human service encounters. Governance-oriented factors, transparency, ethical design, and privacy protection, predict trust in more recent studies reflecting growing regulatory scrutiny of AI (Wang et al., 2024; Rahim et al., 2022), suggesting that the trust antecedent landscape is expanding beyond user experience toward the perceived fairness and safety of AI systems.

Against these positive antecedents, privacy concern functions as a consistent and independent trust inhibitor across all studies that examine it (Alagarsamy & Mehrolia, 2023; Pang et al., 2025; Nguyen et al., 2026). The persistent negative effect of privacy concern on trust persists even after controlling for positive performance and social quality antecedents, suggesting it is not the absence of trust but an active inhibitory force that design improvements alone cannot neutralise. This inhibitory pattern is corroborated qualitatively by Habib et al. (2025), whose grounded theory analysis of US chatbot users identifies technological limitations, including perceived inability to handle complex queries, and personal-perceptual barriers, particularly the preference for human interaction, as the primary forces that truncate chatbot adoption independently of service quality.

A critical limitation of the trust antecedent evidence is its near-exclusive reliance on cross-sectional data. The corpus documents the determinants of initial trust, formed on the basis of first impressions and single-encounter evaluations, but provides almost no evidence on how trust evolves across repeated interactions. The distinction between initial trust and the relational trust that relationship marketing theory identifies as the proximal driver of durable loyalty (Morgan & Hunt, 1994) is theoretically important but empirically invisible in the current literature.

3.2.2 Trust as Mediating Mechanism

The most robustly documented structural finding in the entire corpus is trust's role as the primary mediating mechanism through which chatbot design and service quality attributes generate downstream behavioural outcomes. Across six independent empirical papers, trust significantly mediates the relationship between chatbot interaction features and loyalty-relevant outcomes, including reuse intention (Ye et al., 2026), donation willingness (Sun & Si, 2025), post-recovery satisfaction (Zhang et al., 2024; Lee, 2024), self-disclosure (Choi & Zhou, 2023), and purchase intention (Wang et al., 2025). No study in the corpus that positions trust as a mediator finds it to be non-significant. This convergence across diverse contexts, analytical approaches, and operationalisations is unusual in a field of this heterogeneity and constitutes the review's most defensible empirical foundation.

The structural position of trust in mediation chains is illuminating. Ye et al.'s (2026) sequential mediation (perceived interactivity → social presence → trust → reuse intention) makes explicit that each stage is a necessary but individually insufficient condition for downstream loyalty: merely increasing interactivity without generating social presence is insufficient, and generating social presence without building trust is insufficient to drive behavioural outcomes. In Choi & Zhou's (2023) programme, trust fully mediates the regulatory fit effect on self-disclosure, positioning it not as a distal predictor of relational outcomes but as a proximal psychological gatekeeper conditioning consumers' moment-to-moment engagement decisions.

3.2.3 The Disclosure Paradox

A theoretically coherent but empirically thin cluster of findings points to a disclosure paradox with significant practical and regulatory implications. Luo et al.'s (2019) large-scale observational study, synthesised in Davis & Jin (2024), documents that satisfaction declines at the moment of AI identity disclosure; Wang et al. (2025) provide the mechanism, transparency attenuates social presence, weakening the anthropomorphism-to-trust pathway; and Yu et al. (2024) offer the first actionable mitigation, showing that disclosure timing interacts with service contact level to determine the magnitude of the satisfaction cost. This three-paper cluster is theoretically coherent and practically urgent given proliferating disclosure regulations, but the evidence remains too sparse for strong generalised conclusions. The finding that anthropomorphic visual cues can partially restore trust credibility under disclosure conditions (Sun & Si, 2025) is suggestive but derived from a persuasive communication rather than a service context. Replication across service industries and chatbot capability levels is necessary before firm recommendations can be made.

3.3 Customer Outcomes

The literature documents consumer responses to chatbot interactions along three outcome dimensions that are conceptually distinct but empirically linked: satisfaction with the chatbot encounter itself, loyalty toward the brand the chatbot represents, and engagement as an intermediate relational state that connects the two. Each subsection examines the evidence and the theoretical questions it raises.

3.3.1 Chatbot Quality and Customer Satisfaction

The link between chatbot service quality and customer satisfaction is consistently documented outcome relationship in the corpus. Across e-commerce (Vebrianti et al., 2025; Kusuma et al., 2025), service recovery (Le et al., 2023), AI chatbot use in China (Zhang et al., 2024), and mixed-context samples (Alagarsamy & Mehrolia, 2023; Dwivedi et al., 2023), chatbot service attributes including response speed, reliability, information quality, interactivity, and conversational quality consistently and positively predict customer satisfaction. The effect survives across survey and experimental designs, across diverse national samples, and after controlling for individual difference variables. In Le et al. (2023), interactive quality emerges as the strongest individual predictor of satisfaction in service recovery, consistent with service quality theory's emphasis on the co-productive dimension of service encounters.

The finding is robust but theoretically incremental: it demonstrates that chatbots are subject to the same service quality requirements as other service interfaces, not that chatbots uniquely generate satisfaction through mechanisms unavailable to traditional channels. Its more interesting theoretical contribution comes through moderation: Le et al. (2023) demonstrate that emotional conversational language activates the effectiveness of empathetic and guaranteed quality attributes, indicating that satisfaction formation in chatbot contexts is affectively conditioned rather than purely cognitive.

3.3.2 The Satisfaction-Loyalty Gap

The standard service marketing expectation that satisfaction mediates the path from service quality to brand loyalty receives partial support in the corpus. Multiple papers confirm the path: Lee & Li (2023) document that chatbot exploitation generates brand competence and warmth perceptions that drive customer-chatbot identification and customer-brand identification, both of which significantly predict brand loyalty; Jyothsna et al. (2024) and Vebrianti et al. (2025) confirm the trust and satisfaction-to-loyalty intention chain in Indian and Indonesian samples respectively.

However, Kusuma et al.'s (2025) finding that satisfaction does not significantly predict loyalty for Gen Z Indonesian e-commerce chatbot users represents a theoretically important anomaly that demands theoretical attention rather than dismissal. The result, where service quality and conversational quality improve satisfaction, but satisfaction fails to predict loyalty, may reflect the transactional orientation of digitally native consumers who treat chatbots instrumentally, the low switching costs in highly competitive e-commerce environments, or a habituation effect in which satisfaction with AI interfaces fails to generate brand attachment in contexts where multiple equivalent alternatives are equally accessible. The small sample (N=202) and conference proceedings format mean the finding requires independent replication before strong conclusions are warranted, but its theoretical resonance with the broader literature on digital consumer behaviour justifies treating it as a substantive empirical signal rather than a statistical anomaly.

Lee & Li's (2023) dual-pathway model offers a theoretically important alternative: loyalty is more robustly predicted through identification-based pathways, where interaction with the chatbot generates a psychological connection to both the chatbot and the brand it represents, than through satisfaction alone. Customer-chatbot identification emerges as a stronger predictor of brand loyalty (β=0.42) than customer-brand identification (β=0.18) in this study, suggesting that chatbot-specific relational bonds can serve as conduits for brand-level commitment that circumvent the fragile satisfaction-loyalty logic (Lee & Li, 2023)

3.3.3 Customer Engagement as an Intermediate Relational Outcome

Customer engagement, conceptualised as a motivational state involving cognitive investment, affective involvement, and behavioural activation (Brodie et al., 2011), is documented as a theoretically richer intermediate outcome than satisfaction in several corpus papers, positioned between immediate quality evaluation and terminal loyalty formation. Bhattacharjee et al.'s (2025) two-study investigation establishes that fun conversational style generates stronger engagement than warm style through sense of liberation and hedonic involvement, operating through a hedonic psychological pathway distinct from the social cognition processes that underlie warmth effects. The individualism moderation, fun's advantage over warmth is amplified for high-individualism consumers, provides cross-cultural grounding and connects engagement formation to broader consumer psychology. Youn & Jin's (2021) parasocial interaction study demonstrates that friend-framed chatbots generate stronger parasocial interaction, which in turn mediates positive brand personality perceptions and engagement-relevant outcomes, though paradoxically at the cost of perceived competence, a trade-off that highlights the tension between relational and functional chatbot design objectives.

Nguyen et al.'s (2026) finding that engagement predicts satisfaction but not direct purchase retention suggests that engagement's contribution to loyalty operates through its reinforcement of satisfaction rather than through direct attitudinal commitment, introducing a mediated chain — engagement → satisfaction → retention — that the corpus has not formally verified but that warrants direct empirical investigation.

3.4 Boundary Conditions: Who, Where, and When Chatbots Work

The evidence reviewed in the preceding sections establishes that chatbot effects on trust, satisfaction, and loyalty are not uniform across consumers, contexts, or situations. Three layers of moderation emerge from the corpus: characteristics of the consumer, the service context and product type in which the chatbot operates, and service failure as a distinct and consequential perturbation of the consumer–chatbot relationship.

3.4.1 Consumer-Level Boundary Conditions

The corpus establishes with considerable force, across multiple independent studies using diverse constructs and methodologies, that chatbot interaction outcomes are heterogeneous across the consumer population. No single moderator has accumulated more than two papers of independent evidence, which prevents strong conclusions about any individual boundary condition. However, the collective pattern is theoretically coherent: fundamental individual differences in motivational orientation, cultural values, technology attitudes, and preferences for human versus machine interaction all modulate how consumers respond to identical chatbot designs.

Regulatory focus (Choi & Zhou, 2023), individualism (Bhattacharjee et al., 2025), materialism type (Roy & Naidoo, 2025), and ideological orientation toward AI (Youn & Jin, 2021) each moderate the warmth-competence preference in ways consistent with the theoretical logics of their respective frameworks. The need for human interaction moderates the anthropomorphism-to-competence evaluation path (Kim & Hur, 2024), suggesting structural limits to the effectiveness of humanisation strategies for segments with strong human contact preferences. Technology readiness determines the effectiveness of chatbot experience in generating purchase intentions in emerging market contexts (Becan & Çeber, 2025). These findings collectively imply that a single chatbot design cannot optimise outcomes across heterogeneous consumer populations, and that segmentation-based deployment strategies, matching chatbot personality and design to target segment characteristics, represent an evidence-grounded strategic opportunity. Consistent with this, Rajaobelina & Ricard (2021) identify four distinct consumer segments differentiated by interest in chatbot services, including a persistently disengaged older segment, confirming that population heterogeneity in chatbot engagement is not merely attitudinal but structurally stable across demographic groups.

3.4.2 Service Context and Product Type

The effectiveness of chatbot design is contingent not only on who the consumer is but on what they are trying to accomplish and in what service environment. Chen et al.'s (2023) multi-experiment demonstration that chatbots outperform human agents for search goods but not experience goods is grounded in cognitive fit theory and represents one of the corpus's most practically actionable contextual findings. Igarashi et al.'s (2026) documentation that chatbot design preferences differ between exploration-phase and maturity-phase customers, and that novelty effects decay for one-time purchasers but not for subscribers, establishes that the optimal chatbot design is not static across the customer lifecycle. Yu et al.'s (2024) moderation of disclosure effects by service contact level adds a further contextual dimension that is increasingly relevant given regulatory disclosure mandates. Ye et al.'s (2026) finding that customers significantly prefer human staff over AI chatbots in OTA contexts, even while chatbot interactivity generates positive reuse intentions through trust mediation,provides an important benchmark: documenting that chatbot interactions generate positive outcomes does not establish that they generate outcomes equivalent to human service.

3.4.3 Service Failure as a Critical Moderating Context

Service failure constitutes an important, consequential moderating context in the corpus, representing the moment when accumulated trust faces its most direct test. Zhang et al.'s (2024) mixed-methods programme establishes that system service failures, technical inaccessibility and latency, produce more severe emotional experience damage than information service failures, with emotional experience constituting the primary pathway through which system failures reduce reuse intentions. The differential mediation finding has direct recovery strategy implications: functional restoration is the critical pathway for information failures, while emotional reassurance is additionally necessary for system failures.

The conditional role of anthropomorphism in failure contexts contains an apparent contradiction that requires careful interpretation. Studies drawing on the agency attribution mechanism (Toader et al., 2020; Davis & Jin, 2024, synthesising Crolic et al., 2022) suggest that human-like chatbots amplify consumer anger by elevating expectations that failure then violates. Lee (2024) conversely finds that higher-humanness chatbots enhance recovery effectiveness when recovering from human-caused failures. These findings are not necessarily irreconcilable: the critical distinction is whether the chatbot is the agent responsible for the failure (where anthropomorphism amplifies anger) or the agent performing the recovery of a human-caused failure (where anthropomorphism enables empathetic communication). If this distinction is correct, it carries specific implications for how firms should configure chatbot roles in customer service ecosystems involving both human and AI agents, a prediction that warrants direct experimental verification.

4. DISCUSSION AND CONCLUSIONS

This review synthesised 40 studies examining consumer-chatbot interactions and their consequences for trust, satisfaction, engagement, and brand loyalty in digital marketing contexts. The accumulated evidence, organised around four evidence-grounded themes, addresses the research question, how do the dynamics of consumer-chatbot interactions impact customer outcomes, brand loyalty, and trust in digital marketing, and reveals a field that has achieved meaningful theoretical consolidation in some areas while remaining structurally incomplete in others.

The evidence converges on a sequential causal logic: firms' design decisions regarding chatbot personality style, anthropomorphism level, and transparency configuration shape the quality of the interaction as consumers experience it, specifically the degree of social presence, perceived service quality, and source credibility activated during the encounter. These interaction quality perceptions, in turn, determine whether initial trust is formed, and whether that trust, compounded by satisfaction and engagement across repeated interactions, accumulates into the relational trust that drives functional and relational loyalty. This chain is not invariant: its strength and direction are conditioned by who the consumer is (regulatory focus, individualism, need for human interaction), what service context the chatbot operates in (product type, customer relationship phase, service contact level), and whether the interaction involves service failure, the critical juncture at which accumulated trust faces its most consequential test.

4.1 Theoretical Contributions – the DIAL Framework

The review's principal theoretical contribution is the DIAL framework: Design, Interaction, Accumulation, Loyalty (Figure 1), which organises the accumulated evidence into a sequential, multi-stage model of how chatbot interactions shape brand loyalty over time. DIAL advances beyond the dominant theoretical frameworks in three ways.

In plain terms, the four stages operate as follows. Design refers to the configuration decisions firms make when deploying a chatbot, including personality style (warmth versus competence), level of anthropomorphism, and transparency choices regarding AI disclosure. Interaction denotes the quality of individual consumer–chatbot encounters as consumers experience them, captured by perceived social presence, service quality, and the affective and cognitive responses they elicit. Accumulation captures the longitudinal process through which repeated positive interactions consolidate initial, encounter-based trust into the relational trust that sustains durable brand attachment. Loyalty represents the behavioural and attitudinal outcomes of this cumulative process, distinguishing between functional loyalty, such as repeat purchase and subscription retention, and relational loyalty, such as brand identification, advocacy, and resistance to competitive switching. Each stage is a necessary but individually insufficient condition for the next, and the quality of the translation from one stage to the next is moderated by consumer-level characteristics, service context, and the occurrence of service failure.

The framework extends the Stimulus-Organism-Response model that underpins most empirical work in this corpus by introducing the Accumulation stage as an explicit theoretical construct. Existing SOR applications to chatbot marketing (Le et al., 2023; Ye et al., 2026; Wang et al., 2025) treat the translation from design stimuli to loyalty responses as relatively immediate, collapsing what are in practice temporally extended trust-building processes into a single causal path.

DIAL makes the temporal and repetitive dimension of trust development first-class variables, distinguishing between initial trust (formed on the basis of single-encounter evaluation) and relational trust (accumulated through positive experience sequences across repeated interactions), consistent with developmental trust theory (Lewicki & Bunker, 1996) and relationship marketing's foundational insight that durable commitment requires trust built over time rather than assessed at a moment (Morgan & Hunt, 1994). This distinction is not merely terminological: it implies that cross-sectional measurement of chatbot trust, which accounts for virtually all empirical work in the corpus, captures only the earliest and most fragile stage of the consumer-brand relationship addressed by the research question.

DIAL also advances beyond TAM and UTAUT derivatives by differentiating between functional loyalty (repeat purchase, subscription retention, continued usage) and relational loyalty (brand identification, advocacy, resistance to competitive switching). Existing technology acceptance models treat loyalty as equivalent to continued usage intention, a conflation that obscures the qualitatively different antecedent chains documented in the corpus: functional loyalty is primarily trust-mediated through service quality evaluations, while relational loyalty operates through identification-based pathways in which consumers' psychological connection to the chatbot as a brand representative generates brand-level attachment (Lee & Li, 2023; Youn & Jin, 2021). This distinction has direct implications for research design and for the practical strategies firms employ to build chatbot-mediated brand equity.

The framework's treatment of boundary conditions as a coherent moderating layer rather than isolated study-specific covariates extends the theoretical conversation initiated by the warmth-competence literature. Prior work has tended to identify moderators individually — a single study introduces regulatory focus, another introduces individualism, another introduces product type — without placing them within a common explanatory architecture. DIAL organises these moderators by the stage of the consumer-chatbot relationship at which they operate: consumer-level characteristics primarily moderate the Design → Interaction translation; service context characteristics moderate across multiple stage interfaces simultaneously; and service failure moderates the Accumulation → Loyalty transition. This stage-specific placement makes the moderating effects theoretically tractable and practically actionable in a way that a list of individual moderators does not.

Perceived social presence mediates the path from anthropomorphic design to trust across multiple independent studies (Ye et al., 2026; Wang et al., 2025; Toader et al., 2020). However, the evidence also challenges a simple linear application of social presence theory by documenting conditions under which social presence mechanisms are attenuated or reversed, specifically mandatory disclosure and service failure contexts, suggesting that social presence theory requires boundary condition qualification when applied to AI agents operating under transparency and reliability constraints that do not apply to human service providers.

Figure 1. The DIAL framework: An integrative model of consumer-chatbot relationship dynamics

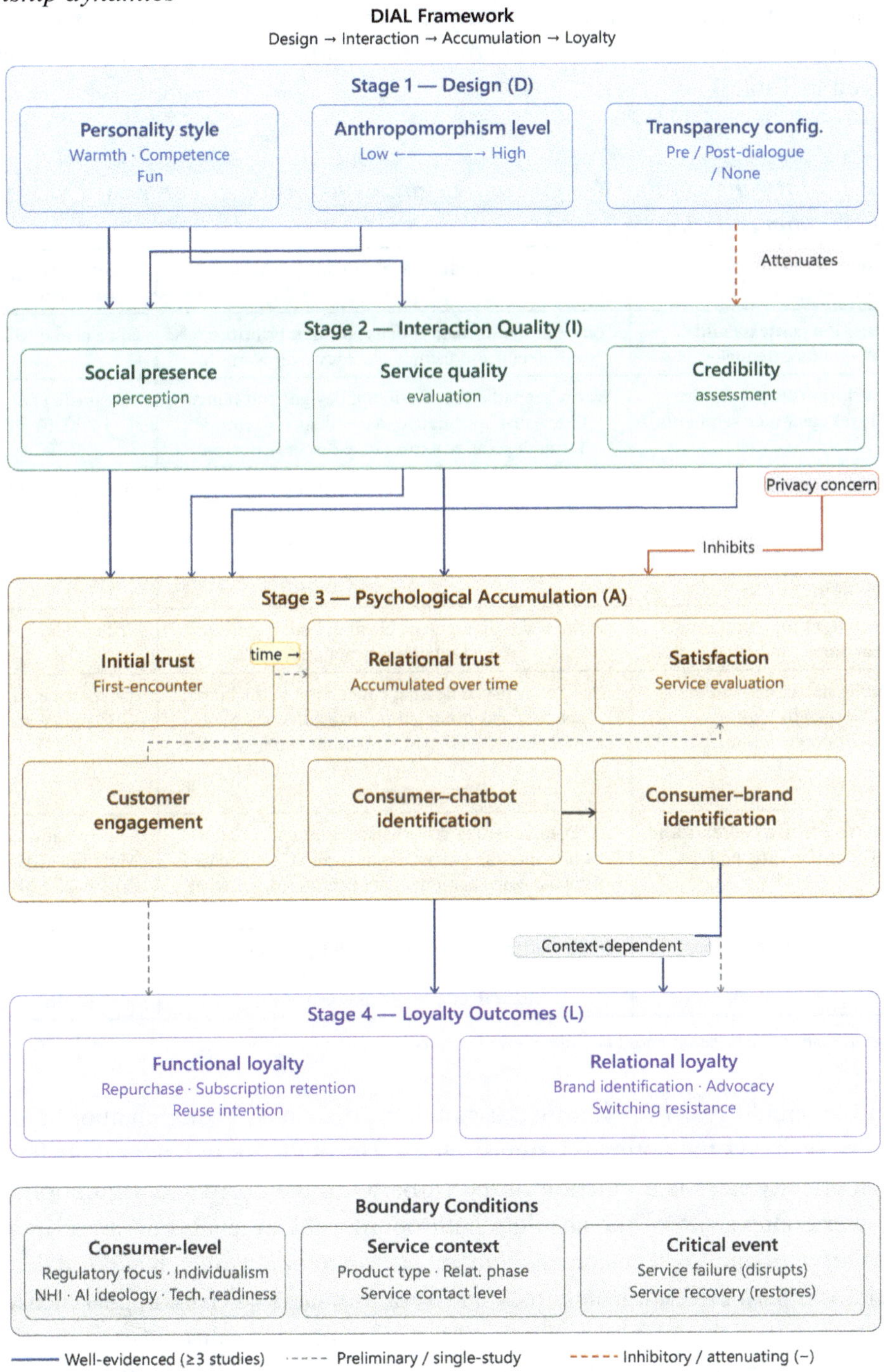

4.2 Practical Implications

The review's findings yield several specific, evidence-based implications for marketing practitioners deploying chatbots in consumer-facing applications, summarized in Table 1.

Table 1. Matching chatbot design configurations to customer contexts: Evidence-based recommendations

Customer context or interaction goal	Recommended chatbot configuration	Supporting evidence
Acquisition contexts and search-goods categories	Competent, information-dense design; prioritise task efficiency and factual accuracy over warmth	Chen et al. (2023)
Subscription-based services and loyal customer segments	Warm, empathetic behavioural design; non-human-like visual appearance may enhance retention through positive expectancy disconfirmation	Igarashi et al. (2026)
High-contact service interactions (complaints, returns, financial or emotionally sensitive exchanges)	Post-dialogue disclosure or disclosure paired with empathetic language and visible brand identity cues; avoid uniform pre-dialogue disclosure	Yu et al. (2024); Wang et al. (2025)
Low-contact informational interactions	Upfront pre-dialogue disclosure; both legally safe and relationally neutral	Yu et al. (2024)
Digitally native consumers (e.g., Gen Z) in high-competition environments	Design for psychological connection to the brand, not only task completion; invest in consistent chatbot personas aligned with brand identity, voice, and values to activate identification-based loyalty pathways	Kusuma et al. (2025); Lee & Li (2023)
Privacy-sensitive contexts and data-intensive interactions	Transparent data governance communication as a trust-building investment: explicit statements on what conversational data is retained, for what purpose, and with what protections	Alagarsamy & Mehrolia (2023); Pang et al. (2025)
Firms with heterogeneous customer bases	Deploy differentiated chatbot configurations across customer lifecycle stages and product categories rather than a single uniform design	Chen et al. (2023); Igarashi et al. (2026)

Source: author's elaboration based on the reviewed corpus.

Firms should resist the intuitive assumption that maximising chatbot human-likeness is always the optimal design strategy. The evidence indicates that chatbot design effectiveness is a function of the fit between the design configuration and customer context, not of the absolute anthropomorphism level. For subscription-based services and loyal customer segments, warm, empathetic behavioural design generates superior retention outcomes, and a non-human-like visual appearance may actually enhance this effect by creating positive expectancy disconfirmation (Igarashi et al., 2026). For acquisition contexts and search-goods categories, competent, information-dense chatbot design is more effective at supporting purchase decisions (Chen et al., 2023). Firms with heterogeneous customer bases should consider deploying differentiated chatbot configurations for different customer lifecycle stages and product categories rather than a single uniform design.

The mandatory disclosure paradox identified in this review has direct strategic implications as regulatory requirements proliferate across jurisdictions. Since pre-dialogue disclosure reduces satisfaction for high-contact services but not for low-contact services (Yu et al., 2024), and since anthropomorphic visual cues partially compensate for the credibility attenuation of AI disclosure in persuasive communication contexts (Wang et al., 2025), firms should develop context-specific disclosure protocols rather than uniform disclosure practices. For high-contact service chatbots — those handling emotionally sensitive interactions such as complaints, returns, or financial advice — post-dialogue disclosure or disclosure paired with empathetic language and visible brand identity cues may minimise relational damage. For low-contact informational chatbots, upfront disclosure may be both legally safe and relationally neutral.

The finding that the satisfaction-to-loyalty translation fails for Gen Z consumers in high-competition digital environments (Kusuma et al., 2025) should prompt firms to reconsider how they measure the effectiveness of their chatbot investments. If satisfaction metrics — the most widely reported KPIs for chatbot performance — do not predict loyalty for digitally native segments, firms relying solely on satisfaction scores risk optimising for a metric that does not capture the relational outcomes that matter for long-term brand equity. The identification-based pathways documented in Lee & Li (2023) — where chatbot exploitation generates brand competence and warmth perceptions that drive customer-chatbot identification, which in turn drives brand loyalty — suggest that firms should invest in chatbot designs that foster psychological connection to the brand, not merely functional task completion. Practically, this means creating chatbot personas with consistent brand identity, voice, and values alignment, such that consumer-chatbot identification can serve as a conduit for brand-level attachment.

Privacy concern is a persistent and independent trust inhibitor that chatbot design improvements alone cannot neutralise (Alagarsamy & Mehrolia, 2023; Pang et al., 2025). Firms should treat transparent data governance communication, explicitly informing consumers about what conversational data is retained, for what purpose, and with what protections, not as a compliance obligation but as a trust-building investment that directly supports the trust-mediated pathway to loyalty. Given that privacy concerns are documented to reduce engagement independently of service quality, firms that neglect this dimension face a structural drag on chatbot-generated loyalty that even excellent interaction design cannot fully offset.

Taken together, these implications point to a common underlying principle: chatbot marketing effectiveness is governed by design–context fit rather than by any universal best configuration. The recommendations above should therefore be read not as a checklist to be applied uniformly, but as a set of conditional prescriptions whose appropriateness depends on customer segment, interaction purpose, service sensitivity, and regulatory environment.

4.3 Methodological Implications

The review reveals a field that has converged on a methodological recipe, cross-sectional online survey, convenience sample of 300–450 prior chatbot users, PLS-SEM analysis, attitudinal or intentional DVs, that is well-suited to establishing the existence of theoretically predicted relationships but poorly suited to generating knowledge about the relational processes that the field's theoretical ambitions require. The near-total absence of behavioural outcome data is a consequential methodological limitation: 94% of empirical papers measure loyalty as intention rather than behaviour, meaning that the corpus's knowledge of how chatbot interactions translate into actual brand loyalty is built almost entirely on self-report proxies that the literature has consistently shown to be imperfect predictors of revealed preference. The single behavioural exception, Igarashi et al.'s (2026) field experiment using actual purchase transaction data, demonstrates that the effort required to generate behavioural evidence is substantial but methodologically tractable, and its findings diverge in theoretically important ways from what intention-based measures alone would have suggested.

The field's systematic reliance on Harman's single-factor test as the primary common method bias mitigation strategy represents a known inadequacy: this test is well-documented as insufficiently sensitive to detect CMB when it is present. Future empirical work should employ more rigorous procedures including the common latent factor approach, marker variable techniques, or, ideally, experimental designs that by construction eliminate the common-source variance problem. The pervasive use of PLS-SEM for confirmatory hypothesis testing when CB-SEM is methodologically more appropriate for theory-testing research represents an additional concern, particularly in papers with sample sizes adequate for maximum likelihood estimation.

4.4 Limitations of the Review

This review is subject to several limitations that qualify the scope of its conclusions. The search was restricted to Web of Science and Scopus, which, while comprehensive for peer-reviewed journal articles, may not capture relevant contributions published in other indexed databases, conference proceedings repositories, or regional journals not indexed in these systems. Some substantive contributions to chatbot marketing research may therefore be absent from the corpus. The restriction to English-language publications likely introduces a systematic geographic bias, as researchers whose primary language is not English may publish significant work in non-English venues that the search strategy cannot retrieve. The thematic synthesis method, while providing flexibility to integrate methodologically diverse evidence, involves interpretive judgements that introduce an element of subjectivity not present in quantitative meta-analysis; an alternative synthesiser might have organised the evidence somewhat differently.

4.5 Future Research Agenda

The review's findings propose a structured research agenda organised around four dimensions.

4.5.1 Under-Researched Themes

Three under-researched themes emerge from the review as priorities for future empirical investigation.

Longitudinal accumulation of trust and loyalty. An important empirical priority is longitudinal investigation of how trust and brand loyalty develop across repeated consumer-chatbot interactions. The corpus provides no evidence on whether the trust generated in individual chatbot encounters accumulates into the relational trust that is the proximal driver of durable brand loyalty, or whether single-encounter trust assessments reset at each interaction without cumulative reinforcement. This question requires panel data or longitudinal experimental designs — specifically, designs in which the same consumers are tracked across multiple chatbot interactions over weeks or months, with trust and engagement measured at multiple time points. Igarashi et al.'s (2026) four-week field experiment represents a methodological template worth extending to longer timeframes and more explicitly relational DVs.

Replication of the identification-based loyalty pathway. The identification-based pathway to loyalty, in which consumer-chatbot identification generates consumer-brand identification, which in turn generates brand loyalty, is documented in a single study (Lee & Li, 2023) and deserves independent replication across service contexts, chatbot capability levels, and consumer populations. If this pathway proves robust, it represents a theoretically distinct route to brand loyalty that operates independently of the satisfaction-mediated logic and may be more effective for digitally native consumers for whom the satisfaction-loyalty translation is weakest.

Generative AI chatbots and the LLM transition. The literature analysed contains virtually no research on generative AI chatbots, those powered by large language models capable of contextually adaptive, open-ended conversation, despite the widespread commercial deployment of such systems since late 2022. Whether the warmth–competence mechanisms, trust formation processes, and loyalty consequences documented for scripted NLP chatbots generalise to LLM-based conversational AI is a theoretically open question with significant practical urgency, given that the technological landscape has shifted substantially relative to the context in which most corpus studies were conducted. Rather (2024) provides an early conceptual framework positioning generative AI-powered ChatGPT within hospitality and tourism contexts, linking AI capabilities to customer engagement and trust, though the framework remains untested empirically, and its applicability to commercial chatbot marketing beyond tourism is yet to be established.

Early empirical contributions addressing generative AI specifically begin to appear in the corpus but remain isolated rather than cumulative. Wang et al. (2025) report that, in generative AI-driven marketing communication, anthropomorphism enhances purchase intention directly and through the mediating effects of perceived social presence and trust, while disclosure of AI-generated content attenuates the effect of anthropomorphism on social presence. Sahut and Laroche (2025), synthesising a set of empirical studies on AI applications in marketing, articulate an integrative perspective in which the effective deployment of AI requires simultaneous attention to personalisation, transparency, authenticity, and hybrid service configurations. These contributions signal a research agenda in which ethical risks are not peripheral concerns but constitutive elements of the generative AI marketing context: privacy protection, security, and the ethics of chatbot deployment have been conceptualised as antecedents of trust and behavioural intentions in adjacent empirical work (Wang et al., 2024).

Future research should therefore investigate generative AI chatbots along three interlocking axes — the generalisability of established warmth–competence and trust mechanisms to LLM-based interactions, the consumer consequences of transparency and disclosure when AI-generated content is indistinguishable from human-authored content, and the ethical and privacy governance conditions under which generative AI chatbots can sustain rather than erode consumer trust.

4.5.2 Contradictory Findings Requiring Resolution

The conditional role of anthropomorphism in service failure contexts requires direct experimental investigation. The apparent contradiction between studies showing that human-like chatbots amplify consumer anger in failure contexts (Toader et al., 2020; Davis & Jin, 2024, synthesising Crolic et al., 2022) and studies showing that high-humanness chatbots enhance recovery effectiveness (Lee, 2024) is potentially resolvable through a factorial design that varies both the locus of failure (chatbot vs. human agent) and the humanness of the recovering chatbot. The theoretical prediction — that anthropomorphism amplifies anger when the chatbot is responsible for the failure but enhances recovery when the chatbot is the recovery agent rather than the failure agent — is specific enough to be directly testable and has clear managerial implications for chatbot deployment in customer service ecosystems that involve both human and AI agents.

The satisfaction-loyalty anomaly documented in Kusuma et al. (2025) for Gen Z consumers requires replication with larger samples, more rigorous loyalty measurement, and explicit comparison across generational cohorts and competitive environments. Before the field accepts or rejects the proposition that the satisfaction-loyalty pathway fails for digitally native consumers, the finding needs to be confirmed in independent samples using validated multi-item loyalty scales that capture both attitudinal and behavioural dimensions of the construct.

4.5.3 Methodological Improvements

Future empirical work in this domain should prioritise three methodological advances. First, field experiments using actual purchase and retention data — following the Igarashi et al. (2026) template — should be actively sought as the gold standard for chatbot effectiveness research. The methodological infrastructure for such research (A/B testing on commercial platforms, integration of chatbot interaction logs with transaction data) is increasingly available to industry-academic research partnerships, and the evidential value of the resulting data substantially exceeds that of survey-based intention measures.

Second, cross-national comparative designs with formal measurement invariance testing are needed to assess the robustness of warmth-competence findings across cultural contexts. The corpus's geographic concentration in East and Southeast Asia and the theoretical expectation that individualism-collectivism moderates chatbot style preferences together motivate multi-country studies that can directly test whether the dominant findings are culturally universal or culturally bounded. Third, research designs that measure both initial and relational trust, using temporal separation between measurement occasions, are needed to test the developmental process proposed in the DIAL framework's Accumulation stage.

4.5.4 Contextual Extensions

Several service and consumer contexts that are underrepresented in the corpus warrant dedicated investigation. High-stakes service categories (financial advice, healthcare consultation, legal guidance) involve chatbot interactions where trust consequences are more severe and failure costs are higher than in the e-commerce and hospitality contexts that dominate the corpus. Whether the trust-building and loyalty-generating mechanisms documented in lower-stakes contexts generalise to these higher-risk settings is theoretically uncertain, given that consumers in high-stakes contexts are likely to maintain higher vigilance and more carefully calibrated trust thresholds. Similarly, the review's geographic evidence base is heavily concentrated in Asia-Pacific contexts, and the generalisability of the primary findings to Western European and North American markets, where privacy norms, regulatory environments, and AI adoption trajectories differ, remains unverified by the current evidence.

The intersection of chatbot deployment and social media marketing, specifically the use of conversational AI agents embedded in social commerce platforms, represents an emerging context that the corpus has only begun to address (Dutta et al., 2025). As social commerce grows in markets from Southeast Asia to Western Europe, the relational patterns of chatbot-consumer interactions in social media environments — where consumer-generated content, peer influence, and brand community co-exist with chatbot service delivery — will require dedicated theoretical and empirical attention.

FUNDING

This work is financed by Portuguese national funds through FCT - Fundação para a Ciência e Tecnologia, under the project UID/05422/2025.

REFERENCES

Alagarsamy, S., & Mehrolia, S. (2023). Exploring chatbot trust: Antecedents and behavioural outcomes. *Heliyon, 9*(5), e16074. DOI: 10.1016/j.heliyon.2023.e16074 PMID: 37206046

Becan, C., & Çeber, B. (2025). How technology readiness influences behavioral and purchasing intention: Serial multiple mediating role of attitude toward AI and AI-driven consumer chatbot experience. *Digital Transformation and Society, 5*(1), 78–104. DOI: 10.1108/DTS-04-2025-0082

Bhattacharjee, D. R., Kuanr, A., Pradhan, D., & Moharana, T. R. (2025). Fun or warm: How conversational style boosts customer engagement. *Journal of Retailing and Consumer Services, 85*, 104293. DOI: 10.1016/j.jretconser.2025.104293

Brodie, R. J., Hollebeek, L. D., Jurić, B., & Ilić, A. (2011). Customer engagement: Conceptual domain, fundamental propositions, and implications for research. *Journal of Service Research, 14*(3), 252–271. DOI: 10.1177/1094670511411703

Chaturvedi, R., Verma, S., Srivastava, V., & Khot, S. S. (2025). Exploring the frontier of anthropomorphism in AI agents: Trends and way forward. *Business and Society Review, 130*(1), 42–80. DOI: 10.1111/basr.70002

Chen, S., Li, X., Liu, K., & Wang, X. (2023). Chatbot or human? The impact of online customer service on consumers' purchase intentions. *Psychology and Marketing, 40*(11), 2186–2200. DOI: 10.1002/mar.21862

Chen, T.-Y., & Chen, K.-J. (2025). Chatbots with swear words? Exploring the roles of humour, aggressiveness, and gender in consumer–chatbot interactions. *Behaviour & Information Technology*, 1–15. Advance online publication. DOI: 10.1080/0144929X.2025.2605484

Choi, S., & Zhou, J. (2023). Inducing consumers' self-disclosure through the fit between chatbot's interaction styles and regulatory focus. *Journal of Business Research, 166*, 114127. DOI: 10.1016/j.jbusres.2023.114127

Crolic, C., Thomaz, F., Hadi, R., & Stephen, A. T. (2022). Blame the bot: Anthropomorphism and anger in customer–chatbot interactions. *Journal of Marketing*, *86*(1), 132–148. DOI: 10.1177/00222429211045687

Davenport, T., Guha, A., Grewal, D., & Bressgott, T. (2020). How artificial intelligence will change the future of marketing. *Journal of the Academy of Marketing Science*, *48*(1), 24–42. DOI: 10.1007/s11747-019-00696-0

Davis, N., & Jin, J. (2024). Beyond code: Consumer response to chatbots. *Current Opinion in Psychology*, *58*, 101841. DOI: 10.1016/j.copsyc.2024.101841 PMID: 38981369

Dutta, S., Ramanathan, A., Sakthi Prasath, G. B., & Edwin, T. S. (2025). AI-powered chatbots in Meta marketing (Facebook and Instagram): A game-changer for brand communication and engagement in e-commerce industries. Journal of Information Technology Teaching Cases. Advance online publication. DOI: 10.1177/20438869251338322

Dwivedi, Y. K., Balakrishnan, J., Baabdullah, A. M., & Das, R. (2023). Do chatbots establish 'humanness' in the customer purchase journey? An investigation through explanatory sequential design. *Psychology and Marketing*, *40*(11), 2244–2271. DOI: 10.1002/mar.21888

Fiske, S. T., Cuddy, A. J. C., Glick, P., & Xu, J. (2002). A model of (often mixed) stereotype content: Competence and warmth respectively follow from perceived status and competition. *Journal of Personality and Social Psychology*, *82*(6), 878–902. DOI: 10.1037/0022-3514.82.6.878 PMID: 12051578

Gatzioufa, P., & Saprikis, V. (2022). A literature review on users' behavioral intention toward chatbots' adoption. Applied Computing and Informatics. Advance online publication. DOI: 10.1108/ACI-01-2022-0021

Habib, M. D., Attri, R., Salam, M. A., & Yaqub, M. Z. (2025). Retail consumers' conundrum: An in-depth qualitative study navigating the motivations and aversion of chatbots. *Journal of Retailing and Consumer Services*, *82*, 104147. DOI: 10.1016/j.jretconser.2024.104147

Hu, X., Xu, X., & Chen, C. (2025). Empowering consumers: The role of avatar choice in consumer-chatbot interaction and psychological ownership. *International Journal of Human-Computer Interaction*, *41*(24), 15311–15322. DOI: 10.1080/10447318.2025.2495845

Huang, M.-H., & Rust, R. T. (2018). Artificial intelligence in service. *Journal of Service Research*, *21*(2), 155–172. DOI: 10.1177/1094670517752459

Huang, M.-H., & Rust, R. T. (2021). A strategic framework for artificial intelligence in marketing. *Journal of the Academy of Marketing Science*, *49*(1), 30–50. DOI: 10.1007/s11747-020-00749-9

Igarashi, M., Onishi, H., Sakai, O., & Hasegawa, S. (2026). How chatbot anthropomorphism shapes customer purchase decisions: Evidence from a field experiment on a cosmetic e-commerce retailer. *Journal of Retailing and Consumer Services*, *91*, 104721. DOI: 10.1016/j.jretconser.2025.104721

Jyothsna, M., Venkata Subbaiah, P., & Kryvinska, N. (2024). Exploring the chatbot usage intention: A mediating role of chatbot initial trust. *Heliyon*, *10*(12), e33028. DOI: 10.1016/j.heliyon.2024.e33028 PMID: 39027428

Kim, W. B., & Hur, H. J. (2024). What makes people feel empathy for AI chatbots? Assessing the role of competence and warmth. *International Journal of Human-Computer Interaction*, *40*(17), 4674–4687. DOI: 10.1080/10447318.2023.2219961

Kusuma, T., Wicaksono, K. A. G., Sihombing, K. D., Wijaya, L., & Phungpumkaew, H. (2025). From conversations to conversions: The role of AI-enhanced chatbots in shaping satisfaction and fostering loyalty in e-commerce. In 2025 17th International Conference on Knowledge and Smart Technology (KST 2025) (pp. 284–288). IEEE. DOI: 10.1109/KST65016.2025.11003290

Le, H. T. P. M., Park, J., & Lee, S. (2023). Emotion and trust in virtual service assistant design for effective service recovery. *Journal of Retailing and Consumer Services*, *74*, 103368. DOI: 10.1016/j.jretconser.2023.103368

Lee, K.-W., & Li, C.-Y. (2023). It is not merely a chat: Transforming chatbot affordances into dual identification and loyalty. *Journal of Retailing and Consumer Services*, *74*, 103447. DOI: 10.1016/j.jretconser.2023.103447

Lee, W.-J. (2024). Service failure by human, service recovery by AI chatbot: The impact of justice, AI efficacy on recovery effort. *Virtual Economics*, *7*(4), 48–63. DOI: 10.34021/ve.2024.07.04(3)

Lewicki, R. J., & Bunker, B. B. (1996). Developing and maintaining trust in work relationships. In Kramer, R. M., & Tyler, T. R. (Eds.), *Trust in organizations: Frontiers of theory and research* (pp. 114–139). SAGE. DOI: 10.4135/9781452243610.n7

Luo, X., Tong, S., Fang, Z., & Qu, Z. (2019). Frontiers: Machines vs. humans: The impact of artificial intelligence chatbot disclosure on customer purchases. *Marketing Science*, *38*(6), 937–947. DOI: 10.1287/mksc.2019.1192

Manigandan, L., & Sivakumar, A. (2024). Chatbot research: Unveiling evolutionary trends and collaborative pathways through bibliometric analysis. *Multidisciplinary Reviews*, *7*(3), e2024045. DOI: 10.31893/multirev.2024045

Mariani, M. M., Perez-Vega, R., & Wirtz, J. (2022). AI in marketing, consumer research and psychology: A systematic literature review and research agenda. *Psychology and Marketing*, *39*(4), 755–776. DOI: 10.1002/mar.21619

Morgan, R. M., & Hunt, S. D. (1994). The commitment-trust theory of relationship marketing. *Journal of Marketing*, *58*(3), 20–38. DOI: 10.1177/002224299405800302

Nguyen, L., Nguyen, C., Do, Q., & Dam, K. (2026). Enhancing customer experience through AI-powered marketing: How AI-driven chatbots impact user engagement, satisfaction and purchase retention? *Concurrency and Computation*, *38*(5), e70630. DOI: 10.1002/cpe.70630

Pang, H., Hu, Z. Y., & Wang, L. (2025). How perceived motivations influence user stickiness and sustainable engagement with AI-powered chatbots: Unveiling the pivotal function of user attitude. *Journal of Theoretical and Applied Electronic Commerce Research*, *20*(3), 228. DOI: 10.3390/jtaer20030228

Puntoni, S., Reczek, R. W., Giesler, M., & Botti, S. (2021). Consumers and artificial intelligence: An experiential perspective. *Journal of Marketing*, *85*(1), 131–151. DOI: 10.1177/0022242920953847

Rahim, N. I. M., & Iahad, A., N., Yusof, A. F., & A. Al-Sharafi, M. (. (2022). AI-based chatbots adoption model for higher-education institutions: A hybrid PLS-SEM-neural network modelling approach. *Sustainability*, *14*(19), 12726. DOI: 10.3390/su141912726

Rajaobelina, L., & Ricard, L. (2021). Classifying potential users of live chat services and chatbots. *Journal of Financial Services Marketing*, *26*(2), 81–94. DOI: 10.1057/s41264-021-00086-0

Rather, R. A. (2024). AI-powered ChatGPT in the hospitality and tourism industry: Benefits, challenges, theoretical framework, propositions and future research directions. *Tourism Recreation Research*, *50*(3), 652–662. DOI: 10.1080/02508281.2023.2287799

Roy, R., & Naidoo, V. (2021). Enhancing chatbot effectiveness: The role of anthropomorphic conversational styles and time orientation. *Journal of Business Research*, *126*, 23–34. DOI: 10.1016/j.jbusres.2020.12.051

Roy, R., & Naidoo, V. (2025). The role of materialism and social judgment in human-chatbot service interactions. *Journal of Services Marketing*, *39*(4), 316–332. DOI: 10.1108/JSM-06-2024-0288

Sahut, J.-M., & Laroche, M. (2025). Using artificial intelligence (AI) to enhance customer experience and to develop strategic marketing: An integrative synthesis. *Computers in Human Behavior*, *170*, 108684. DOI: 10.1016/j.chb.2025.108684

Sun, J., & Si, J. (2025). When AI chatbots ask for donations: The construal level contingency of AI persuasion effectiveness in charity human–chatbot interaction. *Journal of Theoretical and Applied Electronic Commerce Research*, *20*(4), 341. DOI: 10.3390/jtaer20040341

Thomas, J., & Harden, A. (2008). Methods for the thematic synthesis of qualitative research in systematic reviews. *BMC Medical Research Methodology*, *8*(1), 45. DOI: 10.1186/1471-2288-8-45 PMID: 18616818

Toader, D.-C., Boca, G., Toader, R., Măcelaru, M., Toader, C., Ighian, D., & Rădulescu, A. T. (2020). The effect of social presence and chatbot errors on trust. *Sustainability (Basel)*, *12*(1), 256. DOI: 10.3390/su12010256

Vebrianti, R., Aras, M., Putri, M. S. S., & Swandewi, I. A. (2025). AI chatbots in e-commerce: Enhancing customer engagement, satisfaction and loyalty. *PaperASIA*, *41*(2b), 248–260. DOI: 10.59953/paperasia.v41i2b.445

Wang, X., Lin, X., & Shao, B. (2024). Security and privacy protection in developing ethical AI: A mixed-methods study from a marketing employee perspective. *Journal of Business Ethics*, *200*(2), 373–392. DOI: 10.1007/s10551-024-05894-7

Wang, Y., Sauka, K., & Situmeang, F. B. I. (2025). Anthropomorphism and transparency interplay on consumer behaviour in generative AI-driven marketing communication. *Journal of Consumer Marketing*, *42*(4), 512–536. DOI: 10.1108/JCM-04-2024-6806

Yc, H., Law, R., Fong, L. H. N., & Li, N. (2026). How do interactive online travel agencies affect customers' reuse intention? *International Journal of Hospitality Management*, *133*, 104497. DOI: 10.1016/j.ijhm.2025.104497

Youn, S., & Jin, S. V. (2021). 'In A.I. we trust?' The effects of parasocial interaction and technopian versus luddite ideological views on chatbot-based customer relationship management in the emerging 'feeling economy'. *Computers in Human Behavior*, *119*, 106721. DOI: 10.1016/j.chb.2021.106721

Yu, R., Feng, J., Wang, K., Yang, L., & Feng, J. (2024). Who are you talking to? How chatbot identity disclosure affects service satisfaction. *Journal of Travel & Tourism Marketing*, *41*(8), 1090–1106. DOI: 10.1080/10548408.2024.2369755

Zhang, J. N., Lu, X. Y., Zheng, W. Q., & Wang, X. L. (2024). It's better than nothing: The influence of service failures on user reusage intention in AI chatbot. *Electronic Commerce Research and Applications*, *67*, 101421. DOI: 10.1016/j.elerap.2024.101421

Chapter 6

AI-Driven Personalization and the 3S Framework in P2P Aggregators: Implications for Brand Image, Loyalty, and Extension Acceptance

Ayushi Agrawal
http://orcid.org/0009-0004-2388-8513
Christ University, Bengaluru, India

Sachin Pande
http://orcid.org/0009-0006-2228-4149
Christ University, Bengaluru, India

ABSTRACT

This chapter examines how artificial intelligence (AI) strengthens peer-to-peer (P2P) cab aggregators through an integrated 3S framework—service quality, sustainability, and safety—and its impact on brand image, loyalty, and extension acceptance. In decentralized platforms, trust and consistency are critical yet vulnerable. The chapter proposes that AI-driven personalization, predictive analytics, eco-optimization, and fraud detection operationalize the 3S pillars, enhancing reliability, responsibility, and security. A strong AI-enabled 3S foundation reinforces brand image, which mediates loyalty and increases user acceptance of new services such as food delivery or logistics, offering both theoretical and managerial insights.

DOI: 10.4018/979-8-3373-7704-9.ch006

1. INTRODUCTION

In the digital economy, the peer-to-peer (P2P) platforms have transformed the mobility and hospitality and service-based exchanges among consumers. As shown by the examples of Uber, Ola, and Airbnb, collaborative consumption has ceased being a niche concept and became the mainstream service concept. This transformation has dramatically changed consumer demands where digital convenience, personalization, and any other mechanism of fostering trust have a direct impact on engagement and ultimate loyalty. Consequently, P2P platforms have transitioned to an important player in world markets and are disorganizing industries that cannot even be considered stable and unpredictable (Talukder et al., 2024).

This growth has also introduced a series of challenges insurgence coupled with a series of challenges that are unique to this P2P model. Contrary to traditional service organizations whose functions are tightly controlled over employees and operations, P2P platforms act as intermediary agents between a wide range of unrelated providers and consumers. The decentralized form of such interactions can provoke issues of consistency, accountability and trust. A single case, a customer safety breach, or a violation of sustainable standards, could be distributed through the digital networks in several hours and undermine the trust. This reputational risk on such sites is notably more as opposed to the traditional companies. In this context, brand image and trust are vulnerable and essential assets, without which it is difficult to maintain long-term interactions at the platforms (Karaenke et al., 2020).

In the effort to mitigate these vulnerabilities, three aspects of credibility among platforms have been progressively focused upon by the scholars and practitioners; these aspects include service quality, sustainability, and safety. These vulnerabilities directly affect the outcomes of engagement and loyalty, and the creation of the AI-enabled, trust-based brand image is a key to maintaining consumer involvement. These three elements comprise the main triple pillars in consumer confidence with P2P systems in which otherwise the interactions could be impersonal and fully automated. The quality of a service is a reference to the level of reliability, consistency, and responsiveness to the expectations of experiences. Sustainability reflects the level to which platforms are responsible towards social and environmental performance, and this is what matters the most to ethically sensitive buyers. Safety involves both material security of its user in transactions and the cyber security of personal information and privacy. All three dimensions combined, also referred to as the 3S model, are the parameters that contribute to the desirable perception of trustworthiness and credibility of the platform by the consumers (Desai, 2021).

These three dimensions are not simple to handle in practice even though they are quite important. Imparting uniform quality of service in unconcentrated systems involves monitoring of large amount of data and customer actions in true time. Going green requires efficiency in its operations and a long-term perspective that is hard to reconcile with speedy expansion. The area of safety, which is the most delicate one, needs constant attention to identify the safety risks up to the development of fraudulent activities or breach of privacy. The conventional checks and balances are often weak to cover these requirements. The missing aspect is one that can monitor, predict and respond at scale but adapt to the individual user needs (Okeke et al., 2024; Lilly et al., 2024).

With artificial intelligence, this is where it has started to change the way of doing things. It is observed that digital environments are increasingly integrating smart systems into their activities, and this aspect allows them to deal with problems that were a nightmare. Predictive algorithms being used to minimize time spent in waiting lines and optimize routes along with recommendation systems will be able to deliver personalized services and enhance the feeling about service quality (Singh & Farhan, 2024). The use of machine learning tools can help to track sustainability goals by analyzing the best resource distribution, lowering the output of waste, and practices becoming energy efficient. Physical and digital trust in terms of safety is promoted by biometric authentication, anti-fraud systems, and live indicators (Tinkler, 2023). These developments demonstrate that artificial intelligence is not only a convenience in technologies. It is about making the 3S pillars measurable, consistent and value-driven practices that directly plant the impression of the credibility of a platform in the minds of consumers (Thandayuthapani et al., 2024).

The integration further has further implication on brand building. Smart personalization increases the quality of the service that improves the views of the user that the relationship is reliable and responsive. With the assistance of technology, sustainability initiatives can be used to show sincerity about social and environmental responsibility, which will subsequently enhance the reputation of the platforms concerned. The intelligent systems that power off safety mechanisms ensure that, in cases that involve interaction of this user with unknown providers, this gives users a sense of security needed to propagate repeated usage. Taken together, these three forms assist in mitigating the vulnerability of brand trust and turn P2P platforms into solid and reliable members of the digital economy (Kang et al., 2022; Bujak & Kucharski, 2024).

This chapter aims to discuss the ways in which artificial intelligence, once correlated with 3S pillars, strengthens the brand image, gives impetus to consumer loyalty, and contributes to brand extensions for peer-to-peer cab aggregators. In particular, the chapter envisages four goals. The first is the impact of AI-induced personalization strategies of P2P cab aggregators on the brand image. The second is to disperse how an enhanced brand image can lead to increased parent brand equity when the related industry is very competitive and crisis sensitive. The third is to measure the degree of the connection with an already used parent brand and its influence on the readiness of the consumer to accept such new services as food delivery or logistics services, which are offered increasingly often by cab aggregators. Finally, the fourth purpose is to discuss the mediating quality of brand image in structuring loyalty and the contribution of the link to acceptance of services mobilized.

Objectives of the Chapter

- To examine the influence of AI-driven personalization practices on the brand image of peer-to-peer cab aggregators.
- To understand how brand image strengthens parent brand loyalty in a P2P industry.
- To assess how parent brand loyalty drives the acceptance of new service extensions in the peer-to-peer sector.
- To analyse the impact of brand image on brand loyalty and how this relationship influences users' acceptance intention towards brand extensions in P2P sharing platforms.

Contributions

Contributions in this chapter go both theoretical and practical levels. On the theoretical front, it makes the integration of the 3S framework of service quality, sustainability, and safety with the traditional theories of branding. Past studies have tended to explore these dimensions separately, whereas this paper bundles them together and points at artificial intelligence as their facilitator, one that shapes how such aspects may be actualized in peer-to-peer platforms. By relating the 3S pillars to existing body knowledge like customer-based brand equity, the social identity theory, and signaling theory snowballs on the walls of existing body of branding and allows a model that can transcend realities of the digitally mediated environments where any service transaction must take place. This cross-fertilization enhances scholarly perception of how the brand identity and brand image are developed in unstable and trust-sensitive settings and the role technology can plan in influencing a positive outcome.

On the practical front, the chapter gives a systematic model that managers in peer-to-peer organizations can use to help develop executable plans to build a stronger brand image and earn customer trust. In case of other platform driven companies, like Uber, Ola, Airbnb, or Zomato, the framework would show how the investments in smart systems can be directed at maintaining the level of consistent service, environmentally sustainable processes, and even safer systems of controls. These are not merely practices that deal with operational difficulties; they help bolster consumer trust, loyalty and acceptance of brand extensions. The framework hence serves as an analytical tool to scholars and a guideline to practitioners to be competitive in the long-term.

2. BACKGROUND AND LITERATURE REVIEW

2.1 Peer-to-Peer Platforms and the Sharing Economy

The sharing economy has now emerged as one of the major phenomena in the digital market and one that has transformed the ways in which people consume and offer services. The sharing economy is at its most fundamental the process of collaborative consumption whereby underutilized assets of various kinds, including vehicles, rooms, or skills, are shared on an online network that directly pairs peers. P2P platforms provide an opportunity to realize this concept and allow individuals to be providers and consumers of service. Uber, Ola, or Airbnb are examples of companies that showed how this model can completely challenge the existing industries by taking away their reliance on the traditional companies and by providing new values to the direct users of the platforms.

The development history of the P2P platform is not only very fast, but also extremely disruptive. With the aid of the dissemination of smart phones, mobile internet, and safe payment networks, such platforms have grown to a global level within a brief spell. Their growth has also brought about new efficiencies including a reduced cost of conducting transactions and a dynamic pricing mechanism. According to scholars, the popularity of such platforms is explained not only by their low prices and easy access but by the feeling of personalized experiences, which such platforms frequently cause (Babadoğan, 2024). This has increased consumer demands in markets where they previously did not have much differentiation in the services.

But with these opportunities come ethical and regulatory issues within the sharing economy. There is a tendency that the overall decentralized architecture of P2P models confuses lines of accountability among the platforms and service providers. The transparency in pricing process, fair treatment about the treatment of providers, and accountability in the event of failure service are some common concerns (Sahani et al., 2024). Also, crisis sensitivity of these platforms -whether in terms of safety accidents, abusive use of personal information, or environmental criticisms- makes them a constant object of attack (Vetrivel et al., 2024; Patil, 2025).

2.2 Brand Identity and Brand Image in P2P Platforms

The brand identity and brand image are very important aspects used in operation of P2P platforms. Although they are intertwined, these two constructs describe a different sense of the way the brands were developed and perceived. Brand identity is an internal discussion regarding what the brand means, with reference to values, mission and unique positioning. Brand image on the other hand represents actual perceptions and interpretation of brand by the consumers. In the case of P2P, where services are brokered by autonomous mediators and distributed digital platform, alignment of identity with image is even more difficult.

Customer-based brand equity (CBBE), model can help in this dilemma. In this model, one can determine the strength of brand based on how consumers feel about reliability, credibility, and emotional appeal of the brand. But there is also a structural weakness to P2P platforms, namely, that because service encounters can so often be outsourced to third providers, a bad experience can easily destroy consumer confidence. Studies have indicated that one of the main weaknesses of online shopping is that consumers tend to use online reviews, ratings, and peer suggestions as a reduced expression of trust when providing digitally mediated services (Luu et al., 2024). So, brand image is more prone to instability in these settings than in conventional service organizations.

To boost brand equity in such precarious environments, the strategies of personalization and engagement are becoming increasingly popular. Tailored interactions that can encompass customized recommendations and dynamic communication, amongst others, can work to reinforce the brand identity with some impact due to their attention and responsiveness to the needs of the users (Wijethilak et al., 2024). Research shows that not only personalization is associated with increased satisfaction but also it can lead to more emotional connections, which means more loyalty in competitive markets (Venkateswaran et al., 2024). By incorporating such strategies into their service design, P2P platforms are trying to make brand image sound. In the worlds where the consumer opinion may rapidly change, a great deal of work may be done.

Recent studies also suggest the existence of the customer engagement that helps connect between brand identity and brand image. When used with the assistance of data-based intelligence, engagement strategies may help fill the gap between the appearance and the overall perception of a platform (Amin, 2024). Loyalty programs, as such, have proven to be a way of anchoring consumer relationships since they helped to reinforce identity and image by rewarding regular interactions (Kushnarevych & Kollarov a, 2024). These are some strategies that will be important in the P2P where there is intense competition and low switching costs to a consumer.

2.3 Service Quality in P2P Contexts

The quality of service had already been one of the main discussions in service-based economy, and it is even more crucial in peer-to-peer (P2P) services. P2P platforms face problems in delivery of consistet service and experiences as compared to traditional organizations, where there is a tight standardization of the service delivery and clear service blueprint. Early service quality paradigm models like SERVQUAL recognize the reliability, responsiveness, empathy, assurance, and tangibility as key components that help to define consumer expectations. The potential to contrast P2P contexts with this framework provides an additional theoretical basis to the explanation of how AI can be used to improve service consistency. The recognized service quality model identifies five service characteristics including tangibility, reliability, responsiveness, empathy and assurance. Tangibility is the manifestation of touchable surfaces and appearance of services, e.g. the condition of cars in ridesharing or packaging in food delivery services. Reliability indicates how consistently perfection of promises is kept. Responsiveness measures the speed of effective service of the issues. Empathy is an individualized approach to customer demands and assurance is a belief users hold when it comes to the safety and professionalism of the service.

Many of these dimensions of service quality are not controlled by the P2P platforms directly and hence are vulnerable to critique and break in the overall consumer experience leading to backlash for the brand and its image. Thus, the digital platforms are frequently accused of poor regulation of these dimensions. Variations in the performance of the providers and differences between the experiences of different users can contradict the perceptions of the quality. It is here that the artificial intelligence can take a leading role in defining the service quality. They can now utilize AI tools to support predictive analysis, optimized routes, and dynamic customer assist opportunities, which are more likely to minimize variation and customer satisfaction levels. As an example, smart routing systems reduce delays in ride-hailing platforms, like Uber, which maximize the perception of reliability. The same case can apply to food delivery services such as Zomato, which has recommendation systems that customize food choices and allow straight forward ordering, which directly exhibits improved responsiveness and empathy in the service process (Cherukuri, 2024).

It also has a part in service assurance. Fraud detection mechanisms and biometric authentication using driver face IDs to check on factors like authenticity and soberness, as well as live tracking of trips augment the trust subjects feel toward platforms that would otherwise be subject to trust issues. Machine learning can enable firms to predict user concerns and intervene in such a case before the matter occurs, fostering the feeling of reliability and security that would be challenging to sustain by manual control alone (Sundar et al., 2022). Recent studies have pointed out that brand loyalty can be reinforced with the help of smart personalization of the service as it helps enhance consumer engagement (Patil, 2025). These mechanisms allow P2P companies to strike an optimal compromise between decentralization and uniformity of service outcomes, as they incorporate them in their platforms.

Research also indicates that the AI-driven process of personalization of services is shifting the way people derive value and becomes willing to be loyal to the applications, despite the presence of others (Semwal et al., 2024). When the quality of the services is provided proactively such that the consumers do not feel the need to address since it is known before it is felt, it not only lessens friction but also gives an impression of attentiveness and sensitivity. According to scholars, this predictive aspect is emerging as an extension of the traditional service quality model that adapts to the digitally spatial environments (Ganeshkumar et al., 2024).

2.4 Sustainability in P2P Contexts

The traditional basis of sustainability evaluation in service ecosystems is based on the Triple Bottom Line which consists of economic viability, environmental responsibility, and social value creation. By linking AI-based sustainability programs to these pillars, it becomes apparent how P2P platforms indicate sustainable responsibility and credibility in the long-term. Sustainability is another characteristic feature of P2P platform as the platform grows in international markets rapidly and comes under the spotlight of both government and society. TBL framework can provide a valuable window of interpreting sustainability in these settings. It focuses on three pillars: economic viability, environmental responsibility and social contribution. In the case of P2P platforms, economic sustainability is to keep services affordable to users and the providers making decent incomes. Environmental sustainability is about making fewer ecological footprints such as running energy-efficient routes or packaging that does less harm to the environment. Social sustainability touches on the aspects of good labor practices, inclusiveness and trust in digital communities.

Artificial intelligence has been made one of the pillars of sustainability solutions. The creation of algorithms that optimally pool vehicles can reduce carbon emissions and make the environment more sustainable (Babatunde et al., 2024). The task of dynamic allocation of resources and hence avoiding wastage through use of machine learning is also very much relevant in food delivery and logistics (Balli, 2024). As an example, green packaging suggestions based on forecasting mechanisms allows business incurring few costs on environmental protection without compromising its efficiency in operation. The efforts of Airbnb concerning sustainability also show how platforms can incorporate those practices into the brand image. Energy-aware property management and the use of AI-aided data analytics help Airbnb not only develop a positive image in the eyes of socially conscious users but also support property managers, who are likely to describe themselves as environmentally responsible.

On a societal level, AI-supported systems are capable of improving equity and inclusivity as well. Ability to factor in differentiated user requirements through recommendation algorithms and communicating a clear pricing system build trust in one of the most vulnerable aspects of P2P platforms- fair and responsible accessibility. According to researchers, matching AI capabilities in support of sustainable solutions will not only be beneficial to communities, but also the consumers perception of the authenticity of brands (Katikar, n.d.). Consequently, it causes sustainability not only to be practiced in operations but also in the form of reputable asset.

AI is also economically feasible because it permits predictive demand analytics, which can be used to help the platforms better match supply and demand. This minimizes sitting capacity on drivers or service providers thus increasing the network level of income distribution. These practices, coupled with environmentally friendly transportation and socially conducive policies, enhances the sustainability of the platform over the long run. According to the literature, sustainability pledges, especially when supported by intelligent technologies, have a beneficial effect on the brand equity expectation and customer loyalty (Aliarte et al., 2024).

The collaboration between the concept of AI and the TBL model turns the concept of sustainability into a quantifiable practice. By inculcating predictive systems, P2P platforms can prove to be environmentally friendly, possessing economic fairness and social inclusivity in practical terms. The scholars consider that this alignment does not only reduce reputational risks, but it also helps to nurture long-term consumer trust (Babatunde et al., 2024; Ganeshkumar et al., 2024). The programs developed by Airbnb illustrate how one can make sustainability central to business practice and development. The bottom line about sustainability in P2P contexts is not the add-on property but a core aspect of competitiveness in a market where ethical and ethically aware consumers can become drivers of new quality standards.

2.5 Safety in P2P Contexts

The users of peer-to-peer (P2P) platforms are concerned about safety as one of the most important factors to trust. It is an operation that functions on three scales: physical, digital, and psychological. Physical safety is the safeguarding of users during service interactions, e.g. ride safety in cab-sharing or accommodation standards in home-sharing verification. Digital safety refers to information confidentiality, the security of information and protection of sensitive data. Psychological safety is a measure of the users trusting the process of interacting with strangers in an unknown provider by an intermediary platform. In P2P businesses, failure in any of the domains may seriously compromise consumer confidence and long-term loyalty. In a digitally connected world, such failure can amplify the damage it can create on the brand image and reduces its ability to extend its reach and diversification.

Artificial intelligence has in the recent past been playing a pivotal role in enhancing these aspects of safety. Intelligent algorithms are used to power fraud detection systems so that platforms can detect unusual behaviors and take action before an incident takes off (Semwal et al., 2024). Real-time monitoring systems are beneficial to physical security because they monitor rides and predict possible threats, which minimizes uncertainty to the users (Liu et al., 2024). Biometrics verification and identity authentication helps in establishing that service providers and customers are genuine, thereby reducing the risk of impersonating them or engaging in malignant acts (Kandi, 2024). These are not only physical and digital protective mechanisms but also play the role of psychological reassurance as a mark of reliability and accountability.

Practices demonstrate how safety and technology of P2P services can be combined. Uber, as an example has invested in background checks that are aided by automated systems coupled with features to track rides in real-time enabling both customers and family members to be alert of their locations (Rini et al., 2024). Airbnb has implemented credibility regimes that marry up user ratings with automated profile filtering of both a host and a guest to provide a credibility layer system that stands at multiple levels of checking (Kushnarevych, 2024). The scholars emphasize that the role of consumer willingness to use P2P services is directly related to encounters with safety cues as part of the service journey (Aliarte et al., 2024). In addition, marketing that communicates safety features enhances trust in the brand, particularly when it highlights tailored security measures and transparent communication (Agarwal et al., 2023).

Table 1.

Theme	Key Insights from Literature	Implications for P2P Platforms
Peer-to-Peer Platforms and Sharing Economy	P2P platforms redefine access to mobility, hospitality, and services; growth driven by digitalization and consumer demand for convenience. Ethical challenges include accountability, transparency, and reputational sensitivity.	Platforms must address vulnerabilities in trust and accountability to sustain growth and credibility.
Brand Identity and Brand Image	Distinction between identity (internal values) and image (consumer perceptions). Customer-Based Brand Equity (CBBE) highlights vulnerability of brand image in service-based, digitally mediated contexts.	Strong brand identity and consistent delivery are essential to overcome variability in decentralized services.
Service Quality	Dimensions include reliability, responsiveness, empathy, assurance, and tangibility. AI-driven personalization, chatbots, and predictive analytics enhance responsiveness and reliability.	Enhanced service quality builds trust, positions platforms as consumer-centric, and improves brand image.
Sustainability	Triple Bottom Line emphasizes economic, environmental, and social outcomes. AI supports sustainability through route optimization, eco-friendly practices, and resource efficiency.	Eco-branding strengthens brand reputation and appeals to ethically conscious consumers in competitive markets.
Safety	Includes physical, digital, and psychological safety. AI enhances fraud detection, biometric verification, and real-time monitoring.	Safety is a key trust driver; emotional reassurance directly influences loyalty and acceptance of brand extensions.
Theoretical Lenses	Social Identity Theory explains brand belonging; Signaling Theory highlights market signals of responsibility; TAM frames adoption through trust and usefulness; RBV conceptualizes AI as an intangible resource.	Theories provide a foundation for explaining how AI-enabled 3S practices influence brand identity, image, and loyalty.

2.6 Gaps in Existing Literature and Theoretical Integration

Though previous studies investigate the nature of service quality, sustainability, and safety as separate concepts in digital service platforms, only little has studied the areas critically, especially on trade-offs in between. An example is that fast AI-based optimization of service can be more convenient, but create more data privacy challenges; sustainability obligations can be incompatible with competitiveness in high-competition markets. The literature does not analyze much on how these tensions will affect brand image or loyalty formation in a decentralized P2P environment. This gap is taken care of in this chapter.

3. RESEARCH METHODOLOGY

3.1 Research Approach

This chapter adopts a conceptual research design to examine the role of artificial intelligence in shaping service quality, sustainability, and safety (the 3S model) within peer-to-peer (P2P) digital platforms of cab aggregators. Unlike empirical studies that rely on primary data collected through surveys or interviews, a conceptual approach synthesizes existing scholarly work, theories, and case-based evidence to build a structured understanding of an emerging phenomenon. The decision to employ a conceptual design stem from the recognition that research on AI-enabled service transformation in P2P contexts is still at a relatively nascent stage. Empirical data remains limited, fragmented across industries, and often focused on specific applications rather than integrated frameworks. Therefore, theory building based on existing scholarly contributions provides a stronger foundation for advancing knowledge in this domain and potentially provides a framework on which further research can be carried out.

Conceptual approach also makes it possible to integrate insights of other disciplines. The issues of marketing, sustainability management, information systems, and artificial intelligence advances can rarely be considered in terms of their quality. Building on these disparate sources, it is our intention to create an interdisciplinary view on how the 3S model can be reinforced by AI driven practices in P2P platforms that can be considered beyond the business of cab aggregation onto other domains as well

3.2 Sources of Data

The review is largely based on peer-reviewed studies that are indexed in Scopus and Web of science databases. The databases were chosen because they cover extensively high-quality journals in the areas of management study, information systems, marketing, and technology. Certain case studies and conceptual works were included as well when they had something to say about practices of platforms. The result of using established academic sources is that the arguments presented in this chapter are based on evaluated evidence that is not based on hearsay or industry bias.

The search strategy was basing its keywords on topics like artificial intelligence and service quality, AI and sustainability in digital platforms, AI and safety in peer-up to peer services, brand image and digital ecosystems, and sharing economy and trust. The preferred literature review period focused on the works published in 2015 and 2025, since during that time, the theme of AI has reached its modern peak, and

P2P platforms have become highly developed. Previous works have been cited with selectivity where they offer some foundation theoretical work.

3.3 Process of Synthesis

The analysis was conducted through a synthesis of theories, conceptual papers and cases. Relevant studies have been identified and separated/categorized into 3 major pillars in 3S model service quality, sustainability, and safety. The pillars have then been explored with respect to the benefits of integrating AI and how it will contribute to reliability, environmental awareness, and the trust factor in P2P processes.

Second, synthesis of findings was not only isolated, but also interrelated between theories. As an example, research in customer-based brand equity was harmonized with the findings of the Technology Acceptance Model to point out how the enhancements of the service level produced by AI impact adoption and loyalty. Comparably, the views of the Resource-Based View were integrated with the case studies of the highly competitive Uber and Airbnb to provide a detailed idea of how AI capabilities can be used as strategic resources in achieving a competitive advantage through differentiation.

Third, illustrative cases were incorporated to ground conceptual arguments in practical reality. Uber's deployment of AI for background checks, route optimization, and fraud detection exemplifies the role of technology in reinforcing service quality and safety. Airbnb's sustainability initiatives, supported by data-driven systems, illustrate how AI can operationalize environmental and social commitments. Zomato's recommendation algorithms demonstrate how service personalization enhances user experience and strengthens perceptions of reliability. These cases provide tangible evidence of how the 3S model is applied in practice.

Table 2. Search strategy and inclusion rigor

Step	Description
Databases Used	Scopus and Web of Science, chosen for comprehensive coverage of high-quality peer-reviewed journals and conference proceedings.
Keywords and Search Strings	"Artificial intelligence and service quality," "AI and sustainability in digital platforms," "AI and safety in peer-to-peer services," "brand image and digital ecosystems," "sharing economy and trust."
Timeframe	2015–2025, reflecting the period of major AI adoption in P2P platforms and the rapid expansion of sharing economy research.
Language	English-only publications to ensure consistency of interpretation and comparability across studies.
Inclusion Criteria	Peer-reviewed journal articles, book chapters, and reputable conference proceedings that directly address AI, service quality, sustainability, safety, or brand outcomes in digital or P2P contexts.
Exclusion Criteria	Non-peer-reviewed sources, opinion pieces, purely technical AI studies without consumer/brand relevance, and studies outside service-based digital platforms.
Selection Process	Initial screening of titles and abstracts for relevance, followed by full-text evaluation to confirm alignment with the 3S framework.
Final Set of Studies	Literature selected based on conceptual relevance, theoretical contribution, and ability to illustrate the AI-driven 3S framework.

3.4 Summary

In sum, this chapter employs a conceptual research design supported by peer-reviewed literature, systematic synthesis, and illustrative cases to explore the intersection of artificial intelligence and the 3S model in P2P platforms. The methodology is well-suited to theory building in an emerging area of scholarship where empirical research remains limited. By focusing on digital service platforms and drawing on leading examples such as Uber, Airbnb, and Zomato, the chapter develops a structured framework that highlights the theoretical and practical significance of AI in shaping trust, brand image, and loyalty in the sharing economy.

Table 3. Summary of research methodology

Component	Description
Approach	Conceptual research design focusing on theory building rather than primary data collection.
Sources	Peer-reviewed literature from Scopus and Web of Science; selective conceptual papers and case insights.
Process	1. Identification of relevant studies (keywords: AI, service quality, sustainability, safety, P2P platforms). 2. Categorization of findings under 3S pillars. 3. Theoretical integration (CBBE, TAM, RBV, Social Identity, Signaling). 4. Incorporation of illustrative cases (Uber, Airbnb, Zomato).
Rationale	Suitable for theory building in a nascent research area where empirical data is fragmented; enables synthesis of interdisciplinary perspectives.
Scope	Digital service-based P2P platforms with focus on cab aggregators and hospitality-sharing platforms.
Boundaries	Reliance on secondary data only; excludes empirical testing; limited to AI-driven practices within the 3S model.

Figure 1.

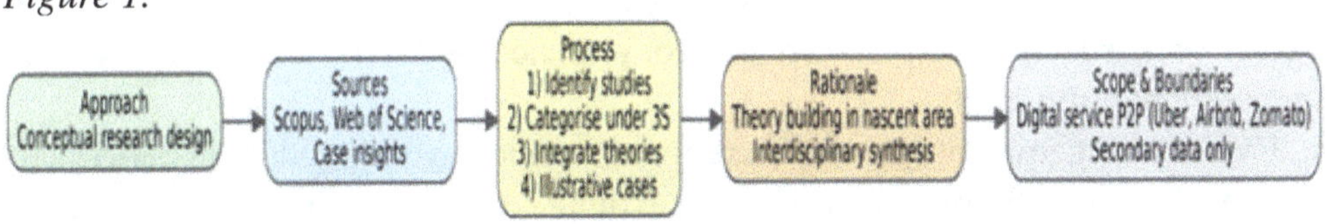

4. ANALYSIS AND DISCUSSION

4.1 AI-Enhanced Service Quality → Brand Image

Service quality has always been a decisive factor in shaping consumer perceptions of brand image, especially in industries where services are intangible and heavily dependent on user experience. In peer-to-peer (P2P) platforms such as ride-hailing and food delivery, maintaining service consistency across thousands of independent providers is particularly difficult. This is where artificial intelligence has emerged as a key enabler of service quality by offering personalization, predictive assistance, and responsive customer care.

One important area where intelligent technologies have contributed is the use of chatbots and virtual assistants. These systems are designed to respond instantly to customer concerns, resolve queries, and escalate issues where needed. Studies indicate that customers usually have the perception that a chat-based communication session creates a sense of responsiveness, thereby, building customer trust in the platform (Reddy, 2024). Service quality is further boosted with regards to personalization. Customizable suggestions represent a desire to empathize and pay attention to the needs of each user, which contributes to the feeling that the platform is aware of their specific needs (Desai, 2022). In this manner, AI-fueled interactions not only add to efficiency but also to relational aspects of service that establishes a brand identity and image.

Predictive analytics has also changed service offerings in that even companies are able to plan before something happens. Companies like Uber use algorithms that forecast waiting times and adjust the number of drivers needed depending on the demand. Predictive capabilities reduce uncertainty and increase reliability and should contribute to a positive brand perception. Research indicates that consumers are keen on the minimization of service friction, and these experiences are attributed to overall judgments made on brand credibility (Ojha, 2023). Analogous activities can also be noted in food delivery, where recommendation engines like those deployed by Zomato use a combination of purchase history and contextual data to present restaurants that most closely match the user tastes. This can be done by predictive personalization that increases convenience, and at the same time develops a reputation of reliability.

Evidence suggests that these interventions extend beyond functional benefits to emotional and psychological reassurance. Young consumers in particular are more receptive to personalized services when they perceive that the system reduces uncertainty and creates a sense of control over the experience (Mathai, 2023). Emotional dimensions of service quality, once considered beyond the scope of automation, are now increasingly mediated through personalized engagement strategies that integrate consumer emotions into the service process (Moe & Alamelu, 2025). This demonstrates that service quality in P2P platforms is no longer confined to the efficiency of delivery but also extends to the ability of brands to establish emotional resonance.

Another aspect of service quality is assurance, which relates to the confidence consumers place in the professionalism and reliability of a service provider. Research indicates that AI-supported personalization strategies reinforce assurance by demonstrating attentiveness to consumer needs in real time (Ramadhana & Hussein, 2022). This sense of assurance strengthens consumer loyalty and indirectly enhances brand image. Similarly, generative technologies such as ChatGPT have been noted for their role in deepening engagement by offering more natural and personalized assistance, further influencing brand loyalty and satisfaction (Patil, Rane, & Rane, 2024). The overall outcome of these changes is constituting a substantial contribution to brand confidence and identity. Chatbots, personalization and predictive systems make the perception that the platform is responsive, empathetic, and reliable. In extremely competitive markets, these attributes become crucial in the differentiation of a brand in the minds of the consumer. Research on the topic confirms that a consistent and personalized customer experience not only enhances their perception of the service provided but also lays a positive foundation with regards to the brand itself (Begum, 2024). In P2P when the variable quality of independent providers can easily mismatch the brand consistency, AI-based service quality has become a crucial requirement in terms of sustaining and improving brand image.

4.2 AI-Driven Sustainability → Brand Image

The areas regarding the strength of the service are often mentioned in operational terms, whereas sustainability is one of the areas of crucial brand image in the digital economy. Consumers are being more environmentally and socially conscious and expect more than that is cost effective and comfortable to their consumer lifestyle. In the case of P2P, it entails that sustainability procedures will be thoroughly examined and can largely determine the level of authenticity and trust.

The use of artificial intelligence has opened up new possibilities to match brand strategy with goals of sustainability. Ride hailing algorithm optimizing the routes can reduce the carbon footprint by suggesting energy efficient routes and enhancing vehicle utilization. The research shows that consumers consider such activities as environmentally friendly, which supports the positive brand association (Liu et al., 2024). In parallel, predictive models to foresee demand enable platforms to optimize the use of resources thus, minimizing wastage in food delivery and logistics. Not only do such technological practices enhance efficiency, but they also communicate to consumers the efforts of the platform to take care of the environment (Bhattacharya, 2025).

Eco-branding has become a competitive-based differentiator. The sustainability efforts offered by Airbnb are a good illustration of how such systems based on data can promote pro-environmental initiatives to hosts, including minimizing energy consumption or forming sustainable tourism experiences. That the platform can observe such behaviors and reward them makes the brand more appealing as responsible social entity. Academics stress that the communication of the stated practices should be secondary only to their realization as visible sustainability can also be used as a market signal that impacts consumer opinion (Patil et al., 2024).

The financial detail of sustainability is also enhanced by the intelligent systems. With predictive analytics, the balance between supply and demand is assessed more efficiently, and this way, it is possible to avoid overloading the idle capacity of service providers in any case. This is a response to one of the criticisms of P2P platforms in that they are perceived to demand exploitation on the part of the providers with all attention being directed to the convenience of the customers. It has been indicated that when sustainability practices are associated with fairness and transparency consumer loyalty and appreciation of the brand will be further contributed (Aguirre et al., 2020).

Social aspect of sustainability also has its own significance. Engagement strategies backed by AI can be deployed to embrace inclusion, e.g. ensuring that underserved communities can access platform services. By conducting visible initiatives, inclusive patches build their social images and attest them to the aspect of being inclusive and fair. As an illustration, a community-oriented action that emphasizes the benefits to other people or fair payment structures appeal to the consumer and contribute to building a reliable brand (Aliarte et al., 2024).

Another area of academic interest associated with AI is the morality of sustainability practices that it entails. Consumers look forward to going green and being socially responsible, but they also want to know how the information they provide is being utilized to make the practices possible (Sarioguz & Miser, 2024). The ethical management of data has in turn come rolling hand in hand with sustainability in brand perception. On the P2P platforms, being environmentally and data responsible will go a long way into making the company popular

Last but not least, sustainability has emerged as a competitive advantage in the market and brand storytelling. In markets where several issues can provide similar comfort to the same cost, the stewardship claims can become an important determinant of the buyer. A body of research documents the rise of consumers choosing to associate their loyalty with socially responsible, authentic, and genuinely committed to sustainability brands (Nalivaikė & Miliukaitė, 2024). In this respect, AI-driven sustainability is not only passed to minimize the ecological footprints but also to position the brand in the category of sustainable and socially conscious technological innovation.

4.3 AI-Enabled Safety → Brand Image

Consumer trust issues in peer-to-peer (P2P) platforms are among the most important elements of platforms safety. Contrary to the established businesses where employees and service delivery are directly under the control of the business, P2P platforms depend on independent providers. Higher risks to safety exist in this decentralized model in terms of physical security during ride-sharing services or data privacy during a digital transaction. This has resulted in the focus on the safety becoming central not only in the process of operations but also brand image and credibility.

As one tool to help resolve the issue of safety, artificial intelligence has become a prominent one. Systems to detect fraud have become real-time monitors of millions of transactions (detecting anomalies). Research indicates that predictive analytics would be faster and more accurate than a manual process to identify suspicious behavior, minimizing exposure to fraudulent behavior (Semwal et al., 2024). On the same note, biometrics authentication and identity verification give users the assurance that they are dealing with genuine customer/service providers, and chances of impersonations are reduced (Kandi, 2024). These technological measures are not just aimed at helping to avoid issues with the performance of the operations but also help to provide the signal that the platform cares about consumer safety, which goes directly towards building brand trust.

Another important aspect of safety is the digital trust. By sharing confidential personal and payment data with sites, users worry about potential abuse or data breaches, and these fears are likely to affect brand image. The research shows that the consumers are more likely to feel confident about the brand and assign it the characteristics of reliability and professionalism once they feel that digital safeguards are stable and transparent (Rini et al., 2024). Such an alignment of safety with brand identity is important when it comes to P2P scenarios where thread of reputational risks circulates rapidly in the social networks or review systems.

Emotional safety has also become a great concept in brand managing. It is the sense of psychological security that helps the consumers feel as they engage the providers that they have never known using mediated platforms. This is complemented with features like a ride tracking, real-time updates and sharing the trip details with trusted contacts. Uber background checks and monitoring processes present a case study on the safety tools aided by AI as a means of improved emotional security of riders (Liu et al., 2024). Airbnb, in its turn, has created a system that checks automatically, as well as peer-to-peer reviews, and has created a multilayered trust environment. These are not mere operational measures that are confined to the functionality aspect but measures that will impact the brand perceived as trustworthy and responsible.

Researchers state that there is a close association between safety and consumer loyalty. In a feeling of safety, customers tend to come back, refer others to the site and accept other services. As another example, the fact that many people trusted the Uber ride-hailing system helped the food delivery service, Uber Eats gain acceptance. Research also mentions that safety signals are seen to be credible market differentiators that enable them to distinguish themselves on competitive environments. This implies that AI-driven safety practices will not only be tools to manage risk but also strategy-oriented brand image-building and brand loyalty generation. Empirical research conducted recently can manifest the positive change in the safety confidence of riders on AI-based driver vetting auto-detection, and real-time monitoring. On the same note, sustainability studies indicate that with algorithmic routing, carbon emission is minimized by a percentage of up to 20 in big mobility markets. The practical applicability is enhanced by the incorporation of such empirical grounding.

4.4 Synergistic Effects of 3S

While service quality, sustainability, and safety are each important in their own right, their interplay creates a more comprehensive foundation for brand equity and image. Together, the 3S model provides a holistic framework that reinforces consumer trust, loyalty, and perceptions of authenticity.

Service quality, as enhanced by chatbots, predictive analytics, and personalization, ensures that users experience reliability and responsiveness (Reddy, 2024). Sustainability demonstrates that the brand is committed to ecological and social responsibility, appealing to ethically aware consumers (Bhattacharya, 2025). Safety mechanisms offer reassurance that both physical and digital risks are being addressed (Semwal et al., 2024). When these three pillars work together, they reinforce one another, creating a self-reinforcing cycle of trust and loyalty.

The interplay between the pillars can be observed in practice. For example, Uber's route optimization not only improves service quality by reducing wait times but also supports sustainability by cutting emissions. Airbnb's sustainability initiatives contribute to environmental goals while simultaneously strengthening perceptions of safety and reliability in community-based hospitality. Zomato's recommendation systems improve service quality through personalization while also reducing waste by aligning demand with supply, contributing to sustainability. These cases illustrate that AI-driven practices often serve multiple dimensions of the 3S model simultaneously.

Comparisons to previous studies explain why this integration is important. Previous literature on service quality within digital platforms used to see them separately compared to sustainability and safety. Newer studies indicate that these dimensions combined altogether influence the view of consumers who are the brand image (Ojha, 2023; Mathai, 2023). An example is with regards to personalization, the strategies that can be used to enhance quality of services also increases psychological safety owing to the reduction in uncertainty. In the same measure, sustainability initiatives gain more authenticity when aided by consistent quality of service delivery and open safety systems (Sarioguz and Miser, 2024).

The 3S model synergies also correspond with the general theories of brand management. Social Identity Theory approach gives reason to believe that consumers will not identify with brands promoting unreliability, irresponsibility, and danger. Signaling Theory also elaborates on how the practices (enabled by AI) in the 3S pillars are credible signals of trustworthiness that differentiates brands in competitive markets. In the Technology Acceptance Model, it is found that adoption is driven by perceived usefulness and trust, which is created by the synergetic influence of service quality, sustainability, and safety. Lastly, the Resource-Based View depicts that AI potentials within the 3S pillars can be described as intangible assets, which possess a high degree of replication challenges and maintains a long-term competitive advantage.

Such simultaneous enhancement of brand image is especially paramount in P2P scenarios in which customer will be very susceptible to input by peers and reputational cues. A system that performs very well in one respect and fails in another may be eroded of credibility. Such as, high service quality cannot off-set perceptions of risk to safety, and sustainability pledges will not be heard when service reliability is lacking. It is an aggregate brand equity brought by the perception on all three dimensions that lays lasting brand equity.

Despite of the advantages, AI can have unintentional negative effects such as algorithmic bias, susceptibility to data privacy, lack of transparency in the process of automatic decisions, and the risk of losing the human touch, which can be significantly disastrous, when not handled. The explainable AI, privacy-sensitive analytics, and human-in-the-loop controls are all safeguards that need to be incorporated to ensure the credibility of the 3S pillars.

4.5 Linking 3S to Loyalty and Extension Acceptance

Among the significant results of the 3S framework, the impact it has made on brand loyalty and on endorsing brand extensions are some of the most important. In markets where P2P can achieve easy substitutions, where consumers can quickly change platforms, customer loyalty could prove to be a leading factor to success in long run. The fact is that AI's contribution to the service quality, sustainability, and safety is essentially in fostering this loyalty by creating positive attributes and trust.

The study reveals that brand loyalty can be seen as a moderator between service perceptions of quality, safety, and sustainability and the readiness to use novel services (Ramadhana & Hussein, 2022). As an example, when users are convinced that Uber provides safe and reliable services continuously, they are more willing to use the Uber Eats. Likewise, the image of Airbnb as a safe and eco-friendly service has led to the adoption of Airbnb Experiences by its users, thus broadening its services to non-accommodation. The above are some examples of how brand loyalty based on the 3S pillars is then translated to acceptance of brand extensions.

The selling idea of the loyalty to mediate has gained considerable reputation in branding literature. Loyalty cannot be viewed as the solely behavioral consequence, but it is also described as an emotional connection which decreases the switching behavior (Begum, 2024). When customers feel safe, appreciated and on the same wavelength with the ethical stance of the company, they will be more receptive to trying new services provided by the same company. This is in line with results that trust-based loyalty augments a responsiveness to innovation and diversification (Nalivaikė & Miliukaitaitė, 2024).

In addition, the personalization through AI enables the enhancement of this mediation impact through the introduction of consistency between the available services and new ones. The predictive recommendations and personalized promotions make consumers feel that the brand knows their tastes even when they launch something new (Desai, 2022). Emotional AI which takes communication a notch higher will adapt some interactions to the mood and responses by the consumer which will further strengthen this commitment of loyalty as it will resonate at a personal level (Moe & Alamelu, 2025). The practices lower risk in adoption of brand extensions as they transfer trust of already trust red services into new solutions.

The recognition of brand extensions is also based on how appropriately they fit in the developed brand image. Scholars believe that extensions work best when they remain in line with the values and attributes of the parent brand (Patil, Rane, & Rane, 2024). With the P2P platforms, the embedded 3S model of the brand image makes extensions part of the brand world and thus, regarded as natural extensions and not opportunistic diversification. As another example, Uber Eats was easily accepted by clients since its expertise in the field of logistics and prompt service was perceived as an offshoot of sister company Uber. Specifically, Airbnb Experiences has caught on because it fell in line with the Airbnb vision of an authentic travel that is community-based.

Lastly, the 3S model alignment with the loyalty and acceptance of the extensions confirm the strategic significance of the AI capacity. The ability to detect fraud, the optimization of routes, environmentally friendly operations, and personalization systems go beyond just being an operational tool, as these tools create a sustainable competitive advantage as they sustain loyalty and enable diversification (Aguirre et al., 2020). Predictive models do not only enhance engagement but also establish malleability that enables brands to innovate across fields as Bhattacharya (2025) observes. Ultimately, such a synergy of the 3S pillars and the AI capabilities makes platforms expand to new markets with increased confidence and keeps trust in the hands of consumers.

5. PROPOSED CONCEPTUAL FRAMEWORK: THE AI-DRIVEN 3S MODEL

The Rapid growth of the peer-to-peer platforms has disrupted service delivery and customer interaction in mobility, hospitality and food services. Simultaneously, these platforms are highly decentralized, and this has presented a consistent difficulty with trust, reliability, and brand reputation. Based on previous literature and case evidence, the chapter advances a conceptual framework in which artificial intelligence (AI) will play a critical role as an enabler of service quality, sustainability and safety (the 3S model). The framework describes how AI-assisted 3S practices increase brand identity, increase brand image, create loyalty and eventually determine acceptability of service prolongations.

5.1 Framework Structure

In this model, AI is not treated as a stand-alone driver but as a cross-cutting enabler that operationalizes and strengthens the 3S pillars. Each pillar contributes directly to the development of a strong brand identity, which in turn enhances brand image. A positive brand image then mediates the effect of the 3S dimensions on brand loyalty. Loyalty, once established, becomes the central mechanism through which users accept brand extensions, such as food delivery, logistics, or hospitality experiences.

Two moderators are introduced to capture contextual influences: crisis intensity and identity–image alignment. Crisis intensity refers to the extent to which a brand is exposed to external shocks, such as safety incidents or reputational scandals. In high-crisis contexts, the impact of AI-enabled 3S practices on brand outcomes is expected to be more pronounced. Identity–image alignment reflects the degree to which internal brand values (identity) are consistent with consumer perceptions (image). High alignment strengthens the relationships in the framework, whereas misalignment weakens them.

Figure 2.

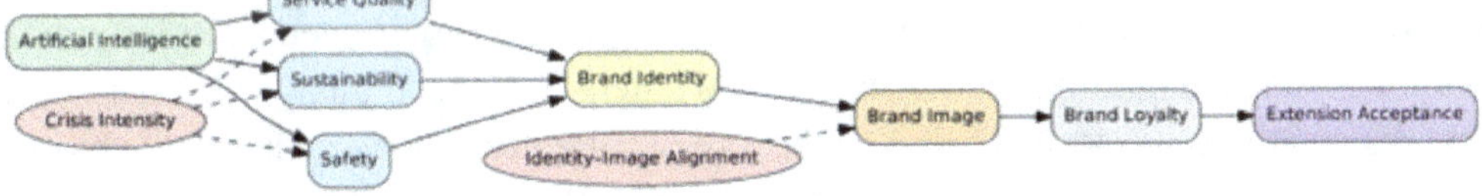

When redefining the conceptual model, make sure that moderator arrows do not relate with dependent constructs, but rather with the relationships among the variables. The moderators ought to have a visual relationship with the linkages and not the outcome variables.

5.2 Moderating Effects

Crisis Intensity moderates the relationships between AI-enabled 3S practices and brand outcomes. In environments where crises are frequent and reputational risks are high, the positive effects of AI-driven service quality, sustainability, and safety are likely to be amplified. Conversely, in stable environments with fewer crises, these effects may be less visible but still significant.

Identity-Image Alignment balances the standing of brand identity and brand image. Once the internal values shared by the brand match with customer perceptions, there is a smooth switch between identity and image, and this increases the level of trust. The misalignment, though, constitutes reputational risk since consumers can think about sustainability or safety claims as fake and only presumed to gain competitive advantage.

Operationalizing Moderators in Practice:

- The severity of crisis can be assessed through such indicators as the rate of safety accidents that occurred on the platform, negative posts of social media, or reported regulatory actions.
- The alignment between identity and image can be determined with either brand authenticity scales, consumer/brand value congruence surveys, or consistency between platform claims and user reviews.

These quantifiable standards make clear the variation of the moderators by market (i.e. markets with stringent mobility controls versus uncontrolled informal ride hailing markets).

5.3 Theoretical Novelty

The proposed framework adds value to the literature because it combines the 3S model framework with branding theories, applied to the AI-facilitated P2P platforms. Although service quality, sustainability, and safety have been analyzed separately, there are no frameworks that bring out how they collectively have an impact in brand identity and image besides building brand loyalty. By locating the technology as an enabling non-disjunctive force this framework shows how technology operationalizes these dimensions in practice.

On a theoretical level, the model can be used to further the Social Identity Theory by demonstrating how AI-sustained 3S practices reinforce the sense of brand-based belongingness. It goes beyond Signaling Theory by indicating the presence of credible market signals in the form of AI-enabled safety and sustainability. The framework further extends Technology Acceptance Model (TAM) by showing that perceived usefulness and trust is determined by the use of AI-enabled 3S practices. Last but not least, it takes into account the Resource-Based View (RBV) by defining AI skills in fraud detention, predictive analytics and eco-optimization as resources that allegedly build competitive advantage.

6. CONCLUSION, IMPLICATIONS, AND FUTURE RESEARCH

6.1 Conclusion

The chapter has discussed how artificial intelligence enhances quality of service, sustainability and safety in peer to peer (P2P) networks, and how all these aspects can contribute to brand identity, brand image and loyalty hence resulting to acceptance of brand extensions. The role of intelligent systems as means of consumer trust and competitive differentiation is certainly reflected in the proposed AI-based 3S framework where reputational risks are abundant.

The discussion has shown that quality of services is improved using predictive analytics, personalized customer care and smart chatbots, thus adding to reliability, responsiveness, and empathy. Eco-friendly logistics and route optimization are some of the latest sustainability initiatives that are fast becoming a driver of brand credibility due to their perceived environmental and social responsibility. Safety systems, complemented by anti-fraud analytics and biometric authentication are tackling the physical and digital risk, with the former serving a psychological safety net to consumers. All these dimensions build up an entire on trust and brand resilience.

The role of the brand identity and brand image as a mediator is also brought out in the framework. The emerging AI-empowered 3S practices do not only precondition the operational efficiency but also form a brand identity, grounded in the values of responsibility, responsiveness, reliability. This identity translates into positive brand image that modulates the connection between service practices and consumer loyalty. Once a loyalty is built, risk perceptions are lower and brand extensions like Uber Eats and Airbnb Experiences are more likely to be accepted.

The conclusion is that AI is not used as a standalone technological tool but gets embedded as a transformation enabler allowing an ethical, sustainable, safety focused P2P platforms. By integrating AI into the 3S pillars, platforms can attain resilience in markets characterized by both volatility and consumer skepticism.

6.2 Theoretical Contributions

Theoretically, the chapter contributes to the branching inquiry by merging the model of 3S with the dynamic of AI in online service venues. Whereas the previous research has tended to either study service quality, sustainability, and safety one-by-one or even contrast/compare them to each other, this work establishes an integrated view of the three in combination, thus highlighting their interdependence.

To begin with, the framework will play a role in advancing the Customer-Based Brand Equity (CBBE) models by integrating values of sustainability and safety as key agents of assessing brand value. The traditional ones usually focused on functional quality and customer perceptions but did not pay full attention to the ethical and safety-related expectations prevailing in digital economies. It is through this correlation of AI-enabled practices with these expectations that the framework adds value to CBBE theory.

Second, the chapter extends Social Identity Theory and Signaling Theory by demonstrating that AI-enabled practices act as credible signals of trustworthiness and allow consumers to align themselves with brands that reflect their values of safety, responsibility, and innovation.

Third, the framework applies the Resource-Based View (RBV) by conceptualizing AI capabilities in personalization, fraud detection, and eco-optimization as intangible resources that provide long-term competitive advantage. In doing so, it positions AI not only as an operational enabler but also as a strategic asset.

6.3 Managerial Implications

Conceptual frameworks give the practitioner the strategic uptake of fragmented evidence into working models. In the case of managers who deal with extremely decentralized P2P conditions, such frameworks show the best AI-enabled leverages that can best foster trust, brand image, and repeat engagement. Managers can use this framework by directly integrating AI tools into the engagement and loyalty strategies. Friction points should be reduced through predictive personalization in all touchpoints, sustainability signals and safety mechanisms should be proactively conveyed through brand-building. These AI powered levers can be used to develop engagement loops that enhance long term loyalty.

Service innovation: Managers must ensure the usage of predictive analytics and intelligent personalization to make sure that the quality of services does not vary across decentralized providers networks. These practices will create stronger brand identity and consumer confidence by eliminating uncertainty during consumer-service interactions.

Eco-branding: Sustainability must be looked beyond compliance. The systems powered by AI have a potential to optimize routing processes, minimize waste, and support environmentally friendly practices, and not only would such practices minimize expenses, but it would also help the platform to improve its brand image as environmentally conscious. Sharing these practices in an open manner is also commendable in the effort to increase the level of competitiveness in markets where the ethically responsibile businesses receive increased attention by the consumers.

Trust mechanisms: Safety initiatives like biometric confirmation, fraud prevention, and real time-monitoring must be connected and marketed as core branding strengths. Platforms are encouraged to feature these mechanisms in their branding initiatives as they can be considered reliable indicators of reliability and can actively contribute to loyalty as well as extension panics.

Approaches that employ this roadmap can help managers develop resilient brands that are not only efficient, but also ethically responsible and trustworthy to consumers.

6.4 Limitations

The chapter has certain limitations that should be acknowledged. The analysis relies on a conceptual approach rather than empirical data. While this approach allows for theoretical integration and interdisciplinary synthesis, it limits the ability to generalize findings across industries and geographies.

The focus is also restricted to a set of high-profile digital P2P platforms such as Uber, Airbnb, Zomato, and Ola. While these cases provide valuable insights, they may not fully represent other forms of sharing economy platforms such as peer-to-peer finance, freelancing markets, or second-hand goods platforms. The conclusions should therefore be interpreted as illustrative rather than universally applicable. Moreover, the extrapolation of insights is restricted since the examples are mostly established and have a high amount of resources in point to P2P brands. New or localized platforms can have various AI adoption obstacles.

6.5 Future Research Directions

Future research should build on this conceptual framework through empirical validation and cross-industry analysis. Several directions are suggested.

Empirical validation: Quantitative studies using techniques such as Structural Equation Modeling (SEM) and Partial Least Squares (PLS) can be conducted to test the propositions advanced in this framework. Large-scale surveys across different geographies would provide empirical support for the mediating and moderating relationships proposed.

Cross-industry comparisons: While this chapter focused on mobility and hospitality platforms, future research could compare the role of AI-driven 3S practices in other industries such as peer-to-peer utility services, finance, education, or healthcare. Such studies would reveal whether the relationships identified are context-specific or generalizable across service domains.

Longitudinal studies: The long-term impact of AI adoption on brand equity and resilience requires longitudinal analysis. Research that tracks consumer perceptions before, during, and after the adoption of AI-driven practices would provide deeper insights into their sustained effectiveness.

Generative AI and governance frameworks: With the rise of generative AI, future work should explore its potential for personalization, customer interaction, and content creation in P2P platforms. At the same time, ethical governance frameworks must be developed to address issues of bias, transparency, and accountability. Such research would expand the framework to reflect the next generation of intelligent systems.

REFERENCES

Agarwal, T., Gopalkrishnan, S., Kale, V., Periwal, D., Kulkarni, A. A., Tharkude, D., & Jaiwani, M. (2023, November). Transforming advertising: Harnessing AI for personalised customer-centricity. In *2023 IEEE International Conference on Technology Management, Operations and Decisions (ICTMOD)* (pp. 1-8). IEEE. DOI: 10.1109/ICTMOD59086.2023.10438160

Aguirre, A., Dempsey, G., Surden, H., & Reiner, P. B. (2020). AI loyalty: A new paradigm for aligning stakeholder interests. *IEEE Transactions on Technology and Society*, *1*(3), 128–137. DOI: 10.1109/TTS.2020.3013490

Aliarte, K. N., Dulay, J. J., & Novilla, N. J. (2024, January 1). Improving marketing personalization with AI: How self-congruency influences consumer engagement. ***International** Journal of Research and Innovation in Social Science*. DOI: 10.47772/IJRISS.2024.8120042

Amin, M. M. (2024, December 1). AI-powered personalized marketing: A deep dive into customer segmentation and targeting. *International Journal of Science, Engineering and Management*. DOI: 10.36647/IJSEM/11.12.A001

Babadoğan, B. (2024, October 29). Unveiling the power of AI-driven personalization: Transforming consumer behavior in the age of digital marketing. *Next Frontier For Life Sciences and AI*. DOI: 10.62802/fj43xy18

Babatunde, S. O., Odejide, O. A., Edunjobi, T. E., & Ogundipe, D. O.Sodiq Odetunde BabatundeOpeyemi Abayomi OdejideTolulope Esther EdunjobiDamilola Oluwaseun Ogundipe. (2024). The role of AI in marketing personalization: A theoretical exploration of consumer engagement strategies. *International Journal of Management & Entrepreneurship Research*, *6*(3), 936–949. DOI: 10.51594/ijmer.v6i3.964

Balli, A. (2024, September 20). The effect of product personalization on consumer purchasing intention, customer satisfaction, brand loyalty and artificial intelligence applications with machine learning. *Fiscaoeconomia*. DOI: 10.25295/fsecon.1449755

Begum, N. (2024, November 28). Beyond automation: How AI service integration is shaping the future of brand management. *Management Dynamics:*. DOI: 10.57198/2583-4932.1339

Bhattacharya, C. B. (2025, January 17). AI-powered predictive models transforming the future of digital marketing and customer engagement. *Journal of Informatics Education and Research*. DOI: 10.52783/jier.v5i1.2015

Bujak, M., & Kucharski, R. (2024, November 5). Balancing profit and traveller acceptance in ride-pooling personalised fares. *arXiv*. https://doi.org//arxiv.2411 .03370DOI: 10.48550

Cherukuri, B. R.Bangar Raju Cherukuri. (2024, June 30). AI-powered personalization: How machine learning is shaping the future of user experience. *International Journal of Science and Research Archive*, *12*(1), 3111–3126. Advance online publication. DOI: 10.30574/ijsra.2024.12.1.0961

Desai, D. (2022). Hyper-personalization: An AI-enabled personalization for customer-centric marketing. In *Customer-Centric Marketing Strategies*. IGI Global., DOI: 10.4018/978-1-7998-7959-6.ch003

Desai, P. (2021). *A strategic approach to enrich brand through artificial intelligence*. Lecture Notes in Networks and Systems., DOI: 10.1007/978-981-15-7106-0_57

Ganeshkumar, M., Karunakaran, S., Muzhumathi, R., & Suguna, R. (2024, October). Ai-driven marketing insights: Harnessing machine learning for enhanced consumer engagement and personalization. In *2024 First International Conference on Software, Systems and Information Technology (SSITCON)* (pp. 1-6). IEEE. DOI: 10.1109/SSITCON62437.2024.10796558

Kandi, A. (2024, November 14). Personalization and customer relationship management in AI-powered business intelligence. *International Journal for Science, Technology and Engineering*. DOI: 10.22214/ijraset.2024.65159

Kang, Y., Mahendra, A., Clarke, C., Tang, L., & Mars, J. (2022). Towards Personalized Intelligence at Scale. *arXiv preprint arXiv:2203.06668*.

Karaenke, P., Schiffer, M., & Waldherr, S. (2020). The customer is always right: A value-based matching mechanism for customer-centered ride pooling. *Proceedings from INFORMS*. DOI: 10.2139/ssrn.5057432

Katikar, H. (n.d.). *Enhancing personalized marketing strategies and customer experiences through AI-driven personalization*. Preprint., DOI: 10.14293/PR2199.000976.v1

Kushnarevych, A. (2024, November 19). Building loyalty programs with AI-powered online tools. *2024 IEEE 24th International Symposium on Computational Intelligence and Informatics (CINTI)*, Budapest, Hungary. DOI: 10.1109/CINTI63048.2024.10830833

Kushnarevych, A., & Kollárová, D. (2024, September 20). The possibilities of artificial intelligence usage in loyalty programs. In *Proceedings of the European Conference on Innovation and Entrepreneurship (ECIE)*. DOI: 10.34190/ecie.19.1.2533

Lilly, A., Rajkumar, R., Kumar, J. V., et al. (2024, January 1). Prominence of artificial intelligence: Upholding customer loyalty via customer relationship management. *Journal of Information and Optimization Sciences*. DOI: 10.47974/JIOS-1767

Liu, T., Zhang, Y., Zhang, M., Chen, M., & Yu, S. (2024, December 18). Factors influencing consumer willingness to use AI-driven autonomous taxis. *Behavioral Sciences (Basel, Switzerland)*, *14*(12), 1216. DOI: 10.3390/bs14121216 PMID: 39767357

Luu, T. M. N., Mittal, S., & Gupta, S. (2024, November 15). Leveraging AI to tailor customer engagement with personalized marketing strategies. In *Advances in Marketing, Customer Relationship Management, and E-Services*. IGI Global. DOI: 10.4018/979-8-3373-0219-5.ch010

Mathai, J. (2023, August 29). Young consumers' perceptions of AI-powered in-car personalized services in a growing market for smart cars. *Journal of Promotion Management*. Advance online publication. DOI: 10.1080/10496491.2023.2251465

Moe, A., & Alamelu, R. (2025, January 4). Harnessing personalized emotional AI for enhanced consumer engagement in intelligent marketing. *Journal of Digital and Computational Advertising*. DOI: 10.71058/jodac.v9i1002

Nalivaikė, J., & Miliukaitė, G. (2024, September 25). Influence of AI-generated avatars on consumer trust in the brand.*14th International Scientific Conference „Business and Management 2024*. DOI: 10.3846/bm.2024.1191

Ojha, A. K. (2023, February 28). Navigating the algorithmic marketplace: How AI is changing consumer psychology and brand loyalty. *Journal of Psychology and Political Science*, . DOI: 10.55529/jpps.32.25.29

Okeke, N. I., Alabi, O. A., & Igwe, A. N.Nnenna Ijeoma OkekeOlufunke Anne AlabiAbbey Ngochindo IgweOnyeka Chrisanctus OfodileChikezie Paul-Mikki Ewim. (2024, October 30). AI-driven personalization framework for SMEs: Revolutionizing customer engagement and retention. *World Journal of Advanced Research and Reviews*, *24*(1), 2019–2035. Advance online publication. DOI: 10.30574/wjarr.2024.24.1.3208

Patil, D. (2025, January 1). Artificial intelligence for personalized marketing and consumer behavior analysis: Enhancing engagement and conversion rates. *SSRN*. DOI: 10.2139/ssrn.5057436

Patil, D. (2025, January 1). Artificial intelligence-driven customer service: Enhancing personalization, loyalty, and customer satisfaction. *SSRN*. DOI: 10.2139/ssrn.5057432

Patil, D., Rane, N. L., & Rane, J. (2024, October 28). The future of customer loyalty: How ChatGPT and generative artificial intelligence are transforming customer engagement, personalization, and satisfaction. In book: The Future Impact of ChatGPT on Several Business Sectors (pp.48-106) Chapter: Publisher: Deep Science Publishing.. DOI: 10.70593/978-81-981367-8-7_2

Patil, R. K. S., Porapur, S. M., & Kagawade, S. (2024). The role of ai-driven social media marketing in shaping consumer purchasing behaviour: An empirical analysis of personalization, predictive analytics, and engagement. In *ITM web of conferences* (Vol. 68, p. 01032). EDP Sciences. DOI: 10.1051/itmconf/20246801032

Ramadhana, M. A., & Hussein, A. S. (2022, October 1). Pengaruh penggunaan artificial intelligence terhadap customer loyalty dengan citra merek sebagai variabel mediasi. *Journal of Marketing & Public Policy*, *1*(4), 522–531. Advance online publication. DOI: 10.21776/jmppk.2022.01.4.11

Reddy, D. R. (2024, October 18). How do customers react to the integration of AI in customer experience. *International Journal for Multidisciplinary Research*. DOI: 10.36948/ijfmr.2024.v06i05.28954

Rini, A. S., Wandrial, S., Lutfi, L., Jaya, I., & Satrionugroho, B. (2024). Data-driven marketing: Harnessing artificial intelligence to personalize customer experience and enhance engagement. *Join: Journal of Social Science*, *1*(6), 282–295. DOI: 10.59613/akx6j040

Sahani, G. S., Chaudhary, M., & Ghouse, S. M. (2024, October 4). Artificial intelligence and hyper-personalization in travel platforms. In *Advances in Hospitality, Tourism and the Services Industry*. IGI Global., DOI: 10.4018/979-8-3693-5678-4.ch006

Sarioguz, O., & Miser, E. (2024, November 30). Assessing the role of artificial intelligence in enhancing customer personalization: A study of ethical and privacy implications in digital marketing. *International Journal of Science and Research Archive*. DOI: 10.30574/ijsra.2024.13.2.2207

Semwal, R., Tripathi, N., Tyagi, P. K., & Nadda, V. (2024). AI-Infused Strategies for Customer Retention. In *Integrating AI-Driven Technologies Into Service Marketing* (pp. 115–134). IGI Global Scientific Publishing. DOI: 10.4018/979-8-3693-7122-0.ch007

Singh, P., & Farhan, M. (2024, July 26). Personalization at scale. In *Advances in Marketing, Customer Relationship Management, and E-Services*. IGI Global. DOI: 10.4018/979-8-3693-7122-0.ch025

Sundar, S. M., Bopp-Bertenbreiter, V., Ziegler, D., Kosuru, R. K., Knecht, C., Pfleging, B., & Widlroither, H. (2022). PersonalAIzation-Exploring concepts and guidelines for AI-driven personalization of in-car HMIs in fully automated vehicles. *Human Factors in Transportation*, *60*, 423–431.

Talukder, M. B., Lina, F. Y., Kumar, S., & Khan, M. R. (2024). Data-Driven Personalization in the Sharing Economy. In *Building Climate Neutral Economies Through Digital Business and Green Skills* (pp. 277–300). IGI Global Scientific Publishing. DOI: 10.4018/979-8-3693-5673-9.ch012

Thandayuthapani, S., Thirumoorthi, P., Elantheraiyan, P., ... (2024, July 26). An exploration of consumer engagement strategies through the lens of artificial intelligence in marketing personalization. In *Advances in Marketing, Customer Relationship Management, and E-Services*. IGI Global. DOI: 10.4018/979-8-3693-7122-0.ch008

Tinkler, A. (2023, December 1). AI, marketing technology and personalization at scale. *Journal of AI Robotics & Workplace Automation*. DOI: 10.69554/CAEO7832

Venkateswaran, P. S., Dominic, M. L., Agarwal, S., Oberai, H., Anand, I., & Rajest, S. S. (2024). The role of artificial intelligence (AI) in enhancing marketing and customer loyalty. In *Data-driven intelligent business sustainability* (pp. 32–47). IGI Global Scientific Publishing.

Vetrivel, S. C., Arun, V. P., Saravanan, T. P., & Maheswari, R. (2024). Harnessing AI for next-generation service marketing. In *Integrating AI-driven technologies into service marketing* (pp. 265–298). IGI Global Scientific Publishing. DOI: 10.4018/979-8-3693-7122-0.ch015

Wijethilak, H. P. G. D., Singh, S. K., & Dhand, S. (2024, November 15). AI for personalizing customer interactions. In *Advances in Marketing, Customer Relationship Management, and E-Services*. IGI Global. DOI: 10.4018/979-8-3373-0219-5.ch011

Chapter 7
Cinematic Storytelling and Neuromarketing in Digital Marketing:
Emotional Engagement, Trust, and Ethics

Aritra Kumar Sarkar
http://orcid.org/0009-0002-0633-8216
Christ (Deemed to be) University, Delhi, India

ABSTRACT

Nowadays, online advertising, shaped by algorithms and brain-based systems, often shakes trust between users and platforms. Instead of tracking habits, immersive film techniques spark feelings naturally. One idea builds on past research - linking hidden surveillance models with smart recommendations to emotional storytelling impacts. A fresh framework emerges: "Cinematic Trust," where mood and scene matter more than machine learning loops. Looking at movie-style storytelling in ads, like Apple, Nike, or Dove, shows that trust grows when people see real intent behind messages. What matters most is openness, informed consent, and respect for cognitive freedom. Honest storytelling supported by transparency and consumer choice strengthens long-term brand relationships. What stands out is how modest personalisation blends into genuine creative expression. This mix shapes enduring, thoughtful online advertising - where imagination meets responsible choices.

DOI: 10.4018/979-8-3373-7704-9.ch007

1. INTRODUCTION

1.1 The Digital Marketing Transformation and Erosion of Trust

Digital marketing has evolved from broad, one-to-many messaging into a highly granular, datafied system in which user behaviour is continuously monitored, analysed, and monetised. Platforms such as Google, Meta, Amazon, and TikTok operate as infrastructures of persuasion, capturing data from every click, pause, scroll, and purchase and feeding it into machine learning models that predict and shape future behaviour. This aligns with Shoshana Zuboff's concept of surveillance capitalism, in which behavioural data is treated as a raw material for predictive analytics and commercial gain (Zuboff, 2019).

The "imperative to collect" ever more detailed behavioural traces has driven the expansion of tracking technologies across apps, devices, locations, and even offline environments. This ubiquity makes data extraction largely invisible to ordinary users and difficult to avoid in everyday life. While these systems enable hyper-personalised content, dynamic pricing, and real-time optimisation, they also convert intimate aspects of human experience into economic assets controlled by a small number of powerful intermediaries.

Consumers have become increasingly aware of these dynamics. Research documents growing discomfort with opaque targeting, algorithmic recommendations, and the perceived loss of control over personal information. This discomfort expresses itself in concrete resistance behaviours: the widespread use of ad-blockers, participation in "digital detox" practices, and enthusiasm for "de-influencing" trends that explicitly reject over-targeted consumption. As a result, the very tools designed to enhance marketing efficiency contribute to structural erosion of trust in digital brands and platforms, as trust depends on perceived integrity and reliability (Mayer et al., 1995).

1.2 Neuromarketing Technologies and Ethical Concerns

Alongside conventional behavioural tracking, neuromarketing technologies extend marketers' reach into the emotional and physiological dimensions of consumer experience. Eye-tracking systems reveal where attention is directed on screens; facial emotion recognition algorithms infer affective states from micro expressions; voice tone analysis gauges sentiment from speech patterns; and biometric sensors record heart rate, skin conductance, and other signals associated with arousal or stress. With AI, these systems create detailed pictures of mental and bodily responses while showing emotions as they unfold moment by moment. Neuromarketing techniques such as electroencephalography (EEG) and functional imaging have been shown to predict consumer responses to marketing stimuli more accurately than self-reported data (Ariely & Berns, 2010; Plassmann et al., 2015).

These findings suggest that advertisements can become more emotionally resonant and contextually relevant. Rather than rely on opinions shaped by preference or bias, brain-based methods track emotions beneath the surface. Yet that closer read can come with significant ethical concerns, particularly regarding manipulation and loss of autonomy (Floridi et al., 2018). Hidden patterns start showing up once feelings and physical signals are gathered and stored. These clues might expose what someone feels deeply but never puts into words. If the main goal is to nudge choices through clever tactics, then advertising stops guiding taste - it begins using mental cracks for advantage.

Fairness sits at the heart of several issues. Because users often miss key details - like exactly what gets tracked, how guesses are built, or how those guesses affect outcomes - true agreement becomes shaky. Then there's the role of feelings in tech systems: now seen like digital pulses under rules like GDPR or the upcoming EU AI law, which tightly control who takes notes, where they go, and how they travel. Fear sits too, around the idea of a real-life "buy button" - even if it sounds basic in science, it taps into common worries. Companies might someday nudge people into decisions they'd never choose on their own. This feels urgent when talking about medicine, money, or power over society.

What worries people most tends to hit the hardest among vulnerable groups - like kids, elderly folks, and people struggling with memory or mood. Because they often can't see how fake feelings might trick them, they become easy marks even if new tools claim to help. Since these individuals are naturally more open to influence, companies aim at them just as much, if not more. Yet behind every clever algorithm sits a choice: build systems that respect minds or push ones that ignore them.

1.3 Cinematic Storytelling as an Alternative Approach

The ethical tensions surrounding surveillance-based marketing and neuromarketing open space for renewed interest in more transparent, aesthetically grounded modes of communication. Cinematic storytelling offers a more straightforward approach. Rather than tracking or modelling that is hidden or complex, it is based on visible, clear elements: composition, lighting, colour, tempo, acting, and sound. These elements work together to build stories that draw audiences into a common emotional space, where the goal is clear but the process is simple to understand.

Narrative transportation theory explains how individuals become mentally immersed in stories, leading to changes in attitudes and beliefs consistent with the narrative (Green & Brock, 2000). When people become engaged in a story, they can identify with characters, feel as if they are inside the story, and experience what is happening as if it is happening to them. This experience can shift attitudes, memories, and future behaviour. The important thing to remember is that this happens because of our natural tendency to organise experience in a storytelling way, not because we are using hidden data.

Studies have found that storytelling enhances memory retention and emotional engagement compared to information presented in abstract formats (Green & Brock, 2000). Stories can take complex ideas and make them concrete and tangible scenes, put abstract concepts into visible choices, and connect brand promises to real life. In marketing, cinematic storytelling allows brands to communicate identity, purpose, and values in a way that feels emotionally authentic while still being clear and interpretable.

Additionally, in a world of media that is filled with algorithm-optimised and algorithm-generated content, audiences are often looking for evidence of human creativity and authenticity. Documentary-style visuals, imperfect textures, and user-generated content can convey authenticity, implying that the messages are from real experiences rather than just optimised machines. When done authentically, cinematic storytelling can convey trust in a way that is very different from the secrecy of behavioural targeting.

1.4 Research Objectives and Significance

This chapter examines the relationships between neuromarketing, movie-style communication and digital ethics. The main goal of this chapter is to examine how, cinematic storytelling can be an ethical counterbalance or at least a complement to the high-tech, (data)-surveillance-based marketing that relies on the use of artificial intelligence technologies. Rather than opposing technologies per se, this chapter investigates the cases in which the use of algorithmic marketing tools may be, at the same time, in line with the principles of movie-style communication and with respect for consumer autonomy.

Four interrelated purposes will guide this chapter:

1. To examine how surveillance capitalism and neuromarketing transform trust and emotional engagement in online marketing.
2. To integrate concepts from narrative psychology and film studies to explain why movie storytelling can build strong and potentially respectful, emotional influence.
3. To examine actual brand campaigns (Apple, Nike, Dove) where cinematic approaches have been applied to address or repair trust issues.

4. To develop a framework called Cinematic Trust in Algorithmic Marketing that integrates aesthetic, ethical, and technical concepts into a coherent model for practice and regulation.

The relevance of this research impacts multiple domains. For marketing scholarship, it contributes to debates on how emotion, authenticity, and aesthetics function in algorithmic environments, moving beyond purely data-analytic or behavioural perspectives. For practitioners, it provides guidance on designing campaigns that leverage cinematic power without resorting to manipulative or opaque tactics. For policymakers and regulators, it illuminates how emotional tracking technologies actually operate in commercial contexts and identifies levers for protecting cognitive liberty without stifling creative expression. For students and emerging professionals, it offers an integrated perspective on how to navigate a field where creative storytelling, AI systems, and ethical scrutiny increasingly intersect.

2. LITERATURE REVIEW

2.1 Surveillance Capitalism and the Trust Deficit in Digital Marketing

Zuboff's concept of surveillance capitalism provides a foundational lens for understanding why trust has become fragile in digital marketing. Trust in digital marketing can be assessed through dimensions such as perceived transparency, credibility, and emotional connection. These dimensions influence consumer attitudes, engagement levels, and long-term brand loyalty, making trust a measurable and actionable construct in marketing strategies. This erosion of trust is closely linked to the growing imbalance between corporate data control and user autonomy (Zuboff, 2019). In this model, digital platforms pursue continuous expansion of data capture and connectivity because their core revenue depends on selling accurate prediction products. Data about user behaviour is extracted not as a secondary by-product but as the main commodity. Consequently, people's online and offline activities are systematically monitored, classified, and nudged in ways that serve commercial optimisation rather than user autonomy.

Subsequent scholars have highlighted the systemic risks produced by this logic. The drive to "collect and connect" increases dependence on digital infrastructures that, when they fail or are misused, can trigger cascading harms, such as data breaches, manipulation of vulnerable groups, and disruptions in essential services. At the everyday level, the opacity of algorithms and complex privacy policies makes it hard for individuals to understand how their data flows through these systems or what inferences and decisions are being made about them.

Empirical research shows that awareness of such practices correlates with reduced trust in brands and platforms. When people discover that their browsing, location, and social interactions are extensively profiled, they are more likely to describe marketing as creepy, manipulative, or unfair. Even when companies offer transparency tools, the underlying power asymmetry between highly resourced platforms and individual users with limited time and expertise remains stark. Within this structure, conventional appeals to "consent" and "choice" often ring hollow.

2.2 Neuromarketing Ethics and Emotional Data

The neuromarketing literature reveals a similar tension between promise and risk. On one hand, technologies such as functional imaging, physiological sensors, and attention-tracking interfaces promise to refine understanding of consumer responses, helping brands design experiences that genuinely resonate and reduce irrelevant noise. Research demonstrates that such techniques can uncover subconscious preferences, raising concerns about ethical boundaries in persuasion (Ariely & Berns, 2010). On the other hand, they intensify longstanding concerns about manipulation, privacy, and exploitation.

Ethical analyses emphasise several issues. First, neuromarketing often operates at the level of subconscious responses; individuals may not fully understand what is being measured or how those measures will later be used to influence them. Second, emotional and biometric data fall into highly sensitive categories because they can reveal health status, psychological traits, and affective vulnerabilities. Third, global regulatory frameworks are uneven: while some jurisdictions strictly regulate biometric data, others provide limited guidance, enabling cross-border exploitation.

Scholars argue that the ethical status of neuromarketing is not determined solely by the tools themselves but by how they are embedded in organisational practices and governance. When used with explicit, informed consent, clear boundaries on secondary uses, and strong data protection, neuromarketing can help design safer, more effective communication. When deployed without such safeguards, the same tools can deepen asymmetries of knowledge and control between firms and individuals.

2.3 Narrative Transportation and Story-Based Persuasion

Narrative transportation theory positions storytelling as a distinct mode of persuasion that operates through immersion, identification, and emotional engagement rather than overt argumentation. Empirical evidence supports that narrative immersion increases persuasion and long-term attitude change (Green & Brock, 2000).

When people become absorbed in a narrative world, they temporarily suspend some critical distance and process information through the lens of characters' experiences and goals. This does not mean they lose agency, but that they engage affectively rather than analytically.

Meta-analytic research across multiple contexts shows that transported audiences are more likely to change attitudes, recall information, and show supportive behaviours aligned with story themes. These effects tend to be durable because stories organise information into coherent, meaningful structures. For marketing, this suggests that ads or campaigns designed as mini-narratives rather than as lists of features or claims can foster deeper brand relationships.

Importantly, narrative persuasion can be ethical or unethical depending on how it is used. Stories can clarify complex issues, represent marginalised voices, and promote informed reflection; they can also obscure trade-offs, romanticise harmful practices, or normalise problematic norms. The key is not whether stories are persuasive, most are, but whether they are truthful, proportionate, and respectful of audiences' ability to interpret and disagree.

2.4 Cinematic Technique and Emotional Resonance

Film studies and visual communication research provide detailed accounts of how cinematic form shapes emotional response. Camera angle, framing, and movement influence perceived power and intimacy; lighting and colour palettes set mood and signal thematic contrasts; pacing and editing sculpt tension and release; and sound design ties imagery to memory and embodied feeling. These elements rarely operate in isolation; rather, they combine into stylistic signatures that audiences may not consciously analyse but feel.

In commercial contexts, cinematic techniques allow brands to express identity and values nonverbally. A slow, lingering shot with natural lighting and ambient sound can evoke contemplation and sincerity; rapid, high-contrast cuts with driving music can signal energy and ambition. When such techniques are chosen thoughtfully and aligned with a brand's real commitments, they can foster perceptions of authenticity. When they are deployed as mere aesthetic veneers over exploitative practices, they risk being read as manipulative or hypocritical.

Research comparing narrative and non-narrative advertising formats suggests that cinematic storytelling is particularly effective at lowering defensive resistance. Viewers encountering a story are less likely to counterargue every claim and more likely to focus on coherence and emotional truth. This "softening" effect increases the ethical responsibility of storytellers: because stories can disarm scepticism, they must be used with care.

2.5 Authenticity, AI, and Brand Narratives

A central theme connecting these literatures is authenticity. Consumers increasingly differentiate between stories that appear grounded in real experiences and values, and those that feel manufactured to trigger emotions on demand. The rise of generative AI intensifies this tension. AI systems can now produce text, images, and video that mimic human style at scale, but often lack depth of insight, vulnerability, or contextual nuance. Audiences may not always consciously detect algorithmic authorship, yet they frequently register a sense of emotional thinness.

Studies comparing human-crafted and AI-generated marketing content suggest that human narratives tend to score higher on perceived authenticity, meaningfulness, and trustworthiness, even when AI content is grammatically flawless and stylistically polished. Hybrid approaches where human creators use AI as a support tool for ideation or production while retaining control over narrative structure and ethical framing show more promise. Such practices align with a broader move toward "human-in-the-loop" systems that combine computational efficiency with human judgment and responsibility.

In this environment, cinematic storytelling can function as a visible anchor of authenticity, especially when it incorporates real people, places, and unscripted elements. However, authenticity cannot be produced purely at the level of style. It depends on alignment between what is shown and what a brand actually does: labour practices, data policies, environmental impact, and more. When this alignment is absent, even the most moving cinematic narrative may ultimately damage trust once discrepancies become visible.

2.6 Ethical Frameworks for Emotion-Driven Marketing

Finally, the literature on digital ethics and AI governance provides criteria for evaluating emotion-driven marketing practices. Scholars and regulators converge on several core principles: transparency about data use and persuasive intent; informed consent for sensitive data collection; fairness and non-discrimination in targeting; protection of vulnerable groups; and accountability mechanisms that allow harms to be identified and addressed.

In practice, these principles imply constraints on how neuromarketing and behavioural AI can be integrated into marketing strategies. Emotional data should not be used to exploit known vulnerabilities or to push individuals toward decisions that conflict with their long-term interests. Dark patterns, hidden experimentation, and undisclosed emotional manipulation violate both emerging legal standards and norms of respectful communication.

Ethical frameworks also highlight the importance of internal governance: cross-functional review boards, ethics guidelines for creative and data teams, training on bias and manipulation, and mechanisms for ongoing audit. Within such structures, cinematic storytelling can be evaluated not only for its aesthetic effectiveness but also for its truthfulness, proportionality, and impact on autonomy.

3. CONSUMER AUTONOMY AND COGNITIVE LIBERTY IN THE DIGITAL AGE

3.1 The Right to Cognitive Liberty

Beyond privacy and transparency, contemporary digital marketing raises deeper questions about consumer autonomy and what some scholars term "cognitive liberty." Autonomy refers to the capacity to make informed, voluntary choices; cognitive liberty extends this to the right to think, feel, and decide without hidden technological interference (Ienca & Andorno, 2017). If marketing continues to influence people's thinking without their knowledge or genuine consent, they may shift from persuasion to manipulation.

Surveillance capitalism and neuromarketing are also raising issues concerning cognitive freedom in many ways. The constant monitoring of behaviour is undermining informational autonomy because people cannot know what is being tracked about them, for how long, and how it will be used. Personalisation systems control what choices and stories are available to people, reducing the information environment in which decisions are made. Such practices can reduce perceived autonomy and trust, particularly when users are unaware of how content is curated (Bleier & Eisenbeiss, 2015). Emotional monitoring and biometric analysis are invading feelings and bodily states that people would otherwise expect to remain private.

The situation is made worse by the fact that many of these technologies are invisible. Unlike the salesman who makes a clear pitch, algorithmic systems operate behind interfaces that appear neutral or even beneficial "for your benefit." Users do not know what aspects of an experience are personalised, what tests are being conducted, or what emotional buttons have been discovered.

3.2 Vulnerability, Power, and Asymmetry

Autonomy concerns are particularly acute when considering power asymmetries between individual consumers and large technology firms. The corporations have big data systems, advanced analytics, and experts in human behaviour. Humans, by contrast, typically have little time, little knowledge, and little access to legal support. This creates a situation where even if privacy policies and consent forms are in place, they may not offer much protection.

Vulnerability is not the same for all people. Children, adolescents, seniors, and people with cognitive or emotional problems may be particularly susceptible to emotional manipulation. People with financial problems may be tempted by short-term gains; people who feel lonely may be more likely to form one-sided relationships with brands. When predictive systems that target feelings are used to display content that triggers these states, the distinction between persuasion and exploitation becomes difficult to make.

Data disparities also make this situation more complex. Corporations tend to know more about a person's behaviour, feelings, and small preferences than the person does. Predictive systems can make educated guesses about things like political beliefs, relationship troubles, or mental health issues based on seemingly innocuous cues. When these predictions are used to craft persuasive messages, they can be used to exploit information that the person does not fully understand or control.

3.3 Criteria for Ethical Persuasion

Given these challenges, ethical marketing in the digital age must address autonomy at both structural and interactional levels. At a minimum, any persuasion system that aims to respect cognitive liberty should meet several criteria:

- **Transparency:** Users should be able to recognise when and how they are being targeted or influenced, and by whom.
- **Informed consent:** Especially for emotional or biometric data, individuals should have clear, accessible explanations of what is collected and for what purposes, with real options to decline.
- **Proportionality:** The intensity and intrusiveness of persuasive techniques should be proportionate to the stakes of the decision and the vulnerability of the audience.
- **Fairness and non-exploitation:** Techniques should not intentionally target or disproportionately affect groups known to be less able to resist or evaluate them.
- **Respect for agency:** Communication should support, rather than circumvent, people's ability to reflect, compare options, and make choices aligned with their own values.

Filmic storytelling may more easily fulfil a variety of criteria for persuasive engagement than the mysterious algorithmic manipulation. The persuasive goal that can be identified in a filmic advertisement is usually clear: viewers understand that they are watching an advertisement or a branded story. The means used in visual storytelling are visible and, in theory, open to analysis. The process is temporally delimited rather than continuously adaptive. This does not make filmic persuasion ethical per se, but it provides a more visible and disputable context for persuasion.

4. THEORETICAL FRAMEWORK: SURVEILLANCE CAPITALISM VS. CINEMATIC TRUST

4.1 The Two Models of Marketing Persuasion

The fundamental thesis of this chapter rests on understanding two contrasting models of how marketing persuasion operates and how they relate to consumer trust:

Model 1: Surveillance-Based Algorithmic Persuasion

This model operates by extracting behavioural data, identifying emotional and cognitive vulnerabilities, and using that information to deliver targeted messages designed to exploit those vulnerabilities. The point is: we observe your behaviour, identify your vulnerabilities, and leverage that to influence you to do what we want. Trust is not required because it's all about manipulation, not a genuine relationship. The person being manipulated doesn't have to believe in or trust the brand; they simply have to be vulnerable to the influence technique.

This method is effective for a short period. It can increase conversions and generate sales. However, it will eventually erode trust because, once people realise they are being manipulated, they become sceptical. The news about Facebook's manipulation of users' emotions, Google's tracking of location data even when location services are turned off, and Amazon's trickery to get people to sign up for Prime does not build trust; it erodes it. Each instance of manipulation leads people to believe that these companies cannot be trusted.

Model 2: Cinematic Trust-Based Persuasion

This model operates by creating narratives that resonate with human values and experiences. The underlying logic is: "We will tell you a genuine story that reflects our values and aspirations. We believe this story will resonate with you because it speaks to common human experiences." Trust is central to this model because the persuasion is based on shared meaning rather than manipulated vulnerability.

This model works differently. It doesn't necessarily drive immediate conversions as effectively as algorithmic targeting. But it builds long-term relationships based on authentic connection. When a consumer feels that a brand genuinely understands them and shares their values, not because of data manipulation but because the brand's narrative authentically speaks to human experiences, they are more likely to develop genuine loyalty and become brand advocates.

4.2 The Trust Paradox

Here lies a critical paradox: the very techniques that make marketing most effective in the short term (surveillance, data extraction, algorithmic targeting) are the techniques that most undermine trust in the long term. Conversely, techniques that require less data extraction and less algorithmic manipulation (authentic storytelling) may be less immediately effective but build more durable trust.

This paradox is not unique to marketing. In interpersonal relationships, people who are transparent and genuine build deeper trust than people who manipulate. In politics, leaders who communicate authentically build more committed followers than leaders who rely on propaganda and emotional manipulation, even if propaganda achieves short-term compliance. In business, companies with transparent practices and genuine commitments to stated values develop more loyal customers than companies that prioritise short-term manipulation.

The question then becomes: can marketing achieve both short-term effectiveness and long-term trust? Can brands balance algorithmic efficiency with authentic storytelling? The "Cinematic Trust in Algorithmic Marketing" framework proposes that they can, but only if they fundamentally restructure their approach around authenticity, transparency, and consumer respect.

4.3 The Framework: Integration Rather Than Opposition

The proposed framework is not asking brands to abandon algorithms completely. The proposed framework is asking brands to adopt a new approach to algorithmic personalisation. Instead of using algorithms to identify and exploit vulnerabilities, they should be used to:

1. **Get real content straight:** Use data to ensure real cinematic stories reach people who will appreciate them, not by appealing to their emotions.
2. **Remain transparent:** Use algorithms to provide clear, understandable explanations of why certain content reaches certain people, rather than remaining a covert manipulator.
3. **Protect vulnerable groups:** Use data to identify people who are more easily manipulated and avoid targeting them with persuasive messages.

4. **Adjust the way stories are told:** Use data to learn cultural preferences and likes so that real stories can be adjusted to fit the culture, while maintaining the underlying truth of the story.
5. **Assess impact ethically:** Use data to determine if marketing is successful while being mindful of consumer choice, rather than using data to hone the manipulation.

The critical difference is the **direction of algorithmic logic**. In surveillance capitalism, algorithmic logic is directed toward: "How can we better predict and manipulate this person's behaviour?" In Cinematic Trust, algorithmic logic is directed toward: "How can we deliver authentic messages more efficiently while maintaining transparency and respecting autonomy?"

5. CINEMATIC STORYTELLING IN MARKETING: VISUAL SEMIOTICS AND NARRATIVE AUTHENTICITY

5.1 Visual Semiotics: How Images Communicate Meaning

Cinematic storytelling in marketing draws on visual semiotics, where images and visual sequences communicate meaning and shape audience perception. Brands use elements such as colour, composition, and visual style to signal identity and values. For example, a brand associated with simplicity may use minimal framing and natural lighting, while a brand focused on innovation may use dynamic visuals and strong contrasts.

These visual choices influence not only immediate emotional responses but also how audiences interpret future brand communication. Over time, a consistent cinematic language creates expectations about brand behaviour. When these expectations align with actual practices, cinematic storytelling reinforces authenticity and builds consumer trust.

5.2 Colour, Composition, and Emotional Tone

Colour and composition play a crucial role in shaping emotional tone and audience perception in cinematic storytelling. Brands strategically use visual elements to evoke specific feelings such as trust, energy, or authenticity, which influence how audiences interpret brand messages.

For example, Apple's campaigns emphasise clarity and precision, Nike's visuals convey energy and movement, while Dove focuses on warmth and natural authenticity. These visual choices are not merely aesthetic but serve as signals of brand identity and values.

By shaping emotional responses and reinforcing consistency in visual communication, these elements contribute to stronger audience engagement and play a significant role in building consumer trust.

5.3 Narrative Structure and Emotional Arc

Narrative structure plays a central role in shaping emotional engagement and meaning in cinematic storytelling. Marketing narratives often follow a progression of challenge, conflict, and resolution, which aligns with how individuals interpret real-life experiences.

Campaigns such as Nike's "Just Do It" and Dove's "Real Beauty" use these narrative structures to create emotionally engaging stories. These narratives allow audiences to connect with characters, experience their journeys, and internalise brand messages.

By guiding emotional responses and creating meaningful story arcs, narrative structures enhance audience immersion and contribute to stronger persuasion and long-term consumer trust.

5.4 Sound, Music, and Affective Memory

Sound design and music are often underestimated elements of marketing communication. Auditory cues can evoke cultural memories, signal genre, and modulate emotional intensity. A well-chosen track can make a short film feel expansive, nostalgic, rebellious, or intimate. Over time, certain sounds become tightly associated with particular brands, functioning as sonic logos that trigger recognition even before visuals appear.

From an ethical standpoint, music and sound can either deepen the authenticity of a narrative or mask its hollowness. Using culturally specific music without understanding or crediting its origins, for example, can amount to appropriation. Conversely, collaborating with artists, communities, or causes connected to the music can embed campaigns in more reciprocal relationships.

These auditory elements strengthen emotional recall and, when used authentically, can enhance consumer trust and reinforce long-term brand relationships.

5.5 Character and Identification

Character identification is a key mechanism in cinematic storytelling, through which viewers relate to characters, adopt their perspectives, and emotionally engage with the narrative. When we become emotionally involved with a character in a film, we are no longer passive observers of a cinematic narrative. Rather than simply watching a movie, we are participating in it. We lose ourselves in its action and feel whatever the protagonist feels.

So, there are a bunch of techniques that you can use to create the identification that your protagonist is real for your audience. Real in the sense that the audience can identify with them and get into the story on an emotional level. One way to do this is to create common situations, common motivations, and the idea of common human vulnerabilities that we can all identify with and a common human process of growth that they are going through as well. And that creates a very humanistic character that our audience can easily step into.

Apple's "Shot on iPhone" ad campaign uses everyday people to capture special moments, while Nike's ads feature a variety of athletes conquering different types of challenges. When we see ourselves in a story, we become more invested in it.

The process of identifying characters serves to further engage the reader in the narrative and is significant in building trust and loyalty towards a brand.

5.6 Documentary and User-Generated Aesthetics

A notable trend in contemporary brand storytelling is the use of documentary or user-generated aesthetics, handheld camera work, natural lighting, unscripted dialogue, and real locations. We're seeing a trend in advertising that's moving away from the typical commercial photography style in favour of more cinematically shot and human moments. Apple's 'Shot on iPhone' campaigns showcase user-generated content, while brands like Nike and Dove have been using a documentary style to feature real-life athletes and women as opposed to airbrushed and unrealistic models.

Each of these aesthetics serves multiple purposes. Each communicates transparency and earthiness and shifts the dynamics of the act of creation so that participants have a somewhat different role to play, and so that audiences can imagine themselves as creators. If these dynamics are managed in a way that builds trust (i.e., in which those who are acting as creators have meaningful input and are fairly depicted), they will have their desired effects. If they are fake or artificially imposed in a way that appears artificial (i.e., if participants do not truly experience themselves as co-creators and audiences do not really feel themselves included as creators), they will be seen for what they are and will undermine their intended meaning.

Authentic disclosure of these types can increase transparency and foster greater trust between companies and consumers.

5.7 Triad Recap

Overall, cinematic storytelling represents a shift from purely data-driven and surveillance-based marketing toward more transparent, human-centred, and engaging communication. As digital environments become increasingly shaped by data-driven targeting, audiences are becoming more aware of issues related to privacy, manipulation, and loss of autonomy. In this context, storytelling approaches that emphasise authenticity, narrative coherence, and meaningful audience connection offer a more ethical alternative to opaque forms of persuasion. By fostering engagement and interpretability, cinematic storytelling not only enhances brand communication but also contributes to the rebuilding of consumer trust in contemporary digital marketing ecosystems.

6. AI AND MARKETING: ALGORITHMIC CAPABILITIES AND ETHICAL LIMITS

6.1 From Personalisation to Predictive Persuasion

Artificial intelligence underpins many aspects of modern marketing: recommendation systems, programmatic ad buying, dynamic pricing, chatbots, content optimisation, and more. In early stages, these technologies were framed as tools for personalisation, helping match people with relevant content and offers. Over time, as models became more powerful and datasets more comprehensive, the focus shifted toward predicting and shaping behaviour in ever finer temporal and contextual granularity.

This shift from descriptive to predictive and prescriptive analytics raises ethical concerns regarding autonomy, transparency, and fairness in AI-driven systems (Floridi et al., 2018). At what point does anticipating preferences become pre-empting deliberation? When interfaces are continually adjusted to maximise engagement or conversion, it can be difficult for users to maintain reflective distance. The same mechanisms that increase efficiency can also entrench habits, amplify impulsivity, and narrow exposure to diverse perspectives.

6.2 Generative AI and Synthetic Media

Recent advances in generative AI add another layer to this landscape. Text, image, audio, and video models can now create synthetic content that is often indistinguishable from human-produced media. For marketers, this promises rapid production of tailored assets at scale: personalised videos, adaptive narratives, and dynamic visual identities. For audiences, it raises new questions about authenticity, authorship, and trust. Ethical frameworks emphasise the importance of transparency and accountability in AI-generated content (Floridi et al., 2018).

If a brand's cinematic story is largely generated by algorithms trained on existing cultural materials, what does it mean to call that story "authentic"? Who is accountable when synthetic media reproduces biases or misrepresents communities? How should disclosures about AI involvement be handled so that viewers can make informed judgments without being overwhelmed by technical detail?

A cautious approach recognises both opportunity and risk. Generative AI can help small teams prototype ideas, localise content, and support accessibility. But it should not replace human oversight in deciding what stories to tell, how people are depicted, and where ethical boundaries lie. In the context of cinematic trust, AI is best treated as an assistive tool within human-led creative and ethical frameworks.

6.3 Aligning AI with Cinematic Trust

The challenge, then, is to align AI-driven capabilities with the values embedded in cinematic storytelling. Several practical principles follow from this aim:

- **Human-centred design:** Start from narratives that reflect real stakeholder experiences and concerns, then use AI to support distribution or adaptation rather than designing stories backwards from what algorithms can optimise.
- **Explainability and disclosure:** Where AI significantly shapes content or targeting, provide accessible explanations and labelling so that audiences are not misled about what they are seeing.
- **Constraint-based optimisation:** Define ethical constraints such as excluding vulnerable profiles from certain forms of emotional targeting before optimisation goals, and encode these into system design.
- **Cross-disciplinary oversight:** Involve ethicists, legal experts, creatives, and user representatives in reviewing emotionally targeted campaigns, not only data scientists and marketers.

Within such guardrails, AI can help cinematic narratives reach appropriate audiences, test variations responsibly, and adapt to diverse cultural contexts without undermining the core principles of transparency and respect for autonomy.

7. CASE STUDIES: CINEMATIC ADVERTISING AS TRUST RESTORATION

7.1 Apple's "Shot on iPhone" Campaign: User-Generated Authenticity

Apple's "Shot on iPhone" platform illustrates how cinematic storytelling can be grounded in everyday experience while still serving clear commercial goals. Instead of relying solely on polished studio shoots, Apple curates' footage captured by users across diverse contexts, landscapes, cities, family moments, sports, and creative experiments. These clips are edited into short films and billboards that foreground image quality but also, crucially, the perspectives of ordinary people.

Cinematically, the campaigns use varied framing, slow motion, time-lapse, and atmospheric soundscapes to construct emotionally resonant vignettes. The phone itself often appears only briefly or not at all; the focus rests on what people are able to see and share through it. This shifts the narrative from a product-centric pitch ("this camera is good") to a participatory story about creativity and connection ("people like you can make cinematic images").

From a trust perspective, several features stand out. The content is clearly branded, so the persuasive context is transparent. Participants are named or credited, signalling partnership rather than extraction. The visual claims about camera performance are verifiable, as viewers can test similar shots with their own devices. While Apple still relies on extensive data ecosystems elsewhere in its business, the "Shot on iPhone" films demonstrate how co-creative cinematic storytelling can build authenticity without requiring intrusive emotional profiling.

7.2 Nike's Inspirational Films: Narrative Transportation and Aspiration

Nike has long used cinematic storytelling to link its products with broader narratives of perseverance, inclusion, and social change. Campaigns featuring athletes who overcome structural barriers or personal adversity, women entering male-dominated sports, para-athletes redefining ability, or players speaking about racial injustice deploy high-impact visuals, voice-overs, and music to create emotionally charged mini-documentaries.

These narratives operate on multiple levels. At the surface, they dramatise the physical intensity and beauty of sport. At a deeper level, they invite viewers to interpret sport as a metaphor for self-definition and resistance. Nike's swoosh and tagline appear as recurring motifs, framing the brand as an enabler of these journeys rather than as the central protagonist.

The trust implications are ambivalent and instructive. On one hand, Nike's films have inspired strong identification and loyalty among audiences who see their own struggles reflected and validated. On the other hand, critics have questioned whether such storytelling sometimes instrumentalises social issues for profit, especially when supply-chain or labour practices appear misaligned with the values portrayed. The campaigns thus illustrate both the power of cinematic narratives to mobilise emotion and the ethical necessity of aligning storytelling with organisational conduct.

7.3 Dove's "Real Beauty" Campaign: Challenging Standards Through Documentary-Style Storytelling

Dove's "Real Beauty" initiatives exemplify documentary-style brand storytelling focused on representation and body image. Many of its films feature non-professional participants reacting to their own reflections, discussing self-esteem, or confronting restrictive beauty norms. The cinematography often uses close-ups, minimal makeup, and plain backgrounds to emphasise faces and voices rather than stylised glamour.

These choices aim to reposition beauty advertising around acceptance and diversity rather than narrow ideals. By showing stretch marks, wrinkles, and varied body types, Dove invites viewers to recognise themselves and question internalised standards. The emotional arc typically moves from self-criticism or discomfort toward recognition, solidarity, and affirmation.

As with Nike, the trust effects are mixed but revealing. Many viewers credit the campaigns with helping to normalise more inclusive images, and research has documented positive shifts in attitudes among some audiences. Yet concerns persist about whether a brand that profits from appearance-related products can ever be a fully disinterested advocate for body neutrality. Critics also note inconsistencies between progressive messaging and broader corporate portfolios or global marketing practices. These tensions underscore that cinematic authenticity must be backed by structural commitments to avoid being perceived as "woke-washing."

8. ETHICAL CONSIDERATIONS IN CINEMATIC, EMOTION-DRIVEN MARKETING

8.1 Manipulation vs Respectful Persuasion

Cinematic storytelling is inherently persuasive: it selects certain perspectives, edits time, and orchestrates emotion. The ethical question is not whether it influences, but how. Ethical persuasion must respect consumer autonomy and avoid exploiting cognitive vulnerabilities (Mayer et al., 1995). Manipulation occurs when stories are designed to bypass or undermine audiences' capacity for reflection, for example, by hiding material conflicts of interest, exaggerating benefits while minimising risks, or deliberately triggering fear, shame, or envy to push consumption.

Respectful persuasion, by contrast, treats audiences as capable agents. It presents emotionally engaging narratives while maintaining truthful representations of products, impacts, and alternatives. It avoids exploiting known psychological vulnerabilities, especially where stakes are high (health, finance, children's development). In practice, the distinction often hinges on intention, proportionality, and transparency: are emotional techniques being used to illuminate genuine value, or primarily to override hesitation?

8.2 Vulnerable Audiences and Protective Boundaries

Because cinematic stories can disarm critical defences, particular care is needed when addressing vulnerable groups. Ads aimed at children, for instance, may anthropomorphise products or blur lines between content and commerce in ways that children cannot easily decode. For individuals experiencing grief, addiction, or financial distress, certain thematic triggers may increase susceptibility to impulsive decisions.

Ethically responsible brands can adopt protective boundaries such as: limiting emotionally intense content in media channels known to have large child audiences; avoiding the use of personal crisis themes for purely commercial ends; and excluding segments flagged as vulnerable from aggressive retargeting or personalised emotional experimentation. These choices may reduce short-term conversion metrics but support long-term trust and regulatory compliance.

8.3 Consistency Between Story and Practice

A recurring theme across the case studies is the importance of "story-practice alignment." Even the most artful cinematic campaigns cannot sustain trust if audiences later discover that a brand's labour policies, environmental impacts, or data practices contradict its on-screen values. Digital transparency and social media scrutiny make such discrepancies more visible than in previous eras.

Ethically, this implies that values-based cinematic storytelling should follow, not lead, substantive organisational change. For example, a company seeking to champion data privacy in its narratives should first ensure robust privacy-by-design processes, clear user controls, and independent audits. Storytelling can then communicate and humanise these commitments rather than serve as a substitute for them.

8.4 Governance, Accountability, and Co-Creation

Finally, ethical cinematic marketing requires governance mechanisms that distribute responsibility across creative, data, and leadership functions. Internal review boards or ethics committees can evaluate proposed campaigns not only for brand fit but also for potential harms and fairness. Clear lines of accountability help ensure that when mistakes occur, such as insensitive representations or undisclosed manipulations, brands can respond with genuine repair efforts.

Increasingly, co-creation with communities, advocacy groups, and participants offers another layer of ethical assurance. Involving stakeholders in the design, scripting, and evaluation of stories can surface blind spots and foster shared ownership. However, such collaboration must be substantive rather than tokenistic; participants should have real influence and be fairly compensated.

9. CONCEPTUAL MODEL: CINEMATIC TRUST IN ALGORITHMIC MARKETING

The **Cinematic Trust in Algorithmic Marketing** framework synthesises the chapter's arguments into a multi-layered model for responsible digital persuasion. It comprises four interlinked layers:

1. Contextual Layer: Surveillance Capitalism and Regulation

This outer layer recognises that all marketing activity is embedded in broader economic and legal structures. Surveillance capitalism's incentives toward data extraction and prediction create persistent pressures toward intrusive tracking and behavioural manipulation. Regulatory regimes, data protection laws, AI governance frameworks, and advertising standards set outer boundaries and obligations. Any trust-oriented strategy must begin by acknowledging these constraints rather than assuming a neutral technological environment.

2. Narrative Layer: Cinematic Storytelling and Realness

The central concept is to leverage cinematic storytelling to emotionally connect. This layer examines the role of visuals, storytelling, casting, audio, and editing to communicate brand values and messages in a way that resonates with viewers to identify with the story. Realness is more than a good look; it's the brand's lived experience, values, and brand representation all aligning.

3. Algorithmic Layer: Helpful, Limited Personalisation

AI is not the driver. It's a helper that assists in matching cinematic stories to the right audience. Personalisation is permitted but governed by strong ethics: avoid certain sensitive predictions, do not let emotional targeting be too intense, and do not use manipulative segmentation. AI should increase relevance and accessibility, not always strive for the most compelling psychological pull.

4. Ethics and Governance Layer: Safeguards for Choice and Fairness

The governance framework is the layer that encircles the other layers to implement ethics such as transparency, consent, fairness, accountability, and protection for vulnerable groups. This includes pre-campaign ethics checks, monitoring of impact, user feedback or complaints, and a willingness to change or delete content if it is causing harm.

Trust is viewed as a long-term result of interactions. This happens when audiences find the brand's cinematic stories true, respectful, and consistent with real-world behaviour, and when people understand that data-driven systems have boundaries that are clearly defined and explained.

The model provides some concepts for future empirical testing, such as:

- Cinematic campaigns that are aligned in story and practice and do not personalise too much will increase long-term trust more than highly emotional campaigns that rely on hidden targeting.
- Authenticity and transparency will play a role in how narrative immersion affects trust in AI-driven environments.
- Clear ethical boundaries (such as labels for AI-created content and the ability to opt out of emotional targeting) will alleviate concerns about manipulation without diminishing the appeal of cinematic storytelling.

10. MANAGERIAL IMPLICATIONS: GUIDELINES FOR RESPONSIBLE VISUAL STORYTELLING

The framework has concrete implications for marketing leaders, creative teams, and organisations seeking to balance effectiveness with ethics.

10.1 Strategic Orientation

First, managers may need to shift key performance indicators from purely short-term metrics (click-through rates, immediate conversions) toward broader trust-related outcomes: repeat engagement, brand advocacy, complaint rates, and sentiment trends. Cinematic storytelling often operates on a longer time horizon, building narrative capital that pays off in loyalty and resilience during crises.

Strategically, this entails viewing audiences not only as targets but as long-term relationship partners whose autonomy and dignity are assets rather than obstacles. Investments in responsible data practices, community partnerships, and internal education should be treated as integral components of brand equity.

10.2 Team Composition and Collaboration

Second, implementing cinematic trust approaches requires interdisciplinary teams. Creatives versed in film language, editors, and sound designers must collaborate closely with data scientists, UX designers, legal counsel, and ethicists. Regular cross-functional workshops or review sessions can help ensure that narrative ideas are evaluated not only for emotional impact but also for fairness, representational accuracy, and compliance.

Building such teams may also involve new roles, such as "ethical design leads" or "trust officers," empowered to question or veto campaigns that cross agreed boundaries. Importantly, these roles should have organisational backing rather than be symbolic.

10.3 Design Guidelines for Campaigns

Third, practical design guidelines can translate the framework into everyday decisions, for example:

- Prioritise stories grounded in real stakeholder experiences; avoid generic, de-contextualised emotional tropes.
- Make persuasive intent and brand involvement clear from the outset; resist blending editorial and commercial content in ways that obscure sponsorship.
- Test cinematic narratives with diverse audience segments for unintended interpretations or harms, not only for recall and liking.
- Use personalisation to tailor language, timing, or channel rather than to dynamically escalate emotional pressure based on detected vulnerabilities.

These guidelines can be codified into internal playbooks and used in agency briefs to align external partners with the organisation's ethical stance.

10.4 Measurement and Feedback

Finally, managers should develop measurement systems that capture both the benefits and potential downsides of cinematic, AI-supported campaigns. In addition to standard analytics, this may include:

- Periodic surveys on perceived transparency, authenticity, and comfort with personalisation.
- Monitoring of user complaints, social media critiques, and advocacy group responses to values-based campaigns.
- Internal post-mortems on controversial or borderline initiatives to identify lessons and adapt safeguards.

Such feedback loops can prevent ethical drift and help refine the practical application of the Cinematic Trust model over time.

11. LIMITATIONS AND DIRECTIONS FOR FUTURE RESEARCH

11.1 Conceptual and Scope Limitations

This chapter is more conceptual and synthetic. This paper uses current marketing science theory and existing example brand advertising campaigns to propose the Cinematic Trust in Algorithmic Marketing (CTAM) framework. It does not empirically validate the proposed framework. So, the assertions in this study regarding cinematic storytelling, authenticity, trust and the ethical governance of online platforms are speculative. A confirmation or elaboration of these assertions should be sought through empirical research.

By taking a particular segment of socially significant actors as its subject, this chapter is also highly selective regarding empirical evidence. It scrutinises only Apple, Nike and Dove, three of the most iconic and, in respect of their global reach, probably the most creative and most financially strong and capaciously managed "corporate celebrities" within the Consumer Goods Industry. Their relative social, economic and communicative distance to the populations they address arguably also turns them into rather less risky objects of sociological inquiry at any rate than local or medium-sized advertising firms would be, and even more so than enterprises faced with stark structural (and therefore cultural) conditions at their core operations.

Similarly, the chapter does not address particularly contentious genres of advertising, such as political propaganda, games or medical advertising.

Another constraint is that the subject matter is overly general, especially in the context of the technical applications of "artificial intelligence" and "neuromarketing." The main objective of this chapter is to discuss the ethical and strategic implications rather than detail the functionalities of the individual tools and technologies, which, in any case, are implemented in such complex and dynamic systems that only technical experts who have implemented and used them regularly can understand the numerous technological variables at play. This general level of treatment is probably more appropriate for the intended readership than the attempted granular comparison of their different functionalities, especially since such comparisons are currently too general and thus unsuited to inform the various strategic choices involving the use of these tools that companies will have to consider over the coming years. Besides, the treatment of technological complexity at the level of individual design choices implicit in any detailed technical comparison, including at the level of source code and training models, is still excessively reductionist and therefore does not reflect the underlying complexity of these systems and the many factors that are often ignored at the code/model level, but will later assume disproportionate importance in their practical uses.

This discussion of vulnerability and cognitive liberty is largely grounded in normative argumentation and secondary research, leaving direct engagement with end-user populations lacking. In addition, children and adolescents, older adults, people with disabilities, and communities often targeted by socially toxic ads have been largely omitted as sources of first-hand information in this analysis, perhaps reinforcing the very dynamics that lead to their exploitation. Their experiences may also undermine some of the sharp category distinctions made here.

11.2 Directions for Future Research

Building on these limitations, several avenues for future research emerge:

1. Empirical testing of the Cinematic Trust model

Quantitative and mixed-methods studies could examine whether campaigns that combine cinematic storytelling with constrained, transparent personalisation indeed generate higher trust and long-term engagement than equally emotional campaigns driven by opaque behavioural targeting. Experimental designs might manipulate levels of narrative authenticity, visible AI involvement, and disclosure of data practices to observe effects on perceived manipulation, autonomy, and brand evaluations.

2. Cross-cultural and contextual comparisons

The way meaning is constructed for visual signs, story formats, and authenticity varies across cultures and regulations. We might examine how trust in cinema is constructed differently in different regions, media landscapes, and sectors of the industry. For instance, we might examine tech brands in Europe and Asia, or the role of values in guiding storytelling in consumer products versus financial services. This research would demonstrate which aspects of the concept are global and which require local adaptation.

3. Audience research with vulnerable groups

In-depth conversations, interviews, focus groups, and co-design research with vulnerable or marginalised groups can demonstrate how they perceive cinematic marketing, where they think the line is between acceptable and unacceptable influence, and what they find meaningful in terms of protection. This would provide a bottom-up perspective on autonomy and harm to the largely top-down discourse on ethics.

4. Organisational and governance studies

Research on companies attempting to implement ethical cinematic storytelling and minimal AI use would highlight real-world challenges, trade-offs, and factors that help. This research could examine how internal review procedures are organised, how tensions between performance metrics and ethical commitments are managed, and what leadership and organisational cultures help to sustain trust-based practices.

5. Technical design for ethical emotional targeting

Technical design could involve collaboration between computer science, design, and ethics experts to develop prototype systems that implement these design principles. These might include recommendation systems that implement ethical design principles, systems that provide explanations for why a given individual views a particular cinematic narrative, or controls that allow individuals to set boundaries on the type of emotional personalisation.

6. Longitudinal impact of values-based storytelling

Longitudinal research on brands that make a large investment in values-based cinematic storytelling could help determine whether these strategies lead to long-term trust or if consumers become sceptical when the company fails to follow through on their values. Outcomes might include sales, tone of the brand, employee engagement, regulatory compliance, and stakeholder activity.

7. Policy and regulatory implications

Policy and regulatory efforts could explore how new AI and data protection regulations might incorporate emotionally targeted cinematic marketing. These might include questions about whether emotional or biometric data used in advertising should be afforded special protection, how to regulate synthetic media and deepfakes in a business context, and how to develop effective disclosure policies for AI-generated content.

By following these directions, future research can move beyond the realm of critique and ideas and instead develop guidelines, tools, and rules that help to use cinematic storytelling in AI-driven marketing in an ethical manner.

12. CONCLUSION

One thing this chapter looks at is how today's online advertising world, built around data tracking and smart algorithms, pulls in opposite directions - ease and personal control. Following user actions, forecasting choices, or reading emotional cues helps tailor messages better, yet makes systems harder to see through, creates uneven access to personal information, and raises the chances people will be misled. When users start noticing these patterns, they trust digital ads less, leading some to push back or question automated targeting.

Facing these conditions, the chapter has argued that cinematic storytelling might offer a better way to connect emotionally with people. Because stories pull viewers into imagined scenes, film uses visual signs that carry weight beyond words. Picture layout, shade control, rhythm of shots, audio layers, and stories centred on people shape how audiences feel involved. When tales draw from actual lives, mirror what a company truly stands for, yet remain open about their aim, bonds form - not through stealthy data gathering or unseen monitoring - but through shared experience.

Looking at Apple's "Shot on iPhone," Nike's inspirational films, and Dove's "Real Beauty" campaigns reveals both potential and challenges. One thing stands out: Apple turns everyday users into visible creators, proving devices can shape stories. Meanwhile, Nike and Dove use emotional journeys to question common beliefs, linking brand identity with meaningful causes. Yet, when company actions clash with what audiences see, trust fades fast. Storytelling wins hearts only if real-world behaviour backs it up.

Putting those pieces side by side, the chapter laid out what became known as the Cinematic Trust in Algorithmic Marketing framework. This setup places cinematic storytelling across four linked parts - starting with how systems like surveillance capitalism and rules shape things now. It also includes ways to build stories so people feel things deeply, then moves into how artificial intelligence can support such aims even when limits apply. Support comes through design, but firm restrictions remain; ethics and oversight form the base holding it together. At its core, data pathways shift from invisible drivers pushing content toward predicted views. Instead, software acts more like a guide, helping meaningful narratives reach suitable listeners without losing control to efficiency-driven logic.

What matters most for those using these tools is less about pushing quick wins, more about building lasting connections - rooted in openness and honesty, care for mental autonomy. Teams need to blend skills from varied fields: creative thinking, tech savvy, law knowledge, moral judgment - not separated but working together. Design rules should support clear stories, avoid pushing emotional buttons without regard. How things are measured should include belief in doing things right, a sense of integrity, not just outcomes shown at first glance.

This part shows how film narratives tie into broader discussions on artificial intelligence, especially around control of data and moral choices. When AI-driven visuals grow common, who decides what counts as truthful storytelling? Issues like hiding digital origins or reshaping credit through editing might rise faster than rules can catch them. Keeping movies persuasive without weakening personal freedom means constant study, shifting policies, and real talk among creators, scholars, and public voices.

What stands behind this thinking isn't wistful, nor opposed to technology. It doesn't call for giving up data or artificial intelligence; just as much, it doesn't praise some earlier period of marketing that relied heavily on trickery. Rather, it argues that with computing now woven through daily life, successful ethical marketing comes from companies using films' emotional depth, yet agreeing to limit how much they watch and control people. When brands share honest narratives, linking them to real actions, their use of algorithms matters less if they are transparent. Showing purpose through narrative gives space for doubt, inviting viewers to question what they see. Trust grows stronger when behaviour matches promise across every frame. This aligns with broader research on trust, which emphasises consistency, transparency, and alignment between actions and communication (Mayer et al., 1995). Instead of noise, storytelling becomes a quiet guide within digital clutter. Ethics aren't extras - they shape how stories move and connect.

Practically, organisations can implement cinematic storytelling by focusing on narrative authenticity, ethical use of consumer data, and emotionally engaging content that prioritises consumer experience over intrusive targeting.

Cinematic storytelling is increasingly relevant to global brands, which are adopting the same techniques used in narrative-driven films to build trust and engagement. The majority of high-profile brand campaigns use narratives and use personal struggle and triumph in order to connect to their audience. For Nike, this can manifest in an empowering sports film, while for Apple, it's showcasing authentic user-generated content through their 'Shot on iPhone' campaign. As such, organisations can build trust with their audience through the use of narrative-driven storytelling, authenticity and responsible use of consumer data in order to deliver emotionally relevant content in the long term.

In addition, the dimension of trust can also be operationalised and expressed in terms of perceived levels of transparency, credibility and emotional connection and measured via consumer engagement metrics and brand loyalty.

REFERENCES

Ariely, D., & Berns, G. S. (2010). Neuromarketing: The hope and hype of neuroimaging in business. *Nature Reviews Neuroscience, 11*(4), 284–292. DOI: 10.1038/nrn2795 PMID: 20197790

Bleier, A., & Eisenbeiss, M. (2015). The importance of trust for personalised online advertising. *Journal of Retailing, 91*(3), 390–409. DOI: 10.1016/j.jretai.2015.04.001

Floridi, L., Cowls, J., Beltrametti, M., Chatila, R., Chazerand, P., Dignum, V., Luetge, C., Madelin, R., Pagallo, U., Rossi, F., Schafer, B., Valcke, P., & Vayena, E. (2018). AI4People—An ethical framework for a good AI society. *Minds and Machines, 28*(4), 689–707. DOI: 10.1007/s11023-018-9482-5 PMID: 30930541

Green, M. C., & Brock, T. C. (2000). The role of transportation in the persuasiveness of public narratives. *Journal of Personality and Social Psychology, 79*(5), 701–721. DOI: 10.1037/0022-3514.79.5.701 PMID: 11079236

Ienca, M., & Andorno, R. (2017). Towards new human rights in the age of neuroscience and neurotechnology. *Life Sciences, Society and Policy, 13*(1), 1–27. DOI: 10.1186/s40504-017-0050-1 PMID: 28444626

Mayer, R. C., Davis, J. H., & Schoorman, F. D. (1995). An integrative model of organisational trust. *Academy of Management Review, 20*(3), 709–734. DOI: 10.2307/258792

Plassmann, H., Venkatraman, V., Huettel, S., & Yoon, C. (2015). Consumer neuroscience: Applications, challenges, and possible solutions. *Journal of Marketing Research, 52*(4), 427–435. DOI: 10.1509/jmr.14.0048

Zuboff, S. (2019). *The age of surveillance capitalism*. Profile Books.

ADDITIONAL READING

Huang, M.-H., & Rust, R. T. (2021). A strategic framework for artificial intelligence in marketing. *Journal of the Academy of Marketing Science, 49*(1), 30–50. DOI: 10.1007/s11747-020-00749-9

Saura, J. R., Škare, V., & Ozretić Došen, D. (2024). Is AI-based digital marketing ethical? *Journal of Innovation & Knowledge, 9*(4), 100597. DOI: 10.1016/j.jik.2024.100597

KEY TERMS AND DEFINITIONS

Algorithmic Persuasion: The use of data-driven algorithms to influence consumer behaviour and decision-making processes.

Authenticity in Marketing: The perception that a brand communicates honestly, transparently, and consistently with its values.

Cinematic Storytelling: A marketing approach that uses film-based narrative techniques to create emotional engagement and communicate brand values.

Cognitive Liberty: Cognitive liberty refers to the right of individuals to control their own mental processes and to be protected from external manipulation of thought and decision-making (Ienca & Andorno, 2017).

Consumer Trust: The confidence consumers place in a brand's integrity, transparency, and reliability in delivering value.

Narrative Transportation: A psychological process in which individuals become mentally immersed in a story, influencing their attitudes and beliefs.

Neuromarketing: The application of neuroscience techniques to understand consumer responses to marketing stimuli and improve decision-making strategies.

Surveillance Capitalism: An economic system based on the large-scale collection and analysis of behavioural data for commercial purposes.

Chapter 8
The Paradox of Credibility:
A Mixed-Methods Study on Consumer Trust and Health Misinformation in the Age of Social Media

Sara Santos
http://orcid.org/0000-0002-3581-6478
CEOS.PP, ISCAP, Polytechnic of Porto, Portugal & NECE–Research Centre for Business Sciences, Portugal & Departamento de Ciências Sociais e Gestão, Universidade Aberta, Portugal

Miguel Pereira
http://orcid.org/0000-0003-3431-1141
ISCA, University of Aveiro, Portugal

Raquel Alves
ISCA, University of Aveiro, Portugal

ABSTRACT

The rapid democratization of health communication through social media has facilitated the global dissemination of public health information while simultaneously escalating the risks associated with digital misinformation. This research employs a dual-methodological approach, comprising a systematic literature review and an empirical survey, to investigate how misinformation influences consumer trust in health content across platforms such as TikTok, YouTube, Instagram, and X. Adhering to the PRISMA framework, the review synthesized 13 relevant articles

DOI: 10.4018/979-8-3373-7704-9.ch008

published between 2022 and 2025, revealing that while professional sources provide superior scientific quality, user-generated content by non-experts achieves higher engagement rates.The findings indicate that users often prioritize emotional resonance, creator relatability, and visual aesthetics over factual accuracy. This study highlights a critical need for platform accountability, enhanced media literacy, and strategic collaborations between healthcare professionals and influencers to restore information integrity.

1. INTRODUCTION

The digital landscape, dominated by platforms such as TikTok, YouTube, Instagram, and Twitter, has revolutionized the dissemination of health information by facilitating rapid communication. While this democratization of health communication expands the reach of public health content, it simultaneously escalates the risks associated with misinformation, posing significant threats to public health outcomes. A critical challenge in this environment is that high levels of engagement do not necessarily correlate with content quality; indeed, content produced by influencers frequently garners higher levels of trust than that originating from expert sources.

Consumer trust is increasingly shaped by emotional resonance, the aesthetics of visual imagery, parasocial relationships, and social validation rather than scientific veracity. When users prioritize perceived credibility over factual accuracy, misleading or harmful content can achieve accelerated reach, fundamentally altering public attitudes and health-seeking behaviors. This phenomenon is particularly evident among young adults and women, who are frequently drawn to the attractive, short-form content prevalent on TikTok and Instagram. Furthermore, platform algorithms systematically prioritize engagement metrics over accuracy, further amplifying misinformation and complicating the efforts of health professionals to share impactful, evidence-based information.

Understanding the intricate interaction between misinformation and consumer perceptions of trust is essential for the development of effective interventions, educational campaigns, and robust health policies. Consequently, this study utilizes a dual approach: a systematic literature review and an empirical survey. The review synthesizes recent research on misinformation and consumer trust using the PRISMA framework to ensure methodological rigor. By identifying major themes, challenges, and existing gaps in the literature, this research aims to provide a comprehensive foundation for future academic inquiry and to inform stakeholders about the systemic risks of health misinformation on social media.

2. METHODOLOGY

This review's central research question is: how does misinformation influence consumer trust in legitimate health content on social media? PRISMA, Preferred Reporting Items for Systematic Reviews and Meta-Analyses checklist, was used as the foundation for structuring the methodology of this study, to give a clearer process for the identification, screening, eligibility assessment, and inclusion of relevant studies that address the research objectives (Page et al., 2021).

Scopus by Elsevier was the database chosen for this systematic literature review. This was the only one for its wide, high-quality coverage and filtering tools.

The research took place on may 19, 2025, and was filtered to include only articles published between 2022 and 2025. The Boolean Operators used on the advanced search mode were: "consumer trust" OR credibility OR perception AND "health information" OR "health content" AND "social media" OR "online platforms" OR Facebook OR Instagram OR TikTok OR Twitter OR YouTube. The keywords and Boolean Operators were adjusted until the results aligned with the research objectives.

Rayyan was used to screen and remove duplicates based on relevance.

VOSViewer was used for creating a data visualization by highlighting the co-occurrence keywords present on the articles chosen for this systematic literature review.

Using the PRISMA methodology, a total of 277 records were identified from the Scopus database. After eliminating duplicates, screening titles and abstracts, 263 records were excluded. Fourteen full-text records were assessed for eligibility, and one was excluded based on the article not being available in full. Thus, a total of 13 records were included in the systematic review (Figure 1).

Figure 1. PRISMA flow diagram for the systematic review process to identify relevant studies

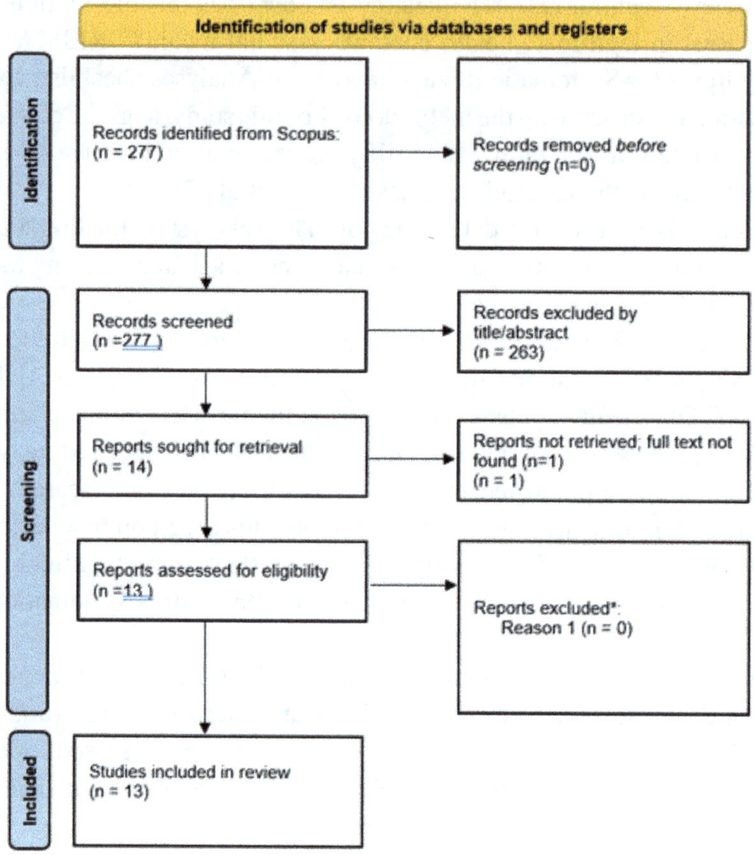

(Adapted from Page et al., 2021)

The 13 studies explore health content credibility and consumer perception across major platforms. The studies utilize quantitative, qualitative, and mixed-method strategies such as cross-sectional surveys, content analysis, experimental framing, and machine learning classification models. A summary of the studies and their aims can be found in Table 1.

Table 1. Description of key characteristics and findings of the studies included in the review

Study no.	Authors	Journal	Study objective	Key highlights
1	Gaysynsky et al. (2024)	JMIR Infodemiology	Explore U.S. adults' interpretations of health misinformation on social media and the effects on health communication behaviors.	Although mental health professionals as social media influencers can support and promote mental health literacy, their overall impact should be examined within a framework of the validity of their content.
2	Wang et al. (2023)	Frontiers in Psychology	Investigate how gain versus loss information would influence a user's willingness to engage with mindfulness content on social media.	According to gain-framed mindfulness messaging, social media promotes more engagement, particularly with individuals who see health as something they can manage themselves.
3	Pretorius, McCashin, and Coyle (2022)	Internet Interventions	Identify popular mental health professionals as influencers on TikTok and Instagram, and explore whether their content adds to mental health literacy.	Being aware of and unclear about misinformation reduces sharing and trusting social media for health-related decisions.
4	Ghavaland and Nabiolahi (2024)	BMC Health Services Research	To rank health information quality criteria on social media, from expert perspectives, using a mixed-methods study design.	The originality and volume of data were viewed as of lesser value. The challenge was the transparency and the need for further accountability measures as goals to help in improving health information quality on social media.
5	De Bérail and Bungener (2022)	Social Network Analysis and Mining	Investigate trust in YouTubers as health information sources and the impact of parasocial relationships on quarantine utility perceptions.	Some YouTubers carry as much credibility as journalists and friends, especially when parasocial relationships are high, having an impact on perceptions of public policies related to health measures.
6	Lim et al. (2022)	Journal of Medical Internet Research	Explore how young adults use different social media platforms to find health-related content and how they evaluate the trustworthiness of information.	YouTube - most trusted for credibility; Instagram - health inspiration; Facebook - shared stakeholder perspectives based on shared group content. Most users acknowledged trusting their intuition and visual appeal over factual evidence of health information.

continued on following page

Table 1. Continued

Study no.	Authors	Journal	Study objective	Key highlights
7	Kirkpatrick and Lawrie (2024)	JMIR Infodemiology	Explore how young women (18-29) in the U.S. use TikTok for health information seeking, how they evaluate credibility, and what their behaviors are for fact-checking information.	Participants preferred content delivered by health professionals. Labelled credentialed people were regarded as more at risk of misinformation than themselves. Increased emotion evoked connection was correlated with increased trust, particularly for TikTok.
8	Idrees, Helmy, and Khedr (2022)	Social Network Analysis and Mining	Assess the credibility aspects of social networks, who and what influences credibility assessment, and how it occurs in health.	Content, source, and community factors gave credibility to health information circulated on social networks. Credibility induction was also improved with NLP and machine learning.
9	Tam, Porter, and Lee (2022)	Urology	Evaluate the accuracy and credibility of UTI-related videos on TikTok and YouTube.	TikTok videos for UTIs had lower levels of accuracy than the ones on YouTube. High levels of engagement don't mean their quality was high.
10	Lukić and Petrović (2023)	Frontiers in Public Health	Examine the quality of information in the most viewed TikTok videos related to dementia using validated scoring systems.	The majority of dementia videos from TikTok were low quality and posted by non-experts. Expert sources had lower rates of engagement.
11	Zhong (2023)	International Journal of Information Management	Examine the temporal and sentiment impact of health-related news stories, their discussion and dissemination on social media channels including Twitter, to identify new ways to combat health misinformation.	Low-rated health news stories on Twitter garnered high engagement compared to high-rated ones.

continued on following page

Table 1. Continued

Study no.	Authors	Journal	Study objective	Key highlights
12	Mohamed and Shoufan (2024)	BMC Public Health	Examine user experiences with health-related content on YouTube and how demographics inform perceptions, usefulness, and decision-making.	Overall, YouTube users found exercise, mental health, and dieting content helpful but were also slightly biased. They recommended promoting verified sources that create health content.
13	Yousefinaghani et al. (2023)	PLOS Global Public Health	Analyze COVID-19 vaccine misinformation on Twitter for the purpose of developing improvement strategies for effective communication.	During COVID-19, vaccine misinformation came from posts by individuals who were about 40 years old and many bot accounts. Misleading accounts' posts had fewer followers and verification badges.

Source: Self-elaboration based on sample articles.

The synthesized literature reveals a multidisciplinary convergence across public health, media studies, and data sciences aimed at addressing the multifaceted complexities of digital health communication. Central themes identified within this research include the significant influence of emotional framing, the role of algorithmic amplification, and the specific credibility cues that drive consumer trust assessments. A critical finding across multiple studies is that emotional appeal consistently acts as a more significant driver of user engagement than factual accuracy. This creates a notable engagement disparity where expert-led content offers superior scientific quality but receives substantially less traction compared to non-professional sources.

Furthermore, a paradox of trust emerges as even skeptical users are prone to acting on content perceived as relatable or popular. These parasocial dynamics between creators and viewers play a vital role in fostering trust, often independent of a source's objective credentials. Research has particularly focused on young adults and women as primary demographics, especially within the context of TikTok and Instagram. Conversely, poor-quality health narratives have been shown to garner high engagement on platforms like Twitter, where older adults and automated bot accounts served as significant vectors for misinformation during the COVID-19 pandemic.

To evaluate these dynamics, researchers have increasingly utilized structured quality assessment frameworks such as DISCERN and HONCode. From a temporal perspective, scholarly interest peaked in 2022, a year in which social media became a formal centerpiece of health communication research following the implementation of misinformation sanctions during the pandemic. This academic momentum has remained steady through 2023 and 2024, reflecting a sustained commitment to understanding the evolution of consumer trust in the digital age.

Figure 2. Temporal distribution of the studies included in the review

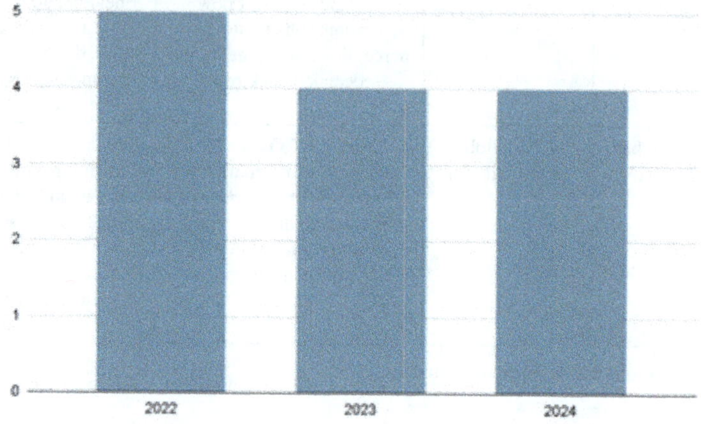

Source: Self-elaboration based on sample articles

Figure 3 illustrates the distribution of studies by scientific area, with most studies grounded in Public Health (38.5%). About a quarter (23.1%) represents Communication and Media Studies, which primarily examines message framing, source trust, and digital engagement. Others originate from Information Science (15.4%), Psychology, Behavioural Science (15.4%), and Computer/Data Science (7.7%). The distribution of studies attests to the multidisciplinary nature of the topic, which requires perspectives from both health and social science disciplines.

Figure 4 shows the classification of the articles by article type. The most common methods of data collection were empirical quantitative studies (53.8%), where researchers typically used surveys and content analysis. The number of mixed-methods studies and qualitative studies was equal (15.4%). Systematic reviews (7.7%) and conceptual papers (7.7%) only made up a small proportion of the literature, and added some theoretical perspectives or syntheses of existing evidence.

Figure 3. Distribution between scientific areas

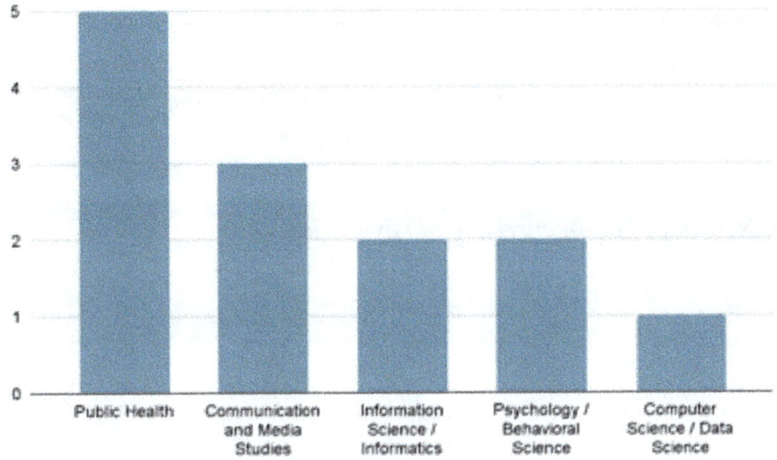

Source: Self-elaboration.

Note: Many articles had interdisciplinary overlaps, especially between public health and communication studies.

Figure 4. Distribution between paper types

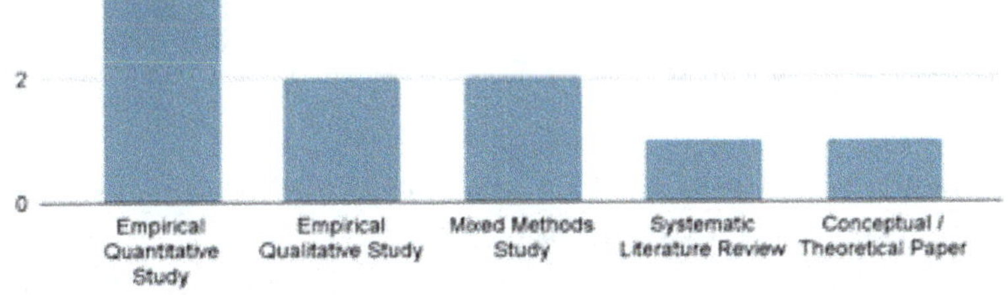

Source: Self-elaboration.

Figure 5 illustrates the VOSViewer keyword co-occurrence network from Scopus-indexed articles. Two clusters visualized: the red cluster, which centers on people and medical terms ("humans", "article", "medical information", "social media"), highlighting the dynamics of trust associated with human involvement; the green cluster, which addresses content flow ("information dissemination", "health information", "social media"). The word "social media" straddles both clusters, bringing the two concepts of trust and information flow together, while "article" and "medical information" provide a connection between trust and the source of information.

Figure 5. Network of co-occurrence of keywords

Source: Self-elaboration with VOSViewer.

3. LITERATURE REVIEW

The literature reviewed shows how users' trust in health content on social media platforms is mostly shaped by misinformation.

The most important themes that emerged are: (3.1) perception of credibility and trust in health information, (3.2) platform dynamics and amplification of misinformation, (3.3) behavioural and psychological effects of health misinformation, (3.4) and contradictions across studies, (3.5).

3.1. Perception of Credibility and Trust in Health Information

To users, credibility is more important than accuracy (Kirkpatrick & Lawrie, 2024; Mohamed & Shoufan, 2024). It can be dangerous, because platforms make it simple to fake credibility (Kirkpatrick & Lawrie, 2024).

Users rely more on their instincts rather than objective criteria, and they judge health information through mental shortcuts, focusing on superficial aspects like tone, language, and the social validation that comes from likes, shares, and comments (Lim et al., 2022). The popularity of the influencers often outweighs objective indicators of credibility (Ghalavand & Nabiolahi, 2024).

Health content often goes viral regardless of its accuracy (Lukić & Petrović, 2023). Parasocial relationships with influencers impact users' trust and behavioral responses (de Bérail & Bungener, 2022). Many users trust influencers more than doctors or journalists (Zhong, 2023).

Studies underline that content quality on social media is very variable, with reliable health professionals and organisations sharing credible and accurate information. However, these high-quality posts are often less popular or less disseminated compared to content that tends to attract more engagement, even if they have a lower scientific accuracy and reliability (Kirkpatrick and Lawrie, 2024; Lukić and Petrović, 2023).

3.2. Platform Dynamics and Amplification of Misinformation

Different social media platforms influence the visibility and credibility of health content differently (Pretorius, McCashin, & Coyle, 2022). YouTube promotes engaging, but often inaccurate videos, while TikTok's short-form videos simplify health messages (Tam, Porter, & Lee, 2022; Kirkpatrick & Lawrie, 2024), but, unlike YouTube, popular videos sometimes show better quality.

Twitter has presented a unique situation, with misinformation peaks during the COVID-19 pandemic, often due to unverified accounts or bots (Yousefinaghani et al., 2023). Controversial and low-quality news triggers discussion and stronger sentiments (Zhong, 2023). Even if the platform puts efforts into moderating content, studies agree that current interventions are not enough to make sure users consistently find reliable health content (Gaysynsky et al., 2024).

TikTok is characterized by short videos, most of which are created by non-experts. Fact-checking and sources' visibility are complicated. The quality of information tends to be low, but many users, especially young women, continue to rely on it for health advice even if they are more likely to act on content from perceived professionals (even if credentials can be easily faked) (Lukić and Petrović, 2023; Kirkpatrick and Lawrie, 2024).

YouTube is more convenient for getting in-depth health information, despite the poor overall quality of health content from a professional perspective. However, users often find these videos useful and trust them due to the educational nature of the platform and parasocial relationships with creators (Mohamed & Shoufan, 2024; de Bérail & Bungener, 2022). Metrics such as likes and views distort the perception of trustworthiness (Zhong, 2023).

Instagram works more as a source of inspiration for health and wellness than as an information source (Lim et al., 2022). In particular, young adults and women follow influencers, models, and celebrities who post content about aspirational lifestyles centered on health ideals such as "healthy eating" and an ideal body image. Health messages are often conveyed visually, through aesthetic posts (Lim et al., 2022). Users tend to associate appearance and authenticity with credibility. Like TikTok, Instagram lacks indicators of informational reliability, while it works well in shaping attitudes and behaviors through social comparison.

Users rely on different cognitive cues on each platform, making it difficult to design and implement universal interventions to counter misinformation.

3.3. Behavioural and Psychological Effects of Health Misinformation

Misinformation awareness should reduce reliance on social media (Gaysynsky et al., 2024). However, users with poor judgment often feel more confident in their judgments and continue to act on what could be false information (Zhong, 2023).

An interesting psychological phenomenon that has been studied is the third-person effect: users believe that others are more vulnerable than they are (Kirkpatrick & Lawrie, 2024). This creates a vicious cycle in which users are confident in their judgments, but believe misinformation without knowing it. Misinformation can spread easily and may contribute to harmful health behaviors, such as delaying medical care (Yousefinaghani et al., 2023) (Ghalavand & Nabiolahi, 2024). Emotionally charged storytellings increase engagement and perceived credibility (Ghalavand & Nabiolahi, 2024; Idrees, Helmy, & Khedr, 2022).

3.4. Contradictions Across Studies

While studies agree on risks of misinformation, some have some conflicting evidence:

- Some studies show that users, being aware of misinformation, are more careful about using social media for health decisions (Gaysynsky et al., 2024), while others show that often misinformation corresponds to greater sharing (Zhong, 2023).

- Engagement doesn't always indicate quality content. On YouTube, a higher engagement often corresponds with lower quality of information (Lukić and Petrović, 2023), while TikTok often shows the opposite (Kirkpatrick and Lawrie, 2024).
- Regarding the diffusion of health behavior, it is unclear if gain-framed (that highlight benefits) or loss-framed (that highlight risks) messages are more effective. Outcomes vary by behavior type (that can be prevention or detection) of the receiver (Wang et al., 2023).
- The connection between age, education, gender, and sensitivity to misinformation is unclear. Some studies find a link between higher education and discernment, while others show no correlation (Gaysynsky et al., 2024).

Most articles use the following methodologies:

- Systematic review of health-related posts or videos, scored for quality and misinformation using DISCERN or JAMA benchmarks.
- Surveys to collect user data on perceptions, trust, and behaviors about health information on social media.
- Qualitative analysis: thematic coding of participant discussions, interviews, and open questions regarding how and why platforms are used for health information.

Some studies combine methods (mixed-methods) for deeper insight. Also, statistical analysis has often been used to interpret the findings.

The synthesis of existing literature underscores a multidisciplinary effort to map the complex landscape of digital health communication, highlighting how emotional resonance and algorithmic structures often supersede factual accuracy in shaping consumer trust. While these studies provide a robust theoretical and systemic foundation, the identified gaps regarding real-time user behavior and the specific influence of visual authority necessitate further primary investigation. Consequently, an empirical study was conducted to transition from theoretical synthesis to the direct observation of how these dynamics manifest among young adults, specifically focusing on the relationship between exposure to misinformation and subsequent verification behaviors.

4. EMPIRICAL STUDY

To complement the findings from the systematic literature review, this research includes an empirical study designed to assess how real-world exposure to health misinformation influences the trust and verification behaviors of social media users. By shifting from secondary data synthesis to primary data collection, this section aims to identify specific behavioral patterns and cognitive shortcuts employed by young adults when interacting with potentially misleading health-related content.

4.1. Data Collection

Lyssna was the platform used to collect the data for this survey. The survey ran from 29/05/25 to 15/06/25. The participants were invited through a link shared by the authors. The survey targeted participants aged 18-25, recruited through the authors' network.

The objective of this survey is to evaluate how exposure to health misinformation on social media influences users' likelihood to trust and verify health information. To answer this question, it's important to understand how people interact and deal with health-related information on social media, specifically when the information might be misleading or incorrect. This survey will help identify behavioral patterns in health-related content consumption by social media users, how users form their trust, and if they check the information by searching for facts to prove its veracity.

4.2. Survey Participants and Screening

The target population consisted of users of social media platforms, aged between 18 and 25, of any gender. Sample included 49 participants, representing a 98% screen-in rate, meaning that only 2% of individuals (1 person) who attempted to take the survey didn´t pass the screening stage. The filter question for the screen stage was: "Do you use social media?" Since this individual answered "no," the survey was closed for this individual.

Of the 49 participants who answered the survey, 25 were from Portugal, 16 were from Romania, and 8 were from Italy. This results' geographic distribution that is beneficial, so the answers of the survey are not only skewed to a single country. Answers from different cultural backgrounds can give different, rich, and insightful perspectives.

4.3. Questions and Types of Tests

The test is an exploratory survey created to investigate users' trust in health content on social media to collect data on perceptions, behaviors, and criteria used to evaluate reliability.

The focus is on the subjective experience, and the cognitive choices users make when they look at posts, videos, or online health suggestions; all this is done through rating scales and multiple-choice questions.

The questionnaire was based on themes from the literature review regarding consumer trust in health content on social media.

The questionnaire explored exposure, trust levels, behaviour, and trustworthiness. Questions have been organised in sections following the thematic areas found in the literature.

Health Information Exposition and Search

The first part of the questionnaire is to understand how much users are exposed, passively or actively, to health content on social media.

- "Has the algorithm ever shown you health-related content (e.g., videos, posts, ads)" (Answers: Yes/No)
- "Have you ever searched for health information directly on social media?" (Answers: Yes/No)

These questions reflect the role and importance of the algorithm in the dissemination of health content to distinguish between automatic exposure and intentional search.

Trust in the Platform

The third question asks users to indicate which platform they consider most trustworthy for health content:

- "Which social media platform do you trust the most for health information?" (Options: YouTube, TikTok, Instagram, Twitter)

The question arises from what has emerged in the literature regarding the differences between platforms in terms of format, perception of credibility, and information quality.

Behaviors Influenced by Health Content

To understand whether users have implemented advice seen online and how they found it:

- "Have you ever tried a health method or advice you saw on social media?" (Answers: Yes/No)

If the answer is yes:

- "Did it work for you?" (Yes/No)
- "Would you trust similar content again?" (Yes/No)

These questions aim to understand how trust in health content translates into concrete actions, also considering the possible consequences of following unverified advice.

Visual Trustworthiness Assessment

The next three sections of the survey presented a visual comparison between three types of health content created by:

1. A girl with an ordinary and informal appearance.
2. A person wearing a doctor-like coat.
3. A creator with a professional tone and use of infographics.

For each image/video, the user was asked:

- "Based on just this image/video, how trustworthy does this content seem to you?" (Scale from 1 = Less trustworthy to 5 = More trustworthy)

This rating aims to understand the role and importance of visual cues, perception of authority, and professional appearance conveyed.

Credibility Signals

To analyse which cognitive signals users rely on to judge health content:

- "When you see health-related content on social media, what signals help you decide whether it's trustworthy?" (Options: expert presence, cited sources, creator's profile, tone of the video, number of likes, number of comments)

This question follows from studies that highlight the use of mental shortcuts when consuming content on social media.

Information Verification

To understand the propensity to check sources before acting, users have been asked:

- "Do you usually check other sources (Google, official websites, health professionals...) before acting on or sharing health advice you saw on social media?" (Options: yes, always/yes, sometimes/rarely/never)

This section examines whether users question health information and seek external confirmation, such as official sources, institutional websites, or opinions of qualified professionals, before following behaviors seen online or sharing health-related content. The goal is to understand users' propensity to adopt a reflective rather than an impulsive attitude.

Experiences With Misinformation

To assess whether users have ever encountered and realized that it was fake news, and how this affected their trust:

- "Have you ever found out that a piece of health information you saw on social media was false or misleading?" (Yes/No)
- "After that experience, how did it affect your trust in health content on social media?" (Options: I only trust certain sources now/I trust it less/my trust stayed the same)

These questions are used to understand how people react when they discover that health content seen on social media is false, misleading, or wrong. This is to see if their trust in social media changes, if they start to trust less, or if they become more careful about what they believe or share.

Followed Sources and Topics of Interest

Finally, the last two questions were used to collect data on the people followed and the health topics most present in the users' feeds:

- "Do you follow any medical professionals or official health organisations on social media?" (Yes/No)
- "What type of health topics do you mostly encounter on social media?" (Multiple choice: mental health, fitness, diet, illness prevention)

These questions contextualise the possible influence of the online community.

5. RESULTS

A large majority of participants (96%) have seen health-related content by algorithms in social media, and 59% have searched for health information on social media. 82% had engaged with health information that they later found out was false or misleading.

Participants indicated moderate-to-high trust in social media health content. Of the respondents, 53% indicated that they most trusted YouTube, followed by TikTok (29%) and Instagram (18%). In addition, 67% indicated that they have tried health advice that they found on social media, and of this group, 85% said that it worked, and 76% said they would be willing to trust this type of content again.

When looking at specific posts, participants shifted their trust upwards if the messages were more visually appealing or emotionally touching. For instance, participants' trust in content shifted from an average of 2.45 (of 5) to 3.43 (of 5); the prominence of visual style and emotional tone can have a considerable impact on perceived trust.

As shown in Figure 6, 65% reported always cross-checking health information with other sources (e.g., Google, official health organizations, or health professionals), but this contradicts their trust and repeated engagement with unvalidated content.

Figure 6. The frequency with which people verify the information from social media

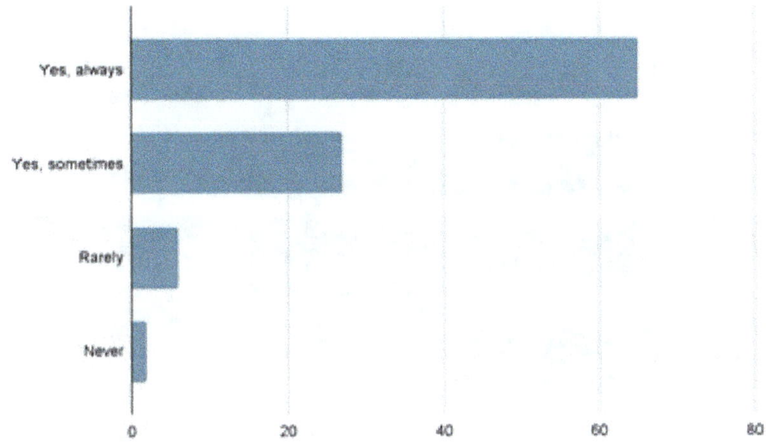

Source: Self-elaboration

The most reported trust cues included:

- Evidence of a medical expert (73%)
- Cited sources (65%)
- Creator Profile/Reputation (63%)

References to the metrics of engagement (likes or comments) in terms of some assessment were noted infrequently, suggesting audiences lean more towards perceived authority rather than popularity.

Exposure to misinformation made an impression - and over half of those who had experienced false content stated they only trust some sources (53%), whilst 33% stated they report lower levels of trust; yet, 15% claimed that their trust was unchanged, indicating a level of overconfidence in their discernible abilities.

Despite the exposure to misinformation, only 49% reported that they followed medical professionals or health-related organizations on social media. Most health content viewed had contact with mental health (71%), fitness (57%), and diet (49%), as explained in Figure7.

Figure 7. Health content categories followed by the respondents

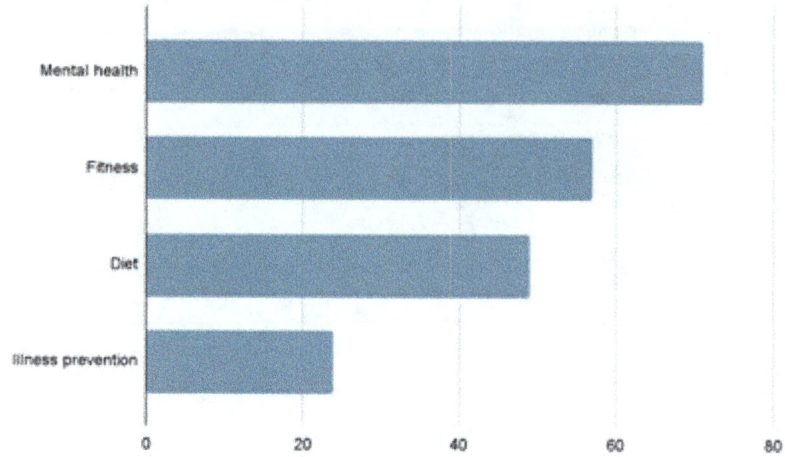

Source: Self-elaboration

6. DISCUSSION

This survey revealed a complex relationship with users of social media and how they engage and trust health-related content, even after finding out the information is false. It was shown that algorithms played a very important role in spreading health-related content, with 96% of the participants of this survey reporting that they found health-related information through social media's algorithm. Additionally, 59% of participants admitted they actively seek health-related information on social media, like YouTube, TikTok, and Instagram. This highlights social media's growing role as a source of health content.

Although 82% of participants said they engaged on social media with health-related content that they later found was misleading, a considerable number of the participants still admitted to have moderately high trust level in this content. This contradiction can make us question users' ability to critically assess health-related information and suggests that they may have developed a habit of relying on such content. Even when the information proves to be inaccurate, users may not discard these types of platforms. As Tam et al. (2022) observed, trust levels remained mostly intact for most users even after exposure to false health-related information, which could indicate a risk of habit to unreliable content. Meanwhile, Gaysynsky et al. (2024) found users tended to perceive themselves as capable of identifying misinformation, which can be determined as an overconfidence and underestimation of the risks of misinformation.

Despite having been confronted with misleading health-related information, only 49% of participants reported that they followed medical professionals or health-related organizations on social media. This means that for a significant number of people, the source of the health-related content may not be tied to the perceived credibility of the content. However, Pretorius et al. (2022) showed that when health professionals act as influencers, it can have a significant influence on the user's willingness to seek help and follow the health advice. Also, Zhong (2023) determined that fact-checking alone is not enough, because the emotional factor and the fast spread of misinformation need a more robust approach to combat it. Authority can indeed be a significant factor for increasing the users´trust on health-related content.

Even though only 15% of participants claimed their trust remained unchanged after being confronted by misleading health-related information, this small percentage should be taken into consideration because it can show a worrying indifference toward the accuracy of health-related content they consume on social media platforms.

YouTube was considered the most trusted platform by 53% of participants, consistent with the content analysis conducted by Tam et al. (2022) on YouTube and TikTok videos, which demonstrated that YouTube scored significantly higher in scientific accuracy and credibility. Additionally, Mohamed et al. (2024) found that users turn to YouTube not only for health information but also as a decision-making tool. Combined with their generally positive attitudes towards content quality on this platform, this can have significant consequences for their health" (Mohamed et al., 2024, p. 1). This shows the important role the YouTube platform plays in shaping users´trust in health-related content, in a way that can lead them to make decisions based on that information. Lim et al. (2023) emphasized that young adults strategically use different social media for different health information needs, indicating that YouTube is used for education, proving once more the YouTube capability to offer credibility to health-related information, as users tend to use this platform to educate themselves on this matter.

Another interesting result was that 67% of participants tried health advice they found on social media. Among the participants who reported positive outcomes, 76% are willing to trust such content again. This is a great outcome since it may indicate that perceived success can reinforce the user's trust in such health-related information. As Wang et al. (2023) study suggested, content framed with positive messages (of gain and good results) can increase user willingness to act on health advice.

As previously demonstrated in Ghavaland et al. (2024), subjective and superficial indicators, such as visual, perceived authority, and emotional factors, influenced the perceived trust in the health-related content. These results determine that aesthetic and emotional factors can sometimes overlap with factual accuracy in shaping user trust perceptions.

This complexity is further reflected by Yousephine et al. (2023), who found that users often rely on engagement metrics (likes, shares, comments) to evaluate the credibility of the vaccine-related content on Twitter during the COVID-19 pandemic. As supported by Bérail et al. (2022), who found that users often trust favorite YouTubers due to parasocial relationships, trusting through the emotional connection they established with that YouTuber. Similarly, Lukić et al. (2023) found that although TikTok videos about dementia were emotionally engaging, they often lacked factual accuracy, showing that emotional factors can increase the visibility and spread of misinformation.

However, aesthetics and emotional factors can influence users' trust in health-related content. The participants of the survey indicated that evidence of medical experts, cited sources, and the content creator's profile/reputation were important aspects that contribute to the credibility of the content. As Idrees et al. (2022) conclude, credibility in social networks can be affected by source, content, and community factors. Kirkpatrick et al. (2024) also determined that young women prefer and are more likely to act on health information provided by health professionals than general users on Tik Tok platform. This highlights the significant influence that the authority of the content creator can have on users' trust in the health-related content.

7. CONCLUSION

This research synthesized findings from a systematic literature review and an empirical study to evaluate how misinformation influences consumer trust in digital health content. The analysis reveals a significant disconnect between user perceptions and actual behaviors; despite frequently encountering false or misleading information, participants reported a moderate to strong trust in social media health posts. This trust is fundamentally driven by emotional resonance, creator relatability, and professional aesthetics rather than scientific accuracy. As noted by Kirkpatrick and Lawrie (2024) and De Bérail and Bungener (2022), these parasocial and emotional factors often supersede factual precision in shaping credibility assessments. Consequently, a substantial number of individuals reported acting on unverified advice without consistently confirming its veracity through reliable sources.

The empirical results further suggest a troubling extent of overconfidence or desensitization, as many participants indicated no change in their trust levels even after being exposed to misinformation. This phenomenon is compounded by limited exposure to professional content, with fewer than half of the respondents following verified medical organizations or health professionals. Such findings align with research by Lukić and Petrović (2023) and Wang et al. (2023), which highlights that non-experts frequently exert a greater influence on user engagement than credentialed authorities. Moreover, the role of platform-specific algorithms in amplifying inaccurate but engaging content, as explored by Tam, Porter, and Lee (2022), remains a critical barrier to information integrity.

Ultimately, these results underscore an urgent need for targeted media literacy campaigns and stronger collaborations between healthcare professionals and digital content creators. While moderation efforts by platforms such as TikTok, YouTube, Instagram, and Twitter are currently insufficient, systemic changes in transparency and algorithmic impact are essential to mitigate public health risks. Future research must build upon these findings by utilizing more representative samples and objective behavior-tracking techniques to observe the real-world impact of misinformation on digital health communication.

8. LIMITATIONS

Limitations of this study should be taken into consideration. The small sample size (n=49) limits the generalizability and statistical significance of the results, since it doesn't represent the population under study.

Since the survey only got answers from Portugal, Romania, and Italy, this limited geographic representation restricts the global applicability of the findings, as cultural differences may influence perceptions of health information. The recruitment method, through a shared survey link, may introduce self-selection bias, as participants might share similar traits, making the sample less representative, and it may limit the generalizability of the results.

Additionally, questions evaluating the trustworthiness of posts and videos on social media may lack context, as only the number of likes, comments, and shares was shown, but full captions were not, and the platform name was not provided. This could result in credibility judgments that differ from real-world evaluations, because the captions and the platform can influence the credibility opinion of the participant and how they assess the trustworthiness of the information.

In addition, two of the questions only provide a screenshot of the video, which may limit the participant's ability to fully evaluate the content´s credibility and full context, as the participant can't access elements such as tone of voice, audio, facial and physical expressions, and movements. These elements are important cues to determine the trustworthiness of the content.

ACKNOWLEDGEMENT

NECE, Research Centre for Business Sciences, Research Centre, and this work are funded by FCT—Fundação para a Ciência e a Tecnologia, IP, project UID/04630/2025 and DOI identifier 10.54499/UID/ 04630/2025.

REFERENCES

Bérail, P., & Bungener, C. (2022). Favorite YouTubers as a source of health information during quarantine: Viewers trust their favorite YouTubers with health information. *Social Network Analysis and Mining, 12*(1), 88. Advance online publication. DOI: 10.1007/s13278-022-00925-5 PMID: 35911482

Gaysynsky, A., Everson, N. S., Heley, K., & Chou, W.-Y. S. (2024). Perceptions of Health Misinformation on Social Media: Cross-Sectional Survey Study. *JMIR Infodemiology, 4*, e51127. DOI: 10.2196/51127 PMID: 38687591

Ghalavand, H., & Nabiolahi, A. (2024). Exploring online health information quality criteria on social media: A mixed-method approach. *BMC Health Services Research, 24*(1), 1311. Advance online publication. DOI: 10.1186/s12913-024-11838-8 PMID: 39478573

Idrees, A. M., Helmy, Y., & Khedr, A. E. (2022). Credibility aspects' perceptions of social networks: A survey. *Social Network Analysis and Mining, 12*(1), 98. Advance online publication. DOI: 10.1007/s13278-022-00924-6

Kirkpatrick, C. E., & Lawrie, L. L. (2024). TikTok as a Source of Health Information and Misinformation for Young Women in the United States: Survey Study. *JMIR Infodemiology, 4*, e54663. DOI: 10.2196/54663 PMID: 38772020

Lim, M. S. C., Molenaar, A., Brennan, L., Reid, M., & McCaffrey, T. (2022). Young adults' use of different social media platforms for health information: Insights from web-based conversations. *Journal of Medical Internet Research, 24*(1), e23656. Advance online publication. DOI: 10.2196/23656 PMID: 35040796

Lukić, S., & Petrović, J. (2023). The quality of information provided by the most popular dementia videos on TikTok. *Frontiers in Public Health, 11*, 1266415. Advance online publication. DOI: 10.3389/fpubh.2023.1266415 PMID: 38089039

Mohamed, F., & Shoufan, A. (2024). Users' experience with health-related content on YouTube: An exploratory study. *BMC Public Health, 24*(1), 86. Advance online publication. DOI: 10.1186/s12889-023-17585-5 PMID: 38172765

. Page, M. J., McKenzie, J. E., Bossuyt, P. M., Boutron, I., Hoffmann, T. C., Mulrow, C. D., ... & Moher, D. (2021). The PRISMA 2020 statement: an updated guideline for reporting systematic reviews. *bmj, 372*.

Pretorius, C., McCashin, D., & Coyle, D. (2022). Mental health professionals as influencers on TikTok and Instagram: What role do they play in mental health literacy and help-seeking? *Internet Interventions : the Application of Information Technology in Mental and Behavioural Health, 30*(100591), 100591. DOI: 10.1016/j.invent.2022.100591 PMID: 36458161

Tam, J., Porter, E. K., & Lee, U. J. (2022). Examination of Information and Misinformation about Urinary Tract Infections on TikTok and YouTube. *Urology, 168*, 35–40. Advance online publication. DOI: 10.1016/j.urology.2022.06.030 PMID: 35809700

Wang, X., Zhu, B., Guo, Q., Wang, W., & Zhao, R. (2023). Designing mindfulness information for interaction in social media: The role of information framing, health risk perception and lay theories of health. *Frontiers in Psychology, 13*, 1041016. DOI: 10.3389/fpsyg.2022.1041016 PMID: 36687971

Yousefinaghani, S., Dara, R., Wang, A., MacKay, M., Papadopoulos, A., & Sharif, S. (2023). Credibility of vaccine-related content on Twitter during the COVID-19 pandemic. *PLOS Global Public Health, 3*(7), e0001385–e0001385. DOI: 10.1371/journal.pgph.0001385 PMID: 37467276

Zhong, B. (2023). Going beyond fact-checking to fight health misinformation: A multi-level analysis of the Twitter response to health news stories. *International Journal of Information Management, 70*, 102626. DOI: 10.1016/j.ijinfomgt.2023.102626

Chapter 9
The Role of Culture in Shaping Loyalty Strategies and Customer Engagement

Sachin Pande
http://orcid.org/0009-0006-2228-4149
Christ University, Bangalore, India

Ayushi Agrawal
http://orcid.org/0009-0004-2388-8513
Christ University, Bangalore, India

ABSTRACT

This chapter examines how culture shapes the design, operation, and effectiveness of customer loyalty programs in a globalized, digitally connected marketplace. Drawing on Social Exchange Theory, Power Distance Theory, and Social Identity Theory, it proposes the 3C Framework of Consumer Cultural Context—Consumer, Culture, and Context—to explain how cultural norms, social values, consumer habits, and global influences affect rewards, engagement, brand voice, user experience, and data practices. Using examples from airlines, retail, and hospitality, the chapter highlights the need for culturally adaptive loyalty strategies and outlines implications for future research on AI, inclusivity, and evolving consumer expectations.

DOI: 10.4018/979-8-3373-7704-9.ch009

1. INTRODUCTION

In an increasingly competitive and customer-centric global marketplace, brands and consumer businesses continue to place high importance on customer loyalty, be it through providing better service, product, and brand experience, or having a loyalty program to engage with customers. While the modern loyalty programs were prominently started with the airlines, with the world witnessing the Airmiles program with Canadian airlines, the idea of actively using a loyalty or a rewards program to drive key business goals and identify with their parent brands spread across multiple sectors such as hospitality, banking (and credit cards), consumer retail, fuel, and subscription services. Many of these sectors rely heavily on data-driven engagement strategies to foster long-term customer relationships and drive sustained growth, where loyalty programs play an active role in leveraging and a channel of communication with the customers.

This chapter provides an in-depth detail of loyalty programs across the globe, it will draw examples and learnings from retail, fuel, subscription services, and similar business sectors, and majorly how cultural aspects influence the main design and operation of these programs. All the topics of the chapter will thoroughly investigate and provide an in depth interpretation about the motivational triggers and actions that vary across different loyalty programs, and the impact of local cultures' influence on such programs. Towards the end, the chapter will also explore views on how the emerging trends on sustainability and woke culture could influence the future of consumer loyalty with the brands in general and specifically in the context of a loyalty program.

We must accept that most of the loyalty programs are born out of the business need for customer engagement for long term profit growth. The goal of a loyalty program is customer retention, engagement, monetization, and relationship building. In the context of overall brand loyalty, factors such as product, customer service, and emotional engagement play an important role. Sustained efforts to maintain the quality of products, improve customer service, introduce brand extensions, and line extensions help a brand grow and sustain through the demographic transitions over generations. However, the longevity of a brand and a loyal customer base come at the cost of many failed experiments, product trials, roll back of some interesting ideas which did not meet customer expectations, and sometimes an outright failure. All those failures serve as a lesson learnt and successful brands use those opportunities to learn, adapt, and continue to grow within their core markets as well as spread their growth across multiple countries, cultures, and markets.

The now-famous case of Coca-Cola introducing the New Coke, which resulted in customer backlash because they felt the company tampered with 'their' brand (Andrivet, 2025) has become a classic case of customers' show of loyalty towards their brands as the brands attain the status of a national icon. The push back from the customers was strong enough for the company to reintroduce Coca-Cola Classic. There are many similar examples where the cultural aspects and customers' reaction to the brands have shaped the growth of the brands that have stood the test of time. Similar influences and experiences are also demonstrated in the context of consumer loyalty programs, where they play an important role in leveraging to engage the customer and provide longevity to the brand itself (Andrivet, 2025).

A loyalty program is a means to have continuous dialogue with the customer, and the rewards are the means that marketers use to engage in a dialogue with their customers. Having said that, the customer is the one who drives the narrative of a business and makes it successful, and loyalty programs are no exception. The programs run successfully only when they resonate with their members, and the parent brand that owns the loyalty program maintains a good reputation and perception with the customers (Pratesi et al., 2021). Some of the biggest loyalty programs today are run by either airline, for example, Miles and More from Lufthansa, or hospitality players like Marriott, Accor group, among others. In the retail and consumer loyalty space, standalone programs from brands like Sephora, Starbucks with its almost 34 Million member base of Starbucks Rewards® continue to stand tall (Masternak, 2025), and multi-partner retail-focused programs like PAYBACK from Germany with more than 33 Million members across Europe (PAYBACK, 2024a) and Ponta from Japan with almost 100 Million members (Loyalty Marketing Inc, 2025) continue to expand their reach across multiple geographies.

Successful brands continue to adapt themselves to meet the customer expectations and cultural aspects. As they are centered around a main product or service, the core offering of product and service needs to be fine-tuned around the localized cultural aspects, and the customer feedback, tastes, and preferences are usually taken into consideration while developing the product. However, this may not always be possible in case of products having a global appeal and their market creation becomes an important aspect for business success. On the other hand, loyalty schemes or rewards programs have several moving parts and customer interaction points. Each of these provides an experience to the customers and requires tuning around the major pillars of interaction.

Through the last decade, one of the biggest blows to the loyalty programs industry has been the folding up of many multi-partner loyalty programs across the world. Airmiles Canada filed for bankruptcy, Nectar Italy wound up, and their program in the UK shrank down to almost a single retail program, Plenti USA experiment by American Express failed, and Flybuys down under also wrapped up. Of multiple reasons that may have varied across these programs, one thing to learn and understand is that most of these programs could not keep up with the changing times and loyalty landscape and evolving expectations of customers and participating retailers. While these programs worked successfully for almost two decades and were well entrenched in the local market cultures, somewhere the finer aspects of the program, its value perception to consumers and retailers, did not meet the expectations of the changing times. Also, many retailers wanted to own the data and protect their respective turf, leading to fragmentation of the program and ultimate decline (Rehnen et al., 2017).

While mutiple studies across and research literature focus on the different factors of loyalty programs which were either successful or were failed during the process, there have been few studies which has discussed and concentrated from the aspects of cultural point of view and compliance with the social thread of the market where they operate. With this as a context, it may help and give purposeful insights in proposing and exploring the understanding of a loyalty program design for success, through a 3C Framework of Consumer Culture Context, which attempts to work for design, measurement, and course correction for loyalty programs so that they can fit into the markets well as well as it evolves with changing consumer preferences and their priorities.

1.1 OBJECTIVES

1. To analyze how cultural factors influence consumer expectations and engagement with loyalty programs across different regions and industries.
2. To study and examine various dimensions of a loyalty program design from the point of view of cultural, societal and technological influences.
3. To evaluate the effectiveness of culturally adapted loyalty programs in fostering brand loyalty, customer retention, and long-term engagement.
4. To provide actionable insights for businesses to tailor loyalty programs that align with local cultural norms while supporting global brand consistency.

1.2 PROBLEM STATEMENT

Loyalty programs are a great insight into consumer behavior and their motivation for showing brand loyalty. Discounts and gift vouchers are regularly used by brands and companies to keep consumers engaged and develop a relationship which would last a test of time. Companies invest money and time to understand the need and want of consumers so that they can deliver on that expectation and thus build a strong connection which will result in loyalty in the long run. However, in today's time, where users are connected digitally and where global stimuli are at play, and technology adaptation is quickly changing consumer dynamics, so the topic requires a revisit to understand the control levers of customer engagement. The design and communication approach of these loyalty programs needs a fresh look based on not only current world dynamics but also based on critical aspects like Culture and the evolving construct of urban culture and consumerism.

Latest technology, innovation, and declining consumer loyalty make it essential for us to revisit the previous models and identify additional frameworks that can add on the existing theories and outline a new direction for evaluation, design, and operation of such loyalty programs.

1.3 Roadmap of the chapter

This chapter is divided into seven main sections. After the introduction, Section 2 provides an in-depth explanation of the objectives, Section 3 reviews the literature of existing theories on social exchange theory and power distance theory, and Section 4 discusses the methodology applied in the chapter. Conceptual framework: A framework is presented in Section 5 to enable us to understand the underlying dynamics of the phenomenon under investigation. Section 6 talks about the discussion and implications, findings, and in the end, Section 7 concludes the chapter by discussing critical learning and future research direction.

2. LITERATURE REVIEW

2.1 Social Exchange Theory

This theory was first explained by Homans (1958) and later redefined by Blau (1964) and serves as a powerful framework for grasping the dynamics of interpersonal and organizational relationships. By emphasizing the importance of reciprocal interactions, this theory helps us know and understand how relationships are built and maintained through mutual benefit and exchange, making it essential for individuals to foster effective connections in both personal and professional contexts. Grounded in behavior psychology and economics, this theory suggests that choices made by people in a relationship are based on the basis of what they will get out of it and what it will cost them. People want to get maximum benefits with minimum cost and with least efforts possible. In this context, it helps in understanding the loyalty of a customer and how they decide to remain loyal to a brand. It is a give and take relationship, where if the brand gives customers maximum benefit in terms of value with least cost involved like time, efforts or cost of the product, Customers will be more likely to stay engaged and loyal to such companies (Cropanzano & Mitchell, 2005).

Social Exchange theory in customer engagement and loyalty - In service marketing, social exchange theory says that customers these days have less time and capacity to put in efforts, so they expect minimum efforts and high value in return to stay loyal towards a brand (Morgan & Hunt, 1994). Loyalty strategies such as personalized communication, emotional bonding with the consumer, and rewards in the form of cash or kind function as a powerful tool within the framework of social exchange theory. These strategies offer meaningful "rewards" that not only help in maintaining a deeper customer engagement but also cultivate lasting relationships. In response, customers demonstrate their loyalty through both positive attitudes and consistent behaviors, reinforcing the value of these initiatives (Palmatier et al., 2006).

Social exchange theory has drawn two major concepts which revolve around trust and commitment. When a customer feels that brand is trustworthy and they start believing that company will deliver what it promises and will take care of the customers' belief and will treat them fairly, this connection of trust helps in building loyalty towards the brand (Garbarino & Johnson, 1999). These trust and commitment constructs are highly relevant in highly involved services or when one is purchasing from a luxury brand, where the emotional and symbolic value of the exchange is particularly significant.

Social exchange theory and the evolution of loyalty programs -

In many areas such as airlines, hospitality, subscription services the concept of loyalty programs has evolved over time. Let us look at it from the lens of social exchange theory which offers the idea of give and take relationship, and it will help in better understanding of why these programs work and how it will work in the best possible way.

From the company's point of view Basically it gives the understanding from that if you as a customer stick with us and be loyal to our brand then we will reward you. Through loyalty programs company gives a customer reward in the form of discounts, points, or perks, this how customer also feels valued, and they are more likely to stay loyal towards the brand.

Loyalty programs have moved beyond points and discounts and now focus on offering rewards which feels more personal and meaningful to the users. Customers tend to feel more connected or rather invested in the company with this approach and thus stick around for longer. Users have evolved today beyond saving money through discounts and reward system, recognition, personalization, and products which resonate with their lifestyle and beliefs are much more in demand. Shift in this lookout highlights the underlying baseline that loyalty programs are built on trust, commitment, and a sense of belonging. These create a air tight bond between customers and brands.

2.2 Power Distance Theory

Power Distance as a concept was introduced by social psychologist Geert Hofstede in his book "Culture's Consequences" (1980) were he talks about how people promote and accept the unequal power in society and companies. With respect to loyalty programs, the concept of power distance plays a critical role in understanding how it impacts the way consumers perceive fairness and exclusivity. If a company understands these dynamics, it will help the organization in maintaining deeper and long-term connections with its customers. Tiered loyalty programs, like exclusive membership programs or premium customer segments, tend to be more effective. They support social hierarchies and provide status-driven incentives that fit cultural norms. In cultures with low power distance, customers prefer programs that are inclusive. They seek equal access and want transparency in how benefits are shared. This preference shows their desire for fairness and equal treatment. Therefore, it is important for companies to focus on their offerings within the system.

2.3 Social Identity theory and Cultural context

People who are from different nations and believe in different cultures and traditions like different kinds of loyalty programs. For instance, Thomson (2015), talks about culture where people prioritize groups over an individual and where authority is respected. There such cultured people prefer loyalty programs which is beneficial for the entire society, rather than their own benefits. Additionally, using the Howard cultural model (Bourdeau et al., 2024) it has been understood that there are people who do not like uncertainty they prefer to have clear and guaranteed rewards system in the loyalty program. Also on the other hand, people from the individualistic culture where they focus on themselves like to have programs where they can choose their own rewards.

As per Johri et al. (2024) marketing effectiveness hinges on cultural adaptability. Their review of two decades of marketing research outlines how firms navigating cultural complexity—such as language, rituals, and identity politics—build stronger brand relationships. Also, the dimensions like masculinity and collectivism affect product evaluations and emotional appeal, especially in entertainment and lifestyle sectors (Song et al., 2017).

To add to this, one should consider the theory of social identity defined by Tajfel (1978), which mentions the idea of value and emotional significance attached to a membership. Brands and, in turn, Loyalty Programs take advantage of this approach to create perceived value and thrive on emotional weight, driving the consumer engagement, be it through reward or fear of missing out. In this context, the cultural aspects coupled with emotional aspects of scarcity, urgency, and loyalty become important to drive customer engagement on a sustained basis. While the emotional aspects may act as a trigger for action, cultural aspects have the power to bring familiarity, acceptance, and quick adaptation to the promises offered by the loyalty programs, thus making the brand affinity stronger, driving towards advocacy.

2.4 Other research

In the recent years, with technology evolving and becoming an integral part of customer engagement and influencer of loyalty, some studies have also attempted to define new benchmarks and measurement approaches for loyalty. The four phased loyalty measurement approach based on cognitive, affective, conative and action originally proposed by Oliver (1999) is taken forward where the study demonstrates that the loyalty is best operationalized through these four discriminate phases (Bourdeau et al., 2024).

Study carried out by Ruvio et al. (2025) further deepens the psychological grounding of loyalty by showing how rewards that "connect to the self" enhance engagement and loyalty via self-concept and self-connection mechanisms. The authors contrast experiential rewards with purely material gifts and incentives and find that the former strengthen the connect with the brands and emotional investment, leading to higher engagement and loyalty. This contribution is especially relevant for loyalty-program and gamified-engagement design (Ruvio et al., 2025).

Covering the physiological aspects in retail loyalty, the study by Liu-Thompkins et al. (2022) focuses on thinking, feeling and social aspects driving customer loyalty. Within the context of retail loyalty, the study documents the dynamic shift that has happened over decades and have changed the relative importance of different drivers; for example, affective experience and personalization gains prominence as shopping becomes more hedonic and digitally mediated (Liu-Thompkins et al., 2022).

However, as noticed that there is still a missing common framework to address loyalty design considering multiple socio-cultural aspects that also include the current trends and technology. Through this chapter, we will see how cultural factors influence the design, operation, and effectiveness of loyalty programs across different regions and industries, and how these culturally informed approaches contribute to market readiness, building brand loyalty, and enhancing customer engagement.

3 RESEARCH APPROACH

This chapter adopts a conceptual research design to examine the role of culture in shaping loyalty strategies and customer engagement. Unlike empirical studies that rely on primary data collected through surveys or interviews, a conceptual approach synthesizes existing scholarly work, theories, and real-life evidence to build a structured understanding of an emerging phenomenon. The decision to employ a conceptual design stems from the recognition that research on strategies for loyalty programs across cultures. Empirical data remains limited, fragmented across industries, and often focused on specific applications rather than integrated frameworks. Therefore, concept and theory building based on existing scholarly contributions and industry practices provides a stronger foundation for advancing knowledge in this domain and potentially provides a proposed conceptual framework on which further research can be carried out. This chapter creates a synthesized explanation by connecting different theoretical points of view and secondary literature and provides a deep insight that contributes to the development of the academic and managerial implications.

The data sources used in this synthesis were well selected to be both of quality and relevance. The sources, based on peer-reviewed articles and conference papers indexed at Scopus and Web of Science, continue to be the most authoritative sites of academic research, and the review heavily refers to them. Additionally, this chapter generously draws its references from industry practices. Employing focused search strings around the central ideas of culture, consumer, and context, and their role in developing strategies for loyalty programs.

The process utilized a rigorous systematic literature review methodology. Initially, we examined the chosen sources to uncover key themes that emerged. Notably, we highlighted the critical role of trust in fostering strong consumer-brand relationships, the fragility of decentralized service delivery, and the substantial reputational risks that ethical controversies can impose on the sharing economy. These insights underscore the necessity for brands to navigate these challenges thoughtfully and strategically.

4. CONTRIBUTION TO THE STUDY

While the individual aspects of loyalty will continue to be studied in detail, a high level framework once defined can potentially provide a direction and help converge the various elements into one operational rule set that can be used by business managers to define their loyalty program design and strategy keeping cultural context in perspective. With that intent, a 3C Framework is proposed that can attempt to cover the multiple aspects of customer loyalty into a single framework.

The proposed 3C Framework of Consumer Cultural Context takes a consumer-centric approach in the design and evaluation of a loyalty program. Sitting in the center, the first layer of the framework addresses the various key aspects of a loyalty program through which a consumer experiences a loyalty program either physically or emotionally.

Rewards and incentives are the backbone of any loyalty program, and the perceived value attached to them makes the program lucrative for consumers to embrace. This forms one of the key motivations for the members to join the program.

Alongside, the brand voice sets the tone of the appeal, which is supposed to trigger the emotional motivators for the consumers to augment their decision to use the program. Continuous engagement through promotional offers, gamification, and communication keeps the engagement going, delivering long-term Customer Lifetime Value. The communication and offers to drive engagement thrive on the cultural aspects and become an important part of the first layer i.e., the program interaction layer.

Lastly, the user interface and user flow journey to attain the rewards make the interaction layer complete. The touchpoints ensure that the loyalty program delivers the desired experience to the members within their natural habits of shopping interaction. Any shift in that behavior usually requires significant rewards and benefits, as we see with the Social Exchange Theory. In the proposed framework, the interaction layer sits in the middle between the consumer and the cultural aspects.

The framework suggests that the cultural aspects are an external influence to the interaction of a consumer with a loyalty program. While some may argue that cultural aspects are an ingredient to how a consumer behaves with a brand or a loyalty program, it becomes imperative to isolate these aspects to break them down into relevant, attainable pieces that can be addressed systematically while designing a loyalty program. The external layer of Cultural Aspects addresses the Cultural Norms, Consumer habits, Social Values and Global Influences. It must be recognized that the post-millennium world is digitally connected, consumers are travelling around the world, and the modern urban culture and consumer habits are getting affected by global influences. Hence, it becomes important to understand and address the impact of each of these aspects on the loyalty program pillars that can shape and reshape the design and progress of a loyalty program.

A loyalty program typically has multiple moving parts to it. It becomes important for a marketer to understand how each of these parts works together to make a successful loyalty program and build a successful brand in turn. This Framework helps define those empirical pieces and proposes a relationship between them to make the program meaningful to the consumers. This model can be effectively used by businesses as a blueprint to ask the right questions and design their loyalty and customer engagement programs.

While it may not be feasible to learn and understand all the cultural aspects of a market immediately, especially in scenarios where the brands are entering the market afresh and do not have a history of operating there, the framework can also serve as a measurement guardrail to evaluate the program regularly and make any course corrections over time.

Figure 1. 3C framework of consumer, culture, context

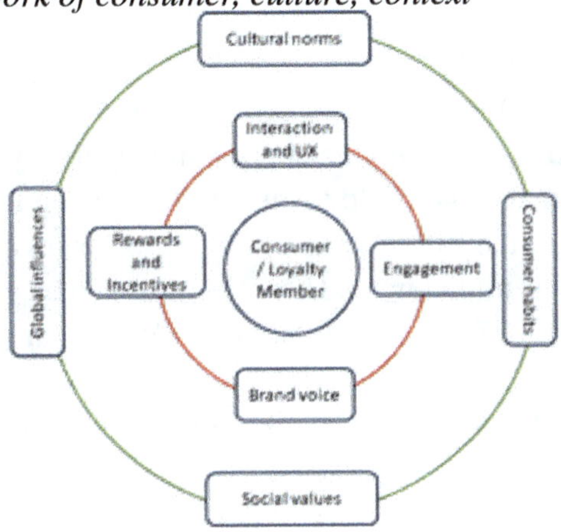

Table 1. Key terms used in the model

Cultural Norms	The prevalent expectations, traditions, and behavioral rules within a society which carry collective emotional value and also act as a guardrail for social behavior of consumers and brands alike.
Consumer Habits	The typical patterns in which consumers interact with a brand or behave in a shopping environment. These include technology adaption, digital habits, shopping habits and willingness to share data and personal information.
Social Values	The collective principles and value systems prevalent in a society or a target market that are considered important by the consumers and consumers use these to evaluate aspects like fairness, transparency and respect for society within a brand.
Global influences	The cross-border transfer of trends, consumer behaviors and expectations, driven by digital connections, knowledge sharing and exposure to foreign cultures, events and news.
Interaction and UX	Interaction of loyalty members with various touch points offered for the usage of loyalty program features - mobile apps, websites, retail counters, or customer service. UX being the experience that a member experiences while interacting with the loyalty program
Engagement	The intensity of a customer's interaction and transaction with a loyalty program and their responsiveness to campaigns and offers demonstrated through active participation.
Brand Voice	The tone and style of a brand and that of a loyalty program communication.
Rewards and incentives	The tangible and intangible benefits offered by a loyalty program as points, discounts, coupons and others. Rewards being the benefits that members can get against those points.

5. ANALYSIS AND DISCUSSION

Let us navigate through the aspects of a loyalty program using the Consumer Culture Context Framework (3C Framework) as shown in Figure 1.

1. Rewards and Incentives

Rewards and Incentives make up the core of any loyalty system and are the reason for customers to engage and build loyalty. Going beyond the product benefits, a loyalty scheme adds value in terms of points, rewards, discounts, and offers to incentivize customers. Let us understand how Rewards and Incentives are influenced through Cultural norms, Consumer Habits, Social Values, and Global Influences.

a. Cultural Norms and Social Values can significantly influence Rewards and Incentives.

Points remain the most common currency of incentive when it comes to transaction-based incentives. The point systems have been actively used through the early 2000s; however, the incentive schemes have a deeper connection to stamps. Traders floated stamps that the customers needed to collect through repeated shopping to get a meaningful reward upon achieving a certain collection milestone.

Loyalty incentive schemes promote deferred gratification as against the instant gratification offered by the discount schemes. To that extent, the rewards come because of the collection of smaller incentives over time. This sets the context for the customers that they must wait and 'show' some loyalty to the brand before they can get the final reward. Nevertheless, point systems work as a meter where customers can track, calculate, and see their journey towards their reward. With points, they can measure their progress in relative terms, based on the goal they may have set for themselves (Nastasoiu & Vandenbosch, 2019).

There are various incentive models and currencies that work across multiple markets. Within one market, multiple currencies can exist and thrive, either specific to an industry or cutting across the categories. Typically, airlines have traditionally worked with 'miles' as the currency, whereas retail has used points and low-frequency high-touch industries like cafes prefer to use stamps. Companies like Starbucks have Starbucks Rewards®, and Germany's PAYBACK program uses points as the currency. However, over time, many of these leading loyalty schemes expanded into multiple domains; however, they have maintained the original incentive currency.

When the airlines diversified their rewards systems of collection of miles across other hospitality sectors and even further to include telecom and retail, miles have remained their currency of choice. Originally, Canada Airmiles was offering Airmiles on travel, but as they added multiple shopping segments into their incentive program to expand the coverage, miles remained their currency throughout. On the other hand, when customers of PAYBACK shop at multiple businesses, including hospitality, insurance,and more, they continue to earn PAYBACK points.

Similarly, miles, points, stamps, badges, stars, or anything that measures as an incentive can be used by loyalty schemes. Points, miles, tickets, stamps, freebies, priority access, special gold card, all these incentives make a statement, either public or personal. Many cultures accommodate customers showing off their status in public, and card tiers have become synonymous with status symbols. Cultures celebrating status upgrades generally see the companies using high loyalty program tiers as a tool to provide privileges to their good customers. In markets where society and culture have high power distance, Thompson and Chmura (2015) the approach of privilege and authority is used to drive high customer engagement and loyalty. Incentives in the form of points and miles remain the standard currency of engagement, but status tools build advocacy and can engage with aspiring customers who wish to move up the value chain.

Similarly, the use of points or stamps to redeem for rewards, benefits, and further discounts is driven by market trends, financial benefits to the company, and usually needs to cover everything from attainable to aspirational rewards and beyond. Concepts like 'Rewards Money Can't Buy' are experiences that can never be purchased directly with money, and companies leverage this to build experiences that go beyond the monetary value of points. However, sometimes offers like this can also work against the parent brand. A widely known case of Pepsi promising a fighter jet was demanded by a customer. This case became famous when Pepsi denied the offer to the customer, the court ruled in favor of Pepsi, but the brand faced severe backlash in the media (Leonard v pepsico,1999). Transparency and integrity are important ingredients that define the social values of a market and become an important part of the culture of a market.

In most cultures worldwide, greed is considered not an acceptable social trait and usually scoffed at, yet loyalty schemes promote greed with a focus on aspirational rewards and indulgence experiences which otherwise the customers would otherwise never purchase directly or may not necessarily need. A free visit to a spa or a hot air balloon ride is a thing which showcases aspirations and indulgences, encouraging customers to engage with the brand.

Some cultures are more open to collection, and consumers are not hesitant to ask for points collection, swipe loyalty cards, cut and redeem coupons, and stamps. While some societies accept the culture of collecting rewards as a normal process, and customers do not feel awkward asking for the points, collecting and redeeming coupons, or asking for discounts. On the other hand, many societies do not look very positively towards the act of collecting incentives openly and are compared to a bargaining attitude, which is sometimes frowned upon, and the customers are rather discreet in collecting incentives and not flashing their loyalty memberships.

While promoting the incentive schemes, companies look at how they promote the incentive collection and what mechanism they choose. For the emerging generation of young customers, gamification around incentive collection and rewards has shown positive effects and engages the customers better with the brands through gamification (Högberg et al., 2019). It becomes imperative to look at Gamification to drive loyalty, leveraging the digital gaming culture of Gen Z, where customers can engage through online and mobile gaming. To top it all, virtual worlds like Metaverse can potentially pose the next big opportunity to engage customers and drive loyalty program participation for the digital natives. Loyalty programs intrinsically designed around the digital and mobile ecosystem and increasingly embracing gamification and virtual, immersive environments can thrive in the future.

Engagement

Customer engagement, driven actively by push communication through emails, social media, and mainline advertising, is increasingly shaped by cultural context. Social Identity theory explains how cultural products drive emotional and cognitive engagement within online communities. Their findings suggest that individuals engage more deeply with brands that resonate with their shared cultural background or values, implying the necessity of cultural relevance in marketing communications. Cultural identification fosters stronger community interactions and increased engagement around cultural products (Zhang & Li, 2022).

Cultural drivers of loyalty engagement can be deeply rooted in collective beliefs, religion, history, and social fabric. Let us take an example of Europe's loyalty program PAYBACK. As they have operated in the markets like India back in 2019 and simultaneously in Germany, Mexico, Poland and Italy, the promotional activities of the programs were respectively aligned with the local festivals of the country, especially in the markets like Germany, India, and Mexico. The Easter Egg campaign promoted by PAYBACK in Germany may not have made sense in India, where most of the customer promotions are planned around the biggest Hindu festivals of Diwali (PAYBACK, 2024b). Aligning the promotional offers and campaigns around a local festive calendar is a widely accepted approach for brands all over, and designing engagement calendars of a loyalty program around the same is no different. This adaptation of culture is no longer desirable but is essential to gain high acceptance among the loyalty program members as they embrace the program as their own and move towards program advocacy. When in the US, events like Fourth of July Weekend and Thanksgiving become an important part of local culture, even if some of these may not be rooted in religion but in historical milestone events or a wide, socially accepted behavior.

Every time a brand or a loyalty scheme enters are new market or needs a re-think on their existing program, it becomes imperative to see whether their efforts are aligned with the local cultural norms, festivals, and societal activities. Events like Independence Day, socio-political, and historical events become a part of the local culture and need to be respected and taken into consideration while designing an engagement plan or promotional calendar. Leveraging these events makes the loyalty program engagement model fit seamlessly into the flow of the target market and its customers and can smooth the acceptance within its target audience. Even locally sensitive opportunities like community support and service can also transform into an act of showing loyalty, and companies like American Express customers benefit from their Small Business Saturday program, where customers can earn loyalty rewards and additional benefits while building an emotional connection with the community (Napoletano, 2024). Supporting the local community helps in building brand trust and is fast-growing as a strong urban subculture in many parts of the world (Habibi et al., 2014).

On the other hand, Global influences also shape the strategy for a program. Taking the Christmas festival as an example, many countries do not particularly have Christmas as their big religious event, yet the markets have adopted Christmas and Santa Claus to engage customers and drive shopping and turned these festive seasons into marketing and shopping events. The last quarter of the year usually provides an ideal time for holidays in a globally connected world where multinational corporations have holidays, consumers tend to plan celebrations, and the overall mood during the month of December is that of shopping, celebrating, and indulging with friends and families.

The retailers worldwide have driven this from the front, leveraging on the global influences catalyzed by the information flow over the internet and social media. Businesses are actively using the marketing opportunities offered by a digitally connected world to further their business growth. Actively using global influences to promote and market their products, brands and loyalty programs have become common nowadays. Loyalty schemes are embracing these events as marketing opportunities and integrating them into their calendars and driving promotional activity. Event properties like Black Friday sales and Cyber Mondays have been actively adopted and promoted by the loyalty programs like PAYBACK in India and Europe, which traditionally did not have any context or background for such events previously. Similarly, Singles' Day, an event property made popular by Alibaba in China around Nov 11 (a play on the number 11.11) has gained traction among other markets as well. These global influences are shaping consumer communication, engagement, and loyalty.

Loyalty programs like PAYBACK have actively embraced this approach and made it a part of their promotional calendar. Being a multi-partner loyalty program, they can leverage such opportunities to drive engagement with their online and e-commerce partners on the network without diluting the core partner network of retail and fuel (PAYBACK, 2024a)

Impact of the rising Woke Culture and inclusivity on loyalty engagement

The rising woke culture around the globe is influencing the urban cultural narrative. While it is yet to be seen whether this is just a transitionary phase in the cultural evolution or it will stay long enough to get intertwined into the fabric of the society. Nevertheless, for organization, brands, and loyalty programs, it is important to adopt their approach towards employees and consumers considering the 'voice of the new consumer'. As Gen Z and Gen Alpha move into the marketplace as new set of consumers, the influences of Woke culture could remain pronounced for a while. The brands will have to ensure that while actively communicating with their consumers, they must be careful in aligning with the topics that consumers are sensitive towards. For loyalty schemes which actively take advantage of consumers life stage and lifestyle data and to drive to create targeted personalized offers and promotions, the aspects of gender neutrality, and communication design colored with gender specific tones poses a direct challenge. The loyalty programs must now re-think how their incentive and reward strategies and their positioning, needs to be tweaked to accommodate the nuances of woke culture. Sometimes, such choices presented without careful consideration of multiple points of view can result in loss of customer trust. Loyalty programs are not untouched with these trends either. Active engagement of customers is one the primary role of a loyalty program and this requires appropriate positioning of the loyalty program to augment the brand equity. Accommodating new dimensions in customer segmentation added by woke culture puts forth a challenge towards the loyalty programs to revisit their strategic approach. In addition, the communication and choices loyalty programs make to position themselves can have its own side effects. The broader society in many markets have not yet accepted the concepts of diversity and inclusivity completely, and creates pockets of customer who distance themselves from these loyalty programs and brands because they see these initiatives are breaking into the social values and cultural 'purity'. In June 2023, the popular retail chain, Target Corporation in the USA included LGBTQ- themed merchandise and as a result faced criticism from conservative groups. Target and partial withdrawal of some Pride items then drew backlash from LGBTQ+ advocates. The brand experienced a direct hit to sales, declining 5.4% in that quarter—their first sales drop in years. Previously too in 2016,

Target faced criticism when they introduced bathroom policy to include transgenders. As a result, company committed themselves to spend around USD 20M to expand their bathroom options in the retail stores. This shows how a relatively new cultural shift taken up by brands can spark consumer and media challenges from both sides (Factora, 2023). There are many such examples with the rising narrative of inclusivity and diversity where the brands have been not able to take a clear position. Of many previous examples, one brand which stood out rather unique and was able to thrive with the positioning on inclusivity was Benetton, with its campaign 'United Colors of Benetton'. But such examples are few and the practice is yet to become mainstream. While designing a loyalty programs, brands and loyalty programs must take measured steps in defining their position within the context of evolving social norms not just in word, but also how they handle their data design at the back end, their customer segmentation methods and personalization strategies. Running pilots to test and include diverse viewpoints might help in rolling out scenarios that have broader acceptance in the market. Simple steps like allowing members to not disclose their gender or offering gender neutrality in the enrolment process or capturing customer preferences on the type of communication they would prefer to receive based on their gender choices can go a long way in building customer trust and earn respect. Despite all this, there may be risk of losing out some customers in the process and loyalty programs and their parent brands may have to make those hard choices at some point (Factora, 2023).

Social and consumer habits also play an important role in defining such promotional calendars for loyalty engagement. There are other aspects of loyalty program engagement communication where members can be sensitive towards certain communications based on local customs. Sending birthday wishes to a loyalty program member in India a week in advance with a promotional coupon may be completely acceptable, whereas in Germany, advance birthday greetings are a strict no-no and considered inauspicious! A finer understanding of such cultural nuances makes a significant difference in building trust and acceptance and is essential to designing the loyalty engagement plan and executing it well within the guardrails of a culture (Nittis, 2025).

Interaction and UX

Consumer habits and, more importantly, digital habits, define the choice of interaction touch points, devices, and user journey in a loyalty program in today's context.

The most prominent influence we have witnessed in the last decade is mobile phone usage and its effect on every aspect of business and consumer interaction.

Mobile adoption has become a key consumer habit that influences how markets and loyalty ecosystems get shaped up. Markets like China and Indonesia saw most of their customers actively using mobile apps through the second decade of this millennium, between 2010-2020. Many companies moved their user experience to mobile and encouraged their loyal customers to adapt to mobile. The companies provide special incentives, coupons, and access for those using the mobile. The customer habits of using the apps, scanning the coupons, and collecting incentives is driving the success of these small programs. This resulted in widespread proliferation of individual store-level loyalty programs where customers would collect incentives digitally and redeem them. The extensive use of smartphones and evolving technology has built a strong consumer habit around smartphone usage, thus defining the mobile-first strategy for companies and loyalty schemes. Features like scan-and-go, tap-and-go became table stakes and are no longer considered innovative. Consumer habits around mobile usage have driven many brands to go beyond mobile-first and adopt a mobile-only strategy for their loyalty programs. Hilton Honors, the loyalty program of Hilton Hotels, provides a classic example of how mobile has been integrated into the customer journey of a loyalty member. Customers using the Hilton Honors mobile app can use the app not just for room bookings and earning rewards, but they can also use the app as a key to access their hotel room. (Hilton, 2025). Such loyalty experiences enhance the customer experience and are seen as building respect for the brand.

Loyalty programs like My Starbucks Rewards® have smartly evolved from a simple punch card in the early 2000s to a My Starbucks Rewards Card through 2016, and eventually into a mobile-based five-Star rewards system, setting a good example of how a successful loyalty program adapts itself to the changing consumer habits and social attitude (Masternak, 2025). Today, ordering a coffee using a mobile app is not just about convenience, but it reflects a certain urban attitude that few brands can come close to. This keeps the brand relevant among the millennials and Gen Z as it continues to grow its loyalty member base (Wassel, 2024).

Extensive and regular use of QR codes, AR features, one-time SMS passwords (OTP), and e-Stamps or digital stamps in the mobile app have become common features and are shaping how loyalty schemes evolve their interaction with customers while collecting incentives.

On the other side, brands like Nike smartly use LINE in Japan, WeChat in China, and WhatsApp in other markets for loyalty engagement with its customers.

In many countries, like India, mobile numbers have become the loyalty program identifier or loyalty number. It is common for customers in India to share their mobile numbers at the check-out for the collection or redemption of rewards. Consumer habits have organically grown from sharing mobile numbers and have become a market standard across retailers, both offline and online. Online platforms and loyalty apps have also adopted mobile number as the loyalty identifier and use double authentication with a One Time Password to verify the customers and provide access to the rewards program. This has also resulted in ease of use for the customers and reduced entry friction into a loyalty program. The need to fill out detailed forms and authenticate customers has been removed and so has the need for customers to remember their passwords. Further, it limits the risks of data breach because the OTP systems work in real-time and do not require customers to remember or store their passwords (Foroudi et al., 2018).

Brand Voice

The brand voice of a loyalty program can be warm, or have dry humor, or scarcity and fear, depending on which market it operates or sometimes simply around a promotion. Like the purpose of a brand communication is to trigger an emotion towards the brand, resulting in purchase, so is the case with a loyalty program.

On the other hand, loyalty programs also need to be avoided or handled carefully while designing the user experience and design in the context of cultural aspects. In many countries or cultures, the use of certain colors triggers a certain historical memory in society, which is better avoided. Be it a red color in Mexico, or any tangential reference to nazi rule in Germany, or a seemingly benign communication that violates a social norm, the brands and their loyalty programs must stay away from such mishaps. While designing a loyalty program, it becomes crucial to decide the role that the loyalty program will play vis-à-vis the brand itself. Whether it stands apart from the parent brand and carries its own identity or should augment the overall brand experience is the choice the loyalty operator must make.

The loyalty program can have its own brand voice, which can be community-led and not be seen as another extension of the brand itself. Also, the loyalty program can position itself as a means to enrich the customer experience with the parent brand. Airlines prominently use the loyalty program to deliver better brand and service experience. Use of tiered programs creates a differentiated brand experience for the loyalty customers. Exploring the concepts of power distance theory, the tiered loyalty program amplifies the differentiated customer experience and attaches more value to the premium services. This cultural aspect feeds into creating layers among the consumers and treats them differently. It's a choice that a brand needs to make based on the society in which it delivers the loyalty experience (Wang et al., 2022).

While an indulgence and positioning breaking the tradition may work well for a loyalty program in the US, a market like Japan, in contrast, requires the principles of hospitality, harmony, respect, and attention to detail to be followed to gain customer trust and respect. Japanese culture of group harmony promotes collective well-being over individual desires and the positioning of businesses, and with loyalty programs being seen as community engagement programs, cannot help but stay in line with a similar thought.

Data and Privacy

Over the past two decades, consumer awareness about data privacy and protection has gone through a complete transformation. Loyalty programs have always remained a strong channel to collect customer data for the purpose of analysis, personalization of communication, as well as monetization with the secondary stakeholders of a business. For example, a retailer uses the shopping data of its loyalty program members to plan assortments in the stores and monetizes the information with the FMCG companies to stock the relevant products.

Culture and social values shape data privacy by defining what is considered sensitive information and ultimately shape the loyalty program around data collection and processing policies. Certain individualistic cultures prioritize individual control over personal data, while cultures with a collectivist attitude go for transparency for group benefit, leading to diverse approaches to data collection, consent mechanisms, and the willingness to share personal information as a trade-off against loyalty program benefits. A loyalty program is meant to collect significant data on customers' personal details as well as their shopping habits and product preferences. Hence, the collection and handling of data becomes an essential topic to address within the context of a loyalty program. The way societies define their private spaces of individuals and co-exist among themselves can define their attitude towards data privacy.

The data policies of a loyalty program are shaped by considering the cultural aspects of a market. The value associated with personal information defines the level of sensitivity the customers will have towards a loyalty program and customers' willingness to share the data. Cultures with high power distance can see customers' willingness to share data with the government authorities as compared to cultures with low power distance demand better transparency and are usually unwilling to openly share the data or marketing consents. (Directory, 2025).

Countries like Chile and Portugal show us that customers can earn loyalty benefits while shopping by quoting their tax identification number. Rather unusual and sometimes a strict no-no in many countries, these markets demonstrate that there are cultural contrasts that exist across the markets when it comes to data privacy.

Consumer habits and how consumer rights are defined in a market is the key pillar that seems to drive the data and privacy habits of the customers and their active protection of their personal information. With the introduction of GDPR and the global shift toward enhanced consumer data protection has started taking shape. However, the value customers associate with their own information in exchange for loyalty benefits continues to be different for each market with some experiments clearly proving that customers are willing to part with personal information in exchange for added benefits. (Beresford et al., 2012). So, using loyalty programs to collect deeper consumer information can remain a key objective for marketers and fits well into most cultures around.

While there may be many aspects of culture affecting the data privacy issues, the primary drivers of data protection remain anchored around the individualistic vs. collectivist society model with one being more open to sharing data compared to the other (Krasnova et al., 2012).

Loyalty programs can build trust and have a lasting positive impact on the brands they represent once they understand the value attached by their customers to their data. Going beyond data storage and protection, the concept of data protection lies in the collection of only relevant data, providing transparency in communication around data handling and the self-worth that the customer associates to their own data.

6. CONCLUSION AND FUTURE RESEARCH

This Chapter looks at how culture in various countries influence the way loyalty programs work. In today's digital world, competition is stronger than ever, and brands often scrap to keep the customers coming back. Staying loyal to a brand has become a critical deal and loyalty programs are one of the most important ways to ensure long-term relationships and support business growth and longevity. In this chapter, we also talked about the 3C framework – Consumer, Culture and Context – which helps us understand how things like people's values, habits, traditions and even global trends impact how loyalty programs are designed, how they are run, and how fruitful they are.

We have observed that successful loyalty programs are not just loyalty tools. These programs serve as a major way to maintain relationships. Loyalty programs are helpful when they meet the requirements and expectations of customers. The parent brand that owns the loyalty program must have a good reputation and positive perception among customers.

FUTURE RESEARCH

Future research can dive deeper into the impact of woke culture on brands and loyalty programs. With corporations embracing diversity and inclusivity at the employee level and widely promoting it into their corporate brand positioning, it will be important to understand two parts of the future journey of the brands. The first part will talk about how the brands shape and maintain their positioning within the value system like diversity, gender equality and inclusivity. Also, the question arises here is are the new startups or MNCs who have adopted such change found it successful or not? Secondly, employees who come from different parts of the world and who have different cultural backgrounds are being comfortable being themselves at work? - how does this change the way a company grows and how its brand is seen? In future research it will be an important aspect to know whether it will make any difference in decision making, resigning or rebranding, and overall future growth of the company. Also, in future researchers can explore the role of AI in shaping different loyalty programs and will how AI will create an impact in understanding the different cultural preferences and behavior. One of the major future directions will be Empirical validation. Future studies should test the proposed model through surveys, experiments, or panel data. Also, longitudinal study can be done with the proposed framework as it will help in understanding how customer taste preference changes over time and thus, loyalty program can evolve accordingly. With the rise of generative AI, future work should explore its potential for personalization, customer interaction, and content creation with respect to different loyalty programs. At the same time, ethical governance frameworks must be developed to address issues of bias, transparency, and accountability. Such research would expand the framework to reflect the next generation of intelligent systems.

LIMITATIONS

This chapter has attempted to maintain its course of analysis, reflection and comparison using the cultural aspects defined using the proposed 3C model of Consumer Culture Context. At the same time, the past research and literature available does not conclusively point towards any elaborate or established framework that guides the design of loyalty programs using any cultural context. Hence, the chapter is only able to address the aspects of a loyalty program design within the scope of available past research, experience of the authors having set up and run successful loyalty programs and opinions drawn from the research, which are limited. On the other hand, since the chapter addresses the loyalty program approach through the proposed model, it may sometimes not be able to address any tangential aspect or emerging market phenomena due to the fitment limitations within the model envisaged. Also, the chapter has not been able to fully address the impact of technology or the emerging cultural narratives like inclusivity and diversity. These aspects have been therefore kept as topics of future research and exploration. Lastly, since there has been no primary research or data included in this chapter, the information is primarily based on the available information, research and the chapter draws heavily on the theories and practices already implemented in the market either by academia or the industry. While the industry practices appear strategic, they do not provide any inside evaluation on the success of these cultural adaptations within the companies. For example, the authors of the chapter cannot directly provide any insider insights on how far the practices of using Black Friday or Singles Day promotional events benefited the PAYBACK loyalty program. These areas will remain unaddressed unless there are direct data and evidence to support the success of such practices. The authors currently proceed with the assumption that while the industry is consistently implementing several such cultural adaptation practices into their marketing mix, these must be adding to the overall positive benefits to a business eventually.

REFERENCES

Andrivet, M. (2025, February 10). New coke: A classic branding case study on a major product change failure. *The Branding Journal*. https://www.thebrandingjournal.com/2025/02/new-coke/

Beresford, A. R., Kübler, D., & Preibusch, S. (2012). Unwillingness to pay for privacy: A field experiment. *Economics Letters*, *117*(1), 25–27. DOI: 10.1016/j.econlet.2012.04.077

Blau, P. M. (1964). Justice in social exchange. *Sociological Inquiry*, *34*(2), 193–206. DOI: 10.1111/j.1475-682X.1964.tb00583.x

Bourdeau, B. L., Cronin, J. J., & Voorhees, C. M. (2024). Customer loyalty: A refined conceptualization, measurement, and model. *Journal of Retailing and Consumer Services*, *81*, 104020. DOI: 10.1016/j.jretconser.2024.104020

Cropanzano, R., & Mitchell, M. S. (2005). Social exchange theory: An interdisciplinary review. *Journal of Management*, *31*(6), 874–900. DOI: 10.1177/0149206305279602

Directory, S. (2025, April 16). What role does culture play in data privacy? → question. *Lifestyle → Sustainability Directory*. https://lifestyle.sustainability-directory.com/question/what-role-does-culture-play-in-data-privacy/

Factora, J. (2023, August 16). Target's sales fell for the first time in 6 years after backlash to pride collection. *Them*. https://www.them.us/story/target-sales-fall-pride-collection-backlash

Foroudi, P., Gupta, S., Sivarajah, U., & Broderick, A. (2018). Investigating the effects of smart technology on customer dynamics and customer experience. *Computers in Human Behavior*, *80*, 271–282. DOI: 10.1016/j.chb.2017.11.014

Garbarino, E., & Johnson, M. S. (1999). The different roles of satisfaction, trust, and commitment in customer relationships. *Journal of Marketing*, *63*(2), 70–87. DOI: 10.1177/002224299906300205

Habibi, M. R., Laroche, M., & Richard, M.-O. (2014). The roles of brand community and community engagement in building brand trust on social media. *Computers in Human Behavior*, *37*, 152–161. DOI: 10.1016/j.chb.2014.04.016

Hilton. (2025). *How to use your Digital Key*. Hilton Help Center. https://www.hilton.com/en/help-center/check-in-and-check-out/how-to-use-your-digital-key/

Högberg, J., Ramberg, M. O., Gustafsson, A., & Wästlund, E. (2019). Creating brand engagement through in-store gamified customer experiences. *Journal of Retailing and Consumer Services*, *50*, 122–130. DOI: 10.1016/j.jretconser.2019.05.006

Homans, G. C. (1958). Social behavior as exchange. *American Journal of Sociology*, *63*(6), 597–606. DOI: 10.1086/222355

Johri, N., Rohit, , Raut, S. K., & Rana, S. (2024). Navigating cultural complexity in global markets: Insights and future directions from two decades of marketing literature. *International Journal of System Assurance Engineering and Management*, *15*(12), 5405–5419. DOI: 10.1007/s13198-024-02520-7

Krasnova, H., Veltri, N. F., & Günther, O. (2012). Self-disclosure and privacy calculus on social networking sites: The role of culture. *Business & Information Systems Engineering*, *4*(3), 127–135. DOI: 10.1007/s12599-012-0216-6

Leonard, pepsico. (n.d.). *Leonard v. Pepsico, inc., 88 F. Supp. 2d 116 (S.D.N.Y. 1999)*. Justia Law. https://law.justia.com/cases/federal/district-courts/FSupp2/88/116/2579076/

Liu-Thompkins, Y., Khoshghadam, L., Shoushtari, A. A., & Zal, S. (2022). What drives retailer loyalty? A meta-analysis of the role of cognitive, affective, and social factors across five decades. *Journal of Retailing*, *98*(1), 92–110. DOI: 10.1016/j.jretai.2022.02.005

Masternak, W. (2025, March 31). Inside the Starbucks Rewards program: A complete diagnosis. *Open Loyalty*. https://www.openloyalty.io/insider/starbucks-rewards-program

Morgan, R. M., & Hunt, S. D. (1994). The commitment-trust theory of relationship marketing. *Journal of Marketing*, *58*(3), 20–38. DOI: 10.1177/002224299405800302

Napoletano, E. (2024, September 30). *How to Help Build Customer Relationships and Deliver Recurring Sales*. Business Class: Trends and Insights | American Express; American Express. https://www.americanexpress.com/en us/business/trends-and-insights/articles/using-small-business-saturday-to-build-customer-relationships-and-deliver-recurring-sales/

Nastasoiu, A., & Vandenbosch, M. (2019). Competing with loyalty: How to design successful customer loyalty reward programs. *Business Horizons*, *62*(2), 207–214. DOI: 10.1016/j.bushor.2018.11.002

Nittis, F. D. (2025, June 20). *Woke culture is a trap, at least sometimes*. Human Centric Group. https://humancg.com/blog/woke-culture-is-a-trap-at-least-sometimes/#When_go_woke_leads_to_go_broke_8211_when_woke_culture_is_a_trap

Palmatier, R. W., Dant, R. P., Grewal, D., & Evans, K. R. (2006). Factors influencing the effectiveness of relationship marketing: A meta-analysis. *Journal of Marketing*, *70*(4), 136–153. DOI: 10.1509/jmkg.70.4.136

PAYBACK. (2024a). *Score, save and win with PAYBACK on "Singles Day" and "Black Week."* Payback.De. https://www.payback.group/en/press/press-releases/detail/beim-singles-day-und-black-week-mit-payback-punkten-sparen-und-gewinnen

PAYBACK. (2024b). *Das ändert sich 2025 bei PAYBACK.* https://www.payback.group/de/presse/pressemeldungen/detail/das-aendert-sich-2025-bei-payback

Pratesi, F., Hu, L., Rialti, R., Zollo, L., & Faraoni, M. (2021). Cultural dimensions in online purchase behavior: Evidence from a cross-cultural study. *Italian Journal of Marketing*, *2021*(3), 227–247. DOI: 10.1007/s43039-021-00022-z

Rehnen, L.-M., Bartsch, S., Kull, M., & Meyer, A. (2017). Exploring the impact of rewarded social media engagement in loyalty programs. *Journal of Service Management*, *28*(2), 305–328. DOI: 10.1108/JOSM-10-2015-0338

Ruvio, A. A., Khodakarami, F., Morgeson, F. V.III, & Voorhees, C. M. (2025). When rewards connect to the self: Unlocking customer engagement through experiential rewards. *Journal of Retailing*.

Song, R., Moon, S., Chen, H., & Houston, M. B. (2017). When marketing strategy meets culture: The role of culture in product evaluations. *Journal of the Academy of Marketing Science*, *46*(3), 384–402. DOI: 10.1007/s11747-017-0525-x

Thompson, F. M., & Chmura, T. (2015). Loyalty programs in emerging and developed markets: The impact of cultural values on loyalty program choice. *Journal of International Marketing*, *23*(3), 87–103. DOI: 10.1509/jim.14.0125

Wang, J. J., Lalwani, A. K., & DelVecchio, D. (2022). The impact of power distance belief on consumers' brand preferences. *International Journal of Research in Marketing*, *39*(3), 804–823. DOI: 10.1016/j.ijresmar.2021.11.004

Wassel, B. (2024, February 1). Starbucks to capitalize on record loyalty membership with app improvements. *Marketing Dive*. https://www.marketingdive.com/news/starbucks-rewards-loyalty-q3-personalization/706322/

Zhang, Z., & Li, W. (2022). Customer engagement around cultural and creative products: The role of social identity. *Frontiers in Psychology*, *13*, 874851. Advance online publication. DOI: 10.3389/fpsyg.2022.874851 PMID: 35548532

Chapter 10
Ad Blockers, Digital Detox, and De-Influencing as Resistance Strategies

Niken Rahma Diasri
http://orcid.org/0009-0003-5449-4210
Universitas Esa Unggul, Indonesia

Binastya Anggara Sekti
http://orcid.org/0000-0001-5489-4888
Universitas Esa Unggul, Indonesia

Vinsens Aji Pamungkas
http://orcid.org/0009-0003-3036-0699
Universitas Esa Unggul, Indonesia

Ryan Putra Laksana
http://orcid.org/0009-0008-5904-1321
Universitas Esa Unggul, Indonesia

Andriyanti M. Asianto
Universitas Esa Unggul, Indonesia

Sawali Wahyu
http://orcid.org/0000-0002-3055-654X
Universitas Esa Unggul, Indonesia

Desfara Angelita Malau
http://orcid.org/0009-0000-8477-9901
Universitas Esa Unggul, Indonesia

ABSTRACT

As digital marketing becomes increasingly driven by algorithmic surveillance and behavioral targeting, consumers are developing resistance strategies to regain autonomy and control over their digital experiences. This chapter examines ad blockers, digital detox practices, and de-influencing movements as socio-technical responses to pervasive monitoring, persuasive design, and platform power. By analyzing these resistance strategies through ethical, political, and cultural lenses, the chapter

DOI: 10.4018/979-8-3373-7704-9.ch010

explores how consumer trust, agency, and accountability are being renegotiated in data-driven marketing ecosystems and considers their implications for the future of responsible digital marketing.

1. INTRODUCTION

The rapid digitalization of marketing has fundamentally transformed the relationship between firms and consumers. Contemporary digital marketing ecosystems are no longer centered on traditional segmentation or mass communication strategies but are increasingly driven by algorithmic decision-making, large-scale data extraction, and real-time behavioral monitoring. Through technologies such as cookies, mobile tracking, biometric identification, predictive analytics, and artificial intelligence-driven personalization, consumer interactions are continuously observed, recorded, and analyzed (Curran, 2023). While these developments promise efficiency, relevance, and personalization, they also introduce pervasive forms of surveillance that reshape power relations between corporations and consumers.

Within this context, surveillance is not merely a technical feature of digital marketing systems but a structural condition that governs how value is produced and captured. Platforms derive economic advantage from asymmetries in information, where consumers are rendered increasingly transparent while algorithmic processes remain opaque. This imbalance has significant implications for trust. Trust has long been recognized as a foundational element of market exchange, enabling consumers to engage with firms under conditions of uncertainty. However, when data collection practices are hidden, excessive, or difficult to contest, trust is gradually eroded. Consumers may perceive that their personal data are exploited beyond their awareness or consent, leading to a sense of vulnerability and loss of control. A lack of security awareness among users remains a significant risk factor, often leading to security breaches, data leaks, and financial losses (Sekti, 2025).

The erosion of trust in digital marketing environments is closely linked to the intensification of surveillance practices. Algorithmic systems infer preferences, emotions, and intentions from behavioral traces, often extending beyond what consumers knowingly disclose. Personalized pricing, targeted political advertising, and behavioral nudging exemplify how surveillance-driven marketing can shape consumer choices in subtle yet powerful ways (Seele, Dierksmeier, Hofstetter, & Schultz, 2021). As a result, consumers may come to view digital platforms not as neutral intermediaries but as actors that actively manipulate attention and decision-making. This perception contributes to a growing legitimacy crisis, in which firms struggle to justify their data practices within prevailing ethical and social norms.

Against this backdrop, consumer resistance has emerged as a salient and increasingly normalized phenomenon. Traditional marketing literature often framed resistance as deviant behavior, irrational opposition, or a barrier to managerial effectiveness. However, such interpretations are insufficient in surveillance-based markets. In highly datafied environments, resistance should be understood as a rational and structurally induced response to perceived power imbalances, opaque governance mechanisms, and the erosion of consumer autonomy. Rather than rejecting markets altogether, consumers develop strategies to renegotiate their position within them.

Consumer resistance in digital contexts takes multiple forms, ranging from individual coping mechanisms to collective and institutionalized actions. On an individual level, consumers may engage in ad avoidance, data obfuscation, or the selective withholding of personal information (Li et al., 2025). The use of ad blockers, privacy-enhancing technologies, and anonymous browsing tools reflects attempts to reassert control over personal data flows. At a collective level, resistance manifests through public discourse, social media activism, and support for regulatory interventions aimed at strengthening data protection and platform accountability. These practices signal a shift from passive consumption toward more reflexive and politicized forms of market participation.

Importantly, the emergence of consumer resistance does not imply a wholesale rejection of personalization or digital innovation. Many consumers continue to value convenience, relevance, and seamless digital experiences (Hardcastle, Vorster, & Brown, 2025). The tension lies in the conditions under which these benefits are delivered. When personalization is perceived as coercive, manipulative, or intrusive, it undermines the very value it seeks to create. Resistance, therefore, functions as a feedback mechanism that exposes the limits of surveillance-driven marketing and challenges firms to rethink the ethical foundations of their strategies.

From a theoretical perspective, the rise of consumer resistance can be situated within broader debates on surveillance capitalism, data governance, and power asymmetry in digital ecosystems. Surveillance-based marketing reconfigures consumers from autonomous decision-makers into data subjects whose behaviors are continuously predicted and shaped. This reconfiguration raises normative questions about consent, agency, and fairness. Resistance emerges at the intersection of these concerns, reflecting consumers' attempts to restore a sense of autonomy and moral legitimacy in their interactions with firms.

Moreover, consumer resistance should be interpreted as a dynamic and context-dependent phenomenon. It evolves alongside technological innovation, regulatory change, and shifting cultural expectations regarding privacy and transparency. As awareness of data practices increases, resistance strategies become more sophisticated and socially legitimized. What was once considered fringe behavior such as blocking ads or questioning data collection has become mainstream in many digital environments. This normalization signals a broader transformation in how consumers understand their rights and responsibilities within data-driven markets.

In positioning resistance as a structural response rather than an anomaly, this chapter challenges managerial and policy-oriented assumptions that equate compliance with trust. Trust cannot be engineered solely through technological optimization or persuasive communication. Instead, it is contingent on governance arrangements that recognize consumers as stakeholders with legitimate claims to transparency, accountability, and control. When such conditions are absent, resistance becomes an expected outcome rather than a failure of consumer understanding.

This introductory discussion establishes the conceptual foundation for the chapter by highlighting the interdependence between surveillance, trust, and consumer resistance in digital marketing. By reframing resistance as an indicator of systemic imbalance, the chapter sets the stage for a deeper examination of the infrastructures, mechanisms, and consequences of surveillance-based marketing practices.

To understand why resistance strategies have become increasingly normalized, it is first necessary to examine the surveillance-based infrastructures that underpin contemporary digital marketing practices.

2. ALGORITHMIC SURVEILLANCE IN CONTEMPORARY DIGITAL MARKETING

Contemporary digital marketing is fundamentally shaped by algorithmic surveillance, which refers to a set of socio-technical mechanisms through which consumer behavior is continuously monitored, analyzed, and acted upon. Unlike traditional marketing research that relied on surveys, panels, or periodic observations, algorithmic surveillance is embedded directly into digital infrastructures and operates in real time. Websites, mobile applications, social media platforms, and connected devices simultaneously function as service interfaces and data extraction systems. As a result, marketing activities are inseparable from ongoing processes of observation and prediction. Social media platforms facilitate direct interaction with consumers, strengthening relationships and engagement (Amalia, Zahira, & Sekti, 2026).

One of the central mechanisms of algorithmic surveillance is behavioral tracking. Digital platforms systematically record user interactions such as clicks, page views, scrolling behavior, dwell time, search queries, and interaction sequences. These data are typically collected passively, without requiring explicit or repeated consent beyond initial acceptance of platform terms. From a marketing perspective, behavioral tracking provides granular insight into consumer habits and attention patterns. It enables marketers to move beyond stated preferences and instead rely on observed behavior as a proxy for consumer intent.

Behavioral tracking is closely connected to the process of datafication, whereby human activities are translated into structured and quantifiable data. Datafication extends beyond observable actions to include inferred attributes such as interests, lifestyle indicators, emotional states, and purchasing propensities. Through the integration of first-party data, third-party data, and algorithmically inferred variables, consumers are transformed into dynamic data profiles (Aimé, Berger-Remy, & Laporte, 2022). These profiles are continuously updated and circulated across digital ecosystems, allowing firms to compare, classify, and rank consumers according to their predicted value or responsiveness.

Once consumer data are collected and datafied, predictive analytics becomes the primary mechanism through which marketing value is generated. Using machine learning and statistical modeling techniques, predictive systems analyze historical and real-time data to identify patterns and correlations (Theodoridis & Gkikas, 2025). The objective is not merely to explain past behavior but to forecast future actions, such as the likelihood of purchase, brand switching, or engagement with specific content. In this context, prediction functions as a strategic resource, enabling firms to intervene in consumer decision-making processes before preferences are fully formed or expressed.

Predictive analytics directly supports automated targeting. Marketing messages, product recommendations, interface designs, and pricing strategies are dynamically adapted based on algorithmic predictions (Spann et al., 2025). These targeting decisions are executed with minimal human oversight and are optimized according to predefined performance metrics such as click-through rates, conversion probabilities, or revenue maximization. For consumers, the criteria underlying these decisions are largely invisible, making it difficult to understand why certain content or offers are presented to them. This opacity contributes to asymmetries of knowledge and control between firms and consumers.

A prominent example of automated targeting is real-time bidding, which plays a central role in digital advertising markets. In real-time bidding systems, advertising space is auctioned within milliseconds when a user accesses digital content. Behavioral and profile data are transmitted to multiple advertisers, who algorithmically determine how much to bid for the opportunity to display an advertisement. This process illustrates how consumer attention is directly monetized through surveillance-based infrastructures. Although real-time bidding is foundational to online advertising, it remains largely invisible to users, reinforcing the hidden nature of data-driven monetization.

To clarify the operational mechanisms of surveillance-based marketing, Table 1 outlines the dominant forms of algorithmic surveillance commonly embedded in digital marketing ecosystems.

Table 1. Forms of algorithmic surveillance in digital marketing

Form of Surveillance	Description	Marketing Purpose
Behavioral tracking	Monitoring clicks, views, and interactions	Predict consumer preferences
Data profiling	Aggregating personal and inferred data	Audience segmentation
Predictive analytics	Forecasting future behavior	Automated targeting
Real-time bidding	Instant ad placement decisions	Monetization of attention

Table 1 illustrates how surveillance operates not as a single isolated practice but as an interconnected system. Behavioral tracking generates raw signals that feed into data profiling, while predictive analytics transforms these profiles into actionable forecasts. Real-time bidding operationalizes these predictions within automated advertising markets, closing the loop between data collection, prediction, and monetization. Together, these mechanisms form a self-reinforcing cycle in which increased data extraction enhances predictive accuracy and further legitimizes expanded surveillance.

From an organizational perspective, algorithmic surveillance is often justified as a source of efficiency and competitive advantage. Firms that possess extensive data resources and advanced analytical capabilities are better positioned to deliver precise targeting and measurable marketing outcomes. However, this logic also concentrates power within actors that control digital platforms and data infrastructures. Smaller firms and consumers become increasingly dependent on dominant intermediaries that govern access to data, audiences disconnect between, and algorithmic tools.

The systematic nature of algorithmic surveillance also raises concerns about transparency and accountability. Data collection and processing practices are typically governed by complex privacy policies and proprietary algorithms that are difficult for consumers to interpret or challenge. Even when consent mechanisms are formally granted, they often serve as procedural requirements rather than meaningful expressions of choice. This formal consent and substantive autonomy contributes to increased skepticism of digital marketing practices.

Furthermore, algorithmic surveillance reshapes the temporal dynamics of marketing decision-making. Automated systems operate at speeds that exceed human deliberation, enabling continuous experimentation and optimization. While this acceleration enhances short-term performance, it reduces opportunities for reflection, contestation, and trust-building. Marketing becomes an ongoing process of behavioral modulation, guided by algorithmic feedback loops rather than relational engagement.

Algorithmic surveillance forms the infrastructural foundation of contemporary digital marketing. Through behavioral tracking, datafication, predictive analytics, and automated targeting, consumer data are systematically collected and monetized.

While these mechanisms enable personalized marketing, they also reshape power relations and challenge consumer autonomy and trust. Their reach is further amplified by the dominance of a small number of digital platforms.

3. PLATFORM POWER AND THE POLITICAL ECONOMY OF DIGITAL MARKETING

The contemporary digital marketing ecosystem is dominated by a small number of large digital platforms, most notably Meta, Google, and TikTok. These platforms function not merely as communication channels or advertising intermediaries but as core infrastructures that organize data flows, algorithmic decision-making, and market access. Their central position enables them to shape how consumer data are collected, processed, and monetized, thereby exerting significant influence over advertisers, consumers, and the broader digital economy. Understanding digital marketing today therefore requires a political economy perspective that foregrounds platform power and structural asymmetries (Narayan, 2024).

Platform power emerges from the ability to integrate multiple functions within a single socio-technical system. Major platforms simultaneously act as data collectors, analytics providers, advertising marketplaces, and content distributors. Through this vertical and horizontal integration, platforms control both the inputs and outputs of digital marketing processes. Consumer interactions generate data, which are processed through proprietary algorithms, transformed into predictive insights, and sold back to advertisers in the form of targeted access to audiences. This closed-loop system limits external scrutiny and reinforces platform dependence. Digital marketing serves as a dynamic platform for consumer-brand interaction, shaping brand image through user-generated content, influencer marketing, and community engagement (Rianisa, Anggraini, & Sekti, 2026).

A defining characteristic of platform-based marketing is algorithmic opacity. Algorithms that determine content visibility, ad placement, pricing, and performance metrics are treated as proprietary assets. While advertisers and consumers interact with platform interfaces, the underlying decision-making processes remain largely inaccessible. This opacity prevents meaningful evaluation of how targeting decisions are made, how biases may be embedded, or how competing interests are prioritized (Coglianese & Lehr, 2019). As a result, accountability mechanisms that rely on transparency and contestability are weakened.

For advertisers, platform opacity creates a paradox. On the one hand, platforms promise efficiency, precision, and measurable outcomes. On the other hand, advertisers have limited insight into how algorithms allocate attention, rank content, or attribute conversions. Performance metrics are defined and controlled by the platforms themselves, creating potential conflicts of interest. Advertisers must often accept platform claims at face value, reinforcing asymmetric dependence and reducing their capacity to challenge or audit marketing outcomes.

For consumers, algorithmic opacity has even more profound implications. Consumers are subject to continuous data extraction and behavioral inference, yet they lack visibility into how their data are used or how algorithmic classifications affect the content they see. Recommendation systems, personalized feeds, and targeted advertisements shape attention and choice without offering clear explanations or avenues for redress. This invisibility undermines informed consent and limits consumer agency within digital markets.

The concentration of platform power also reflects broader dynamics of the political economy of data. Data function as a key economic resource, but access to large-scale, high-quality data is unevenly distributed (Sen, 2022). Dominant platforms benefit from network effects, where increased user participation generates more data, which in turn improve algorithmic performance and attract additional users and advertisers. This cumulative advantage creates high barriers to entry and consolidates market power within a small number of firms.

Moreover, platforms operate as private regulators of digital marketing ecosystems. Through terms of service, content moderation policies, and advertising guidelines, platforms define the rules under which market actors operate. These governance mechanisms are typically unilateral and subject to change without negotiation. While platforms justify such control as necessary for efficiency or safety, it effectively shifts regulatory authority from public institutions to private corporations, raising concerns about democratic accountability.

Within this context, surveillance-based marketing is not simply a managerial strategy but a structural outcome of platform capitalism. Platforms incentivize extensive data collection and predictive analytics because these practices directly support revenue generation through advertising and monetization of attention. The logic of optimization prioritizes engagement, predictability, and scalability, often at the expense of transparency, fairness, and consumer autonomy. As long as revenue models remain tied to targeted advertising, surveillance practices are likely to intensify rather than diminish.

Figure 1 visualizes the structural relationship between platforms, advertisers, algorithms, and consumers within surveillance-driven marketing ecosystems.

Figure 1. Platform power and surveillance-based marketing ecosystem

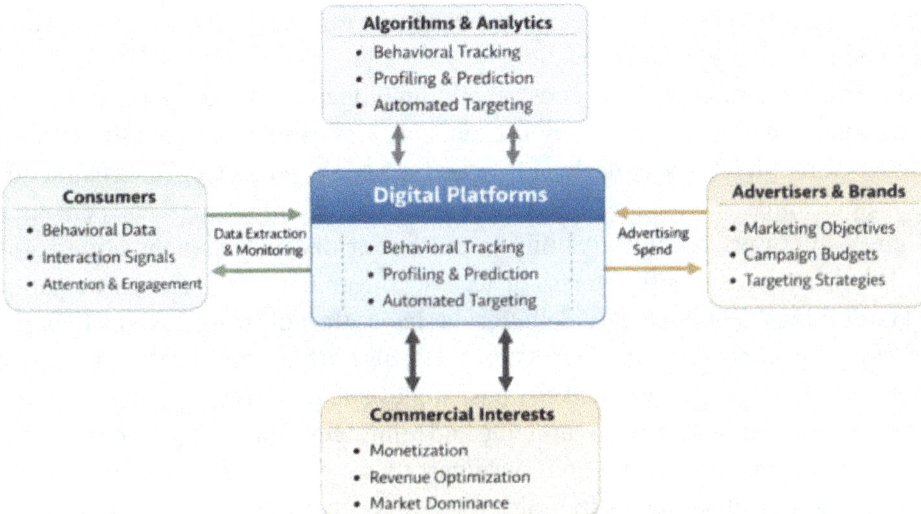

The figure conceptually represents platforms as central mediators that connect consumer data, algorithmic processing, and commercial interests. Consumer interactions generate behavioral data that flow into platform-controlled databases. Algorithms transform these data into predictions and classifications, which are then leveraged by advertisers to reach targeted audiences. Platforms manage visibility, pricing, and performance metrics, positioning themselves as indispensable intermediaries.

Figure 1 highlights how platforms consolidate power by controlling data flows, algorithmic visibility, and monetization processes, leaving consumers with limited agency. While advertisers and consumers participate in the ecosystem, their roles are constrained by platform-defined rules and opaque decision-making systems. Consumers, in particular, have minimal influence over how their data are used or how algorithmic outcomes affect their market experiences.

The political economy perspective also draws attention to how platform power shapes regulatory debates. Platforms often present themselves as neutral technological intermediaries rather than active market actors. This framing complicates efforts to impose accountability, as responsibility for outcomes can be diffused across complex algorithmic systems. At the same time, platforms possess substantial resources to influence policy discussions, further entrenching their position within digital markets.

Asymmetrical power relations between platforms, advertisers, and consumers have direct implications for trust. When platforms operate as opaque and self-regulating entities, trust becomes increasingly fragile. Consumers may perceive that their interests are subordinated to commercial optimization, while advertisers may question the fairness and reliability of performance metrics. In this environment, skepticism toward platform governance becomes a rational response rather than an expression of resistance to innovation.

Importantly, platform power does not eliminate agency altogether, but it reshapes the conditions under which agency is exercised. Consumers navigate digital environments through interfaces designed to maximize engagement and data extraction. Their choices are structured by algorithmic curation, default settings, and persuasive design. While users retain the ability to opt out or disengage, such actions often entail significant trade-offs in terms of access, convenience, or social participation.

The dominance of large digital platforms shapes the political economy of digital marketing. By controlling data infrastructures, algorithms, and market rules, platforms consolidate power and weaken transparency and accountability. This structure normalizes surveillance-based marketing and reinforces asymmetrical relationships between platforms, advertisers, and consumers. In response, consumers increasingly adopt technological strategies to limit exposure to surveillance and persuasion.

4. AD BLOCKERS AS TECHNOLOGICAL RESISTANCE

The widespread adoption of ad blockers represents one of the most visible forms of technological resistance within surveillance-based digital marketing ecosystems. Unlike symbolic or discursive forms of resistance, ad blockers operate directly at the level of technical infrastructure, intervening in the data flows and monetization mechanisms that sustain platform economies. By preventing advertisements from being displayed and, in many cases, blocking tracking scripts, ad blockers enable users to reassert a degree of control over their digital environments.

The emergence of ad blockers is closely tied to growing consumer dissatisfaction with intrusive advertising practices. Excessive ad volume, disruptive formats, and persistent tracking have contributed to negative user experiences across digital platforms (Redondo & Aznar, 2018). For many users, ad blockers are initially adopted as pragmatic tools to improve usability, reduce cognitive overload, and enhance browsing speed. Over time, however, their use often becomes associated with broader concerns about privacy, autonomy, and fairness in digital markets.

From a motivational perspective, ad blocker adoption reflects both instrumental and normative considerations. Instrumentally, users seek to avoid unwanted interruptions, protect personal data, and reduce exposure to manipulation (Celik, Çam, & Köseoglu, 2022). Normatively, ad blockers can express disapproval of surveillance-driven business models that prioritize data extraction over user well-being. In this sense, ad blocking functions not merely as a convenience tool but as a moral stance toward the perceived excesses of digital advertising.

Ad blockers disrupt surveillance-based marketing by interfering with key mechanisms of data collection and targeting. Many ad blockers prevent third-party trackers from monitoring user behavior, thereby limiting the data available for profiling and predictive analytics. This reduction in data quality challenges the effectiveness of automated targeting systems and weakens the feedback loops that underpin algorithmic optimization. As a result, ad blockers directly affect the economic foundations of platform advertising models.

The ethical implications of ad blocker use are subject to ongoing debate. From the user perspective, ad blocking can be justified as a legitimate response to non-consensual data collection and attention exploitation. Users may argue that platforms have failed to respect reasonable boundaries of privacy and transparency, thereby forfeiting claims to unimpeded access to user attention. Ad blockers, in this view, restore balance by allowing individuals to set their own limits.

From the platform and publisher perspective, ad blockers raise concerns about free-riding and revenue loss. Many digital services rely on advertising income to fund content creation and platform maintenance. When users block ads, they benefit from services without contributing to their financial sustainability. This tension highlights the structural contradictions of advertising-based business models, which depend on user participation while often undermining user trust.

The conflict between ad blockers and platforms has led to an ongoing technological arms race. Platforms and advertisers develop countermeasures such as anti-ad-blocking scripts, native advertising, and paywalls, while ad blocker developers continuously update their tools to bypass detection. This escalation reflects deeper disagreements about who has the right to control digital interfaces and data flows. Rather than resolving underlying ethical concerns, technical countermeasures often intensify adversarial relationships between users and platforms.

Ad blockers also raise questions about the collective dimensions of resistance. While individual users may experience immediate benefits, widespread ad blocking can have systemic effects on digital ecosystems. Smaller publishers and independent content creators may be disproportionately affected by advertising revenue losses, even though they have limited influence over surveillance practices. This uneven impact complicates the moral evaluation of ad blocking and underscores the need for broader governance solutions.

At the same time, the normalization of ad blocker use signals a shift in consumer expectations. Practices that were once accepted as the cost of accessing free content are increasingly questioned. Users demonstrate a willingness to intervene technologically when institutional mechanisms fail to protect their interests. In this sense, ad blockers function as indicators of legitimacy deficits within digital marketing systems rather than isolated acts of defiance.

From a governance perspective, ad blockers expose the limits of self-regulation by platforms. If advertising practices were widely perceived as fair, transparent, and respectful of user autonomy, the demand for ad blocking tools would likely be lower. Their widespread adoption suggests that existing consent mechanisms and privacy assurances are insufficient to address user concerns. Ad blockers thus highlight the gap between formal compliance and lived experience in digital environments.

Moreover, ad blockers reshape the dynamics of trust between users and platforms. While platforms often frame ad blocking as harmful or unethical, users may interpret platform resistance as evidence that their interests are being subordinated to revenue optimization. This mutual distrust reinforces cycles of surveillance and resistance, making cooperative solutions more difficult to achieve.

A widely cited example of technological resistance can be observed in the global adoption of browser-based ad blocking tools such as uBlock Origin and Adblock Plus. Industry reports indicate that hundreds of millions of internet users employ these tools to prevent intrusive advertisements and tracking scripts. The popularity of these technologies reflects growing dissatisfaction with advertising saturation and surveillance-based targeting practices. For many users, ad blockers represent a practical means of reclaiming control over their browsing experience while signaling disapproval of opaque data collection practices.

Ad blockers represent a technological form of consumer resistance against surveillance-based digital marketing. Motivated by concerns about usability, privacy, and autonomy, users employ these tools to reduce intrusive advertising and data collection. Beyond technical intervention, ad blockers signal structural imbalances in platform-based marketing ecosystems and highlight broader patterns of resistance. Resistance also extends beyond technology through behavioral withdrawal from digital environments perceived as intrusive or exhausting.

5. DIGITAL DETOX AND THE REJECTION OF CONTINUOUS SURVEILLANCE

The concept of digital detox has gained increasing prominence as individuals seek relief from the psychological, cognitive, and emotional burdens associated with continuous connectivity. In the context of surveillance-based digital marketing, digital detox represents more than a lifestyle trend or wellness strategy. It functions as a response to the pervasive monitoring, data extraction, and algorithmic modulation of everyday life. As digital environments become increasingly saturated with personalized content and behavioral nudges, some consumers choose to disengage as a means of restoring autonomy and mental balance.

Digital detox practices are closely linked to experiences of digital fatigue and surveillance anxiety. Continuous exposure to notifications, targeted advertisements, and algorithmically curated feeds can produce feelings of overload and loss of control (Lyu, Guo, & Chen, 2023). Users may become acutely aware that their online behaviors are constantly tracked and evaluated, leading to heightened self-monitoring and stress. In this sense, digital fatigue is not solely a consequence of excessive screen time but also of persistent awareness of being observed.

Digital detox practices are increasingly visible across social media cultures. For example, periodic campaigns such as "No Social Media November" or "digital minimalism" movements encourage individuals to temporarily disengage from social platforms in order to reduce algorithmic exposure and reclaim attention. These practices illustrate how withdrawal from digital environments can function not only as a wellness strategy but also as a form of resistance against surveillance-driven engagement economies.

From a psychological perspective, digital detox can be understood as a coping mechanism aimed at reducing cognitive strain and emotional exhaustion. Temporarily disconnecting from digital platforms allows individuals to regain attentional focus, improve well-being, and reestablish boundaries between work, consumption, and private life (Mizrak, Demirel, Yaşar, & Karakaya, 2025). These short-term detox practices are often framed in therapeutic terms, emphasizing self-care and mental health rather than political or economic critique.

However, digital detox also has a cultural and ethical dimension. For some users, disengagement reflects a broader rejection of surveillance-driven business models and attention economies. Avoiding specific platforms or limiting data-generating activities becomes a way to contest the normalization of constant monitoring. In this context, digital detox operates as a symbolic practice that communicates dissatisfaction with the values embedded in digital infrastructures.

Digital detox practices vary significantly in duration, intensity, and motivation. Some individuals engage in temporary breaks, such as abstaining from social media for a few days or disabling notifications. Others adopt medium-term strategies, including the avoidance of particular platforms known for aggressive data collection or targeted advertising. At the most sustained level, lifestyle-oriented detox involves long-term or permanent reconfiguration of digital habits, often grounded in ethical or philosophical commitments to privacy, minimalism, or technological restraint.

To distinguish different forms of digital disengagement, Table 2 categorizes common digital detox practices and their underlying motivations.

Table 2. Characteristics of digital detox practices

Detox Practice	Duration	Primary Motivation
Temporary detox	Short-term	Mental well-being
Platform avoidance	Medium-term	Privacy concerns
Lifestyle detox	Long-term	Ethical rejection

Table 2 shows that digital detox ranges from temporary coping mechanisms to long-term ethical stances against surveillance capitalism. While short-term detox focuses on alleviating stress and fatigue, longer-term practices reflect deeper concerns about autonomy, identity, and the moral legitimacy of data-driven platforms. These distinctions highlight that digital detox is not a uniform phenomenon but encompasses diverse forms of resistance and self-regulation.

The symbolic nature of digital detox is particularly important in understanding its broader social implications. By disengaging, individuals signal that constant availability and data transparency are neither inevitable nor universally desirable. Digital detox challenges the assumption that participation in surveillance-based ecosystems is a prerequisite for social and economic inclusion. Even when practiced by a minority, detox narratives can influence public discourse and reshape cultural expectations around connectivity and privacy.

At the same time, digital detox is characterized by significant limitations and tensions. Complete disengagement is often impractical, given the integration of digital platforms into work, education, and social life. As a result, detox practices may remain partial, temporary, or unevenly distributed across social groups (Mbare, Perkiö, & Koivusalo, 2024). Individuals with greater socioeconomic resources are typically better positioned to opt out or reduce dependence on dominant platforms, raising questions about inequality and privilege in resistance practices.

Moreover, digital detox does not directly challenge the structural foundations of surveillance capitalism. While it may reduce individual exposure to monitoring and persuasion, it leaves platform business models largely intact. In some cases, detox may even be commodified, as wellness industries and digital tools market disconnection as a purchasable experience. This commercialization risks neutralizing the critical potential of detox by framing it as a personal lifestyle choice rather than a systemic issue.

Despite these limitations, digital detox remains an important indicator of legitimacy crises within digital marketing ecosystems. Its growing visibility reflects widespread unease with continuous surveillance and algorithmic influence. As with ad blockers, detox practices reveal gaps between user expectations and platform governance, highlighting the need for structural solutions that go beyond individual self-regulation.

In summary, digital detox represents a multifaceted response to the psychological and cultural consequences of continuous surveillance. It operates simultaneously as a coping strategy, an ethical practice, and a symbolic form of resistance. By examining digital detox within the context of surveillance-based marketing, this chapter underscores how consumer resistance extends beyond technological tools to include broader reconfigurations of digital life.

While ad blockers and digital detox operate largely at the individual level, resistance also emerges collectively through cultural and discursive movements.

6. DE-INFLUENCING AND THE POLITICS OF AUTHENTICITY

The rise of de-influencing reflects a growing cultural response to the saturation of influencer marketing and the broader persuasive economies that dominate digital platforms. Influencer marketing has become a central component of algorithmic advertising strategies, leveraging personal identity, intimacy, and perceived authenticity to shape consumer preferences. Against this backdrop, de-influencing emerges as a symbolic form of resistance that challenges both the credibility of influencer culture and the commercial logics that underpin it.

De-influencing refers to practices in which content creators or consumers actively discourage excessive consumption, question sponsored recommendations, or expose the economic incentives behind influencer endorsements. Rather than promoting products, de-influencers often highlight overconsumption, misleading claims, or the psychological pressures created by curated online lifestyles (Moir, 2025). This shift reflects growing skepticism toward influencer marketing as audiences become more aware of its strategic and monetized nature.

Figure 2. Consumer resistance strategies in surveillance-based digital marketing

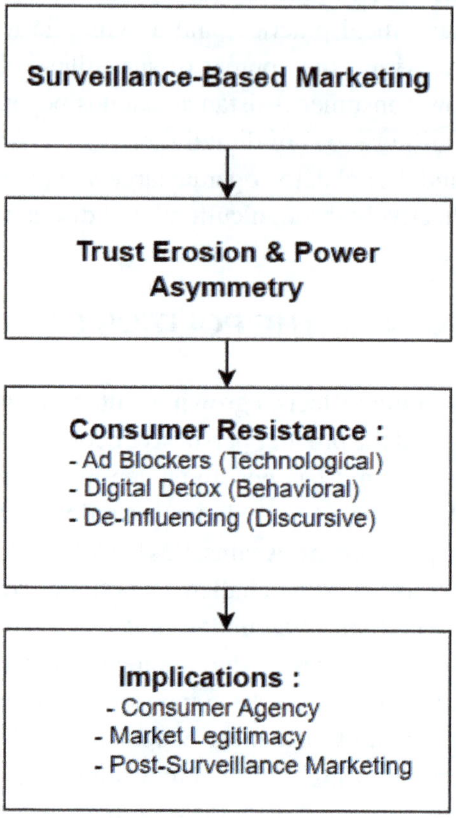

Figure 2 synthesizes the relationship between surveillance-based marketing practices and emerging forms of consumer resistance. Surveillance infrastructures based on behavioral tracking, algorithmic profiling, and platform power generate asymmetries of information and control. These asymmetries contribute to declining consumer trust and perceptions of manipulation.

In response, consumers adopt different resistance strategies operating at three levels. Technological resistance is expressed through ad blockers that directly interfere with data collection and advertising infrastructures. Behavioral resistance appears in the form of digital detox practices that reduce participation in surveillance environments. Discursive resistance emerges through de-influencing movements that challenge persuasive cultures in social media ecosystems.

Together, these responses highlight a feedback mechanism through which consumer resistance signals legitimacy deficits in surveillance-driven marketing systems and motivates the transition t

A prominent example of de-influencing emerged on TikTok, where creators began producing videos explicitly advising viewers not to purchase trending products that were widely promoted by influencers. These videos often highlight issues such as overconsumption, misleading advertising claims, and unnecessary product accumulation. The popularity of such content demonstrates growing audience skepticism toward influencer marketing and the commodification of authenticity.

At the core of de-influencing lies the politics of authenticity. Influencer marketing relies heavily on the perception that recommendations are genuine expressions of personal experience rather than commercial persuasion (Wellman, Stoldt, Tully, & Ekdale, 2020). However, the increasing visibility of sponsorship disclosures, affiliate links, and algorithmic amplification has complicated this perception. De-influencing capitalizes on this tension by revealing how authenticity itself has become a marketable asset, strategically produced and optimized within platform economies.

The critique advanced by de-influencing is not limited to individual influencers but extends to the structural conditions of digital platforms. Algorithms reward engagement, visibility, and emotional resonance, incentivizing influencers to continuously perform relatable identities. As personal narratives become data points optimized for reach and monetization, identity itself is increasingly commodified. De-influencing challenges this process by questioning the sincerity and ethical implications of identity-based persuasion.

Transparency plays a central role in de-influencing practices. De-influencers often emphasize disclosure, critical evaluation of product claims, and awareness of marketing tactics. By foregrounding the commercial context of influencer content, they seek to reintroduce critical distance between recommendation and consumption. This emphasis on transparency contrasts with traditional influencer marketing strategies that blur the boundaries between personal expression and advertising.

De-influencing also reflects broader cultural shifts in how consumers engage with digital content. Audiences are no longer passive recipients of influencer messaging but increasingly participate in evaluative and critical discourse (Mady, Salaheldeen, Refaat, & Battour, 2025). Comment sections, reaction videos, and platform-native debates contribute to a more reflexive consumption culture. In this environment, de-influencing functions as both content genre and discursive practice, shaping norms around credibility and trust.

From an economic perspective, de-influencing introduces friction into persuasive economies that depend on seamless transitions from exposure to purchase. By encouraging hesitation, reflection, or refusal, de-influencers disrupt the efficiency of influencer marketing funnels. While their impact on overall consumption patterns remains contested, their symbolic significance lies in challenging assumptions about aspiration, desirability, and social status embedded in influencer culture.

However, de-influencing is not without contradictions. As it gains visibility, it can itself be incorporated into platform logics of attention and monetization. De-influencing content may attract sponsorships, algorithmic amplification, or commercial partnerships that replicate the dynamics it seeks to critique. This incorporation raises questions about whether de-influencing represents a sustainable alternative or a cyclical adaptation within persuasive economies.

Moreover, the politics of authenticity in de-influencing is inherently unstable. Authenticity is socially constructed and context-dependent, making it difficult to define or verify conclusively. While de-influencers may position themselves as more honest or ethical, they are not immune to strategic self-presentation or audience management. This ambiguity highlights the limits of authenticity as a regulatory principle in digital markets.

Despite these tensions, de-influencing plays an important role in reshaping public discourse around influencer marketing. It legitimizes skepticism and critical engagement as acceptable responses to persuasive content. By articulating dissatisfaction with commodified identities and opaque sponsorship practices, de-influencing contributes to a broader redefinition of consumer agency in algorithmic environments.

In summary, de-influencing represents a form of symbolic resistance that interrogates the cultural and economic foundations of influencer marketing. By foregrounding issues of authenticity, transparency, and identity commodification, it challenges the persuasive logics of digital platforms. While susceptible to co-optation, de-influencing nonetheless signals shifting expectations regarding trust and agency in contemporary digital marketing.

Taken together, these resistance strategies invite deeper reflection on how consumer agency and trust are being redefined in algorithmic marketing environments.

7. CONSUMER AGENCY, TRUST, AND ETHICAL IMPLICATIONS

The emergence of consumer resistance strategies such as ad blockers, digital detox, and de-influencing reflects a broader reconfiguration of consumer agency within surveillance-based digital marketing ecosystems. Rather than isolated reactions, these practices represent interconnected responses to persistent data extraction, algorithmic persuasion, and declining trust in platform governance. Examining these strategies together allows for a deeper understanding of how agency and trust are being renegotiated under conditions of algorithmic marketing.

Consumer agency in digital environments has traditionally been conceptualized as the ability to make informed and voluntary choices. However, algorithmic personalization and predictive targeting complicate this notion by shaping choices before they are consciously articulated (Nokhiz & Ruwanpathirana, 2025). In this context, resistance practices function as corrective mechanisms through which consumers attempt to reclaim autonomy. Ad blockers intervene at the technical level, digital detox restructures patterns of participation, and de-influencing reshapes discursive norms around consumption. Although distinct in form, each strategy reflects an effort to counteract perceived losses of control.

Trust plays a central role in mediating the relationship between consumer agency and resistance. Trust in digital marketing is not solely a matter of brand reputation but is embedded in the governance of data practices and algorithmic systems. When consumers perceive that platforms and marketers prioritize surveillance and persuasion over transparency and respect, trust erodes (Markou, Serdaris, Antoniadis, & Spinthiropoulos, 2025). Resistance then emerges as a rational response to this erosion rather than as a rejection of digital innovation itself.

The ethical implications of consumer resistance are multifaceted. From the consumer perspective, resistance strategies can be seen as morally justified attempts to protect autonomy, privacy, and psychological well-being. Ad blockers limit non-consensual data collection, digital detox asserts the right to disengage, and de-influencing exposes hidden commercial interests. Together, these practices articulate an ethical critique of surveillance-based persuasion that challenges its legitimacy.

From the perspective of brands and marketers, consumer resistance presents ethical dilemmas that extend beyond performance metrics. Brands must confront questions about the fairness of targeting practices, the transparency of influencer partnerships, and the sustainability of attention-based revenue models. Continued reliance on opaque or manipulative strategies risks further undermining trust and provoking stronger forms of resistance. Ethical marketing, in this sense, requires more than compliance with formal regulations. It demands a reassessment of how consumer data and attention are valued and governed.

Platforms occupy a particularly complex ethical position. As infrastructure providers, they mediate interactions between consumers and advertisers while simultaneously benefiting from surveillance-based monetization. When resistance emerges, platforms often frame it as a technical or behavioral problem to be mitigated through design changes or enforcement mechanisms. This framing risks obscuring the structural role platforms play in shaping incentives and outcomes. Ethical responsibility cannot be fully delegated to individual users without addressing platform-level governance.

A key ethical risk highlighted by consumer resistance is the shifting of responsibility from institutions to individuals. By emphasizing tools such as ad blockers or practices like digital detox, the burden of protecting privacy and autonomy may be placed disproportionately on consumers. This individualization of responsibility assumes that users possess the resources, knowledge, and capacity to manage complex digital risks. In reality, such capacities are unevenly distributed, raising concerns about equity and fairness.

To synthesize the ethical dimensions of consumer resistance, Table 3 compares key resistance strategies and their implications for trust and accountability.

Table 3. Resistance strategies and ethical implications

Strategy	Form of Resistance	Ethical Implication
Ad blockers	Technological	Reassertion of autonomy
Digital detox	Behavioral	Ethical refusal
De-influencing	Discursive	Challenge to persuasion

Table 3 demonstrates that resistance strategies vary in form but converge in their critique of surveillance-based persuasion. Each strategy highlights a different ethical dimension of consumer agency, ranging from technical control to moral expression and cultural critique. Together, they underscore the inadequacy of viewing consumer protection solely through the lens of individual choice.

The convergence of these resistance practices also suggests that trust is increasingly conditional. Consumers may continue to engage with digital platforms and brands, but their engagement is shaped by skepticism and selective participation. Trust becomes provisional and revocable, contingent on perceived respect for autonomy and transparency. This shift challenges traditional marketing assumptions that equate personalization with value creation.

Importantly, consumer resistance does not absolve brands, marketers, or platforms of ethical responsibility. On the contrary, it signals the need for structural interventions that reduce reliance on surveillance and persuasion. Ethical marketing practices should aim to minimize asymmetries of information and power rather than exploit them. This includes clearer data governance, meaningful consent mechanisms, and accountability for algorithmic outcomes.

In summary, ad blockers, digital detox, and de-influencing collectively illuminate how consumer agency and trust are being redefined in algorithmic marketing environments. These resistance strategies function as ethical critiques of surveillance-based persuasion and expose the limitations of individual-level solutions. Addressing the concerns they raise requires a shift from reactive resistance toward proactive governance and ethical design.

These ethical tensions raise important questions about whether existing regulatory and governance frameworks are sufficient to address consumer concerns.

8. GOVERNANCE, REGULATION, AND THE LIMITS OF INSTITUTIONAL RESPONSES

As concerns over data privacy, algorithmic manipulation, and consumer surveillance intensify, institutional governance and regulatory frameworks have emerged as the primary formal responses to the excesses of data-driven digital marketing. Regulations such as the General Data Protection Regulation (GDPR) in the European Union and the California Consumer Privacy Act (CCPA) in the United States are frequently presented as milestones in rebalancing power between platforms, marketers, and consumers (Miller, Lukic, & Skiera, 2025). These frameworks aim to enhance transparency, limit unlawful data processing, and restore individual control over personal information. However, despite their symbolic and legal significance, regulatory approaches face substantial limitations when confronted with the structural dynamics of surveillance-based marketing ecosystems.

At their core, GDPR and CCPA are grounded in a compliance-oriented logic that treats privacy as a matter of procedural correctness. Concepts such as informed consent, lawful processing, data minimization, and user rights to access or deletion are intended to operationalize consumer protection within complex digital systems. In practice, however, these principles are often translated into standardized interfaces, lengthy privacy notices, and consent banners that shift responsibility for data governance onto individual users. As a result, consumers are formally empowered while remaining practically constrained, navigating environments where meaningful choice is limited and understanding is partial.

One of the most persistent critiques of contemporary data protection regimes concerns the notion of consent itself. While consent is framed as an expression of autonomy, it frequently operates as a ritualized formality rather than a genuine decision-making process. Users are expected to agree to opaque data practices in order to access essential platforms and services, creating what many scholars describe as coerced or forced consent. This dynamic is particularly pronounced in digital marketing contexts, where personalization and targeting rely on extensive behavioral data that consumers cannot realistically evaluate or negotiate. Regulatory compliance, in this sense, legitimizes surveillance rather than fundamentally challenging it.

Algorithmic opacity further compounds the limitations of regulatory oversight. Even when platforms comply with formal disclosure requirements, the underlying mechanisms of data aggregation, inference, and predictive modeling remain largely inaccessible to regulators and consumers alike. The complexity of machine learning systems, combined with claims of trade secrecy and intellectual property protection, restricts the ability of institutions to audit or contest algorithmic decision-making.

As a result, power asymmetries persist, with platforms retaining control over visibility, ranking, and monetization processes that directly shape consumer experience.

Another structural limitation of governance frameworks lies in their jurisdictional scope. Digital marketing platforms operate globally, while regulatory regimes remain territorially bounded. This mismatch enables regulatory arbitrage, allowing companies to adapt compliance strategies selectively while maintaining core surveillance practices across markets. Smaller firms and advertisers may bear disproportionate compliance costs, while dominant platforms leverage their resources to absorb regulatory burdens without altering their business models. Consequently, regulation may inadvertently reinforce market concentration rather than democratizing the digital economy.

From the perspective of consumers, these institutional responses often fail to address the ethical dimensions of surveillance-based marketing. While regulations emphasize legality and rights, they rarely engage with lived experiences of manipulation, loss of trust, or emotional fatigue. Feelings of being constantly tracked, profiled, and targeted are not easily resolved through access requests or opt-out mechanisms (Goncalves, Hu, Aliagas, & Cerdá, 2024). This gap between formal governance and ethical perception helps explain why consumer resistance frequently emerges outside institutional channels, taking the form of ad blockers, digital detox, and discursive critique rather than legal mobilization.

Moreover, the focus on individual rights risks obscuring the collective and structural nature of surveillance harms. By framing privacy as a personal responsibility, regulatory models align with broader neoliberal logics that prioritize individual action over systemic reform. Consumers are encouraged to manage their own risk through settings and preferences, while platforms continue to extract value from aggregated data at scale. These dynamics raise critical questions about whether the current governance paradigm is capable of addressing the political economy of digital marketing or simply regulating its surface manifestations.

Recent debates on data governance increasingly call for a shift beyond compliance toward more substantive forms of accountability. Proposals such as transparency-by-design, algorithmic impact assessments, and shared responsibility models seek to redistribute ethical obligations across platforms, advertisers, and regulators. These approaches emphasize not only whether data practices are legal, but whether they are socially acceptable, proportionate, and aligned with public values. However, such frameworks remain unevenly implemented and often lack enforcement mechanisms comparable to traditional regulatory tools.

In this context, governance should be understood as a necessary but insufficient condition for restoring trust in digital marketing. Legal protections play a crucial role in setting boundaries and articulating norms, yet they cannot alone resolve the deeper tensions produced by surveillance-driven persuasion. As long as data extraction and behavioral prediction remain central to marketing logics, regulatory compliance risks functioning as a legitimizing layer rather than a transformative force.

Ultimately, the limitations of institutional responses underscore the need to rethink digital marketing beyond surveillance-centered paradigms. Rather than relying exclusively on regulation to correct market failures, alternative models must be explored that prioritize consumer autonomy, ethical engagement, and sustainable trust. These considerations open the space for reimagining marketing practices that are less dependent on continuous monitoring and more attentive to relational and value-based interactions.

Given the limitations of regulation alone, alternative marketing models must be considered to rebuild trust in post-surveillance environments.

9. TOWARD POST-SURVEILLANCE AND RESPONSIBLE DIGITAL MARKETING

The growing normalization of consumer resistance highlights the limitations of surveillance-based digital marketing as a sustainable model for value creation. Practices such as ad blocking, digital detox, and de-influencing reveal not only dissatisfaction with specific tactics but also deeper concerns about autonomy, trust, and ethical legitimacy. In response, scholars and practitioners increasingly call for alternative approaches that move beyond intensive data extraction and predictive persuasion. This chapter explores emerging directions for post-surveillance and responsible digital marketing that seek to realign marketing practices with consumer agency and social trust.

A central principle in post-surveillance marketing is transparency-by-design. Unlike traditional transparency measures that rely on lengthy privacy policies or retrospective disclosures, transparency-by-design integrates clarity and intelligibility into the architecture of digital systems. Data collection purposes, targeting logic, and algorithmic decision-making processes are communicated in accessible ways at the point of interaction (Magrizos, Campora, Lamprinakos, Giovanis, & Christofi, 2025). This approach treats transparency not as a legal obligation but as a core design value that enables informed participation.

Transparency-by-design challenges the assumption that opacity is necessary for competitive advantage. While firms often argue that algorithmic secrecy protects innovation, excessive opacity undermines trust and fuels resistance. Responsible marketing recognizes that long-term legitimacy depends on consumers understanding how their data are used and how marketing decisions affect them. By reducing informational asymmetries, transparency-by-design supports a more balanced relationship between marketers and consumers.

Another emerging direction is slow marketing, which deliberately resists the acceleration and hyper-optimization characteristic of algorithmic persuasion. Slow marketing emphasizes quality of engagement over quantity, prioritizing meaningful interactions rather than continuous behavioral nudging. This approach draws inspiration from broader slow movements that value reflection, sustainability, and human-centered design. In digital marketing contexts, slow marketing may involve limiting targeting frequency, reducing intrusive personalization, or favoring contextual relevance over individual profiling.

Slow marketing reframes success metrics away from short-term conversions and toward long-term relationships. Rather than maximizing attention capture, it seeks to cultivate trust and mutual respect. This shift requires marketers to reconsider the ethical costs of constant optimization and to acknowledge that not all consumer behavior should be predicted, influenced, or monetized. By accepting limits to persuasion, slow marketing affirms consumer autonomy as an intrinsic value rather than an obstacle to efficiency.

Responsible digital marketing also entails a broader ethical reorientation that places consumer autonomy at the center of strategic decision-making. Autonomy in this context refers not only to freedom of choice but also to the conditions under which choices are made. Ethical marketing practices aim to preserve consumers' capacity for reflection and self-determination by avoiding manipulative design, excessive personalization, and exploitative use of behavioral insights (Kamila & Jasrotia, 2023). This perspective aligns marketing ethics with principles of respect, fairness, and dignity.

Importantly, post-surveillance approaches do not imply the rejection of data or technology altogether. Instead, they call for restraint and proportionality in data use. Data should be collected only when necessary, used for clearly defined purposes, and governed by accountability mechanisms that extend beyond individual consent. Responsible marketing recognizes that consent alone is insufficient in complex algorithmic environments and must be complemented by ethical standards and institutional oversight.

From an organizational perspective, adopting post-surveillance marketing requires cultural and structural change. Firms must move beyond compliance-driven ethics and integrate ethical reflection into innovation processes. This includes interdisciplinary collaboration between marketing, design, legal, and ethics teams to anticipate unintended consequences of data-driven strategies. Ethical impact assessments and participatory design methods can help organizations evaluate how marketing systems affect different stakeholders.

Platforms play a particularly influential role in shaping the feasibility of post-surveillance marketing. As infrastructural intermediaries, they determine the tools, metrics, and incentives available to marketers. Supporting transparency-by-design and slow marketing may require platforms to revise revenue models that depend on intensive targeting and engagement maximization. While such changes pose economic challenges, they also present opportunities to rebuild trust and legitimacy in increasingly skeptical markets.

The transition toward responsible digital marketing is not without obstacles. Competitive pressures, entrenched business models, and expectations of personalization create resistance to change. Moreover, ethical approaches may initially appear less efficient or profitable when evaluated through conventional performance metrics. However, continued reliance on surveillance-driven logics risks deepening trust deficits and provoking stronger regulatory and consumer backlash. From a long-term perspective, ethical restraint may enhance resilience and reputational capital.

At a societal level, post-surveillance marketing aligns with broader debates about the role of markets in shaping digital life. Marketing does not merely respond to consumer preferences but actively constructs norms, aspirations, and identities. By adopting ethical and transparent practices, marketers can contribute to healthier digital environments that support well-being rather than exploitation. This reframing positions marketing as a social practice with responsibilities that extend beyond transactional outcomes.

In summary, post-surveillance and responsible digital marketing offer a pathway beyond the legitimacy crises associated with algorithmic persuasion and continuous monitoring. Through principles such as transparency-by-design, slow marketing, and respect for consumer autonomy, these approaches seek to rebalance power relations and restore trust. While challenging to implement within existing economic structures, they represent a necessary evolution in response to growing resistance and ethical concern.

These emerging approaches signal a broader shift toward reimagining marketing beyond surveillance-driven logics.

9.1 Managerial Implications for Post-Surveillance Marketing

The normalization of consumer resistance carries important implications for firms and marketers operating in digital environments. First, marketers must recognize that practices perceived as intrusive or opaque can undermine long-term brand trust, even if they generate short-term engagement metrics. Designing marketing strategies that prioritize transparency and respect for consumer autonomy may reduce the likelihood of resistance behaviors such as ad blocking or digital disengagement.

Second, brands should reconsider their reliance on hyper-personalization and intensive behavioral tracking. While predictive analytics can enhance relevance, excessive targeting may trigger perceptions of manipulation or surveillance. Responsible marketing therefore requires a careful balance between personalization benefits and respect for consumer privacy expectations.

Finally, firms should engage with emerging cultural shifts such as de-influencing and authenticity debates. Rather than viewing these movements as threats, marketers can treat them as signals of evolving consumer values that prioritize honesty, transparency, and ethical consumption. Brands that adapt to these expectations are more likely to build durable trust and legitimacy in increasingly skeptical digital markets.

CONCLUSION

This chapter has examined the growing normalization of consumer resistance within surveillance-based digital marketing ecosystems and its implications for trust, agency, and ethical governance. By situating practices such as ad blocking, digital detox, and de-influencing within broader socio-technical and political-economic contexts, the chapter has argued that resistance should not be understood as anomalous or antagonistic behavior. Rather, it represents a structurally induced and rational response to pervasive data extraction, algorithmic persuasion, and asymmetries of power embedded in contemporary digital markets.

At the core of this analysis lies the recognition that digital marketing has evolved into a system of continuous surveillance. Algorithmic infrastructures enable the real-time monitoring, profiling, and prediction of consumer behavior at unprecedented scale and granularity. While these mechanisms promise efficiency and personalization, they also reconfigure consumers into data subjects whose attention, identity, and decision-making processes are continuously optimized for commercial purposes. As the chapter has demonstrated, such transformations place significant strain on trust, which remains a foundational condition for market legitimacy.

Consumer resistance emerges precisely at this point of tension. The widespread adoption of ad blockers illustrates how consumers intervene technologically to reclaim control over data flows and attention economies. Digital detox practices reveal behavioral and ethical refusals of constant monitoring, reflecting both psychological fatigue and normative critique. De-influencing, meanwhile, operates at the cultural and discursive level, challenging the commodification of authenticity and the persuasive authority of influencer marketing. Although these strategies differ in form, duration, and scope, they converge in their critique of surveillance-driven persuasion and opaque governance.

Importantly, the chapter has emphasized that resistance does not signal a rejection of digital marketing or personalization per se. Consumers continue to value relevance, convenience, and innovation. What they increasingly contest are the conditions under which these benefits are delivered—particularly when data practices are excessive, manipulative, or difficult to contest. Resistance, therefore, functions as a feedback mechanism that exposes legitimacy deficits in existing marketing models and calls for ethical recalibration.

The ethical implications of these resistance practices extend beyond individual consumer behavior. While ad blockers, detox, and de-influencing enable forms of self-protection, they also risk shifting responsibility away from institutions and onto individuals. This individualization of ethical burden assumes that consumers possess equal resources, literacy, and capacity to manage complex digital risks, an assumption that is both unrealistic and inequitable. As the chapter has argued, consumer agency cannot substitute for institutional accountability.

The examination of governance and regulatory responses further underscores this limitation. Frameworks such as GDPR and CCPA represent important normative advances, yet they remain largely compliance-oriented and procedurally focused. By emphasizing consent and individual rights without addressing structural incentives and algorithmic opacity, regulation often legitimizes surveillance rather than transforming it. The persistent gap between formal legality and lived ethical experience explains why resistance frequently unfolds outside institutional channels.

In response to these challenges, the chapter has outlined emerging directions toward post-surveillance and responsible digital marketing. Principles such as transparency-by-design, slow marketing, and the prioritization of consumer autonomy offer alternative pathways that move beyond optimization-centered logics. These approaches do not reject data or technology but advocate restraint, proportionality, and ethical reflection in their use. By foregrounding trust, dignity, and relational value, post-surveillance marketing repositions ethical legitimacy as a strategic and societal asset rather than a regulatory constraint.

In conclusion, consumer resistance should be interpreted not as a failure of marketing communication or consumer understanding, but as a meaningful signal of systemic imbalance within surveillance-based digital markets. Addressing this signal requires more than technological fixes or legal compliance. It demands a reimagining of digital marketing as a socio-technical practice grounded in accountability, transparency, and respect for consumer autonomy. Only through such a reorientation can sustainable trust be rebuilt in increasingly datafied and algorithmically governed environments.

REFERENCES

Aimé, I., Berger-Remy, F., & Laporte, M.-E. (2022). The brand, the persona and the algorithm: How datafication is reconfiguring marketing work☆. *Journal of Business Research, 145*, 814–827. https://doi.org/https://doi.org/10.1016/j.jbusres.2022.03.047. DOI: 10.1016/j.jbusres.2022.03.047

Amalia, F., Zahira, T., & Sekti, B. A. (2026). Influence of Social Media and Virtual Reality on Consumer Behavior. In *Modern Consumer Behavior at the Intersection of AI and Social Media* (pp. 91–121). DOI: 10.4018/979-8-3373-2747-1.ch004

Celik, F., Çam, M., & Köseoglu, M. A. (2022). Ad avoidance in the digital context: A systematic literature review and research agenda. *International Journal of Consumer Studies, 47*(6), 2071–2105. DOI: 10.1111/ijcs.12882

Coglianese, C., & Lehr, D. (2019). TRANSPARENCY AND ALGORITHMIC GOVERNANCE. *Administrative Law Review, 71*(1), 1–56.

Curran, D. (2023). Surveillance capitalism and systemic digital risk: The imperative to collect and connect and the risks of interconnectedness. *Big Data & Society, 10*(1), 20539517231177620. DOI: 10.1177/20539517231177621

Goncalves, M., Hu, Y., Aliagas, I., & Cerdá, L. M. (2024). Neuromarketing algorithms' consumer privacy and ethical considerations: Challenges and opportunities. *Cogent Business & Management, 11*(1), 2333063. DOI: 10.1080/23311975.2024.2333063

Hardcastle, K., Vorster, L., & Brown, D. M. (2025). Understanding Customer Responses to AI-Driven Personalized Journeys: Impacts on the Customer Experience. *Journal of Advertising, 54*(2), 176–195. DOI: 10.1080/00913367.2025.2460985

Kamila, M. K., & Jasrotia, S. S. (2023). Ethics and marketing responsibility: A bibliometric analysis and literature review. *Asia Pacific Management Review, 28*(4), 567–583. https://doi.org/https://doi.org/10.1016/j.apmrv.2023.04.002

Li, Y., Tsang, Y. P., Ho, D. C. K., Ozden, M., Lee, C. K. M., & Hu, H. (2025). Unraveling consumer resistance to innovative marketing in web 3.0: Empirical findings and large language model insights. *Enterprise Information Systems, 19*(1–2), 2462069. DOI: 10.1080/17517575.2025.2462069

Lyu, T., Guo, Y., & Chen, H. (2023). Understanding the privacy protection disengagement behaviour of contactless digital service users: The roles of privacy fatigue and privacy literacy. *Behaviour & Information Technology, 43*(10), 1–17. DOI: 10.1080/0144929X.2023.2237603

Mady, K., Salaheldeen, M., Refaat, H., & Battour, M. (2025). The impact of social media on consumer boycotts: Mediating roles of animosity, behavioral control, and efficacy. *Social Sciences & Humanities Open*, *12*, 102041. https://doi.org/https://doi.org/10.1016/j.ssaho.2025.102041. DOI: 10.1016/j.ssaho.2025.102041

Magrizos, S., Campora, M., Lamprinakos, G., Giovanis, A., & Christofi, M. (2025). Transparency by design: The effect of privacy policies visualisation on brand trust and perceived intrusion. *Behaviour & Information Technology*, •••, 1–13. DOI: 10.1080/0144929X.2025.2520594

Markou, V., Serdaris, P., Antoniadis, I., & Spinthiropoulos, K. (2025). Personalization, Trust, and Identity in AI-Based Marketing: An Empirical Study of Consumer Acceptance in Greece. *Administrative Sciences*, *15*(11), 440. Advance online publication. DOI: 10.3390/admsci15110440

Mbare, B., Perkiö, M., & Koivusalo, M. (2024). Algorithmic management, wellbeing and platform work: Understanding the psychosocial risks and experiences of food couriers in Finland. *Labour & Industry*, *34*(4), 386–411. DOI: 10.1080/10301763.2024.2423442

Miller, K. M., Lukic, K., & Skiera, B. (2025). The impact of the General Data Protection Regulation (GDPR) on online tracking. *International Journal of Research in Marketing*. https://doi.org/https://doi.org/10.1016/j.ijresmar.2025.03.002

Mizrak, F., Demirel, H. G., Yaşar, O., & Karakaya, T. (2025). Digital detox: Exploring the impact of cybersecurity fatigue on employee productivity and mental health. *Discover Mental Health*, *5*(1), 25. DOI: 10.1007/s44192-025-00149-x PMID: 39998759

Moir, A. (2025). Deinfluencing TikTok During the Cost-of-Living Crisis: Neoliberal Logics of (Over)Consumption Across Popular Media. *Television & New Media*, *26*(8), 914–930. DOI: 10.1177/15274764251348596

Narayan, D. (2024). The political economy of digital platforms: Key directions. *Platforms & Society*, *1*, 29768624241263070. DOI: 10.1177/29768624241263071

Nokhiz, P., & Ruwanpathirana, A. K. (2025). Consumer Autonomy or Illusion? Rethinking Consumer Agency in the Age of Algorithms. *Journal of Social Computing*, *6*(3), 184–208. DOI: 10.23919/JSC.2025.0015

Redondo, I., & Aznar, G. (2018). To use or not to use ad blockers? The roles of knowledge of ad blockers and attitude toward online advertising. *Telematics and Informatics*, *35*(6), 1607–1616. https://doi.org/https://doi.org/10.1016/j.tele.2018.04.008. DOI: 10.1016/j.tele.2018.04.008

Rianisa, A., Anggraini, D. S., & Sekti, B. A. (2026). Role of AI in Consumer Decision-Making Processes. In *Modern Consumer Behavior at the Intersection of AI and Social Media* (pp. 123–151). DOI: 10.4018/979-8-3373-2747-1.ch005

Seele, P., Dierksmeier, C., Hofstetter, R., & Schultz, M. D. (2021). Mapping the Ethicality of Algorithmic Pricing: A Review of Dynamic and Personalized Pricing. *Journal of Business Ethics, 170*(4), 697–719. DOI: 10.1007/s10551-019-04371-w

Sekti, B. A. (2025). Information Security Awareness. In *User-Centric Cybersecurity Implications for Sustainable Digital Transformation* (pp. 111–145). DOI: 10.4018/979-8-3373-3171-3.ch004

Sen, A. (2022). Are data markets a solution to big tech market power? A competitive analysis. *Journal of Government and Economics, 7*, 100052. https://doi.org/https://doi.org/10.1016/j.jge.2022.100052. DOI: 10.1016/j.jge.2022.100052

Spann, M., Bertini, M., Koenigsberg, O., Zeithammer, R., Aparicio, D., Chen, Y., . . . Yoo, H. (2025). Algorithmic pricing: Implications for marketing strategy and regulation. *International Journal of Research in Marketing*. https://doi.org/https://doi.org/10.1016/j.ijresmar.2025.05.001

Theodoridis, P. K., & Gkikas, D. C. (2025). Maximizing Social Media User Engagement Through Predictive Analytics in Retail Tourism: Identifying Key Performance Indicators That Trigger User Interactions. *Applied Sciences (Basel, Switzerland), 15*(21), 11720. Advance online publication. DOI: 10.3390/app152111720

Wellman, M. L., Stoldt, R., Tully, M., & Ekdale, B. (2020). Ethics of Authenticity: Social Media Influencers and the Production of Sponsored Content. *Journal of Media Ethics, 35*(2), 68–82. DOI: 10.1080/23736992.2020.1736078

KEY TERMS AND DEFINITIONS

Ad Blockers: Technological tools used by consumers to prevent advertisements and tracking scripts, functioning as a form of technical resistance.

Algorithmic Surveillance: The automated monitoring and analysis of consumer actions through digital infrastructures to enable profiling, prediction, and targeting.

Consumer Agency: The capacity of consumers to exercise autonomy and make reflective choices within algorithmically mediated environments.

De-Influencing: A discursive and cultural form of resistance that critiques influencer marketing, overconsumption, and the commodification of authenticity.

Digital Detox: Behavioral practices of disengaging from digital platforms to reduce exposure to surveillance, persuasion, and digital fatigue.

Platform Power: The structural dominance of digital platforms in controlling data flows, algorithms, and market access within digital marketing ecosystems.

Post-Surveillance Marketing: An emerging approach to digital marketing that minimizes reliance on continuous monitoring and prioritizes trust, autonomy, and ethical engagement.

Surveillance Capitalism: An economic logic in which personal data are extracted and monetized to predict and shape behavior for commercial gain.

Surveillance-Based Marketing: Marketing practices that rely on continuous data collection, behavioral tracking, and algorithmic prediction to influence consumer behavior.

Transparency-by-Design: An ethical design principle that embeds clarity and intelligibility about data practices directly into digital systems and interfaces.

Chapter 11
The Importance of Digital Marketing in Non-Professional Sports Organizations

Hugo Filipe Fernandes da Silva
http://orcid.org/0009-0005-6628-803X
Polytechnic of Porto, Portugal

Jorge Remondes
http://orcid.org/0000-0002-5259-4379
CEOS.PP, ISCAP, Polytechnic of Porto, Portugal

Sandrina Teixeira
http://orcid.org/0000-0002-5859-0002
CEOS.PP, ISCAP, Polytechnic of Porto, Portugal

ABSTRACT

The Portuguese sports landscape reflects a well-established tradition and the central role of sport in national identity. Based on a pyramid structure, it has its foundation in Non-Professional Sports Organizations (ODNP), which differ from professional structures in that they have no formal contracts and are mostly run by volunteers. This study analyzes the impact of Digital Marketing on the visibility, notoriety, and recruitment of members of these organizations. Based on a questionnaire answered by 203 participants, it assesses the perception of fans and members regarding the digital strategies adopted. The results show that social networks are decisive for engagement, emotional connection, and loyalty, reinforcing the identity and bond between the club and the community.

DOI: 10.4018/979-8-3373-7704-9.ch011

INTRODUCTION

Marketing and communication in sports should be strategically designed, using authentic narratives that reflect the club's values and history, thus creating differentiation in the competitive market (Chanavat & Desbordes, 2014).

For non-professional clubs, the accessibility provided by digital tools represents a golden opportunity. Digital platforms allow for two-way and personalized communication, where clubs can not only disseminate information but also collect feedback, increasing the sense of community and belonging among their fans (Filo et al., 2014). Furthermore, according to the same authors, these platforms foster an ongoing, long-term relationship based on mutual exchange and interactivity.

On the other hand, sponsorships remain a crucial source of funding, especially for clubs with limited resources. Chanavat and Desbordes (2014) state that "sponsorship activities are perceived as a unique marketing tool that perfectly complements a marketing communication program " (p. 46).

Research Problem

All sports organizations worldwide recognize that their 'product' can only grow if it is supported by a professionally managed marketing campaign (Smith et al., 2024).

Fans with a high degree of identification with the club or team tend to invest more time, resources, and money in the relationship to demonstrate their loyalty and the unwavering connection that unites their affiliation (Soares, 2023, citing Pontes et al., 2020).

Since this is the target audience for most non-professional sports clubs, this is the base of sponsors these organizations tend to rely on (Carreiro, 2023). However, according to the same author, clubs seeking greater investment capacity prioritize partnerships with larger national and international entities, as is the case with Clube Sport Marítimo.

Clubs that develop management skills to diversify revenue streams and implement effective marketing strategies have demonstrated greater growth potential and less financial vulnerability (Jëol et al., 2024).

Several cases have identified attracting sponsors as a significant benefit of using social media in marketing communication. (Marthinus et al., 2024).

The main research problem then focuses on understanding how Non-Professional Sports Organizations (NPSO) can effectively implement digital marketing strategies to overcome typical challenges, such as limited budgets and staff shortages: How does the use of digital marketing impact non-professional sports organizations in terms of brand awareness, visibility, fan attraction, and membership growth?

Chapter Structure

This chapter is structured into logically and sequentially organized sections, reflecting the research path from contextualizing the topic to the conclusions and practical implications.

The first section reviews the literature, exploring the main theoretical concepts and prior studies on the topic. The second section is dedicated to the research methodology, detailing the procedures adopted for data collection and analysis. It describes the research design, the sample definition, and the participant selection criteria, as well as the data-collection instrument: a questionnaire administered to fans, members, and supporters of non-professional sports clubs. In the third section, the results are analyzed and discussed, interpreting the data obtained through the questionnaire. Finally, in the fourth and final section, the study's conclusions are presented, summarizing the research's main contributions and the potential impact of the results on sports organizations. The theoretical and practical implications of the research are explored, with suggestions on how NPSO can optimize their digital presence and maximize their results. Furthermore, the study's limitations are discussed, and directions for future research are proposed.

BACKGROUND

The Portuguese Sports Landscape and the Sports Pyramid Model

According to Neves (2013), on a typical weekend in Portugal, for every game played between two professional football teams, an average of about thirty official games are played between amateur teams. Therefore, according to Pires (2024) the top of the pyramid, it can only aspire to a product of excellence if it takes care of its base.

This pyramidal structure is then characterized by a broad participation of athletes in the lower levels, which serves as a foundation for the development of talents who progressively ascend to the higher levels of competition (Pires, 2024). Using once again the example of Portuguese football, the "king of sports" in our country, according to Coelho (2004) this sports pyramid structure, is particularly evident, as can be seen in Figure 1.

Figure 1. Representation of the competitive pyramid in Portugal (Coelho, 2004)

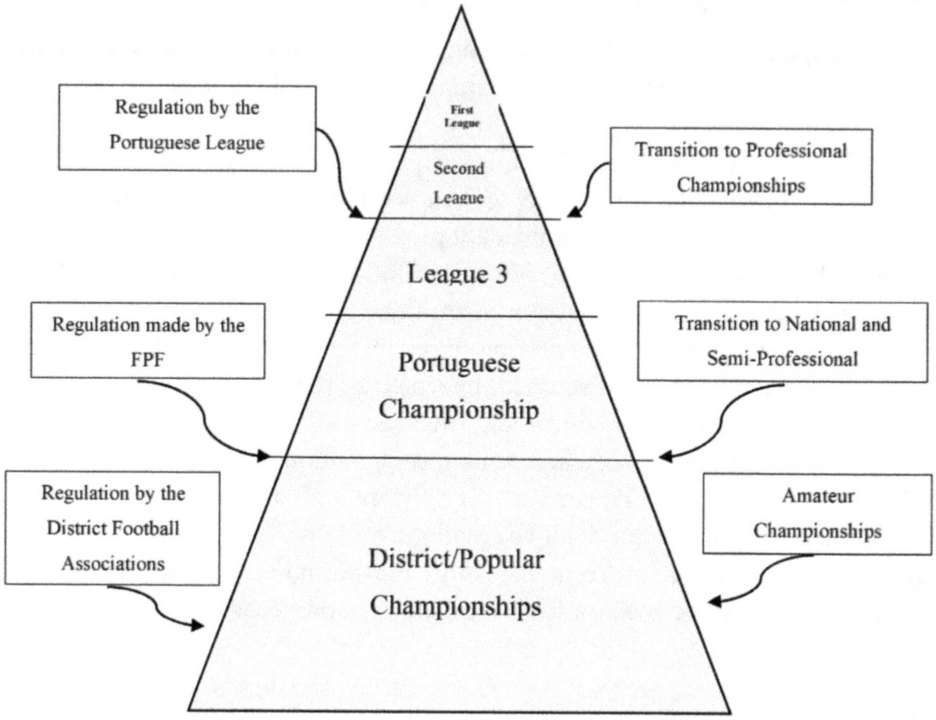

However, this model faces significant challenges. The financial sustainability of grassroots clubs is a constant concern, as many depend on limited support and volunteer work (Reis, 2024). Furthermore, the lack of talent retention and adequate infrastructure for sports practice is a pressing issue (XXIV Portuguese Government, 2024). These have been a recurring criticism of various organizations in positions of power, highlighting the need for greater attention from the competent authorities (Reis, 2024).

The Portuguese sports pyramid still faces the challenge of maintaining international competitiveness. According to García-Fernández et al. (2022) the top of the pyramid, there needs to be greater competitive balance, which will allow smaller clubs a greater capacity to compete with the larger ones. In this sense, significant progress is needed to achieve more solid and sustainable economic and sporting success, according to the same authors. Although there are success stories, most sports struggle to achieve outstanding results abroad. This scenario raises questions about the effectiveness of the current model and the need for reforms that promote greater professionalization and investment in grassroots sports (Tenreiro, 2014).

National sports federations thus play a crucial role in regulating and promoting the various sports, ensuring the organization of competitions and compliance with standards that guarantee the integrity and development of sport in the country (Portuguese Football Federation, 2025).

Characterization of NPSO and Challenges in Their Management

According to Anchieta (2008), "sport, like all areas of human activity, is in constant mutation and development. Globalization and technological advancement are infallible realities, and sports managers have the mission of ensuring that it survives this new reality, taking advantage of its benefits, without losing its essence, its values, and its principles" (p. 1).

In parallel, NPSO in Portugal play a fundamental role in the promotion and development of sport at the local and community level (Carvalho, 2024).

Generally constituted as non-profit associations, their main objective is the promotion and organization of physical and sporting activities, being crucial for the democratization of access to sport. They provide opportunities for sports practice to a wide range of participants, regardless of their age, gender, or social condition, thus contributing to social cohesion and community development (Basic Law of Physical Activity and Sport, 2007).

Nevertheless, Seaton (2010) notes that non-professional sporting event organizations share many of the characteristics of small businesses. They therefore face organizational problems related to the recruitment and retention of members, volunteers, and coaches, as well as the club's financial situation (Wicker & Breuer, 2012). In the world of sport, every product or company represents competition, meaning that this market is highly competitive, and the common goal for all clubs is to win over the spectator. The main objective of the clubs is to transform these spectators into fans and subsequently into members (Vieira, 2017).

The dependence on public subsidies and local patronage makes them vulnerable to economic and political fluctuations, according to Pereira (2024) "sponsorships represent approximately 45% of the total budget of senior men's teams, constituting the largest source of funding. Municipalities contribute 19%, while the remaining 36% comes from other sources, including subsidies and various support" (p. 29).

Furthermore, the management of non-profit sports organizations is frequently ensured by leaders who combine technical and administrative functions, often without specific training in sports management (Leão, 2018). According to Augusto (2015) the volunteer sports leader is characterized by living in a state of uncertainty, which daily opposes the effective exercise of their function.

Therefore, according to Seaton (2010), while it is true that professional sports organizations tend to be characterized by large, well-structured commercial enterprises managed by industry professionals, non-professional organizations are the opposite – there is a contrasting lack of skills that limits the ability of NPOs to implement marketing processes.

The Role of Community and Supporter Involvement in NPSO

According to Carvalho (2025), sport acts as an economic catalyst in communities, creating employment opportunities and boosting local commerce.

Sports events organized by NPSO generate jobs for coaches, managers, referees, and other professionals, and can also promote sports tourism, benefiting sectors such as hotels and restaurants. For example, a tournament in a small village can significantly increase hotel occupancy and sales in local restaurants (Carvalho, 2025). This information is corroborated by the European Commission: Directorate-General for Education (2016), which states that sport requires human intervention and therefore has a significant impact on job creation at the local level, not only in the activity itself but also in the construction and maintenance of infrastructure. In short, sport has a high employment multiplier effect.

The Portuguese government has implemented several policies and initiatives aimed at promoting community involvement in non-professional sport. The "National Sport for All Programme" is a notable example. This program is a structural measure designed to support projects that encourage the widespread practice of informal, recreational, or competitive sports, emphasizing the role of sport in the holistic development of individuals, promoting inclusion through sport, and improving health, quality of life, and well-being (Portuguese Institute of Sport and Youth, 2024) Nevertheless, Arroba et al. (2022) state that it is the history of the team itself, as well as the city, the style of play, the players and coaches (past and present), the nationality, the community or the actions carried out for the benefit of a particular community, that are significant factors in truly attracting fans who identify with a football team to form communities.

Additionally, these fans can transform their own perception of the team, developing loyalty over time. This loyalty leads them to experience everything involving the club more intensely, becoming more attentive to both positive and negative actions (Arroba et al., 2022).

Vieira (2017) states that brand attachment influences fans to be more confident, committed, and satisfied with their beloved club, thus making them more likely to actively participate and financially support the organization. Furthermore, fans in Portugal are, in general, quite attached to their clubs and couldn't be more loyal (Vieira, 2017).

According to Allison (2013), clubs that adopt a customer- centric philosophy, organizations that implement effective Customer Relationship Management (CRM) across the entire organization and develop social media platforms as part of their

CRM strategy are better positioned to understand their fans and adapt their marketing strategies to strengthen loyalty and brand advocacy, which, in the long term, will result in profitability and sustainable growth. Since winning is within reach of only a few each season, a strategy that places the fan at the center of the club will prove beneficial for most clubs, at all levels, in the long term (Allison, 2013).

Beyond the economic benefits, non-profit sports organizations are fundamental in promoting social inclusion. Sporting activities unite individuals of different backgrounds, ages, and cultures, fostering an inclusive environment and combating social isolation, especially in smaller localities (Carvalho, 2025). Sports clubs become meeting points and centers of social activity, where community members can interact and strengthen social ties.

Digital Marketing in the Sports Context

With the rise of the internet, buying and selling relationships have been transformed, both for the consumer and the seller. The market has become more dynamic, with economic transactions happening instantly around the world (de Oliveira et al., 2024).

The expansion of internet marketing is due to the various opportunities it offers. Among these, the most notable are convenience, speed, low costs, communication, closer relationships, and the possibility of collecting data in a more detailed way (de Oliveira et al., 2024).

The customer thus has unlimited access to information, made possible by the digital revolution, which allows for greater interaction between the company and consumers, and among consumers.

This social and digital phenomenon is generating changes in the interactions between consumers and brands in a very particular way (Tsai & Men, 2013). Companies need to be present where audiences are and spend the most time, such as on social networks (Bleize & Antheunis, 2019). These platforms currently play a highly relevant role in shaping consumer behaviors and attitudes (ML Cheung et al., 2021).

In fact, Araújo (2015) considers social networks powerful strategic tools for the online sales market, a phenomenon known as viral marketing. Social networks thus represent a non-traditional method of advertising with high effectiveness. In this way, it is possible not only to know the market but also to understand its technologies and benefit from collective interactions efficiently.

According to Marthinus et al. (2024) several cases, attracting sponsors has been identified as an important benefit of using social networks in marketing communication, which, as previously mentioned, is fundamental for NPSO.

Digital Sports Marketing and its Impact on the Connection Between Clubs and Fans/Members

Marketing can be considered as: a specific application of theoretical marketing principles to sports products and services; as marketing of non-sports products and services through an association with sport; and as marketing of sports organizations, including their events, activities, strategies, and image (Havrysh & Fen, 2022).

According to Mihai (2013), there are three stages in the strategic planning process of sports marketing, even in non-professional settings: identifying marketing opportunities; determining the strategy; and implementing, evaluating, and adjusting the strategy, respectively. Each of these stages has some inherent steps.

According to Mihai (2013), "all sports organizations, whether for profit or non-profit, develop social marketing programs to influence the behavior of their target audiences and improve the well-being of the groups to which they belong." (p. 234).

Additionally, citing Smith et al. (2024) all sports organizations in the world, including amateur ones, recognize that their 'product' can only grow if it is supported by a professionally managed marketing campaign.

According to Sá and Sá (2008), it is necessary to understand that sports consumers do not limit their interest solely to the sport itself, as there is a whole experience that spans the pre- and post-match phases. Miguel (2022) then explains that fans use social networking sites to obtain information or seek content that brings them emotionally closer to their favorite clubs.

Thus, in a digital context, the creation of online platforms, such as websites and social networks, is fundamental, where fans can obtain information about events, buy tickets, or register for activities related to the club, that is, the appropriate channels for each club to communicate (Miguel, 2022).

Digital Marketing in Membership Acquisition and Renewal

To assess the impact of digital marketing on membership acquisition and renewal, it is ideal to combine the effects of two branches of Marketing in the digital realm: Sports Marketing and Relationship Marketing.

Relationship marketing focuses on managing the relationships between an organization and its stakeholders, with the goal of developing loyal, mutually beneficial, and long-term relationships (Ravald & Grönroos, 1996). Although some non-profit organizations may lack sufficient financial or human resources to implement an elaborate marketing strategy, relationship marketing leverages many of the capabilities already existing within these organizations, such as interactions with volunteers and other valuable stakeholders (Mato- Santiso et al., 2023).

Sports marketing aims primarily to attract sports consumers through various means, positioning the brand and simultaneously conveying its original message. It seeks to create direct connections that involve brand experiences, targeting markets that encompass groups of people with similar affinities, united by the passion that sport generates (Suárez et al., 2023). Additionally, specific research findings by Funk et al. (2009) indicate that marketing communication should emphasize the benefits associated with the emotion, performance, and prestige of attending professional sporting events.

For example, according to Beličková (2024), digital marketing offers, through Artificial Intelligence (AI), the possibility of attracting and retaining members through highly segmented and personalized campaigns. Digital Network Professionals (DNP) can anticipate behaviors and trends and quickly adjust their strategies to maximize engagement. AI also contributes to greater cost efficiency by automating processes and ensuring better resource allocation. By facilitating communication personalization and audience segmentation, it allows DNP to target their campaigns to fans with greater potential for membership, strengthening engagement and encouraging the conversion of occasional fans into loyal members (Beličková, 2024).

Therefore, and according to Soares (2023), digital marketing actions and strategies in sports function as a tool that strengthens long-term connections and, therefore, increases levels of loyalty, fidelity, and passion among fans.

According to Achen (2017) social networks, such as Instagram, X (formerly Twitter), TikTok, etc., are an ideal setting for sports marketing activities, as these fan bases already have an established interactive community. Therefore, De Masters et al. (2024) state that the emergence of platforms such as TikTok, Snapchat, and Instagram offers non-profit organizations an opportunity to rethink their social media strategy. These networks require users to create short videos that combine audio and text, allowing organizations to open new lines of communication with their stakeholders . (DeMasters) et al., 2024).

According to Filo et al. (2014), the accessibility provided by digital tools, it represents a golden opportunity for non-professional clubs. These tools enable multidirectional (omnichannel) and personalized communication, allowing clubs not only to disseminate information but also to collect feedback, increasing the sense of community and belonging among their fans.

In a sporting context, NPSO can benefit from members who adopt omnichannel behaviors. They can, for example, cross-reference and analyze behavioral data from these members regarding their use of online and offline channels, thus adjusting their communication strategies (Mato-Santiso et al., 2023).

Marketing strategies and actions, therefore, play a vital role in building and strengthening the loyalty of followers, offering relevant and exclusive content, activities, special promotions, or interactive experiences (Soares, 2023).

The Supporter Engagement Scale Model

In the words of Stokburger-Sauer et al. (2008), one of the main competitive advantages of any club is its fans and, therefore, knowing and understanding them is fundamental to the success of a marketing strategy.

Beyond behavioral characteristics, fans can be differentiated by their degree of attachment to a team, that is, by their attitudinal loyalty towards it (Stokburger-Sauer et al., 2008).

These statements are consistent with the work of Rein et al. (2007), who introduced the Fan Engagement Scale, which categorizes fans based on their level of engagement with the sporting product. For easier understanding, this scale is represented in the form of an inverted pyramid – see Figure 2.

Figure 2. Fan involvement scale (Rein et al., 2007)

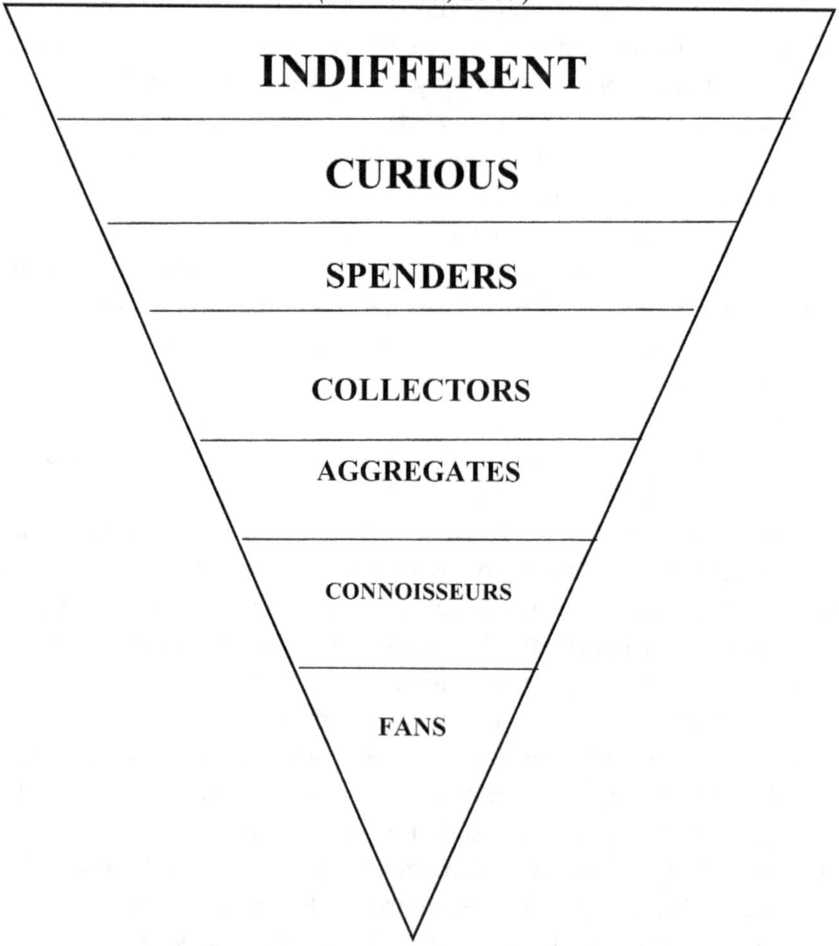

Looking then at the representation of the Scale in Figure 2, you can see that the degree of involvement of the followers increases as you go down the structure.

At the top, with a more superficial involvement, are the indifferent consumers, who have little or no interest in sports. Just below them are the curious consumers, who watch sporting events sporadically, without a deep connection to a team or sport, and whose relationship with sports is essentially mediated. Next are the spendthrift fans, who regularly follow sports and demonstrate a willingness and predisposition to invest money purely for sporting pleasure, still without any connection to any team. As involvement increases, and already in the middle of the pyramid, come the collector fans, who demonstrate some emotional connection to a specific club and are also willing to spend money on products that symbolize something related to the sport and/or club. Following them are the devoted fans, who already show a strong bond with the club and a desire to meet and interact with their idols, thus standing out from the rest of the fan base. It is at the next level that we find knowledgeable fans who are deeply connected to the sport and have access to and participate in the sporting events themselves. Finally, at the base of the pyramid are the fanatical supporters, who identify completely not only with the sport but also with their team. They rarely fail to provide their support, whether personally, financially, or through digital platforms (Teixeira, 2017).

The connection and love that spectators reveal towards their club reach levels of great closeness and involvement. Tribal behaviors are thus observed even in the sporting context (Teixeira, 2017). According to Soares (2023) a large part of the fan community, which was led to sympathize with the club due to family influences or traditions, and by chance, which causes these communities to follow and apply tribal elements in their sporting relationship.

Therefore, one of the most promising strategies for sports marketing professionals to boost consumer preferences and loyalty involves creating strong, positive, and distinctive beliefs about the club, that is, building a brand with a solid identity, fostering the image that the club and its fan base resemble a family and/or tribe (Stokburger-Sauer et al., 2008, Soares, 2023).

Digital Strategies and Tools for NPSO

The massification of digital communication and the enormous development of social media platforms have introduced a major change in the communication processes between people and organizations/football clubs and fans' (Gonçalves, 2015). Digital platforms, especially social networks are essential tools for sports marketing professionals and managers, allowing them to create and increase consumer/fan engagement with the brand (Machado et al., 2020).

Additionally, according to Dima (2015) the digital reach a club acquires is directly linked to the institution's revenue; that is, the more followers and supporters they attract, the greater the revenue generated. This statement is corroborated by Sutton et al. (1997) those who state that the more identified the fans are, the more willing they will be to buy club merchandise, namely jerseys, scarves, and/or flags.

Clubs should therefore orient this same communication strategy in order to enhance the connection with fans, since digital platforms end up facilitating interaction with fans, such as, for example, greeting or responding to fan comments on publications (da Costa, 2022).

Marketing objectives with ensuring adequate spaces for expressing opinions with the club and other fans, and providing effective and necessary communication, regardless of whether it is desired by the public, as a way to minimize uncertainty and strengthen trust, is vital so that, as seen previously, consumers move down the Fan Engagement Scale model (Soares, 2023, Teixeira, 2017, Rein et al., 2007).

Behavior of Supporters/Members in the Digital Environment

Currently, followers have become much more informed and attentive individuals, forcing clubs/organizations to define their strategy and establish precise communication (Félix, 2023).

The study by Haugh and Watkins (2016) indicates that fans do not limit themselves to passively consuming sports content, but also use social networks, for example, to access real-time information, express support for teams, and interact with other fans.

The interaction provided by digital platforms strengthens the relationship between NPOs and their supporters. According to Félix (2023), exclusive content, live event broadcasts, and the possibility of active participation through comments and sharing increase the feeling of belonging and loyalty among fans. This emotional connection is fundamental for retaining members and supporters and for growing the support base.

Thus, and again according to Haugh and Watkins (2016), sports fans use various social networks to obtain information about their favorite teams, with Facebook, Twitter, Instagram, and Snapchat being the most prominent. Furthermore, fans tend to use Facebook and Twitter for more informational purposes, while Instagram and Snapchat are used for emotional reasons, such as entertainment and escapism (Haugh & Watkins, 2016).

Measuring fan engagement is an essential element in sports marketing content strategy on social media, according to Ahiabor et al. (2023). Engagement metrics such as consumption, contribution, and the creation of relevant content of relevant (metrics related to content), are used to assess the level of interest and interaction of fans with the content. By analyzing these metrics, clubs can identify which types of content generate the greatest impact among these fans and adjust their strategy accordingly (Ahiabor et al., 2023).

Online communication for sports organizations stems from how they establish contact and interact with their audience. Therefore, it is fundamental to have a good strategy, to define achievable goals and objectives, and subsequently to measure and analyze the results so that improvements can be made or the chosen path can be established (Gonçalves, 2015).

Social Media Marketing as a Means of Engagement With Members, Supporters, and Sympathizers

Regardless of its form, any organizational promotion strategy has an objective and a target audience. In the context of sports, this target audience has very specific characteristics. On the one hand, there is the participating consumer, who promotes behaviors of integration or involvement in the sports organization. On the other hand, there is the spectator consumer, who may be watching through the media or "live" (Gonçalves, 2015).

The customer engagement then reflects the investment of cognitive, emotional, behavioral, and social resources by the customer (or consumer, in this case, the fan/member/supporter) during, or in relation to, specific interactions with the brand (Hollebeek et al., 2019). Although this investment of resources can have both positive and negative consequences, high fan engagement with a sports team is generally considered beneficial for several reasons (Huettermann et al., 2022). Following the reasoning of Huettermann et al. (2022) one reason is that engaged fans generate a constant source of income through purchase transactions (e.g., season tickets, merchandise), regardless of fluctuations in the team's performance on the field. Another reason is the positive influence these fans exert on other consumers.

Thus, as highlighted by Filo et al. (2014), social networks promote the co-creation of value between clubs and their audiences, providing more meaningful and personalized experiences. Furthermore, these platforms foster a continuous, long-term relationship based on mutual exchange and interaction.

Abeza et al (2017) corroborate these claims, arguing that social networks offer clubs/organizations the opportunity to educate and shape identity, while remaining accessible to their followers. They also mention that content shared on social networks should be clear, dynamic, and engaging, so that interaction with followers becomes increasingly strong and close.

According to Kim (2021), "when composing a plan to measure marketing results and, consequently, engagement, the first stage involves defining the Key Performance

Indicators (KPI), that is, the primary objectives to be achieved for the campaign to be successful." (p. 39).

It is therefore essential that these sports brands understand what drives fan engagement in order to encourage passive users to become more active participants on their digital platforms (Machado et al., 2020).

Elements That Drive Digital Engagement and Interaction Between the Club and its Fans

Engagement can be analyzed in three dimensions: cognitive, emotional, and behavioral, according to Borel and Christodoulides (2016). The cognitive aspect reflects the need for information and understanding among fans; emotional engagement relates to the trust and affective involvement that fans develop with the club; and the behavioral aspect translates into active participation, whether through interactions on social networks or through the generation of content by users themselves. The success of a digital strategy depends on the club's ability to foster these three dimensions in a balanced and integrated way (Borel & Christodoulides, 2016).

Furthermore, digital engagement can be influenced by electronic WOM, which refers to electronic recommendations made by fans about the club. Although positive electronic WOM has a significant impact on attracting new fans and building the club's reputation, periods of crisis can lead to inertia in recommendations and even a predisposition to share negative opinions (Cheung et al., 2008).

Regarding the elements that drive engagement and digital interaction between sports clubs and their fans and members, these can be divided into intrinsic and extrinsic factors (Trkulja et al., 2024). Intrinsic motivations, such as personal identity, entertainment, and brand love, are strong catalysts for high-quality engagement behaviors, including meaningful comments and active participation in discussions. Extrinsic motivations, particularly the role of social interaction, were more associated with the frequency of content publication and sharing. Emphasizing content that creates emotional connections, aligns with fan identity, and provides entertainment can enhance engagement (Trkulja et al., 2024).

According to Trkulja et al. (2024), the combination of intrinsic and extrinsic motivators allows sports organizations to create dynamic digital communities and strengthen fan loyalty.

In a similar vein, Mastromartino et al. (2020) state that the behavior of fans in the digital environment is strongly influenced by how the club manages its communication and promotes fan participation. Studies have shown that digital engagement is not limited to the quantity of interactions (likes, comments, and shares), but also to the quality of these interactions and the level of emotional involvement among fans. In positive moments, a significant increase in interaction and support for the club is observed, while in negative moments, there is a reduction in participation and an increase in public criticism (Mastromartino et al., 2020, Soares. 2023).

Content Marketing: Maximizing Engagement Through Quality and Frequency of Content

Content marketing is a marketing process focused on creating and distributing valuable and engaging content to attract, win over, and involve a clearly defined and understood target audience, with the goal of driving profitable actions from consumers (Pulizzi & Piper, 2023). It therefore has a significant impact on maximizing engagement, with the quality and frequency of content being crucial for fan interaction with sports clubs (Yarkin et al., 2024).

According to McCarthy et al. (2022), for the successful implementation of a marketing strategy, especially on social media, clubs are increasingly focused on the quality of the content published. In addition to quality, the frequency of content publication also influences engagement. An active and regular digital presence allows clubs to keep fans involved, ensuring constant communication and avoiding prolonged periods without interaction (McCarthy et al., 2022). Research by Yarkin et al. (2024) demonstrates that brands that maintain a consistent content publication strategy achieve a higher level of engagement and loyalty from consumers. Therefore, it is only logical that clubs with a well-implemented marketing strategy tend to use a content calendar to plan their publications throughout the season and pre-season, ensuring strategic alignment across platforms (McCarthy et al., 2022).

According to Kharmalki and Raizada (2020), fan engagement with clubs' social media channels is driven by needs similar to those identified in broader social media contexts (uses and gratifications theory, applied to sports marketing). Their study highlights that fans are particularly motivated to interact with content that strengthens their connection to the club, provides valuable and up-to-date information, and facilitates social interactions with other fans (Kharmalki & Raizada, 2020). The interactive nature of social media platforms allows sports clubs to effectively apply uses and gratifications theory, adapting their content to meet these specific needs (Trkulja et al., 2024).

Therefore, according to de Vasconcelos' study (2024) the main form of social interaction for Generation Z is through social networks, and they agree that they value sharing content on social networks and trusting other users more. Thus, sports organizations, especially professional ones, understand that many fans interact on various platforms because each offers a different experience. Facebook's algorithm favors long-form content, while Twitter is used as an information feed and Instagram as a more visual platform (McCarthy et al., 2022). Therefore, it is also concluded that diversifying content formats is another fundamental aspect of maximizing engagement. The combination of videos, images, live streams, and interactive posts enables the targeting of different fan segments and the addressing of various motivations. The use of interactive content, such as surveys, quizzes, and live streams, stimulates fan participation and strengthens their emotional connection with the club (Yarkin et al., 2024).

These characteristics are important to consider in marketing strategies, given the importance and value of the insights they provide (de Vasconcelos, 2024).

The Influence of Storytelling and the Digital Identity of Clubs

Professional sports organizations have a long tradition of using stories as part of their marketing efforts. Storytelling in the sports sector is becoming integrated into social media (Laurell & Söderman, 2018). Combined with the narrative skill of the storyteller, a narrative can capture the audience's attention, entertain, persuade, and shape new ways of thinking (Nicoli et al., 2021). Additionally, according to de Vasconcelos (2024) Generation Z tends to prefer viewing storytelling- related content on social media, especially Instagram. It is therefore natural that organizations are increasingly investing in creating content for different platforms, including social media, video streaming, and podcasts. Digital storytelling is designed to build bridges among citizens around the world, promoting greater understanding across generations and ethnicities. This approach allows an entity's diverse audience to develop mutual understandings on various issues (Nicoli et al., 2021).

On social media, narratives unfold over time through a process known as 'distributed linearity', emerging from the 'environmental affiliation' of individual users (Dawson & Mäkelä, 2020). This means that stories are not created in isolation by a single author, but are constructed collectively as users interact, share, and comment on content. According to Dawson and Mäkelä (2020), social media allows multiple perspectives to intertwine, giving rise to dynamic and constantly evolving narratives.

Borges (2018) states that sports organizations have become producers of their own content. In this way, they have come to exercise greater control over the symbolic elements and the narrative surrounding events, enhancing the club's visibility and promotion. This ability to shape discourse is essential to building a solid and enduring brand, as it helps consolidate the club's values and identity (Borges, 2018). In the words of Borges (2018), there is no sport without the media, and even less so without engagement with members and supporters.

Creation and Management of Online Communities

The feeling of unity generates motivation, which leads to better organization, thus ensuring the continuity of club activities and, consequently, good management (Ubah & Malcourant, 2018).

According to Stevens et al. (2024), identification with an experience can convert pre-experience interactions into positive post-experience evaluations, demonstrating the importance of the pre-experience phase.

Organizations can and should therefore begin developing meaningful relationships with consumers early on, including those encountering an offer for the first time. This approach can bring significant benefits, since identification with the experience positively influences loyalty to the service provider, which, in turn, reinforces word-of-mouth (WOM) and satisfaction with the experience (Stevens et al., 2024).

According to Saraiva G. and Silva (2023), based on the experiences of Taylor and Shanka (2008), there is no correlation between frequent visitors to sporting events and their level of education, and that they actually prefer to communicate with each other, with this WOM process being a catalyst for the origin of communities around clubs.

Thus, new fan communities have formed in recent years, especially with the growth of social networks. These online communities have created an element in fan culture, replacing the centrality of club success. They promote the idea of a common interest and romanticize the sport's simplicity (Levental, 2023).

It is in this sense that inclusion through NPSO emerges as a platform capable of improving social connections, promoting social integration, social justice, and active citizenship, that is, the development of social capital (Pedro, 2017).

Online communities differ from traditional brand communities by nature. Firstly, online fan communities allow overcoming the physical barriers of time and distance, becoming a powerful platform for strengthening relationships between fans (Kim & Manoli, 2023).

According to Young et al. (2011), online sports communities continue to grow in popularity and sophistication, becoming an essential means for geographically dispersed fans to stay connected. They are frequently used as sources of knowledge and repositories of information, where members share their real-life experiences. They also allow people with common interests to actively share information, debate relevant and irrelevant topics, establish online connections, and build a sense of belonging in a dynamic virtual community. However, for these communities to exist and thrive, the active participation of their members is essential (Young et al., 2011).

Studies by Farzan et al. (2011) demonstrate that social presence on digital platforms can be manipulated to strengthen bonds and shared identities, increasing user commitment and engagement. The team selection process and active participation in community dynamics increase user engagement.

In general, identification of sports fans with the online community is a determining factor for all constructs: identification with the team, intention to attend events, and intention to have a positive WOM experience (Kim & Manoli, 2023).

Therefore, and according to Kim and Manoli (2023), the online community should be considered a central element for a sports organization in understanding the real behavior of sports fans.

METHODOLOGY

Main Research Problem

The aim of this study is to analyze how the use of digital marketing affects the organizations under investigation in terms of increased brand awareness and visibility, recruitment of new supporters, and growth in membership numbers.

The choice of methodology was guided by the exploratory nature of the topic, which required a quantitative approach and, consequently, the collection of primary data via a questionnaire survey.

Thus, the problem and the main research question were defined as follows: How does the use of digital marketing impact non-professional sports organizations in terms of brand awareness, visibility, fan attraction, and membership growth?

Specific Problems

The specific research problems were defined in detail to deepen the understanding of the main problem. These problems allow for segmentation of the analysis, focusing on different dimensions of the relationship between digital marketing and the success of non-professional sports organizations.

Each specific problem reflects a central question that will be explored in the study, guiding data collection and theoretical discussion. This approach facilitates a more focused and structured analysis, ensuring that all relevant aspects of the topic are considered. The questions guiding this research are presented below.

1. How can social media increase the awareness and/or visibility of a Non-Professional Sports Organization?
2. Which digital platforms are most valued by fans for interacting with clubs and fostering the creation of an online community?

3. To what extent does digital marketing influence the level of engagement and loyalty of fans and members?

Research Objectives

The main objective of this research is to analyze the impact of digital marketing on NPSO in terms of increasing visibility and attracting and retaining new fans.

The increasing digitalization of the sports sector has created opportunities for clubs with limited resources to compete for attention and recognition in the digital environment, making it essential to understand how these organizations can structure effective strategies to differentiate themselves in the market and maximize the return on their digital initiatives, promoting more efficient management of their online communication channels.

Thus, the aim is to understand how the strategic use of social media, the frequency and quality of digital content, and the choice of the most appropriate platforms can directly impact fan engagemen*t* and the conversion of fans into active members.

To achieve the main objective, the following specific objectives were defined, which delve into different dimensions of the impact of digital marketing:

1. To analyze how social media can be used to increase the visibility of non-professional sports organizations. This objective seeks to understand how the strategic use of social media can improve the visibility and recognition of these organizations.
2. Identify which digital platforms are most used by fans, members, and supporters to follow the clubs. This objective focuses on identifying which digital platforms are most successful in improving fan and member engagement with the club.
3. Measure the impact of digital marketing on loyalty and the level of emotional engagement of fans. This objective focuses on investigating the relationship between the creation of relevant and appealing digital content and the growth of an online community of fans and members.

These objectives structure the research more precisely, enabling a deeper analytical understanding of the impact of digital marketing on the management and development of such organizations. Furthermore, they enable the creation of a strategic framework to guide future implementations in the sports digital marketing sector.

Research Hypotheses

The hypotheses of this study focus on the relationship between digital marketing and NPSO success, evaluating the impact of digital awareness, fan engagement, and member loyalty. The theoretical model constructed considers the influence of digital marketing variables on follower engagement and loyalty, highlighting social media and communication personalization as key elements.

H1: The Strategic Use of Social Media Positively Impacts the Visibility of Non-Professional Sports Organizations (NPSO)

An active and well-structured digital presence contributes to increasing the reach and reputation of clubs, making them more recognized by the public (McCarthy et al., 2022). Furthermore, according to Soares (2023), digital media, particularly social networks, act as bridges of proximity and identification between clubs and their fans. Additionally, according to Achen (2017), social media platforms such as Instagram, Facebook, and TikTok are an ideal setting for sports marketing activities .

H2: There are Digital Platforms That Stand Out More Than Others When it Comes to Increasing Visibility and Fan Engagement With the Club

Followers have become much more informed and attentive individuals, forcing clubs/organizations to define their strategy and establish precise communication (Félix, 2023).

Strategies that segment the audience and offer personalized content increase the perception of closeness and exclusivity, making fans more likely to maintain a long-term commitment (Yarkin et al., 2024).

As mentioned above, fans use social media platforms to obtain information or seek content that brings them closer emotionally to their clubs (Miguel, 2022).

H3: The Quality and Frequency of Digital Content Influence the Level of Engagement. of the Supporters, Facilitating the Conversion of Followers Into NPSO Members

Relevant and regular content increases follower interaction, encouraging active participation on social media and promoting greater emotional engagement (Pulizzi & Piper, 2023).

Continuous interaction through digital platforms strengthens the emotional bond with the club, increasing the likelihood of joining membership programs and providing financial support (Kharmalki & Raizada, 2020).

Highly engaged and loyal club brand supporters are more likely to contribute financially, whether through the purchase of merchandise, tickets, or membership subscriptions (Dima, 2015).

Theoretical Model

An investigation model was constructed based on the previously formulated hypotheses, yielding the theoretical framework shown in Figure 3.

Figure 3. Theoretical research model

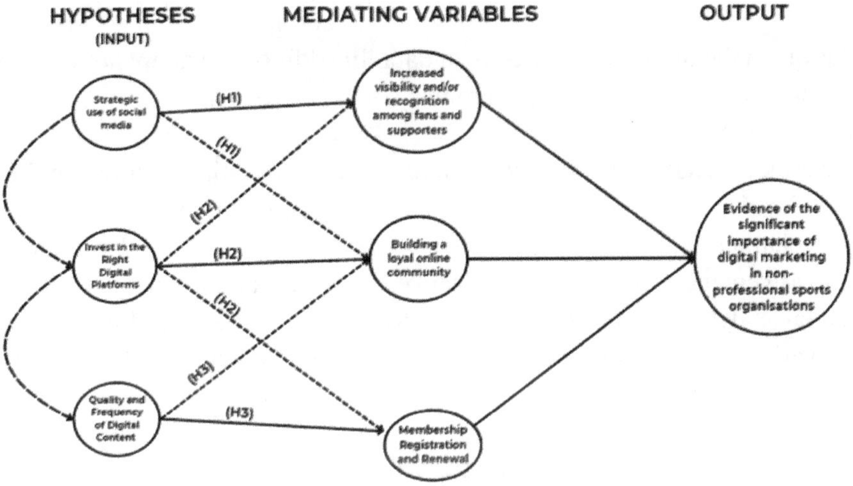

The theoretical model presented in Figure 3 is structured around three main independent variables. These variables influence three mediating variables, with the ultimate goal of measuring the importance of digital marketing in NPSO.

The relationship between these variables is complex, reflecting the dynamic interaction between digital strategies and their results. For example, the strategic use of social media (H1) not only increases visibility but also fosters a loyal online community. On the other hand, investing in the right platforms (H2) can simultaneously influence membership, visibility, and/or brand awareness. Finally, the quality of digital content (H3) can impact not only membership and renewal but also the creation of a more loyal online community, ultimately increasing the organization's visibility/brand awareness.

Data Collection Method

Before large-scale application, the questionnaire underwent a pre-test conducted by academics involved in Digital Marketing. The objective was to assess the clarity and relevance of the questions, identify ambiguities, and ensure that the questionnaire addresses the topics relevant to the study (Becker et al., 2012).

The questionnaire was made available on the Google Forms platform, chosen for its security, ease of access, and ability to generate preliminary reports. Participants were invited to respond via private messages on WhatsApp and on the social networks Instagram, Facebook, X (formerly Twitter), and LinkedIn. To maximize the response rate, an eight-week period was established, from April 10th to June 5th. All responses were collected anonymously and processed in accordance with legislation on the protection of personal data. In addition, participants were offered the option to receive an executive summary of the study's main results as an incentive to participate.

The collected data were analyzed using specialized statistical tools, in this case, SPSS software, allowing for descriptive and inferential analyses. The descriptive analysis characterizes the respondents' profile, identifying variables such as their roles, involvement with sports organizations, and digital marketing practices. The inferential analysis included correlation and regression tests to explore relationships among variables, including social network use, digital campaign effectiveness, and fan engagement.

Sample Definition and Selection Criteria

Anyone could answer this questionnaire, the main focus being on members, supporters, and sympathizers of NPSO, that is, anyone involved in the world of non-professional sports. Therefore, it can be said that the target population includes two main groups:

1. Members, supporters, or sympathizers of non-professional sports clubs, contributing to the perception of the impact of the campaigns;
2. Fans who don't feel as connected to their nearest non-professional sports club need to understand the best ways to attract them to the club.

These groups were chosen because they are directly involved in assessing the success of digital marketing strategies.

The study aimed to collect at least 200 valid responses. Sample sizes between 200 and 400 are considered adequate to ensure robust and reliable results (Kline, 2023), also allowing a safety margin for data cleaning and exclusion of invalid responses.

The collection platform enabled real-time progress monitoring, ensuring the minimum number of participants was reached within the stipulated timeframe.

RESULTS

Sample Characterization

The sample for this study comprises 203 respondents, whose sociodemographic characteristics are detailed below.

Most participants are between 35 and 54 years old (33.5%), followed by the 18-24 age group (31.0%) and the 25-34 age group (25.6%). Only 4.9% of respondents are 55 or older, and another 4.9% are under 18. This distribution reveals a predominance of individuals in the active-adult age group, reflecting the audience most involved in or affected by NPSO digital marketing practices.

The gender distribution shows a slight male predominance (52.2%), compared to 45.8% female. Only 2.0% of participants identified with another gender.

Regarding geographical location, 98.0% of participants reside in Portugal, with only 2.0% living outside the country.

Preferred Channels and Average Daily Usage of the Same

The frequency of digital channel use by the target audience directly influences the reach and impact of the clubs' actions. Table 1 shows the digital channels most used by respondents.

Table 1. Respondents' preferred digital channels

Digital Channel	Response Frequency	Total Percentage
Social media	200	98.5%
Emails / Newsletters	65	32%
Advertisements	36	17.7%
Mobile App	23	11.3%
Website / Blog	67	33%
Podcast	14	6.9%
Partnerships with Influencers	32	15.8%
SMS	21	10.3%

The most used digital channels by respondents are Social Networks, as expected, with an almost 100% response rate (98.5%). Websites/Blogs are the second-preferred digital channel (33%), with Emails and Newsletters following closely behind (32%). Also noteworthy are Advertisements (17.7%) and Influencer Partnerships (15.8%), which were not forgotten in the questionnaire responses. It is also worth noting that the frequency exceeds 100% because respondents were asked to choose up to 3 of the existing options.

Analysis of data on the average daily time respondents spend on social media reveals a strong digital presence in the sample. A significant majority (approximately 43%) of participants report using social media between 1 and 3 hours per day, followed by those reporting between 3 and 6 hours per day (approximately 31%). These two groups account for almost three-quarters of the sample, demonstrating regular, continuous use of social networks.

On the other hand, only 1% of respondents say they use social media for more than 10 hours a day, with about 13% using between 6 and 10 hours, and 12% using less than 1 hour. This data shows that, despite some extremes, the dominant pattern is moderate to high usage.

Follow-up Frequency by Gender

It is noted that males demonstrate greater and more regular engagement, particularly in the "A few times a week" and "Daily" categories. Women show a more dispersed distribution, with sharper peaks in "Rarely," "A few times a month," and "A few times a week," reflecting less and more irregular engagement. Those who identify with other genders show residual values in all options, preventing robust conclusions from being drawn.

Frequency of Use of Specific Platforms

Facebook continues to show a significant presence among respondents. With over 62% (126 respondents) giving positive responses compared to approximately 38% (77 respondents) giving negative responses.

Instagram stands out with an even more significant difference: more than 150 respondents (75.4%) say they use it, compared to only about 50 (24.6%) who do not.

This reflects the clear predominance of these platforms among respondents, enabling a more relevant and applicable analysis of non-profit organizations' digital strategies. Even so, the TikTok and X data are important for contextualizing emerging trends and may be useful for clubs that wish to explore niches or prepare their adaptation to new platforms.

Sports in Which the Clubs Supported by the Respondents are Included

Table 2 shows the distribution of sports in which the most followed non-professional sports clubs belong, according to the respondents.

The results reveal an overwhelming predominance of football, mentioned by 92.6% of participants (n = 188), highlighting the centrality of this sport in the Portuguese sporting landscape, even at the non-professional level. Futsal ranks second at 19.7% (n = 40), followed by athletics at 17.7% (n = 36), indicating some diversity in the sample, although these values are much lower than those for football.

Table 2. Sports in which the NPSO supported by the respondents are included

Sport	N	%
Soccer	188	92.6%
Futsal	40	19.7%
Athletics	36	17.7%
Volleyball	32	15.8%
Basketball	14	6.9%
Handball	9	4.4%
Swimming	8	3.9%
Roller Hockey	7	3.4%
Others)	9	4.4%

Other sports, such as volleyball (15.8%), basketball (6.9%), swimming (3.9%), and roller hockey (3.4%), are also represented, though at significantly lower percentages. The presence of several sports with only one or two mentions is also noted, such as surfing, judo, rugby, gymnastics, and cycling, among others, representing a residual fraction of the sample.

It is important to note that the question allowed multiple answers, which explains why the sum of the percentages exceeds 100%. Even so, the data confirm football's hegemony as the most popular sport among national digital games, which may have implications for how clubs communicate digitally and invest in marketing, given the greater pressure and media attention associated with this sport.

Impact of Digital Strategies on the Notoriety and Visibility of Clubs

Social media plays a significant role among adults up to 55 years old, with this age group being the one that most frequently reports discovering non-professional sports clubs through these platforms. The 25-34 age group clearly stands out with the highest number of affirmative responses, closely followed by the 35-54 age group. Among those under 18 and over 55, the impact is much smaller.

This pattern suggests that social media is an effective channel for attracting a young adult audience, which is particularly relevant to clubs' digital communication and marketing strategies.

The overwhelming majority of respondents selected options 4 and 5, on a scale of 1 (strongly disagree) to 5 (strongly agree), with particular emphasis on the maximum score (5), which had more than 150 responses (approximately 75% of respondents). This result demonstrates a largely positive perception among participants of social networks' role as a visibility tool for clubs.

To complement this analysis, data were also collected on how frequently users discovered clubs through social media and on how social media affects a fan's connection to the NPSO. The relationship between respondents' gender and the discovery of clubs through social media. It is noted that both male and female individuals report discovering non-professional clubs through this channel, although the percentage is significantly higher among men: approximately 74% of male respondents state that they have discovered a non-professional club through social media. In turn, the percentage of female respondents who also report having done so is around 56%.

Finally, we assess the respondents' level of identification with the statement 'I feel more connected to a NPSO due to its presence on social networks and other digital platforms'. It can be concluded that there is a clear trend: approximately 70% of respondents agree, either partially or fully.

Hypothesis Testing and Validation of the Conceptual Model

Correlation and regression analyses were conducted to assess the strength and direction of relationships among the variables, as well as the predictive validity of the proposed model.

The descriptive statistics for the perception scales used in the conceptual model are shown in Table 3.

The results generally show a fairly positive trend among respondents regarding the statements presented, with averages ranging from 3.30 to 4.64. The variable with the highest average was "Social networks help increase the notoriety/visibility of non-professional sports clubs" (Average = 4.64; Standard Deviation = 0.740), reflecting a fairly consensual perception of the role of social networks in institutional promotion.

Table 3. Descriptive statistics of the perception scales

Statistics	Social media helps increase the notoriety/ visibility of non-professional sports clubs	I feel more connected to a NPSO due to its presence on social media and other digital platforms	The frequency and quality of content published by a club affect my level of interest and interaction with them	Interaction with other fans through social media increases my engagement with the club	I prefer clubs that have an active and interactive digital presence	Quality Influences Support	Channels Influence Loyalty
N Valid	203	203	203	203	203	203	203
N Missing	0	0	0	0	0	0	0
Mean	4.64	4.00	4.17	3.82	4.09	3.70	3.90
Median	5.00	4.00	4.00	4.00	4.00	4.00	4.00
Mode	5	5	5	5	5	5	4
Std. Error	0.740	1.027	0.991	1.077	1.040	1.231	1.026
Minimum	1	1	1	1	1	1	1
Maximum	5	5	5	5	5	5	5

High averages are also highlighted in variables such as "I prefer clubs that have an active and interactive digital presence" (Average = 4.09; Standard Deviation = 1.040) and "The frequency and quality of content published by a club affect my level of interest and interaction" (Average = 4.17; Standard Deviation = 0.991), demonstrating that digital content is recognized as a factor that significantly contributes to engagement with the club.

On the other hand, the variable with the lowest average was "Interaction with other fans through social media increases my involvement with the club" (Average = 3.30; Standard Deviation = 1.077), although it remains above the midpoint of the scale. This result may suggest that digital engagement among fans is not, by itself, sufficient to significantly boost engagement, or that its impact is perceived as more indirect.

With regard to the quality of content and digital channels as factors of support and loyalty, the averages (Average = 3.87 and Average = 3.90, respectively) are equally encouraging, supporting the relevance of communication dimensions in building lasting relationships with fans, members, and supporters.

Based on these statistics, all variables show favorable trends and align with the conceptual model's assumptions.

Table 4 presents the results of Spearman's correlation coefficients, which measure the relationship between the variables studied, at a significance level of 0.01.

Table 4. Calculation of Spearman correlation coefficients between the variables studied

	Social networks help to increase the awareness/ visibility of NPSO.	**I feel more connected to NPSO because of its presence on social media and other digital platforms.**	**The frequency and quality of content published by a club affect my level of interest in and interaction with it.**	**Interacting with other fans through social media increases my involvement with the club.**	**I prefer clubs that have an active and interactive digital presence.**	**The quality of a club's digital communication influences my willingness to support it (e.g., attend a game, become a member).**	**The digital channels of the NPSO influence my engagement and loyalty as a supporter.**
Social networks help to increase the awareness/visibility of NPSO.	1	,419**	,438**	,401**	,350**	,310**	,273**
I feel more connected to NPSO because of its presence on social media and other digital platforms.	,419**	1	**,576****	,429**	**,515****	**,500****	,473**
The frequency and quality of content published by a club affect my level of interest in and interaction with it.	,438**	**,576****	1	**,530****	,494**	**,545****	,482**
Interacting with other fans through social media increases my involvement with the club.	,401**	,429**	**,530****	1	**,514****	,493**	,447**
I prefer clubs that have an active and interactive digital presence.	,350**	**,515****	,494**	**,514****	1	**,657****	**,557****
The quality of a club's digital communication influences my willingness to support it (e.g., attend a game, become a member).	,310**	**,500****	**,545****	,493**	**,657****	1	**,687****
The digital channels of the NPSO influence my engagement and loyalty as a supporter.	,273**	,473**	,482**	,447**	**,557****	**,687****	1

** Correlation is significant at the 0.01 level [2 extremes]

The results demonstrate a strong and significant correlation ($\rho = 0.419$; Sig. < 0.001) between the perception that social media increases NPSO awareness and visibility and fans' emotional connection to the organization due to its digital presence. Additionally, a positive and significant correlation is found between the use of social media to increase awareness and the quality and frequency of published content ($\rho = 0.438$; Sig . < 0.001).

In turn, the correlation between "The frequency and quality of content published by a club affect my level of interest and interaction with it" and "I prefer clubs that have an active and interactive digital presence" ($r = .494$, $p < .001$) suggests that the quality and frequency of digital content influence fan engagement, indirectly supporting the relevance of certain platforms.

Finally, Table 7 shows a significant correlation between the frequency and quality of content and fans' level of interest and interaction with the club ($\rho = 0.576$; Sig. < 0.001). Furthermore, this variable shows a significant relationship with fan engagement through social media interactions ($\rho = 0.530$; Sig . < 0.001) and with fan loyalty ($\rho = 0.482$; Sig . < 0.001), indicating that high-quality content published regularly promotes greater engagement and loyalty, and the conversion of followers into members.

Correlation Analysis for Hypothesis Validation

Spearman's correlation analysis provides a better understanding of the relationship between social media use and fans' engagement with the NPSO, particularly regarding loyalty, interest, and preference for clubs with an active digital presence.

There is a positive and statistically significant correlation ($\rho = 0.515$; $p < 0.001$) between fans' connection to a non-profit organization and their preference for clubs with an active, interactive digital presence, suggesting that this preference is related to visibility and digital engagement. The value indicates that individuals who feel more connected to non-profit organizations through their social media activity also tend to prefer clubs that adopt a more active and engaging digital communication strategy.

A moderate and statistically significant positive correlation was found between the perception that digital channels influence loyalty and the frequency and quality of content published by the clubs ($\rho = 0.482$; $p < 0.001$). Similarly, this perception of the influence of digital channels on loyalty shows an equally moderate correlation with the preference for clubs that maintain an active and interactive digital presence ($\rho = 0.557$; $p < 0.001$). Finally, the frequency and quality of published digital content are positively correlated with this preference for digitally active clubs ($\rho = 0.494$; $p < 0.001$). These data reinforce the notion that consistent, high-quality, and regularly published digital content contributes not only to increasing fan interest but also to strengthening the emotional connection with clubs and promoting their loyalty.

Weak but significant negative correlations were found between loyalty and the use of *Facebook* ($\rho = -0.109$; $p = 0.120$), Instagram ($\rho = -0.182$; $p = 0.009$), Tik-

Tok (ρ = -0.223; p = 0.001), and *X* (excluding Twitter) (ρ = -0.140; p = 0.047). These results can be interpreted as a reflection of greater demand from the most frequent users of these platforms, who, despite being more exposed to clubs' digital presence, do not always feel sufficiently impacted or loyalized by the strategies used. In other words, the simple fact that a club is present on these networks does not, in itself, seem to be sufficient to positively influence fan loyalty.

In turn, a preference for clubs with an active and interactive digital presence also shows a negative correlation with the use of Instagram (ρ = -0.196; p = 0.005), TikTok (ρ = -0.230; $p < 0.001$), and *X* (Ex -Twitter) (ρ = -0.147; p = 0.036).

The frequency and quality of digital content show a moderate positive correlation with the support given to the club (ρ = 0.545; $p < 0.001$), suggesting that effective digital communication can reinforce fans' sense of support and identification. Conversely, a significant negative correlation is observed with the influence on going to the stadium (ρ = -0.326; $p < 0.001$) and with the influence on participation in any activity promoted by a non-profit sports organization (ρ = -0.278; $p < 0.001$), which may indicate that, in contexts of more intense digital communication, sports consumption tends to shift to the digital environment, reducing the need for physical presence or direct practice. These negative relationships are also reflected among the other variables involved, such as the relationship between support and going to the stadium (ρ = -0.275; $p < 0.001$) or between the influence on going to the stadium and the influence on participating in some activity promoted by a non-profit organization (ρ = 0.562; $p < 0.001$), the latter being a positive exception that suggests that those who go to the games also tend to be more active in the activities (physical or digital) created by a non-profit organization.

Scale Reliability

The reliability analysis of the scale was conducted by calculating Cronbach's alpha, which assesses the internal consistency of the variables comprising the scale used in the questionnaire. The data presented in Table 5 provide statistical information, enabling the impact of each variable on the scale's overall reliability to be identified.

Table 5. Reliability table for the scale using Cronbach's Alpha

Items	Scale Mean if Item Deleted	Scale Variance if Item Deleted	Corrected Item-Total Correlation	Squared Multiple Correlation	Cronbach's Alpha if Item Deleted
Social media helps increase the notoriety/visibility of non-professional sports clubs.	23.67	23.688	.485	.295	.853
I feel more connected to a Non-Professional Sports Organization due to its presence on social media and other digital platforms.	24.32	21.059	.596	.380	.839
The frequency and quality of content published by a club affect my level of interest and interaction with them.	24.14	20.905	.645	.445	.832
Interaction with other fans through social media increases my involvement with the club.	24.49	20.568	.614	.393	.836
I prefer clubs that have an active and interactive digital presence.	24.22	20.015	.713	.527	.821
QualityInfluenceSupport	24.61	18.775	.697	.575	.824
ChannelsInfluenceLoyalty	24.41	21.036	.599	.454	.838

Cronbach's alpha for the total scale is 0.854, indicating high internal consistency among the items. All variables show corrected item-total correlations greater than 0.3, indicating that they contribute positively to the scale. According to Nunnally and Bernstein (1978), Cronbach's alpha is an essential measure of an instrument's internal reliability, with a minimum value of 0.70 recommended for instruments in the early stages of development. Higher values, such as 0.80 or above, are advised when the instrument is used in applied or highly demanding contexts.

Excluding any item does not improve overall reliability, suggesting that all items are relevant and should be retained.

Thus, it can be concluded that the questionnaire's scale is reliable for measuring the impact of digital marketing on NPSO and, consequently, suitable for validating the research hypotheses and objectives.

DISCUSSION

The results obtained throughout this study aim to offer a relevant contribution to understanding the role of digital marketing in NPSO. Through correlation analysis and hypothesis testing, it was possible to verify that digital channels significantly influence fans' perceptions, loyalty, and engagement with clubs, especially when there is an active, attractive, and interactive digital presence. These findings align with the words of Stokburger-Sauer et al. (2008), who state that one of the main competitive advantages of any club is its fans; therefore, knowing and understanding them is fundamental to the success of a marketing strategy.

Firstly, the data demonstrate that the digital presence of non-profit organizations is strongly associated with a sense of emotional connection among supporters, validating the premise that digital media, particularly social networks, serve as bridges of proximity and identification. This statement is also corroborated by Soares (2023) what was mentioned above. The positive and significant correlation between feeling more connected to the organization and the preference for clubs with an active digital presence reinforces this idea. This suggests that, in a context where the resources of non-profit organizations are generally limited, investing in digital content can be an efficient strategy to strengthen the club's identity within its community.

Similarly, it was found that both the frequency and quality of published digital content directly affect fans' interest and interaction, as well as their willingness to support the club, attend games, or participate in initiatives promoted by the organization. There is a positive relationship between the perceived quality of content and declared support for the club, and an inverse relationship between content's influence on the decision to attend live games. This last point suggests that although digital content encourages overall engagement, it does not completely replace the in-person experience; rather, it complements the sporting experience. These statements are also supported by studies by Gonçalves (2015), Machado et al. (2020), and da Costa (2022), who argue that digital platforms ultimately facilitate interaction with fans – the key word being 'facilitate' and not 'replace'.

Additionally, the results show that the influence of digital channels on loyalty is significantly correlated with a preference for clubs that are more digitally active and with perceptions of content quality and frequency. This supports the idea that loyalty to the club brand in non-digital organizations is built not only through sporting results but also through relational and communicative elements. Thus, as also argued by Arroba et al. (2022) this, loyalty makes it easier to convert fans into members, as they experience the club more intensely.

Finally, it is worth highlighting the relationship between digital presence and the predisposition to participate in club-promoted activities, such as raffles, voting, or special events. The significant correlations between positive perceptions of content and active participation reveal that digital channels not only keep the public informed but also have mobilization potential that warrants exploration. This ability to convert communication into action represents a fundamental strategic resource for NPSO that intend to increase their social impact and the loyalty of their community, as substantiated by DeMasters et al. (2024) and Achen (2017), as mentioned above.

Thus, the results obtained validated all the initial hypotheses. Hypothesis H1, which posited that the digital presence of non-profit organizations positively impacts their notoriety, was confirmed by the positive and significant correlations between perceptions of digital presence and both the degree of interest and the level of emotional connection. Hypothesis H2, which suggested that some digital platforms stand out more than others in terms of increasing the visibility and engagement of fans with the club, was also validated. Finally, Hypothesis H3, which argued that the quality and frequency of digital content influence the level of fan engagement, thereby facilitating the conversion of followers into members of non-profit organizations, was also validated. The results revealed positive correlations between perceptions of digital presence and the predisposition to engage in initiatives such as events, raffles, and polls.

In summary, the results obtained confirm the importance of a well-defined digital *marketing strategy* in the context of NPSO. The data reinforce the idea that digital presence and performance not only influence feelings of belonging and loyalty but also actively contribute to fans' engagement and participation. Thus, NPSO should view digital marketing not as a cost, but as a strategic investment in their sustainability and relational growth.

Table 6. Validating research hypotheses

Hypotheses	Content	Result (True/ False)
H1	The strategic use of social media positively impacts the visibility of NPSO.	True
H2	There are digital platforms that stand out more than others when it comes to increasing visibility and fan engagement with the club.	True
H3	The quality and frequency of digital content influence the level of engagement of the supporters, facilitating the conversion of followers into NPSO members.	True

Table 6 presents the results for all hypotheses, indicating the number of each hypothesis, its basis or content, and the result obtained from the research.

CONCLUSION

This chapter aimed to analyze the impact of digital marketing practices, especially digital

presence on social networks and other platforms, on fans' engagement with NPSO. Using a quantitative approach and a questionnaire administered to 203 participants, data were obtained to validate the three formulated hypotheses.

The results revealed a positive and significant correlation between NPSO digital presence and fans' sense of connection, demonstrating that the greater the perception of an active, interactive presence on digital platforms, the stronger the emotional connection between the public and the clubs. It was also found that the quality and frequency of published content significantly affect fan loyalty, particularly the preference for clubs that maintain consistent and engaging digital communication.

Finally, the data showed that digital presence influences the willingness of fans to participate in initiatives promoted by the NPSO, such as events, raffles, and voting. These results reinforce the strategic role of digital marketing not only as a communication tool but also as an engine for engagement, loyalty, and activation of the sports community.

Theoretical and Practical Implications

At a theoretical level, this research contributes to the scarce existing literature on digital marketing in the non-professional sports context, offering an empirically supported conceptual model that links digital practices to fans' affective connection, loyalty, and active participation. The results validate assumptions of relationship marketing and digital communication theories, suggesting that even in contexts with more limited resources, such as NPSO, online presence can play a transformative role in the relationship with audiences.

From a practical standpoint, the results offer valuable guidance for managers, communication managers, and NPSO volunteers. Firstly, the importance of maintaining an active, regular, and high-quality digital presence with relevant and appealing content that promotes fan engagement becomes evident. Secondly, the strategic management of social media should go beyond simply sharing sporting results and focus on content that stimulates interaction, fosters a sense of belonging, and encourages community participation. Initiatives such as polls, contests, live streams, and digital engagement campaigns have proven to impact loyalty and participation in club activities.

In short, the data show that investing in digital marketing is not a luxury reserved for professional sports but rather a real opportunity for NPSO to strengthen itself institutionally, expand its support base, and ensure greater sustainability and relevance within the social fabric in which it operates.

Limitations of the Study

Despite being conducted with methodological rigor and using a sample relevant to the proposed objectives, this study has some limitations that should be considered when interpreting the results.

Firstly, this is a quantitative study based exclusively on a questionnaire, which may limit the depth of the analysis. The absence of qualitative methods, such as interviews or focus groups, may prevent a deeper understanding of the respondents' perceptions, motivations, and experiences regarding the role of digital marketing in NPSO.

Secondly, although large, the sample was collected via convenience sampling and social networks, which may introduce bias, namely the over-representation of younger and digitally active individuals. This may have influenced the results, leading to a greater emphasis on social networks.

Additionally, the data collected covers a specific period, making it impossible to track temporal evolution in fan behavior or in clubs' adoption of digital strategies.

Finally, it is important to mention that the study focuses on a specific geographical and cultural reality, the Portuguese context, and, in particular, the district, which may limit its generalization to other countries or levels of competition.

Future Research Directions

Based on the identified limitations and the results obtained, several avenues for future research emerge to deepen the understanding of the importance and impact of digital marketing in non-professional sports.

Firstly, it would be relevant to complement this type of study with qualitative approaches. Conducting interviews with managers, athletes, or communications managers at non-professional clubs would allow for a more detailed exploration of the strategies used, the challenges faced, and internal perceptions of digital marketing's effectiveness.

Secondly, it is recommended to broaden the sample to include greater diversity across regions, age groups, and levels of digital literacy, as well as other stakeholders, such as local sponsors and municipal representatives, whose perspectives can be fundamental to analyzing the sports ecosystem.

Another interesting line of investigation would be a longitudinal analysis of the impact of social media over time, observing, for example, growth in fan base, digital engagement, or revenue as a function of the strategies implemented by the clubs.

Finally, it would be relevant to conduct comparative studies between clubs across different sports or between countries, with the aim of identifying best practices, digital communication patterns, and successful models adaptable to the Portuguese context.

ACKNOWLEDGMENTS

The authors would like to thank NotebookLM and Grammarly for their AI tools, which helped to refine the language and grammar of this manuscript and to create tables and figures. The authors reviewed the text, edited the content as necessary, and took full responsibility for the final publication.

REFERENCES

Abeza, G., O'Reilly, N., Seguin, B., & Nzindukiyimana, O. (2017). Social Media as a Relationship Marketing Tool in Professional Sport: A Netnographical Exploration. *International Journal of Sport Communication*, *10*(3), 325–358. DOI: 10.1123/ijsc.2017-0041

Achen, R. M. (2017). Measuring social media marketing: Moving towards a relationship-marketing approach. *Managing Sport and Leisure*, *22*(1), 33–53. DOI: 10.1080/23750472.2017.1379883

Ahiabor, D. K., Kosiba, J. P. B., Gli, D. D., Tweneboah-Koduah, E. Y., & Hinson, R. E. (2023). Satellite fans engagement with social networking sites influence on sport team brand equity: A UGT perspective. *Digital Business*, *3*(2), 100064. DOI: 10.1016/j.digbus.2023.100064

Allison, N. (2013). *Going beyond on-pitch success: Fan engagement as a catalyst for growth* [University of London]. https://core.ac.uk/download/pdf/141220628.pdf

Anchieta, T. (2008, November). What are the challenges of sports management as a sports manager? *efdeportes*. https://www.efdeportes.com/efd126/desafios-da-gestao-desportiva-enquanto-gestor%20desportivo.htm

Araújo, R.F. (2015). Digital scientific marketing and alternative metrics for journals: From visibility to engagement. *Perspectives in Information Science, 20* .

Arroba, T., Gea García, G., Sánchez-Sáez, J. A., & Conde, E. (2022). Fan identification as a precursor of loyalty towards a football team. *Systematic Reviews*, *11*, 22–60.

Augusto, P. M. C. (2015). *Profile of Non-Professional Football Sports Leaders – A case study on Sports Leaders in the Lisbon District* [University of Lisbon]. https://repositorio.ulisboa.pt/bitstream/10400.5/8643/1/Perfil%20dos%20Dirigentes%20Desportivos%20de%20Futebol%20N%C3%A3o%20Profissional%20-%20Doc%20Final%20-%20Pedro%20Augusto%20-%20Altera%C3%A7%C3%A3o.pdf

Basic Law on Physical Activity and Sport. No. 161, Assembly of the Republic (2007). https://diariodarepublica.pt/dr/legislacao-consolidada/lei/2007-58896796

Becker, S., Bryman, A., & Ferguson, H. (2012). *Understanding research for social policy and social work: Themes, methods and approaches* (2nd Edition). Policy Press. https://books.google.pt/books?hl=pt-PT&lr=&id=QB-LaGf05z0C&oi=fnd&pg=PP8&dq=Bryman+2012&ot s=m7eR7HMlTT&sig=TICshqJjvS6kU-PeqkYs3S9btmSs&redir_esc=y#v=onepage&q=Bryman%202012&f=false

Beličková, P. (2024). AI-powered Insights: Strengthening Nonprofit Communication through Neuromarketing. *Media & Marketing Identity*, 22–29. DOI: 10.34135/mmidentity-2024-02

Bleize, D. N. M., & Antheunis, M. L. (2019). Factors influencing purchase intention in virtual worlds: A review of the literature. *Journal of Marketing Communications*, *25*(4), 403–420. DOI: 10.1080/13527266.2016.1278028

Borel, L., & Christodoulides, G. (2016). *Branding and digital analytics* .

Borges, F. (2018). Always Together: How Football Clubs Want Constant Connections with Fans. *ATHENS JOURNAL OF SPORTS*, *5*(4), 263–278. DOI: 10.30958/ajspo.5-4-2

Carreiro, H. S. O. (2023). *Importance of marketing in football: A comparative analysis between clubs* [University of the Azores]. http://hdl.handle.net/10400.3/7039

Carvalho, E. (2024, January 26). 6 Challenges that Youth Sports Clubs Face. *emjogo.pt*. https://emjogo.pt/blog/6-desafios-que-os-clubes-de-desporto-de-formacao-enfrentam/

Carvalho, E. (2025, January 30). The Impact of Sport on Local Communities. *emjogo.pt*. https://emjogo.pt/blog/o-impacto-do-desporto-nas-comunidades-locais/

Chanavat, N., & Desbordes, M. (2014). Sponsorship and ambush marketing in sport. In *Routledge handbook of sports marketing* (2nd ed., p. 46). Routledge., https://www.researchgate.net/publication/339237351

Cheung, C. M. K., Lee, M. K. O., & Rabjohn, N. (2008). The impact of electronic word-of-mouth. *Internet Research*, *18*(3), 229–247. DOI: 10.1108/10662240810883290

Cheung, M. L., Pires, G. D., Rosenberger, P. J.III, & De Oliveira, M. J. (2021). Driving COBRAs: The power of social media marketing. *Marketing Intelligence & Planning*, *39*(3), 361–376. DOI: 10.1108/MIP-11-2019-0583

Coelho, J. N. (2004). Waving the Flag: Football and National Identity. *International Relations, 2*, 22. https://ipri.unl.pt/index.php/pt/publicacoes/revista-ri/arquivo-de-revista-ri/83-relacoes-internacionais-n-2

da Costa, G. J. C. (2022). *Digital Sports Communication in the midst of the Covid-19 pandemic: The cases of FC Paços de Ferreira and Rio Ave FC* [ISCTE - University Institute of Lisbon]. https://repositorio.iscte-iul.pt/bitstream/10071/29473/1/master_guilherme_conceicao_costa.pdf

Dawson, P. A., & Mäkelä, M. (2020). The Story Logic of Social Media: Co-Construction and Emergent Narrative Authority. *Style (Fayetteville), 54*(1), 21. https://api.semanticscholar.org/CorpusID:226735125. DOI: 10.5325/style.54.1.0021

de Oliveira, E. R., & Ferreira, P. (2014). *Research Methods: From Questioning to Scientific Discovery*. Vida Economica Editorial. https://books.google.pt/books?id=Xku7BAAAQBAJ

de Vasconcelos, B. C. (2024). *Content strategies on social media for Generation Z: TikTok and Instagram* [ISCAP - Instituto Superior de Contabilidade e Administração do Porto]. http://hdl.handle.net/10400.22/26040

DeMasters, C., Morgan, K., Schwoerer, K., & Wiley, K. (2024). Forging Connections: Nonprofits, TikTok, and Authentic Engagement – A Mixed-Methods Study. *Journal of Public and Nonprofit Affairs, 10*(1). Advance online publication. DOI: 10.20899/jpna.dky82f18

Dima, T. (2015). Social Media Usage In European Clubs Football Industry. Is Digital Reach Better Correlated With Sports Or Financial Performance? *Romanian Economic Journal, 18* (55), 117–128. https://ideas.repec.org/a/rej/journl/v18y2015i55p117-128.html

European Commission: Directorate-General for Education, Y., Sport and Culture. (2016). *Study on the contribution of sport to regional development through the structural funds – Final report* . Publications Office. DOI: 10.2766/940310

Farzan, R., Dabbish, L. A., Kraut, R. E., & Postmes, T. (2011). Increasing commitment to online communities by designing for social presence. *Proceedings of the ACM 2011 Conference on Computer Supported Cooperative Work*, 321–330. DOI: 10.1145/1958824.1958874

Félix, B. J. (2023). *Strategic communication plan for the dissemination of acrobatic gymnastics in Portugal* [ISCTE - University Institute of Lisbon]. http://hdl.handle.net/10071/30262

Filo, K., Lock, D., & Karg, A. (2014). Sport and social media research: A review. *Sport Management Review, 18*(2), 166–181. DOI: 10.1016/j.smr.2014.11.001

Funk, D. C., Filo, K., Beaton, A. A., & Pritchard, M. (2009). Measuring the motives of sport event attendance: Bridging the academic-practitioner divide to understanding behavior. *Sport Marketing Quarterly, 18*(3), 126–138. https://digitalcommons.cwu.edu/cobfac/276/. DOI: 10.1177/106169340901800302

García-Fernández, J., Grimaldi-Puyana, M., & Bravo, G. (2022). *Sport in the Iberian Peninsula*. Routledge., DOI: 10.4324/9781003197003

Gonçalves, R. G. (2015). *Sports organizations and new media: Trends and good practices* [University of Aveiro]. http://hdl.handle.net/10773/14627

Haugh, B., & Watkins, B. (2016). Tag Me, Tweet Me if You Want to Reach Me: An Investigation Into How Sports Fans Use Social Media. *International Journal of Sport Communication, 9*(3), 278–293. DOI: 10.1123/ijsc.2016-0044

Havrysh, I. I., & Fen, K. S. (2022). Sports marketing: Essence, specificity and basic subjects. *Economic Sciences Series, 66*(66), 61–68. DOI: 10.24025/2306-4420.66.2022.268591

Hollebeek, L., Srivastava, R., & Chen, T. (2019). SD logic–informed customer engagement: Integrative framework, revised fundamental propositions, and application to CRM. *Journal of the Academy of Marketing Science, 47*(1), 161–185. Advance online publication. DOI: 10.1007/s11747-016-0494-5

Huettermann, M., Uhrich, S., & Koenigstorfer, J. (2022). Components and Outcomes of Fan Engagement in Team Sports: The Perspective of Managers and Fans. *Journal of Global Sport Management, 7*(4), 447–478. DOI: 10.1080/24704067.2019.1576143

Jëol, M., Terrien, M., & Chanavat, N. (2024). Challenges, risks, and development opportunities for amateur sports clubs: The case of French handball clubs. *Managing Sport and Leisure*, •••, 1–17. DOI: 10.1080/23750472.2024.2305909

Kharmalki, G., & Raizada, S. (2020). Social Media Marketing in Sports: The Rise of Fan Engagement through Instagram. *Annals of Tropical Medicine and Public Health, 23*(17). Advance online publication. DOI: 10.36295/ASRO.2020.231721

Kim, S. (2021). Mapping social media analytics for small business: A case study of business analytics. *International Journal of Fashion Design, Technology and Education, 14*(2), 218–231. DOI: 10.1080/17543266.2021.1915392

Kim, S., & Manoli, A. E. (2023). From horizontal to vertical relationships: How online community identification fosters sport fans' team identification and behavioral intentions. *International Journal of Sports Marketing & Sponsorship*, *24*(1), 1–19. DOI: 10.1108/IJSMS-09-2021-0188

Kline, R. B. (2023). *Principles and practice of structural equation modeling.* (5th Edition). Guilford Publications. https://books.google.pt/books?hl=pt-PT&lr=&id=t2CvEAAAQBAJ&oi=fnd&pg=PP1&dq=Kline,+R.+B.+(2023).+Pri nciples+and+Practice+of+Structural+Equation+Modeling+(5%C2%AA+ed.).+Guilford+Press.&ots=sWUCS5b1fO&s ig=z6tiHh-5ux7uxlniaZw6Z_NnuJ8&redir_esc=y#v=onepage&q=Kline%2C%20R.%20B.%20(2023).%20Principles%20a nd%20Practice%20of%20Structural%20Equation%20Modeling%20(5%C2%AA%20 ed.).%20Guilford%20Press.&f=false

Laurell, C., & Söderman, S. (2018). Sports, storytelling and social media: A review and conceptualization. *International Journal of Sports Marketing & Sponsorship*, *19*(3), 338–349. Advance online publication. DOI: 10.1108/IJSMS-11-2016-0084

Leão, R. R. S. (2018). *Sports Leaders in Portugal: A case study on roller hockey* [University of Évora]. https://dspace.uevora.pt/rdpc/bitstream/10174/23498/1/Mestrado %20-%20Dire%C3%A7%C3%A3o%20e%20Gest%C3%A3o%20Desportiva%20 -%20Ricardo%20Rafael%20Soares%20Le%C3%A3o%20-%20Os%20dirigentes %20desportivos%20em%20Portugal...%20.pdf

Levental, O. (2023). Online sports fan communities: Humor, trivial knowledge, and anti-modern tendencies. *Frontiers in Sports and Active Living*, *5*, 1280519. Advance online publication. DOI: 10.3389/fspor.2023.1280519 PMID: 37901392

Machado, J. C., Martins, C. C., Ferreira, F. C., Silva, S. C., & Duarte, P. A. (2020). Motives to engage with sports brands on Facebook and Instagram–The case of a Portuguese football club. *International Journal of Sports Marketing & Sponsorship*, *21*(2), 325–349. DOI: 10.1108/IJSMS-06-2019-0066

Marthinus, J., Duffett, R. G., & Knott, B. (2024). Social media adoption as a marketing communication tool by non-professional sports clubs: A multiple case study approach. *International Journal of Sports Marketing & Sponsorship*. Advance online publication. DOI: 10.1108/IJSMS-04-2024-0082

Mastromartino, B., Ross, W., Wear, H., & Naraine, M. (2020). Thinking outside the 'box': A discussion of sports fans, teams, and the environment in the context of COVID-19. *Sport in Society*, *23*(11), 1–17. DOI: 10.1080/17430437.2020.1804108

Mato-Santiso, V., Rey-Garcia, M., & Sanzo, M. J. (2023). Volunteer omnichannel behavior in nonprofit organizations: Key antecedents and implications for management. *Nonprofit Management & Leadership*, *34*(2), 433–463. Advance online publication. DOI: 10.1002/nml.21579

McCarthy, J., Rowley, J., & Keegan, B. J. (2022). Social media marketing strategy in English football clubs. *Soccer and Society*, *23*(4–5), 513–528. DOI: 10.1080/14660970.2022.2059872

Miguel, L. B. (2022). *The use of Instagram during lockdown: The case of the main Portuguese sports clubs* [ISCTE - Instituto Universitário de Lisboa]. http://hdl.handle.net/10071/26568

Mihai, A. L. (2013). The Strategic Sport Marketing Planning Process. *Manager Journal, 17* (1), 230–236. https://ideas.repec.org/a/but/manage/v17y2013i1p230-236.html

Neves, A. J. G de A. (2013). *The Phenomenon of Football in Portugal—A Case Study of the Municipality of Guarda* [University of Beira Interior]. https://ubibliorum.ubi.pt/bitstream/10400.6/3512/1/relat%C3%B3rio_estagio_armandoneves_Mestr_ensinoEF.pdf

Nicoli, N., Henriksen, K., Komodromos, M., & Tsagalas, D. (2021). Investigating digital storytelling for the creation of positively engaging digital content. *EuroMed Journal of Business*. Advance online publication. DOI: 10.1108/EMJB-03-2021-0036

Nunnally, J. C., & Bernstein, I. H. (1978). *Psychometric Theory* (2nd Edition). McGraw-Hill. https://archive.org/details/dli.scoerat.1556psychometrictheorysecondedition/page/18/mode/2up

Oliveira, J. S., Santos de Souza Vasconcelos, M. N., & Gomes Lopes Pinheiro, A. (2024). Digital Marketing: A scientific approach to business success in the digital age. *RevistaFT*, *29*(140). Advance online publication. DOI: 10.69849/revistaft/ni10202411101149

Pedro, S. D. G. (2017). *Innovation and Strategic Development in Sports Organizations Aimed at Inclusion and Social Change* [Lusófona University of Humanities and Technologies]. https://recil.ulusofona.pt/server/api/core/bitstreams/e3384686-b649-4456-843e-594210d1573c/content

Pereira, J. P. H. M. M. (2024). *Sports Sponsorship of Amateur Teams in Portugal: A Study of the First Divisions of Men's Sports in Five Sports* [University of Porto]. https://repositorio-aberto.up.pt/bitstream/10216/163973/2/699921.pdf

Pires, H. (2024). *Valuing the base of the pyramid.* Liga Portugal. https://www.ligaportugal.pt/opinion/637/valorizar-a-base-da-piramide

Portuguese Institute of Sport and Youth. (November 12, 2024). *National Sport for All Program.* Portuguese Institute of Sport and Youth. https://ipdj.gov.pt/programa-nacional-de-desporto-para-todos

Pulizzi, J., & Piper, B. W. (2023). *Epic Content Marketing, Second Edition: Break through the Clutter with a Different Story, Get the Most Out of Your Content, and Build a Community in Web3* (2nd). McGraw Hill LLC. https://epiccontentmarketing.com/wp-content/uploads/2023/02/Epic-Content-Marketing-Second-Edition-WM.pdf

Ravald, A., & Grönroos, C. (1996). The value concept and relationship. *European Journal of Marketing*, *30*(2), 19–30. DOI: 10.1108/03090569610106626

Rein, I., Kotler, P., & Shields, B. R. (2007). *The Elusive Fan: Reinventing Sports in a Crowded Marketplace.* McGraw Hill LLC. https://books.google.pt/books?id=6Vf4gg20ZVkC

Reis, A. (2024, August 12). *Sport in Portugal: What the Portuguese need to know (in 11 points).* Community Culture and Art. https://comunidadeculturaearte.com/o-desporto-em-portugal-o-que-os-portugueses-precisam-de-saber-em-11-pontos/

Sá, D., & Sá, C. (2008). *Sports marketing, the new rules of the game.* Editions of the Portuguese Institute of Marketing Administration, Marketing School for Business. https://books.google.pt/books?id=bJ4Va0aMghwC

Seaton, S. S. (2010). *Measuring Return on Marketing Investment in Non-Professional Sports Event Organizations* [University of Southern Queensland]. https://research.usq.edu.au/item/q0x84/measuring-return-on-marketing-investment-in-non-professional-sports-event-organisations

Silva, NDBSG e. (2023). *The Role of Social Networks in the Digital Sports Marketing of Football Clubs—The Case of Sporting Clube de Portugal* [Instituto Superior de Gestão]. https://comum.rcaap.pt/bitstream/10400.26/45829/1/Dissertacao%20MSc%20Marketing_%20Nuno%20Guerra%20e%20Silva_impressa.pdf

Smith, A. C., Stavros, C., Skinner, J., Geurin, A. N., & Burch, L. M. (2024). *Introduction to Sport Marketing* (3rd ed.). Routledge., DOI: 10.4324/9781003391319

Soares, L. F. S. (2023). *Tribal Consumption: An Analysis of the Role of Digital Strategies in the Context of a Sports Crisis—The Case of Sporting Clube de Portugal* [ISCAP - Instituto Superior de Contabilidade e Administração do Porto]. http://hdl.handle.net/10400.22/23578

Stevens, J., Gleim, M., & Waites, S. (2024). Experience identification: Connecting online engagement to offline loyalty. *Journal of Services Marketing, 38*(8), 1012–1029. Advance online publication. DOI: 10.1108/JSM-12-2023-0466

Stokburger-Sauer, N., Bauer, H., & Wannow, S. (2008). Brand Image and Fan Loyalty in Professional Team Sport: A Refined Model and Empirical Assessment. *Journal of Sport Management, 22*(2), 205–226. DOI: 10.1123/jsm.22.2.205

Suárez, MAV, León López, LW, León López, OD, & León Vélez, RM (2023). Impact of digital communication strategies for the promotion of healthy sporting activities and integration. *RECIMUNDO, 7* (2), 171–183. https://doi.org/.(2).jun.2023.171-183DOI: 10.26820/recimundo/7

Sutton, W. A., McDonald, M. A., Milne, G. R., & Cimperman, J. (1997). Creating And Fostering Fan Identification In Professional Sports. *Sport Marketing Quarterly, 6*(1), 15–22. DOI: 10.1177/106169349700600104

Teixeira, A. R. M. (2017). *Tribal Marketing: The Behavior of the Sports Consumer: The Case of Sporting Clube de Portugal* [University of Coimbra]. https://estudogeral.uc.pt/bitstream/10316/82203/1/Marketing%20Tribal%20SCP.pdf

Tenreiro, F. (June 26, 2014). *The National Sport Model Ran Out Years Ago*. https://www.publico.pt/2014/06/26/desporto/noticia/o-modelo-do-desporto-nacional-esgotouse-ha-anos-1660460

Trkulja, Ž. M., Primorac, D., & Martinčević, I. (2024). The Influence of Consumer Motivation on Engagement with Sports Club Social Media: An Intrinsic and Extrinsic Analysis. *Business Systems Research Journal, 15*(1), 91–109. DOI: 10.2478/bsrj-2024-0005

Tsai, W.-H. S., & Men, L. R. (2013). Motivations and Antecedents of Consumer Engagement With Brand Pages on Social Networking Sites. *Journal of Interactive Advertising, 13*(2), 76–87. DOI: 10.1080/15252019.2013.826549

Ubah, O., & Malcourant, E. (2018). *Governance within sports organizations: Exploring how non-professional sports organizations motivate and retain their volunteers.* [Louvain School of Management]. http://hdl.handle.net/2078.1/thesis:13378

Vieira, C. B. (2017). *Affectivity and consumer behavior in sports contexts: The case of football fans in Portugal.* [University of Minho]. https://repositorium.sdum.uminho.pt/bitstream/1822/49466/1/Carla%20Barbosa%20Vieira.pdf

Wicker, P., & Breuer, C. (2012). Understanding the importance of organizational resources to reduce organizational problems: Evidence from nonprofit sport clubs in Germany. *Voluntas, 17* (2), 24 (461-484). DOI: 10.1007/s11266-012-9272-2

XXIV Portuguese Government. (November 22, 2024). *Sport "promotes well-being and values of life in society"*. Portuguese Republic - XXIV Government. https://www.portugal.gov.pt/pt/gc24/comunicacao/noticia?i=desporto-promove-bem-estar-e-valores-da-vida-em-sociedade

Yarkin, Z., Dogan, E., & Kiliç, Ç. (2024). Content Brand Journalism Impact on Consumption and Consumer Behavior of «Big Five» Football Clubs' Digital Products. *Revista de Cercetare si Interventie Sociala, 85*(85), 15. DOI: 10.33788/rcis.85.10

Young, B., Takeda, H., & Cuellar, M. (2011). Investigating the Impact of Offline Events on Group Development in an Online Sports, Proceedings of the Southern Association for Information Systems Conference Community, Atlanta, GA, USA, March 25th-26*th,* 206-211.

KEY TERMS AND DEFINITIONS

Digital Marketing: Refers to the use of online channels and technology to promote products, services, or organizations. It enables organizations to reach target audiences, foster connections, and monitor outcomes.

Digital Strategy: Structured plan outlining how an organization utilizes online tools and platforms to achieve its objectives. It ensures that all online activities align with the organization's primary goals.

Engagement: The degree of interaction and connection between an organization and its audience. It is commonly measured by metrics such as likes, comments, shares, and audience participation.

Non-Professional Sports Organizations: Groups that do not aim to make a profit. They usually depend on volunteers and limited resources, and they support community involvement, growth, and amateur sports.

Notoriety: The extent to which an organization is known and remembered by its target audience. It is closely associated with the organization's visibility and recognition.

Social Media: Online platforms where people and organizations can create, share, and interact with content. These sites help users communicate, connect, and build online communities.

Chapter 12
Comparing Restaurant and Influencer Social Media Posts:
Effects on Consumer Perceptions and Visit Intentions

Suzanne Amaro
http://orcid.org/0000-0001-9263-6951
Polytechnic Institute of Viseu, Portugal

Carla Henriques
Polytechnic Institute of Viseu, Portugal

Ana Beatriz Saraiva
Polytechnic Institute of Viseu, Portugal

ABSTRACT

Social media is a critical element of restaurant marketing, yet limited research has simultaneously examined the role of content source and format in shaping consumer responses. Using the Stimulus–Organism–Response framework, this study examines how the source of social media content (restaurant vs. influencer) and format (photo vs. video) affect cognitive–emotional–sensory appeal, perceived credibility, and restaurant visit intention. A between-subjects experimental design (2 × 2) was used, in which participants viewed different combinations of content source and format. Data were collected via an online questionnaire with 507 valid responses. The results show that restaurant posts perform better with photo-based content, while influencer posts tend to generate stronger responses with video content. In

DOI: 10.4018/979-8-3373-7704-9.ch012

addition, video content is associated with higher perceived credibility across both sources. Both cognitive–emotional–sensory appeal and perceived credibility are positively associated with restaurant visit intentions.

INTRODUCTION

Previous research has largely shown that social media affects consumers' decisions in the tourism and hospitality industry (e.g., Gretzel & Yoo, 2017; Liu et al., 2022; Ramos & Hassan, 2021). In particular, restaurants benefit from their presence on social media and community engagement (Alnsour & Al Faour, 2019; Lima et al., 2019), as this has been found to influence people's choice of restaurants (Yarış & Aykol, 2021) and intentions to visit a restaurant (Alnsour & Al Faour, 2019; Lima et al., 2019), especially when it is their first time visiting the restaurant (Huifeng & Ha, 2021). As a result, social media has become a critical component of restaurant marketing strategies, with 90% of restaurants stating that social media is either very or extremely important in their digital marketing approach (Deloitte, 2025).

In this context, the increasing visibility of social media influencers has become a key factor in influencing consumer decision-making in the travel industry (Pop et al., 2021) and is becoming increasingly relevant in the restaurant industry (Lee et al., 2021). Influencers are perceived as relatable content creators who share personal experiences, often fostering trust and authenticity among their followers (Wang & Chan-Olmsted, 2024; Zniva et al., 2023). In the restaurant context, influencers frequently share their restaurant experiences with photos and videos. Previous research has shown that Instagram influencers play a significant role in shaping consumers' restaurant choices and positively influence their intention to visit and dine at promoted establishments (Anjos et al., 2022; Szakály et al., 2025). At the same time, restaurants actively produce and disseminate their own social media content, which has also been shown to affect consumers' purchase intentions (Lima et al., 2019). Despite evidence supporting the effectiveness of both sources, direct empirical comparisons between influencer-generated and restaurant-generated posts remain scarce. Consequently, it is not yet clear which source exerts a stronger influence on consumers' cognitive and affective evaluations, such as perceived appeal and credibility, as well as on their behavioural intentions in the restaurant context.

Moreover, beyond the question of source, relatively little attention has been given to the role of content format. Social media posts are typically presented as either static photos or short videos, yet few studies have examined how these formats may differentially shape consumers' cognitive–emotional–sensory responses and perceived credibility, particularly when combined with different content sources. This chapter addresses these gaps by comparing influencer-generated and restaurant-generated posts across both photo and video formats.

Understanding how source (restaurant versus influencer) and content format (photo versus video) influence consumers' cognitive–emotional–sensory evaluations, perceptions of credibility, and intention to visit is particularly relevant for restaurant managers, who must decide how to allocate resources between owned social media content and influencer collaborations.

The findings contribute to the literature on digital restaurant marketing by providing clearer evidence regarding the relative effectiveness of different communication approaches. In doing so, it offers practical insights to support more informed social media content planning and collaboration decisions.

LITERATURE REVIEW

Social Media in Restaurant Marketing

In recent years, social media has become an essential marketing tool in the restaurant industry, serving as a preferred channel through which marketers can digitally reach restaurant customers (Kim et al., 2015; Li et al., 2021). Given the cost constraints typically faced by restaurants, social media provides an attractive marketing option because it allows businesses to promote their offerings at a relatively low cost while reaching a significant number of consumers (Lima et al., 2019; Needles & Thompson, 2013). Through social media platforms, restaurants can share information about their products and services, increase visibility, interact with consumers, and maintain ongoing communication that helps build long-term customer relationships, stimulate engagement, and encourage electronic word-of-mouth (Gruss et al., 2020; Ibrahim et al., 2021; Kim et al., 2015; Lima et al., 2019; Oksüz et al., 2025). Research has further demonstrated that restaurants' social media activity can positively influence firm value (Kim et al., 2015), which demonstrates another aspect of its importance, beyond communication and engagement outcomes.

Consumers increasingly rely on social media platforms to search for restaurant recommendations, view food images, and evaluate dining experiences before deciding where to dine (Gruss et al., 2020; Lima et al., 2019; Philp et al., 2022). Consequently, maintaining an active and engaging presence on social media has become increasingly important for restaurants seeking to attract new customers, influence dining decisions, and remain competitive in a competitive industry (Lima et al., 2019; Philp et al., 2022).

Visual content plays a particularly important role in restaurant communication on social media, as restaurants frequently rely on visual posts to attract attention and engage consumers online (Philp et al., 2022). Restaurants frequently use photographs and videos to showcase their dishes, atmosphere, and dining experiences in ways that capture consumers' attention and stimulate interest (Chan et al., 2023; Philp et al., 2022). Food consumption is a highly sensory experience, therefore visual representations of food can evoke sensory responses and shape consumers' perceptions of restaurants (Chan et al., 2023). Moreover, since restaurant services are largely intangible and experiential (Gruss et al., 2020), potential customers often rely on online information and visual cues to reduce uncertainty when selecting a dining establishment (Yarış & Aykol, 2021; Zhang et al., 2024). Consequently, consumers increasingly turn to both user-generated and brand-generated online content to search for dining options, evaluate alternatives, and reduce uncertainty before making a visit decision (Gretzel & Yoo, 2017). Research has shown that visually appealing food-related content shared on social media can influence how consumers evaluate restaurants and form intentions to visit them (Chen et al., 2026; Lima et al., 2019). As a result, visual content has become a central component of restaurant marketing strategies on social media platforms.

Source of Social Media Content

Social media content in the restaurant industry originates from different sources, including restaurants themselves and third parties, such as consumers and influencers. Restaurants are increasingly using social media as a marketing channel to promote their services, connect with customers, and strengthen relationships with their audiences (Lima et al., 2019). Through these platforms, restaurants can share information about their offerings, including food images, menus, promotions, and details about the dining experience (Oksüz et al., 2025; Yarış & Aykol, 2021). Such firm-generated content allows restaurants to showcase menu items, highlight the restaurant atmosphere, and communicate elements of their brand identity, while simultaneously maintaining engagement with existing customers and attracting potential diners (Li et al., 2021). By providing visual and informational cues about the restaurant experience, this type of content may shape consumers' attitudes toward the restaurant and influence their purchase intentions (Anas et al., 2023). Restaurant-generated content represents a controlled form of communication in which businesses manage the message and presentation of their offerings (Kumsawat et al., 2025).

However, social media environments are also characterized by the increasing presence of user-generated content, which includes posts, reviews, and recommendations shared by consumers and influencers (Zhang et al., 2024). User-generated content has become particularly influential in the hospitality and restaurant contexts because consumers frequently rely on the experiences and opinions of others when evaluating dining options (Lima et al., 2019).

Among different forms of user-generated content, social media influencers have emerged as particularly important actors in digital marketing environments (De Veirman et al., 2017). Social media influencers can be defined as independent third-party individuals who create content on social media platforms and have the ability to shape the attitudes and behaviours of their audience through the information and opinions they share (Freberg et al., 2011). Unlike traditional celebrities who gain recognition through mass media, social media influencers are ordinary individuals who become online opinion leaders by creating and sharing content on social media, often focusing on specific areas such as food, travel, lifestyle, or fashion (Lou & Yuan, 2019).

Influencer-generated content is often perceived as more authentic and trustworthy than traditional advertising because it is communicated through individuals who share personal experiences and interact directly with their followers (Haddad, 2025, De Veirman et al., 2017; Lou & Yuan, 2019). Influencers can play a key role in helping brands engage with their target audience and build trust with them (Wang & Chan-Olmsted, 2024). Therefore, it is not surprising that the global influencer marketing market size has more than tripled since 2020 (Navarro, 2025) and is projected to continue to grow steadily in the coming years (Business Research Insights, 2026).

This trend is also evident in the restaurant sector, where influencer marketing has grown rapidly, as it provides a relatively quick and cost-effective way for businesses to attract potential customers (Lee et al., 2021). In the restaurant context, influencers typically create and share content such as photos, reviews, videos, and live broadcasts on social media that showcase restaurants, food, and their positive experiences (Lee et al., 2021).

Research has evidenced that restaurant influencers have an impact on consumers' restaurant visit intentions (Anjos et al., 2022; Leung et al., 2022; Olfat et al., 2025; Szakály et al., 2025), attitude towards the restaurant (Pereira et al., 2025), brand awareness (Lee et al., 2021), engagement (Lee et al., 2021; Ting & Ahn, 2026) and restaurant satisfaction (Olfat et al., 2025). Moreover, influencers facilitate trust transfer from themselves to the restaurant brands they endorse, which strengthens restaurant brand credibility and brand equity (Wang & Chan-Olmsted, 2024).

Content Format Effects: Photo Versus Video

Regardless of whether content is generated by restaurants or influencers, both must decide which format is most effective in achieving their communication objectives. Given the wide range of content formats available on social media, prior research has consistently shown that text-only content is less effective in capturing attention and generating engagement compared to visual formats (Cvijikj & Michahelles, 2013; Li & Xie, 2020; Sabate et al., 2014). Consequently, marketing communication on social media has become predominantly visual, with photos and videos emerging as the dominant formats used by brands and content creators (Highfield & Leaver, 2016; Philp et al., 2022).

Despite both being visual formats, important differences exist between photos and videos in terms of how they communicate information and influence consumers. Photos rely primarily on static visual cues, which may limit their ability to convey complex or multisensory experiences (Harsanto et al., 2025; Peng & Lu, 2024). This limitation may reduce their persuasive power compared with more dynamic formats such as video (Harsanto et al., 2025).

Video content is characterized by higher media richness, as it integrates motion, sound, and narrative elements, enhancing vividness and facilitating mental imagery (Peng & Lu, 2024; Sui et al., 2023). In addition, videos are often considered more powerful in eliciting emotional responses, as they can "tell a story or portray a drama" (Tellis et al., 2019, p. 1). Furthermore, video content has been shown to be particularly effective in encouraging content sharing, as it can elicit strong emotional responses such as warmth and happiness among audiences (Pansari & Kumar, 2017). Consistent with this, a different study found that tweets containing videos achieved higher favourites compared to posts featuring photos (Thongmak, 2024).

However, existing evidence does not consistently show that videos always outperform photos in terms of engagement. Several studies indicate that photos can generate equal or even higher levels of engagement, i.e., likes, comments, and shares, than videos (Annamalai et al., 2021; Moran et al., 2020; Reimer, 2023). For instance, while both formats significantly enhance customer engagement compared to non-visual content, photos have been shown to increase likes by 190%, comments by 66%, and shares by 260%, whereas videos increase likes by 140% and comments by 51%, but generate higher levels of sharing, with an increase of 400% (Gruss et al., 2020). This suggests that although videos may be particularly effective in stimulating content diffusion, photos can be more effective in driving immediate user reactions. Photos also demand fewer cognitive resources to process and are quicker to consume (Liu et al., 2022; Reimer, 2023), making them especially effective in fast-scrolling environments and for capturing immediate attention.

These distinctions are particularly relevant in the restaurant context, where marketing communication is highly dependent on sensory cues and experiential representations (Silaban et al., 2023). Existing research indicates that both photos and videos can positively influence consumers' perceptions and behavioral intentions. Restaurant photos act as concrete representations of the dining experience, offering potential customers visual insights into the food, ambiance, and overall atmosphere of the establishment (Safeer et al., 2025), stimulating their desire to experience the food (Chen et al., 2026). The growing importance of sharing food images on social media has led to the emergence of the term *foodstagramming*, defined as "the capturing and sharing of food-related photography on social media platforms" (Chang, 2022, p.3). Foodstagramming posts, particularly those with high aesthetic appeal and popularity, significantly increase restaurant visit intentions, largely driven by consumers' desire to mimic the dining experiences seen online (Chen et al., 2024a). Restaurant food photos and user-generated food photos shared on social media have been found to have a positive impact on intentions to visit the restaurant (Chen et al., 2026; Safeer et al., 2025) and foster digital brand engagement (Sohaib et al., 2025). Moreover, Chan et al. (2023) found that the higher the number of photos included in a post, the higher the visit intention to the restaurant and also makes the restaurant more memorable. The nature of the content is also relevant: despite the common belief that highly stylised "Instagrammable" dishes attract more attention, simpler and more familiar foods tend to generate greater engagement due to their ease of cognitive processing (Philp et al., 2022).

In the restaurant context, video content may better simulate the dining experience by presenting food preparation, ambience, and social interaction. Food videos can stimulate sensory imagination and appetite by showing aspects such as preparation processes, textures, and consumption experiences (Truong et al., 2025). Consequently, videos may have the potential to evoke stronger sensory and emotional reactions than static images. Video-based content created by influencers, such as food vlogs, also plays a particularly important role in shaping consumer responses. Research shows that such content has a significant positive effect on consumers' attitudes and intention to visit restaurants (Malik et al., 2025).

Overall, both photos and videos play important but distinct roles in restaurant social media communication. While photos may facilitate rapid processing and immediate engagement, videos provide richer and more immersive representations of the dining experience, enhancing emotional and sensory responses. Consequently, understanding how these formats differentially influence consumer perceptions and behavioural intentions is essential for optimising social media strategies in the restaurant context.

Stimulus–Organism–Response (S–O–R) Framework

The Stimulus–Organism–Response (S–O–R) theory suggests that external stimuli influence a person's internal state (organism), which then leads to a behavioral response (Mehrabian & Russell, 1974). As a well-known theory, previous research has used this framework in the Marketing field to explain, for example, brand loyalty (Yu et al., 2021), the effects of social media on consumer online impulse buying intentions (Safeer, 2024), and customer engagement (Naqvi et al., 2021).

The theory is very useful to elucidate consumers' internal states and behavioral responses to stimuli in digital settings (Safeer, 2024). In the restaurant context, consumers rely on mediated stimuli, such as social media posts, to form expectations about the dining experience. These stimuli can trigger cognitive evaluations (e.g., perceived attractiveness or interest), emotional responses (e.g., pleasure or excitement), and sensory imagination (e.g., anticipated taste, smell, or atmosphere) that can then lead to a behavioral response.

Taking the S–O-R framework as the baseline, this study considers that restaurants and influencers' posts with a photo or video are the stimuli, that the organismic reactions are consumers' perceptions of the post's credibility and their cognitive, emotional and sensory evaluation of the post and that the response is intentions to visit the restaurant.

Cognitive–Emotional–Sensory Appeal

Cognitive–emotional–sensory appeal refers to the multidimensional experiential responses elicited by marketing stimuli, encompassing cognitive processing, affective reactions, and sensory stimulation (Lacroix et al., 2020; Rajaobelina et al., 2019). Cognitive appeal relates to the extent to which content captures attention and stimulates mental processes such as curiosity, elaboration, and interpretation, thereby facilitating information processing (Rajaobelina et al., 2019). Emotional appeal reflects the ability of content to evoke affective responses such as pleasure, excitement, or enjoyment, which are central to attitude formation and behavioural intentions (Rajaobelina et al., 2019). Sensory appeal refers to the stimulation of the senses through elements such as visuals, colours, music, and motion (Rajaobelina et al., 2019).

Prior research has shown that visual and experiential digital content can evoke both cognitive and emotional reactions that shape consumers' evaluations and decision-making processes (Lacroix et al., 2020. Content that is more engaging, emotionally appealing, and capable of eliciting sensory imagination is more likely to positively influence consumers' perceptions and behavioural intentions (Choi et al., 2018; Lacroix et al., 2020).

For the purpose of this study, the cognitive–emotional–sensory appeal refers to the extent to which the social media post captures attention, generates positive affect, and stimulates imagined sensory experiences. In digital food marketing, such appeal is particularly relevant because consumers cannot directly experience the product and must rely on mediated representations. Visual stimuli that effectively trigger emotional and sensory anticipation may increase the attractiveness of the restaurant and lead to higher intentions to visit.

Perceived Credibility of Social Media Content

Perceived credibility refers to the extent to which information is considered trustworthy and believable by consumers (Shin et al., 2020). In social media environments, where information is abundant and often unverifiable prior to consumption, credibility becomes a critical determinant of how users interpret and rely on content. Consumers' evaluations of product claims are shaped by how credible they perceive the information source to be, especially when those claims relate to attributes that cannot be assessed before purchase (Jain & Posavac, 2001). This is particularly relevant in the restaurant context, where many attributes such as food quality or dining experience cannot be assessed before the visit. Information perceived as more credible has been shown to positively influence attitudes and behavioural intentions, including intentions to visit or purchase (Choi et al., 2018).

Different sources can produce distinct psychological effects, shaping how the same content is interpreted (Choi et al., 2018). For instance, user-generated content (UGC), including customer reviews and food photos, is generally perceived as more authentic and trustworthy than firm-generated content, as it is seen as less biased and more experience-based (Chen et al., 2026; Simonetti & Bigne, 2022). Similarly, visual attention to such content has been shown to influence key outcomes such as restaurant visit intention and expectations (Simonetti & Bigne, 2022).

More recently, influencer-generated content has emerged as a particularly powerful source of credibility. Evidence suggests that influencers are perceived as more credible than restaurant operators themselves, and even more than other consumers in certain contexts, due to their perceived expertise, authenticity, and relatability (Kumsawat et al., 2025). This higher perceived credibility translates into stronger behavioral outcomes, including greater engagement with content and increased purchase intentions (Kumsawat et al., 2025). In line with this, influencer credibility has been found to significantly influence restaurant visit intentions (Malik et al., 2025), with specific influencer characteristics—such as trustworthiness and expertise—playing a key role, particularly among younger consumers such as Generation Z (Pereira et al., 2025).

Behavioural Intentions

According to the theory of reasoned action, behavioural intentions is a strong predictor of actual behaviour (Ajzen, 1985). For the purpose of this study, behavioural intentions are the intention to visit the restaurant, reflecting the likelihood that a consumer will choose a particular restaurant.

Numerous studies have examined intentions rather than behaviour in the hospitality industry (e.g., Casais et al., 2025; Nazli et al., 2025) and in particular on restaurant visit intentions (e.g., Chen et al., 2026; Malik et al., 2025; Pereira et al., 2025; Truong et al., 2025). Prior research shows that restaurant visit intentions are shaped by multiple factors, including restaurant content-related features such as informativeness, entertainment, and vividness (Truong et al., 2025), credibility of Instagram food vloggers and parasocial relationships between followers and food vloggers (Malik et al., 2025), user generated food photos (Chen et al., 2026), influencer's characteristics (Pereira et al., 2025) and consumers' satisfaction with the information, entertainment, and social interaction provided on the restaurant's Instagram page (Oksüz et al., 2025). However, existing research has largely examined these factors in isolation and has not explicitly compared the effects of different content sources (e.g., influencers versus restaurants) and content formats (e.g., photos versus videos), highlighting an important gap in the literature. Therefore, understanding how different characteristics of social media posts influence intention to visit is therefore of practical and theoretical importance. This study proposes to analyse which sources and formats have higher impacts on intentions to visit the restaurant.

Hypotheses and Proposed Model

The source of social media content represents a key heuristic used by consumers when evaluating online information (Choi et al., 2018). Influencer-generated content is typically perceived as more authentic, experience-based, and relatable, which enhances trust and reduces perceptions of persuasive intent (De Veirman et al., 2017; Lou & Yuan, 2019; Wang & Chan-Olmsted, 2024). In contrast, restaurant-generated content is often recognised as firm-controlled and promotional, which may trigger scepticism and reduce perceived authenticity.

These differences are likely to extend beyond credibility and influence how consumers process and experience the content itself. Content perceived as more authentic and relatable tends to generate stronger emotional engagement and facilitates mental imagery, thereby enhancing cognitive processing and sensory imagination (Lacroix et al., 2020; Choi et al., 2018). In the restaurant context, where consumption is inherently experiential, such effects may be particularly pronounced. Accordingly, the following hypotheses are proposed:

H1a: Post source (restaurant vs. influencer) has an effect on perceived cognitive–emotional–sensory appeal.

H1b: Post source (restaurant vs. influencer) has an effect on perceived credibility.

Content format represents another important stimulus characteristic influencing how information is processed in digital environments. According to media richness theory, richer formats enhance message vividness and reduce ambiguity, thereby facilitating understanding and engagement (Sui et al., 2023).

Video content, due to its dynamic nature and integration of motion, sound, and narrative, provides higher levels of vividness and immersion, which can enhance emotional responses and stimulate sensory imagination (Tellis et al., 2019; Peng & Lu, 2024). This is particularly relevant in the restaurant context, where videos can simulate aspects of the dining experience, such as food preparation, textures, and ambience (Truong et al., 2025).

In contrast, photographs offer static but often highly curated visual representations that can enhance aesthetic appeal and facilitate rapid cognitive processing, especially in fast-scrolling environments (Liu et al., 2022; Reimer, 2023). While less immersive, photos may still effectively capture attention and stimulate desire through visual attractiveness.

Given these differences, content format is expected to influence both perceived credibility and the cognitive–emotional–sensory appeal of social media content. Thus, the following hypotheses are proposed:

> H2a: Post format (photo vs. video) has an effect on perceived cognitive–emotional–sensory appeal.
> H2b: Post format (photo vs. video) has an effect on perceived credibility.

Within the S–O–R framework, internal evaluations triggered by external stimuli are expected to shape behavioural responses. Perceived credibility represents a key cognitive evaluation, reflecting the extent to which consumers consider information to be trustworthy and reliable. Prior research has shown that higher perceived credibility positively influences attitudes and behavioural intentions in tourism and hospitality contexts (Choi et al., 2018; Shin et al., 2020).

Similarly, cognitive–emotional–sensory appeal captures consumers' affective and experiential reactions to social media content, including its ability to generate positive emotions, attract attention, and stimulate sensory imagination. Such responses have been shown to play a central role in shaping consumer attitudes and intentions (Lacroix et al., 2020; Rajaobelina et al., 2019). Therefore, both perceived credibility and cognitive–emotional–sensory appeal are expected to positively influence consumers' intention to visit a restaurant.

> H3: Perceived credibility of social media content positively affects consumers' intention to visit the restaurant.

H4: Cognitive–emotional–sensory appeal of social media content positively affects consumers' intention to visit the restaurant.

Figure 1 presents the conceptual framework, illustrating the hypotheses.

Figure 1. Conceptual framework

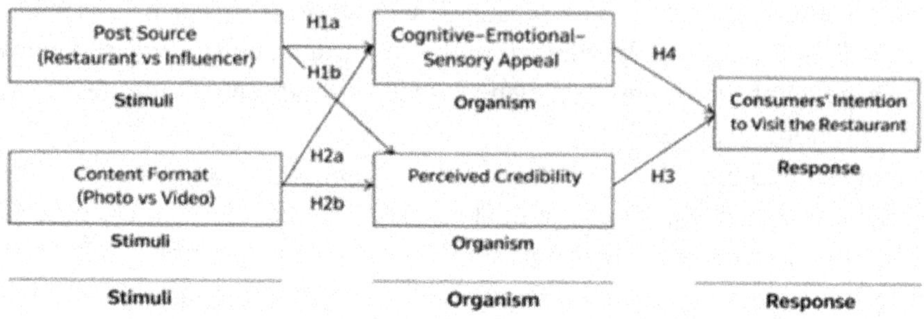

METHODOLOGY

Questionnaire Design

This study was conducted through a survey using a questionnaire as the data collection instrument. The questionnaire was developed based on the objectives of the study and the literature review.

The questionnaire was developed in Portuguese, as the authors are from Portugal and Brazil, and the aim was to distribute it in these two countries. Although both nationalities share the same language, certain words have different meanings in each country, and the currency also differs. Therefore, the questionnaire was adapted to both Brazilian and Portuguese respondents. Whenever terminology or contextual elements differed, alternative wording was provided to ensure mutual understanding.

The questionnaire began with a brief introduction to the study and an initial screening question regarding nationality. Respondents who selected "Brazilian" or "Portuguese" were allowed to proceed, while those who selected "Other" were directed to the end of the survey.

The remaining structure of the questionnaire was divided into three sections. The first section included sociodemographic questions aimed at characterising the respondents, such as gender, age and education level. In the second section, participants indicated whether they followed influencers. Respondents who answered "yes" continued the questionnaire, while those who answered "no" were directed to the end of the survey. This section also included questions about the number of influencers followed and whether influencers affected their restaurant choice decisions. In the third and last section, participants were exposed to a hypothetical social media scenario that included two posts: one photograph of a Japanese dish from a restaurant and one video of a dessert from another restaurant. The stimuli used in both experimental conditions were similar in structure and content, ensuring comparability across scenarios.

The key difference between conditions concerned the source attribution of the posts. In one condition, the posts were presented as having been published by a restaurant (Figure 2), whereas in the other condition they were framed as having been published by an influencer who was physically present at the restaurant (Figure 3). Thus, the manipulation focused on the post source, while maintaining similar visual content across conditions.

Figure 2. Experimental stimuli: Restaurant-attributed social media posts

Figure 3. Experimental stimuli: Influencer-attributed social media posts

To allocate participants to the experimental conditions without influencing their responses, respondents were asked to randomly choose a number between 1 and 10 upon reaching this section. This procedure aimed to ensure that approximately half of the respondents evaluated restaurant-generated posts and the other half evaluated influencer-generated posts, allowing comparison between the two sources.

Participants who selected odd numbers were directed to the section featuring posts published by restaurants, while participants who selected even numbers were directed to a section featuring posts published by influencers.

Respondents were presented with the following hypothetical scenario: “Imagine that you are browsing social media and come across the following post from a restaurant/influencer.” After the scenario was presented, respondents were asked questions that were identical regardless of the scenario. The questions and sources are presented in Table 1. A five-point Likert scale was used for these items, ranging from 1 = Strongly disagree to 5 = Strongly agree.

Table 1. Measurement scales and item sources

Construct	Item	Source
Cognitive, Emotional and Sensory Evaluation	The post is pleasant	Adapted from Lacroix et al. (2020)
	The post is visually attractive	
	The post captures my attention	
	The post evokes positive emotions	
Perceived Credibility	The post offers credible information	Adapted from Choi et al. (2018)
	The post provides trustworthy information	

Data Collection

Prior to distributing the online questionnaire using Google Forms, a pre-test was conducted with a group of 11 individuals selected through non-probabilistic convenience sampling. Based on their feedback, minor issues were identified and corrected, resulting in a clearer final version of the questionnaire. The survey was subsequently disseminated online through Instagram, Facebook and email between 16 June and 1 August 2023. The data collection was conducted simultaneously in Portugal and Brazil.

Data Analysis

The data were initially organised and processed using Microsoft Excel and subsequently coded and analysed in SPSS (Statistical Package for the Social Sciences). A significance level of 0.05 was adopted.

The Sign test and the Wilcoxon signed-rank test were used to perform comparisons between paired samples (e.g., comparison of respondents' evaluations regarding the attractiveness of a post presented as a photo versus video). The Wilcoxon test was applied only in cases where the differences between paired observations exhibited an approximately symmetrical distribution. The Mann–Whitney U test was used to assess the significance of the differences between restaurant and influencer posts. Spearman's correlation coefficients were calculated to assess the association between intention to visit the restaurant and both perceived credibility and perceived cognitive–emotional–sensory constructs.

Results and Discussion

Sample profile

In the present study, 507 valid responses were obtained from a sample of 338 (67%) Brazilian and 169 (33%) Portuguese participants. Women constitute the vast majority of responses, representing 77.7%, whereas men account for 21.9%. The participants' mean age was 30 years old, with a standard deviation of 10 years. In terms of education, more than 80% of participants held a college degree or higher.

Over 60% of respondents follow their favourite restaurants on social media (95% CI: 61–70%), and over 60% often follow digital influencers (95% CI: 62–70%). Among respondents who follow influencers, 81% (95% CI: 77–85%) report following five or more influencers. Such consistently high percentages reinforce the central role of social media in shaping consumer engagement with both restaurants and influencers.

Following the analysis of influencer-following behaviour, respondents were asked whether an influencer's recommendation could affect their decision to visit a restaurant (Table 2). Results indicate that 63% of participants agree or strongly agree that influencer recommendations influence their decision-making. In contrast, only 11% disagree or strongly disagree, while 26% remain neutral. These findings suggest that influencer recommendations play a meaningful role in shaping restaurant visitation intentions among the majority of respondents.

Table 2. Perceived influence of influencer recommendations on restaurant visitation

Response Category	**n (%)**
Strongly disagree	12 (3.6%)
Disagree	25 (7.4%)
Neither agree nor disagree	88 (26.2%)
Agree	124 (36.9%)
Strongly agree	87 (25.9%)
Total	336 (100%)

Comparative Analysis of Post Source and Format Effects

Figures 4 and 5 display box plots for *Cognitive-Emotional-Sensory Evaluation* and *Perceived Credibility, respectively,* across post source (restaurant vs. influencer) and post format (photo vs. video). In each box plot, the median is indicated by the bold horizontal line within the box, while the lower and upper edges represent the first and third quartiles, respectively. The 'whiskers' extending from the boxes represent the range of the data, excluding outliers.

Figure 4. Box plots of cognitive–emotional–sensory evaluation across post source (restaurant vs. influencer) and post format (photo vs. video)

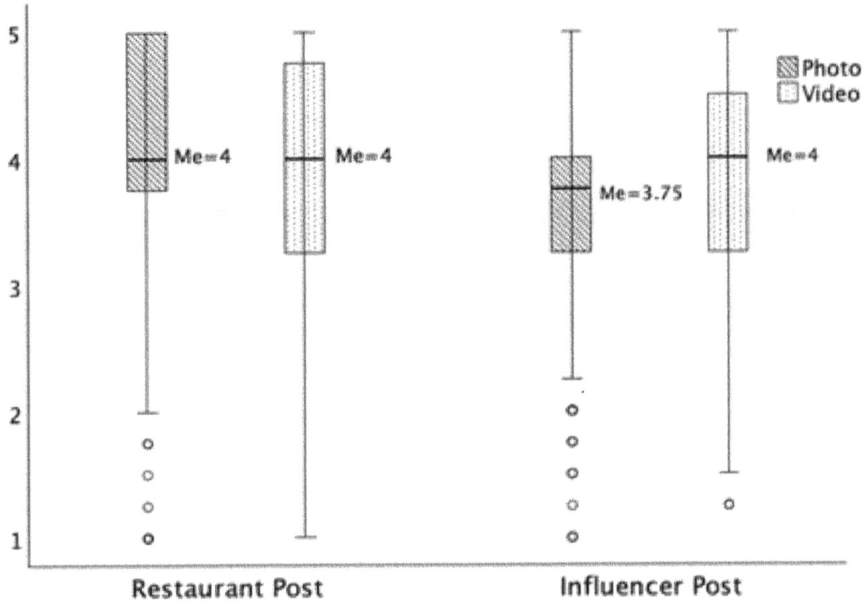

Regarding *cognitive-emotional-sensory evaluation* (Figure 4), the box plots for restaurant and influencer posts in the video condition are very similar, with equal median values, indicating that participants evaluated both types of posts in a comparable manner. Consistently, no significant differences were found between restaurant and influencer video posts.

However, for photo posts, Figure 4 shows a higher position of the box plot for the restaurant, compared to the influencer. The restaurant post received significantly higher evaluations than the influencer post ($p < 0.001$). This means that hypothesis $H_{1a,}$ which predicted an effect of source on perceived cognitive–emotional–sensory appeal, is supported for photos but not for videos. When comparing formats, a cross-over pattern emerges. For the restaurant, the photo format was rated higher than the video ($p=0.03$), whereas for the influencer, the video post had higher evaluations ($p = 0.01$). Thus, hypothesis H_{2a} is supported both for videos and photos, although the direction of the effect differs depending on the post source.

Figure 5. Box plots of perceived credibility across post source (restaurant vs. influencer) and post format (photo vs. video)

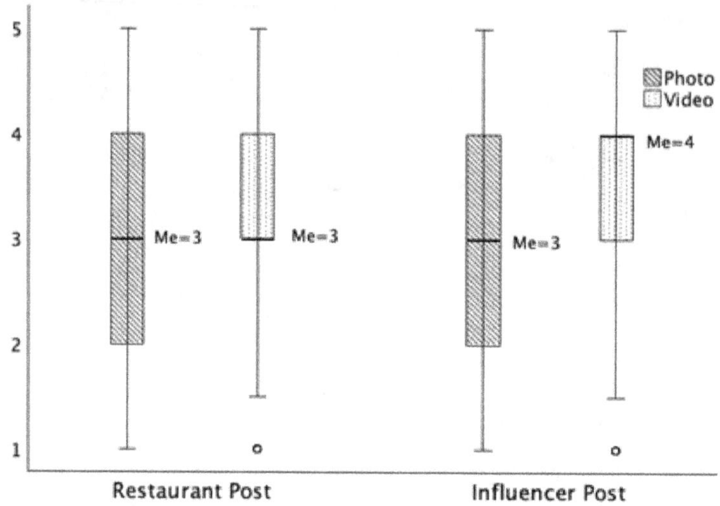

For *perceived credibility* (Figure 5), no significant differences were found between restaurant and influencer photos, as reflected in the equal box plots for the photo condition. However, within the video format, the influencer post demonstrated a relative advantage in perceived credibility than the restaurant post (Median = 4 *vs.* 3; $p = 0.006$). Thus, hypothesis H_{1b} is again partially supported (evidence in its favour exists for video but not for photos). When comparing formats, video perceived credibility had significantly higher ratings than photos, both for restaurant and influencer posts ($p < 0.001$), supporting H_{2b}.

Spearman's correlation coefficients were calculated to assess the association between intention to visit the restaurant and both perceived credibility and perceived cognitive–emotional–sensory appeal (Table 3). All correlations were positive and statistically significant ($p < 0.001$). The 95% confidence intervals indicate that Spearman's rho (ρ) exceeds 0.50 across all conditions, suggesting moderate to strong associations between the variables. These findings support H3 and H4, indicating that higher perceived credibility and cognitive–emotional–sensory appeal are associated with greater intention to visit the restaurant.

Table 3. Spearman's correlations between intention to visit and key constructs (ρ, 95% CI)

Variable	Restaurant (Photo)	Restaurant (Video)	Influencer (Photo)	Influencer (Video)
Cognitive–emotional–sensory appeal	0.603 (0.59-0.73)	0.751 (0.69-0.80)	0.640 (0.56-0.71)	0.752 (0.68-0.80)
Perceived credibility	0.607 (0.52 - 0.68)	0.662 (0.59-0.73)	0.660 (0.58-0.73)	0.736 (0.67-0.79)

Table 4 provides a summary of the hypothesis testing results, indicating the level of support for each proposed relationship.

Table 4. Hypotheses tests results

Hypothesis	Result
H_{1a}: Post source (restaurant vs. influencer) has an effect on perceived cognitive–emotional–sensory appeal.	Partially Supported
H_{1b}: Post source (restaurant vs. influencer) has an effect on perceived credibility.	Partially Supported
H_{2a}: Post format (photo vs. video) has an effect on perceived cognitive–emotional–sensory appeal.	Supported
H_{2b}: Post format (photo vs. video) has an effect on perceived credibility.	Supported
H_3: Perceived credibility of social media content positively affects consumers' intention to visit the restaurant.	Supported
H_4: Cognitive–emotional–sensory appeal of social media content positively affects consumers' intention to visit the restaurant.	Supported

CONCLUSION

This study aimed to examine how the source of social media content (restau rant vs. influencer) and content format (photo vs. video) influence consumers' cognitive–emotional–sensory appeal, perceived credibility, and intention to visit a restaurant. Grounded in the S–O–R framework, the findings provide several relevant insights.

First, the results show that content format plays a more consistent role than content source, as hypotheses related to format were largely supported, whereas those related to source were only partially supported. This suggests that how content is presented may be a particularly important factor in shaping consumers' perceptions and behavioural intentions, although the effect of the content source appears to depend on the specific context. This finding aligns with prior research highlighting the importance of media richness and vividness in influencing consumer responses (Peng & Lu, 2024; Sui et al., 2023), as well as with studies demonstrating that video content can enhance emotional engagement and sensory stimulation (Tellis et al., 2019; Truong et al., 2025).

Second, although influencer-generated content is often assumed to be more credible and persuasive (De Veirman et al., 2017; Lou & Yuan, 2019), the results of this study only provide partial support for the superiority of influencers over restaurant-generated content. This suggests that restaurants' own content can be equally effective in certain contexts, possibly due to perceived expertise and greater control over message quality. This finding is consistent with research showing that firm-generated content can positively influence consumer attitudes and intentions (Lima et al., 2019; Li et al., 2021), while also complementing studies that highlight the role of influencers in shaping restaurant visit intentions (Anjos et al., 2022; Malik et al., 2025).

Third, the findings reinforce the importance of cognitive–emotional–sensory appeal and perceived credibility as key organismic responses, supporting prior literature that demonstrates the role of experiential and affective reactions in shaping behavioural intentions (Choi et al., 2018; Lacroix et al., 2020). In line with the S–O–R framework, the results suggest that social media stimuli influence internal evaluations, which in turn contribute to consumers' intention to visit a restaurant.

Overall, this study contributes to the literature by simultaneously examining content source and format, an area that has received limited attention in previous research. While prior studies have focused on individual factors such as influencer characteristics (Pereira et al., 2025), food vlogs (Truong et al., 2025), or user-generated content (Chen et al., 2026), this research provides a more integrated perspective by comparing different types of social media stimuli within the same framework. Although influencer marketing has gained significant attention, studies focusing specifically on the restaurant sector remain limited, further reinforcing the relevance of the present study.

Practical Implications

The findings of this study offer several important implications for restaurant managers and digital marketing practitioners. First, the results highlight that the effectiveness of content format depends on the content source. For restaurant-generated content, photos appear to be more effective in enhancing cognitive–emotional–sensory appeal, whereas for influencer-generated content, videos yield stronger evaluations. This suggests that managers should align content format with the communication source to maximise impact. The results also indicate that perceived credibility is higher for video content, either for restaurant or influencer posts. Videos allow a better simulate of the dining experience by showcasing food preparation, textures, and ambience, which can increase consumers' trust and desire to visit (Truong et al., 2025). However, photos should not be disregarded, as they remain effective in capturing attention quickly and facilitating fast processing in social media environments (Liu et al., 2022; Reimer, 2023). Therefore, an integrated content strategy combining both formats is recommended.

Second, the results suggest that restaurants should not rely exclusively on influencers. While influencer collaborations can enhance reach and credibility, restaurant-generated content can also be effective in influencing perceptions and intentions. Managers should therefore adopt a balanced approach, combining owned media (restaurant posts) with earned media (influencer collaborations), depending on campaign objectives, target audience, and budget constraints.

Third, given the importance of cognitive–emotional–sensory appeal, restaurants should design content that is visually attractive, emotionally engaging, and capable of stimulating sensory imagination. This includes using high-quality visuals, storytelling elements, and immersive content that evokes taste, smell, and atmosphere.

Finally, as perceived credibility remains a key determinant of behavioural intentions, restaurants and influencers should focus on enhancing authenticity and transparency in their communication. This can be achieved through genuine storytelling, realistic portrayals of the dining experience, and avoiding overly promotional or artificial content, which may reduce trust.

Limitations and Directions for Future Research

Despite its contributions, this study presents several limitations that open avenues for future research. First, the use of a convenience sample and the focus on respondents from Portugal and Brazil limit the generalisability of the findings. Future studies should replicate this research using more representative samples and across different cultural contexts, as cultural differences may influence how social media content is perceived and evaluated.

Second, the study employed specific experimental stimuli, namely a limited number of posts with particular types of food and presentation formats. Future studies could test a wider variety of stimuli, including different cuisines, levels of visual aesthetics, and alternative content styles, to enhance the robustness and generalisability of the findings.

Third, the analysis focused primarily on the main effects of content source and format, without exploring moderating variables. Future research could examine moderating factors such as age, gender, social media usage intensity, or familiarity with influencers.

Finally, although influencer marketing has gained increasing attention, research focusing specifically on the restaurant context remains relatively limited. Future studies could further explore this domain by analysing different types of influencers (e.g., micro vs. macro influencers) and different platforms (e.g., Instagram vs. TikTok).

ACKNOWLEDGMENT

This work is funded by National Funds through the FCT - Foundation for Science and Technology, I.P., within the scope of the project Ref. UIDB/05583/2020. NECE and this work are supported by FCT - Fundação para a Ciência e Tecnologia, I.P. by project reference UID/04630/2025 and DOI identifier 10.54499/UID/04630/2025 Furthermore, we would like to thank the Research Centre in Digital Services (CISeD) and the Instituto Politécnico de Viseu for their support.

REFERENCES

Ajzen, I. (1985). From intentions to action: A theory of planned behavior. In Kuhl, J., & Beckman, J. (Eds.), *Action control: From cognitions to behaviors* (pp. 11–39). Springer., DOI: 10.1007/978-3-642-69746-3_2

Alnsour, M., & Al Faour, H. R. (2019). The Influence of Customers Social Media Brand Community Engagement on Restaurants Visit Intentions. *Journal of International Food & Agribusiness Marketing, 32*(1), 79–95. DOI: 10.1080/08974438.2019.1599751

Anas, A. M., Abdou, A. H., Hassan, T. H., Alrefae, W. M. M., Daradkeh, F. M., El-Amin, M. A. M. M., Kegour, A. B. A., & Alboray, H. M. M. (2023). Satisfaction on the driving seat: Exploring the influence of social media marketing activities on followers' purchase intention in the restaurant industry context. *Sustainability (Basel), 15*(9), 7207. DOI: 10.3390/su15097207

Anjos, C. J. F., Marques, S., & Dias, A. (2022). The impact of Instagram influencer marketing in the restaurant industry. [IJSSMET]. *International Journal of Service Science, Management, Engineering, and Technology, 13*(1), 1–20. DOI: 10.4018/IJSSMET.297496

Annamalai, B., Yoshida, M., Varshney, S., Pathak, A. A., & Venugopal, P. (2021). Social media content strategy for sport clubs to drive fan engagement. *Journal of Retailing and Consumer Services, 62*, 102648. DOI: 10.1016/j.jretconser.2021.102648

Business Research Insights. (2026). *Influencer Marketing Market: Size & Trend Projection 2026–2035*. https://www.businessresearchinsights.com/market-reports/influencer-marketing-market-117468

Casais, B., Coelho, T., & Escadas, M. (2025). Sensory marketing in the metaverse for tourism preview and tourism pre-experience: The effect on the intention to visit tourist destinations. *Tourism Review, 80*(8), 1558–1577. DOI: 10.1108/TR-06-2024-0540

Chan, I. C. C., Chen, Z., & Leung, D. (2023). The more the better? Strategizing visual elements in social media marketing. *Journal of Hospitality and Tourism Management*, *54*, 268–289. DOI: 10.1016/j.jhtm.2022.11.007

Chang, R. C. Y. (2022). Developing a taxonomy of motivations for foodstagramming through photo elicitation. International *Journal of Hospitality Management, 107*, 103347. 7 https://doi.org/DOI: 10.1016/j.ijhm.2022.103347

Chen, Y. V., Jin, X., Gardiner, S., & Wong, I. A. (2024b). How foodstagramming posts influence restaurant visit intention: The mediating role of goal relevance and mimicking desire. *International Journal of Contemporary Hospitality Management*, *36*(12), 4319–4337. DOI: 10.1108/IJCHM-12-2023-1881

Chen, Y. V., Jin, X. C., & Gardiner, S. (2026). How user-generated food photos influence tourists' restaurant visits: The effect of aesthetics, familiarity, and regulatory focus. *International Journal of Hospitality Management*, *133*, 104509. DOI: 10.1016/j.ijhm.2025.104509

Chen, Y. V., Wong, I. A., Leong, A. M. W., & Huang, G. I. (2024a). Having fun in micro-celebrity restaurants: The role of social interaction, foodstagramming, and sharing satisfaction. *International Journal of Hospitality Management*, *120*, 103768. DOI: 10.1016/j.ijhm.2024.103768

Choi, Y., Hickerson, B., & Kerstetter, D. (2018). Understanding the sources of online travel information. *Journal of Travel Research*, *57*(1), 116–128. DOI: 10.1177/0047287516683833

Cvijikj, I. P., & Michahelles, F. (2013). Online engagement factors on Facebook brand pages. *Social Network Analysis and Mining*, *3*(4), 843–861. DOI: 10.1007/s13278-013-0098-8

De Veirman, M., Cauberghe, V., & Hudders, L. (2017). Marketing through Instagram influencers: The impact of number of followers and product divergence on brand attitude. *International Journal of Advertising*, *36*(5), 798–828. DOI: 10.1080/02650487.2017.1348035

Deloitte. (2025). *Serving up an impactful social media strategy for restaurants.* https://www.deloittedigital.com/us/en/insights/perspective/social-media-strategies-restaurants.html

Freberg, K., Graham, K., McGaughey, K., & Freberg, L. (2011). Who are the social media influencers? A study of public perceptions of personality. *Public Relations Review*, *37*(1), 90–92. DOI: 10.1016/j.pubrev.2010.11.001

Gretzel, U., & Yoo, K. H. (2017). Social media in hospitality and tourism. In Dixit, S. K. (Ed.), *The Routledge handbook of consumer behaviour in hospitality and tourism* (pp. 339–346). Routledge., DOI: 10.4324/9781315659657-38

Gruss, R., Kim, E., & Abrahams, A. (2020). Engaging restaurant customers on Facebook: The power of belongingness appeals on social media. *Journal of Hospitality & Tourism Research (Washington, D.C.), 44*(2), 201–228. DOI: 10.1177/1096348019892071

Haddad, J. (2025). *Why Influencer Marketing Beats Traditional Ads in 2025.* Torro Media. https://torro.io/blog/why-influencer-marketing-beats-traditional-ads-in-2025

Harsanto, P. W., Wisetrotomo, S., & Prasetya, H. B. (2025). The Declining Impact of Product Advertising Photography on Consumer Purchase Decisions. *Dirasat: Human and Social Sciences, 52*(2), 316–327. Advance online publication. DOI: 10.35516/hum.v52i2.5203

Highfield, T., & Leaver, T. (2016). Instagrammatics and digital methods: Studying visual social media, from selfies and GIFs to memes and emoji. *Communication research and practice, 2*(1), 47-62. https://doi.org/DOI: 10.1080/22041451.2016.1155332

Huifeng, P., & Ha, H. Y. (2021). Temporal effects of online customer reviews on restaurant visit intention: The role of perceived risk. *Journal of Hospitality Marketing & Management, 30*(7), 825–844. DOI: 10.1080/19368623.2021.1897053

Ibrahim, B., Wang, X., & Bourne, H. (2021). Exploring the effect of user engagement in online brand communities: Evidence from social media. *Sustainability, 13*(2277), 1–16. DOI: 10.3390/su13042277

Jain, S. P., & Posavac, S. S. (2001). Prepurchase attribute verifiability, source credibility, and persuasion. *Journal of Consumer Psychology, 11*(3), 169–180. DOI: 10.1207/S15327663JCP1103_03

Kim, S., Koh, Y., Cha, J., & Lee, S. (2015). Effects of social media on firm value for US restaurant companies. *International Journal of Hospitality Management, 49*, 40–46. DOI: 10.1016/j.ijhm.2015.05.006

Kumsawat, P., Suttikun, C., & Mahasuweerachai, P. (2025). Does credibility matter on TikTok: The influence of food content creator types on restaurants' social media engagement and purchasing intentions. *Journal of Global Marketing, 38*(3), 234–251. DOI: 10.1080/08911762.2024.2440093

Lacroix, C., Rajaobelina, L., & St-Onge, A. (2020). Impact of perceived experiential advertising on customers' responses: A multi-method approach. *International Journal of Bank Marketing, 38*(6), 1237–1258. DOI: 10.1108/IJBM-12-2019-0451

Lee, P. Y., Koseoglu, M. A., Qi, L., Liu, E. C., & King, B. (2021). The sway of influencer marketing: Evidence from a restaurant group. *International Journal of Hospitality Management*, *98*, 103022. DOI: 10.1016/j.ijhm.2021.103022

Leung, X. Y., Sun, J., & Asswailem, A. (2022). Attractive females versus trustworthy males: Explore gender effects in social media influencer marketing in Saudi restaurants. *International Journal of Hospitality Management*, *103*, 103207. DOI: 10.1016/j.ijhm.2022.103207

Li, F., Larimo, J., & Leonidou, L. C. (2021). Social media marketing strategy: Definition, conceptualization, taxonomy, validation, and future agenda. *Journal of the Academy of Marketing Science*, *49*(1), 51–70. DOI: 10.1007/s11747-020-00733-3

Li, Y., & Xie, Y. (2020). Is a picture worth a thousand words? An empirical study of image content and social media engagement. *JMR, Journal of Marketing Research*, *57*(1), 1–19. DOI: 10.1177/0022243719881113

Lima, M. M. D., Mainardes, E., & Cavalcanti, A. L. (2019). Influence of social media on restaurant consumers: A case study of Crab island restaurant. *Journal of Foodservice Business Research*, *22*(5), 413–432. DOI: 10.1080/15378020.2019.1631657

Liu, H., Feng, S., & Hu, X. S. (2022). Process vs. outcome: Effects of food photo types in online restaurant reviews on consumers' purchase intention. *International Journal of Hospitality Management*, *102*, 103179. DOI: 10.1016/j.ijhm.2022.103179

Lou, C., & Yuan, S. (2019). Influencer marketing: How message value and credibility affect consumer trust of branded content on social media. *Journal of Interactive Advertising*, *19*(1), 58–73. DOI: 10.1080/15252019.2018.1533501

Malik, G., Saini, P., Kumar, A., & Singh, K. (2025). Examining the impact of Instagram food vloggers on restaurant visit intentions: Structural equation modelling approach. *International Journal of Business and Systems Research*, *19*(1), 71–94. DOI: 10.1504/IJBSR.2025.143556

Mehrabian, A., & Russell, J. A. (1974). *An Approach to Environmental Psychology*. MIT.

Moran, G., Muzellec, L., & Johnson, D. (2020). Message content features and social media engagement: Evidence from the media industry. *Journal of Product and Brand Management*, *29*(5), 533–545. DOI: 10.1108/JPBM-09-2018-2014

Naqvi, M. H. A., Jiang, Y., & Naqvi, M. (2021). Generating customer engagement in electronic-brand communities: A stimulus–organism–response perspective. *Asia Pacific Journal of Marketing and Logistics*, *33*(7), 1535–1555. DOI: 10.1108/APJML-01-2020-0053

Navarro, J. G. (2025). *Influencer marketing market size worldwide from 2015 to 2025*. Statista. https://www.statista.com/statistics/1092819/global-influencer-market-size/

Nazli, M., Bulut, C., & Ozarslan, Y. (2025). Gen Z travel intentions and museum visits in the metaverse: Case of Egypt, Scotland, and Turkey. *Current Issues in Tourism*, *28*(15), 2447–2465. DOI: 10.1080/13683500.2024.2376885

Needles, A. M., & Thompson, G. M. (2013). Social media use in the restaurant industry: a work in progress. Cornell Hospitality Report 13 (7), 6–17 https://ecommons.cornell.edu/server/api/core/bitstreams/acc22f42-8dca-402b-b8e2-1c1845442272/content

Oksüz, B., Altinay, L., & Ciftci, S. (2025). Digital or physical satisfaction? The role of social media marketing in restaurant customer satisfaction. *International Journal of Hospitality Management*, *118*, 103630. DOI: 10.1016/j.ijhm.2024.104011

Olfat, M., Hedayati, M. H., Mirzaei, H., Nasir, M., Amani, M. H., & Hassanzadeh, M. (2025). "Our communications made me loyal; it's delicious now!": Commercial food influencers' interactive practices and follower retention. *British Food Journal*, *127*(12), 4811–4836. DOI: 10.1108/BFJ-05-2025-0635

Pansari, A., & Kumar, V. (2017). Customer engagement: The construct, antecedents, and consequences. *Journal of the Academy of Marketing Science*, *45*(3), 294–311. DOI: 10.1007/s11747-016-0485-6

Peng, Y., & Lu, L. (2024). Untangling influence: The effect of follower-followee comparison on social media engagement. *Journal of Retailing and Consumer Services*, *78*, 103747. DOI: 10.1016/j.jretconser.2024.103747

Pereira, P., Piramanayagam, S., Mallya, J., & Patwardhan, V. (2025). How restaurant influencers' characteristics impact Gen Z's restaurant visit: An elaboration likelihood perspective. *Cogent Business & Management*, *12*(1), 2532858. DOI: 10.1080/23311975.2025.2532858

Philp, M., Jacobson, J., & Pancer, E. (2022). Predicting social media engagement with computer vision: An examination of food marketing on Instagram. *Journal of Business Research*, *149*, 736–747. DOI: 10.1016/j.jbusres.2022.05.078

Pop, R. A., Săplăcan, Z., Dabija, D. C., & Alt, M. A. (2021). The impact of social media influencers on travel decisions: The role of trust in consumer decision journey. *Current Issues in Tourism*, *25*(5), 823–843. DOI: 10.1080/13683500.2021.1895729

Rajaobelina, L., Lacroix, C., & St-Onge, A. (2019). Does experiential advertising impact credibility? *International Journal of Bank Marketing*, *37*(1), 171–191. DOI: 10.1108/IJBM-01-2017-0021

Ramos, C. M., & Hassan, A. (2021). Evaluation of the tourist experience using a framework for the analysis of the influence of social media on tourist behaviour. *International Journal of Tourism Policy, 11*(3), 207–221. DOI: 10.1504/IJTP.2021.118663

Reimer, T. (2023). Environmental factors to maximize social media engagement: A comprehensive framework. *Journal of Retailing and Consumer Services, 75*, 103458. DOI: 10.1016/j.jretconser.2023.103458

Sabate, F., Berbegal-Mirabent, J., Cañabate, A., & Lebherz, P. R. (2014). Factors influencing popularity of branded content in Facebook fan pages. *European Management Journal, 32*(6), 1001–1011. DOI: 10.1016/j.emj.2014.05.001

Safeer, A. A. (2024). Harnessing the power of brand social media marketing on consumer online impulse buying intentions: A stimulus-organism-response framework. *Journal of Product and Brand Management, 33*(5), 533–544. DOI: 10.1108/JPBM-07-2023-4619

Safeer, A. A., Abrar, M., & Zhou, Y. (2025). Leveraging the potential of social media: Unveiling the influence of customer-generated photos on customer behavior. *PLoS One, 20*(9), e0330201. DOI: 10.1371/journal.pone.0330201

Shin, Y., Noone, B. M., & Robson, S. K. (2020). An exploration of the effects of photograph content, photograph source, and price on consumers' online travel booking intentions. *Journal of Travel Research, 59*(1), 120–139. DOI: 10.1177/0047287518817399

Silaban, P. H., Chen, W. K., Eunike, I. J., & Silalahi, A. D. K. (2023). Traditional restaurant managers' use of sensory marketing to maintain customer satisfaction: Findings from PLS-SEM and fsQCA. *Cogent Business & Management, 10*(1), 2196788. DOI: 10.1080/23311975.2023.2196788

Simonetti, A., & Bigne, E. (2022). How visual attention to social media cues impacts visit intention and liking expectation for restaurants. *International Journal of Contemporary Hospitality Management, 34*(6), 2049–2070. DOI: 10.1108/IJCHM-09-2021-1091

Sohaib, M., Safeer, A. A., & Majeed, A. (2025). Social media food photos and brand engagement: Role of content source, authenticity, brand stereotypes and online community influence. *Journal of Hospitality and Tourism Technology*, •••, 1–20. DOI: 10.1108/JHTT-05-2025-0388

Sui, M., Hawkins, I., & Wang, R. (2023). When falsehood wins? Varied effects of sensational elements on users' engagement with real and fake posts. *Computers in Human Behavior, 142*, 107654. DOI: 10.1016/j.chb.2023.107654

Szakály, O., Pinke-Sziva, I., & Smith, M. K. (2025). The impact of digital influencers on attitude and intent to consume and travel in restaurant choice–evidences from Hungary. *British Food Journal, 127*(9), 3498–3511. DOI: 10.1108/BFJ-11-2024-1186

Tellis, G. J., MacInnis, D. J., Tirunillai, S., & Zhang, Y. (2019). What drives virality (sharing) of online digital content? The critical role of information, emotion, and brand prominence. *Journal of Marketing, 83*(4), 1–20. DOI: 10.1177/0022242919841034

Thongmak, M. (2024). Twitter content strategies to maximize engagement: The case of Thai Banks. *Computers in Human Behavior, 152*, 108081. DOI: 10.1016/j.chb.2023.108081

Ting, L., & Ahn, J. (2026). The effects of a multidimensional parasocial relationship with an influencer on customer behavioral intention in restaurants. *Journal of Hospitality and Tourism Technology*, •••, 1–20. DOI: 10.1108/JHTT-02-2025-0126

Truong, T. A., Piscarac, D., Kang, S., & Yoo, S. C. (2025). Virtual culinary influence: Investigating the impact of food vlogs on viewer attitudes and restaurant visit intentions. *Information (Basel), 16*(1), 44. Advance online publication. DOI: 10.3390/info16010044

Wang, R., & Chan-Olmsted, S. (2024). Brand communication through social media influencers: Trust building and trust transfer mechanisms. *International Journal of Business Communication, 23294884241255911*, 23294884241255911. Advance online publication. DOI: 10.1177/23294884241255911

Yarış, A., & Aykol, Ş. (2021). The impact of social media use on restaurant choice. *Anatolia, 33*(3), 310–322. DOI: 10.1080/13032917.2021.1931379

Yu, Z., Klongthong, W., Thavorn, J., & Ngamkroeckjoti, C. (2021). Understanding rural Chinese consumers' behavior: A stimulus–organism–response (SOR) perspective on Huawei's brand loyalty in China. *Cogent Business & Management, 8*(1), 1880679. DOI: 10.1080/23311975.2021.1880679

Zhang, R., Yu, Z., & Yao, W. (2024). Navigating the complexities of online opinion formation: An insight into consumer cognitive heuristics. *Journal of Retailing and Consumer Services, 81*, 103966. DOI: 10.1016/j.jretconser.2024.103966

Zniva, R., Weitzl, W. J., & Lindmoser, C. (2023). Be constantly different! How to manage influencer authenticity. *Electronic Commerce Research, 23*(3), 1485–1514. DOI: 10.1007/s10660-022-09653-6

Compilation of References

Abeza, G., O'Reilly, N., Seguin, B., & Nzindukiyimana, O. (2017). Social Media as a Relationship Marketing Tool in Professional Sport: A Netnographical Exploration. *International Journal of Sport Communication, 10*(3), 325–358. DOI: 10.1123/ijsc.2017-0041

Abidin, C. (2021). Mapping Internet celebrity on TikTok: Exploring attention economies and visibility labours. *Cultural Science Journal, 12*(1), 77–103. DOI: 10.5334/csci.140

Achen, R. M. (2017). Measuring social media marketing: Moving towards a relationship-marketing approach. *Managing Sport and Leisure, 22*(1), 33–53. DOI: 10.1080/23750472.2017.1379883

Acquisti, A., Brandimarte, L., & Loewenstein, G. (2015). Privacy and human behavior in the age of information. *Science, 347*(6221), 509–514. DOI: 10.1126/science.aaa1465 PMID: 25635091

Agarwal, T., Gopalkrishnan, S., Kale, V., Periwal, D., Kulkarni, A. A., Tharkude, D., & Jaiwani, M. (2023, November). Transforming advertising: Harnessing AI for personalised customer-centricity. In *2023 IEEE International Conference on Technology Management, Operations and Decisions (ICTMOD)* (pp. 1-8). IEEE. DOI: 10.1109/ICTMOD59086.2023.10438160

Aggarwal, C. C. (2016). An Introduction to Recommender Systems. In *Recommender Systems* (pp. 1–28). Springer International Publishing., DOI: 10.1007/978-3-319-29659-3_1

Aguirre, A., Dempsey, G., Surden, H., & Reiner, P. B. (2020). AI loyalty: A new paradigm for aligning stakeholder interests. *IEEE Transactions on Technology and Society, 1*(3), 128–137. DOI: 10.1109/TTS.2020.3013490

Aguirre, E., Roggeveen, A. L., Grewal, D., & Wetzels, M. (2016). The personalization-privacy paradox: Implications for new media. *Journal of Consumer Marketing, 33*(2), 98–110. DOI: 10.1108/JCM-06-2015-1458

Ahiabor, D. K., Kosiba, J. P. B., Gli, D. D., Tweneboah-Koduah, E. Y., & Hinson, R. E. (2023). Satellite fans engagement with social networking sites influence on sport team brand equity: A UGT perspective. *Digital Business, 3*(2), 100064. DOI: 10.1016/j.digbus.2023.100064

Aimé, I., Berger-Remy, F., & Laporte, M.-E. (2022). The brand, the persona and the algorithm: How datafication is reconfiguring marketing work☆. *Journal of Business Research, 145*, 814–827. https://doi.org/https://doi.org/10.1016/j.jbusres.2022.03.047. DOI: 10.1016/j.jbusres.2022.03.047

Ajzen, I. (1985). From intentions to action: A theory of planned behavior. In Kuhl, J., & Beckman, J. (Eds.), *Action control: From cognitions to behaviors* (pp. 11–39). Springer., DOI: 10.1007/978-3-642-69746-3_2

Alagarsamy, S., & Mehrolia, S. (2023). Exploring chatbot trust: Antecedents and behavioural outcomes. *Heliyon, 9*(5), e16074. DOI: 10.1016/j.heliyon.2023.e16074 PMID: 37206046

Ali, A., & Hastuti, H. (2024). Predictive analytics and marketing decision-making: A systematic review of data-driven influence. *Journal of Business Research, 164*, 113963.

Aliarte, K. N., Dulay, J. J., & Novilla, N. J. (2024, January 1). Improving marketing personalization with AI: How self-congruency influences consumer engagement. ***International** Journal of Research and Innovation in Social Science*. DOI: 10.47772/IJRISS.2024.8120042

Allison, N. (2013). *Going beyond on-pitch success: Fan engagement as a catalyst for growth* [University of London]. https://core.ac.uk/download/pdf/141220628.pdf

Alnsour, M., & Al Faour, H. R. (2019). The Influence of Customers Social Media Brand Community Engagement on Restaurants Visit Intentions. *Journal of International Food & Agribusiness Marketing, 32*(1), 79–95. DOI: 10.1080/08974438.2019.1599751

Amalia, F., Zahira, T., & Sekti, B. A. (2026). Influence of Social Media and Virtual Reality on Consumer Behavior. In *Modern Consumer Behavior at the Intersection of AI and Social Media* (pp. 91–121). DOI: 10.4018/979-8-3373-2747-1.ch004

Ameen, N., Tarhini, A., Reppel, A., & Anand, A. (2021). Customer experiences in the age of artificial intelligence. *Computers in Human Behavior, 114*(1–2), 106548. DOI: 10.1016/j.chb.2020.106548 PMID: 32905175

Amin, M. M. (2024, December 1). AI-powered personalized marketing: A deep dive into customer segmentation and targeting. *International Journal of Science, Engineering and Management*. DOI: 10.36647/IJSEM/11.12.A001

Anas, A. M., Abdou, A. H., Hassan, T. H., Alrefae, W. M. M., Daradkeh, F. M., El-Amin, M. A. M. M., Kegour, A. B. A., & Alboray, H. M. M. (2023). Satisfaction on the driving seat: Exploring the influence of social media marketing activities on followers' purchase intention in the restaurant industry context. *Sustainability (Basel)*, *15*(9), 7207. DOI: 10.3390/su15097207

Anchieta, T. (2008, November). What are the challenges of sports management as a sports manager? *efdeportes*. https://www.efdeportes.com/efd126/desafios-da-gestao-desportiva-enquanto-gestor%20desportivo.htm

Andrivet, M. (2025, February 10). New coke: A classic branding case study on a major product change failure. *The Branding Journal*. https://www.thebrandingjournal.com/2025/02/new-coke/

Anjos, C. J. F., Marques, S., & Dias, A. (2022). The impact of Instagram influencer marketing in the restaurant industry. [IJSSMET]. *International Journal of Service Science, Management, Engineering, and Technology*, *13*(1), 1–20. DOI: 10.4018/IJSSMET.297496

Annamalai, B., Yoshida, M., Varshney, S., Pathak, A. A., & Venugopal, P. (2021). Social media content strategy for sport clubs to drive fan engagement. *Journal of Retailing and Consumer Services*, *62*, 102648. DOI: 10.1016/j.jretconser.2021.102648

Araújo, R.F. (2015). Digital scientific marketing and alternative metrics for journals: From visibility to engagement. *Perspectives in Information Science, 20* .

Ariely, D., & Berns, G. S. (2010). Neuromarketing: The hope and hype of neuroimaging in business. *Nature Reviews Neuroscience*, *11*(4), 284–292. DOI: 10.1038/nrn2795 PMID: 20197790

Arora, N., Dreze, X., Ghose, A., Hess, J. D., Iyengar, R., Jing, B., Joshi, Y., Kumar, V., Lurie, N., Neslin, S., Sajeesh, S., Su, M., Syam, N., Thomas, J., & Zhang, Z. J. (2008). Putting one-to-one marketing to work: Personalization, customization, and choice. *Marketing Letters*, *19*(3–4), 305–321. DOI: 10.1007/s11002-008-9056-z

Arora, P. (2019). *The next billion users: Digital life beyond the West*. Harvard University Press. DOI: 10.4159/9780674238879

Arroba, T., Gea García, G., Sánchez-Sáez, J. A., & Conde, E. (2022). Fan identification as a precursor of loyalty towards a football team. *Systematic Reviews*, *11*, 22–60.

Augusto, P. M. C. (2015). *Profile of Non-Professional Football Sports Leaders – A case study on Sports Leaders in the Lisbon District* [University of Lisbon]. https://repositorio.ulisboa.pt/bitstream/10400.5/8643/1/Perfil%20dos%20Dirigentes%20Desportivos%20de%20Futebol%20N%C3%A3o%20Profissional%20-%20Doc%20Final%20-%20Pedro%20Augusto%20-%20Altera%C3%A7%C3%A3o.pdf

Babadoğan, B. (2024, October 29). Unveiling the power of AI-driven personalization: Transforming consumer behavior in the age of digital marketing. *Next Frontier For Life Sciences and AI*. DOI: 10.62802/fj43xy18

Babatunde, S. O., Odejide, O. A., Edunjobi, T. E., & Ogundipe, D. O.Sodiq Odetunde BabatundeOpeyemi Abayomi OdejideTolulope Esther EdunjobiDamilola Oluwaseun Ogundipe. (2024). The role of AI in marketing personalization: A theoretical exploration of consumer engagement strategies. *International Journal of Management & Entrepreneurship Research*, *6*(3), 936–949. DOI: 10.51594/ijmer.v6i3.964

Balli, A. (2024, September 20). The effect of product personalization on consumer purchasing intention, customer satisfaction, brand loyalty and artificial intelligence applications with machine learning. *Fiscaoeconomia*. DOI: 10.25295/fsecon.1449755

Bansal, G., Zahedi, F. M., & Gefen, D. (2015). The role of privacy assurance mechanisms in building trust and the moderating role of privacy concern. *European Journal of Information Systems*, *24*(6), 624–644. DOI: 10.1057/ejis.2014.41

Basic Law on Physical Activity and Sport. No. 161, Assembly of the Republic (2007). https://diariodarepublica.pt/dr/legislacao-consolidada/lei/2007-58896796

Baumeister, R. F., & Leary, M. R. (1997). Writing Narrative Literature Reviews. *Review of General Psychology*, *1*(3), 311–320. DOI: 10.1037/1089-2680.1.3.311

Becan, C., & Çeber, B. (2025). How technology readiness influences behavioral and purchasing intention: Serial multiple mediating role of attitude toward AI and AI-driven consumer chatbot experience. *Digital Transformation and Society*, *5*(1), 78–104. DOI: 10.1108/DTS-04-2025-0082

Becker, S., Bryman, A., & Ferguson, H. (2012). *Understanding research for social policy and social work: Themes, methods and approaches* (2nd Edition). Policy Press. https://books.google.pt/books?hl=pt-PT&lr=&id=QB-LaGf05z0C&oi=fnd&pg=PP8&dq=Bryman+2012&ot s=m7eR7HMlTT&sig=TICshqJjvS6kU-PeqkYs3S9btmSs&redir_esc=y#v=onepage&q=Bryman%202012&f=false

Beer, D. (2017). The social power of algorithms. *Information Communication and Society*, *20*(1), 1–13. DOI: 10.1080/1369118X.2016.1216147

Begum, N. (2024, November 28). Beyond automation: How AI service integration is shaping the future of brand management. *Management Dynamics:*. DOI: 10.57198/2583-4932.1339

Beličková, P. (2024). AI-powered Insights: Strengthening Nonprofit Communication through Neuromarketing. *Media & Marketing Identity*, 22–29. DOI: 10.34135/mmidentity-2024-02

Bérail, P., & Bungener, C. (2022). Favorite YouTubers as a source of health information during quarantine: Viewers trust their favorite YouTubers with health information. *Social Network Analysis and Mining*, *12*(1), 88. Advance online publication. DOI: 10.1007/s13278-022-00925-5 PMID: 35911482

Beresford, A. R., Kübler, D., & Preibusch, S. (2012). Unwillingness to pay for privacy: A field experiment. *Economics Letters*, *117*(1), 25–27. DOI: 10.1016/j.econlet.2012.04.077

Bhambri, P., & Kant, S. (2025a, February 1-2). A taxonomy of bias in machine learning: Classification, sources, and implications for ethical AI [Paper presentation]. Lincoln-SPAST Global Sustainability Programme (SGS-24), 1st International Conference of LGPR Program, Lincoln University College, Malaysia. SPAST Proceedings, 1(2). https://spast.org/techrep/article/view/5387/724

Bhambri, P., & Kant, S. (2025b, April 26-27). Ethical AI systems: A comprehensive framework for bias mitigation and fairness in machine learning [Paper presentation]. Lincoln-SPAST Global Sustainability Programme (SGS-24), 2nd International Conference of LGPR Program, Lincoln University College, Malaysia. SPAST Proceedings, 1(2). https://spast.org/techrep/article/view/5385/698

Bhambri, P., & Kant, S. (2025c, August 2-3). Navigating the AI trade-offs: A sector-level study on fairness, performance, and explainability [Paper presentation]. Lincoln-SPAST Global Sustainability Programme (SGS-24), 3rd International Conference of LGPR Program, Lincoln University College, Malaysia. SPAST Proceedings, 1(4). https://spast.org/techrep/article/view/5734/862

Bhambri, P. (2025). Innovative systems: Entertainment, gaming, and the metaverse. In Ho, R. C., Song, B. L., & Tee, P. K. (Eds.), *Managing customer-centric strategies in the digital landscape* (pp. 483–514). IGI Global., DOI: 10.4018/979-8-3693-5668-5.ch018

Bhambri, P., & Kautish, S. K. (2024). Analytic hierarchy process and business value creation. In Kautish, S. K. (Ed.), *Using strategy analytics for business value creation and competitive advantage* (pp. 54–77). IGI Global., DOI: 10.4018/979-8-3693-2823-1.ch003

Bhambri, P., & Khang, A. (2024a). The human-machine nexus with art-making generative AIs. In Hai-Jew, S. (Ed.), *Making art with generative AI tools* (pp. 73–85). IGI Global., DOI: 10.4018/979-8-3693-1950-5.ch004

Bhambri, P., & Khang, A. (2024b). Challenges and future directions on business intelligence. In Özsungur, F. (Ed.), *Generating entrepreneurial ideas with AI* (pp. 117–146). IGI Global., DOI: 10.4018/979-8-3693-3498-0.ch006

Bhandari, V., & Sreenivasan, S. (2023). India's Digital Personal Data Protection Act: Promise and pitfalls. *Economic and Political Weekly*, *58*(34), 14–18.

Bhattacharjee, D. R., Kuanr, A., Pradhan, D., & Moharana, T. R. (2025). Fun or warm: How conversational style boosts customer engagement. *Journal of Retailing and Consumer Services*, *85*, 104293. DOI: 10.1016/j.jretconser.2025.104293

Bhattacharya, C. B. (2025, January 17). AI-powered predictive models transforming the future of digital marketing and customer engagement. *Journal of Informatics Education and Research*. DOI: 10.52783/jier.v5i1.2015

Blau, P. M. (1964). Justice in social exchange. *Sociological Inquiry*, *34*(2), 193–206. DOI: 10.1111/j.1475-682X.1964.tb00583.x

Bleier, A., & Eisenbeiss, M. (2015). Personalized Online Advertising Effectiveness: The Interplay of What, When, and Where. *Marketing Science*, *34*(5), 669–688. DOI: 10.1287/mksc.2015.0930

Bleier, A., & Eisenbeiss, M. (2015). The importance of trust for personalized online advertising. *Journal of Retailing*, *91*(3), 390–409. DOI: 10.1016/j.jretai.2015.04.001

Bleize, D. N. M., & Antheunis, M. L. (2019). Factors influencing purchase intention in virtual worlds: A review of the literature. *Journal of Marketing Communications*, *25*(4), 403–420. DOI: 10.1080/13527266.2016.1278028

Bodó, B., Helberger, N., & de Vreese, C. H. (2017). Political micro-targeting: A Manchurian candidate or just a dark horse? *Internet Policy Review*, *6*(4). Advance online publication. DOI: 10.14763/2017.4.776

Boerman, S. C., Kruikemeier, S., & Zuiderveen Borgesius, F. (2021). Online behavioral advertising: A literature review and research agenda. *Journal of Advertising*, *50*(3), 341–362.

Borel, L., & Christodoulides, G. (2016). *Branding and digital analytics* .

Borges, F. (2018). Always Together: How Football Clubs Want Constant Connections with Fans. *ATHENS JOURNAL OF SPORTS*, *5*(4), 263–278. DOI: 10.30958/ajspo.5-4-2

Borgesius, F. Z., Helberger, N., & Reyna, A. (2017). The perfect match? A closer look at the relationship between EU consumer law and data protection law. [Kluwer Law International.]. *Common Market Law Review, 54*(5), 1427–1465. DOI: 10.54648/COLA2017118

Bourdeau, B. L., Cronin, J. J., & Voorhees, C. M. (2024). Customer loyalty: A refined conceptualization, measurement, and model. *Journal of Retailing and Consumer Services, 81*, 104020. DOI: 10.1016/j.jretconser.2024.104020

Bradshaw, S., & Howard, P. N. (2019). *The global disinformation order*. Oxford Internet Institute.

Braun, V., & Clarke, V. (2006). Using thematic analysis in psychology. *Qualitative Research in Psychology, 3*(2), 77–101. DOI: 10.1191/1478088706qp063oa

Brent Mittelstadt, B. (2019). Principles alone cannot guarantee ethical AI. *Nature Machine Intelligence, 1*(11), 501–507. DOI: 10.1038/s42256-019-0114-4

Brodie, R. J., Hollebeek, L. D., Jurić, B., & Ilić, A. (2011). Customer engagement: Conceptual domain, fundamental propositions, and implications for research. *Journal of Service Research, 14*(3), 252–271. DOI: 10.1177/1094670511411703

Bujak, M., & Kucharski, R. (2024, November 5). Balancing profit and traveller acceptance in ride-pooling personalised fares. *arXiv*. https://doi.org//arxiv.2411.03370DOI: 10.48550

Burtell, M. (2023). Artificial influence: Ethics of AI-driven persuasion and behavioral optimization. *AI & Society, 38*(4), 1567–1581.

Business Research Insights. (2026). *Influencer Marketing Market: Size & Trend Projection 2026–2035*. https://www.businessresearchinsights.com/market-reports/influencer-marketing-market-117468

Calder, B. J., Malthouse, E. C., & Schaedel, U. (2009). An Experimental Study of the Relationship between Online Engagement and Advertising Effectiveness. *Journal of Interactive Marketing, 23*(4), 321–331. DOI: 10.1016/j.intmar.2009.07.002

Caliskan, A., Bryson, J. J., & Narayanan, A. (2022). Fairness and discrimination in algorithmic decision-making. *Communications of the ACM, 65*(6), 54–63. DOI: 10.1145/3531146

Carreiro, H. S. O. (2023). *Importance of marketing in football: A comparative analysis between clubs* [University of the Azores]. http://hdl.handle.net/10400.3/7039

Carvalho, E. (2024, January 26). 6 Challenges that Youth Sports Clubs Face. *emjogo.pt*. https://emjogo.pt/blog/6-desafios-que-os-clubes-de-desporto-de-formacao-enfrentam/

Carvalho, E. (2025, January 30). The Impact of Sport on Local Communities. *emjogo.pt*. https://emjogo.pt/blog/o-impacto-do-desporto-nas-comunidades-locais/

Casais, B., Coelho, T., & Escadas, M. (2025). Sensory marketing in the metaverse for tourism preview and tourism pre-experience: The effect on the intention to visit tourist destinations. *Tourism Review*, *80*(8), 1558–1577. DOI: 10.1108/TR-06-2024-0540

Celik, F., Çam, M., & Köseoglu, M. A. (2022). Ad avoidance in the digital context: A systematic literature review and research agenda. *International Journal of Consumer Studies*, *47*(6), 2071–2105. DOI: 10.1111/ijcs.12882

Chanavat, N., & Desbordes, M. (2014). Sponsorship and ambush marketing in sport. In *Routledge handbook of sports marketing* (2nd ed., p. 46). Routledge., https://www.researchgate.net/publication/339237351

Chang, R. C. Y. (2022). Developing a taxonomy of motivations for foodstagramming through photo elicitation. International *Journal of Hospitality Management, 107*, 103347. 7 https://doi.org/DOI: 10.1016/j.ijhm.2022.103347

Chan, I. C. C., Chen, Z., & Leung, D. (2023). The more the better? Strategizing visual elements in social media marketing. *Journal of Hospitality and Tourism Management*, *54*, 268–289. DOI: 10.1016/j.jhtm.2022.11.007

Chaturvedi, R., Verma, S., Srivastava, V., & Khot, S. S. (2025). Exploring the frontier of anthropomorphism in AI agents: Trends and way forward. *Business and Society Review*, *130*(1), 42–80. DOI: 10.1111/basr.70002

Chen, J., & Stalla-Bourdillon, S. (2023). Algorithmic persuasion and autonomy in digital markets. *Computer Law & Security Review*, *49*, 105775.

Chen, S., Li, X., Liu, K., & Wang, X. (2023). Chatbot or human? The impact of online customer service on consumers' purchase intentions. *Psychology and Marketing*, *40*(11), 2186–2200. DOI: 10.1002/mar.21862

Chen, T.-Y., & Chen, K.-J. (2025). Chatbots with swear words? Exploring the roles of humour, aggressiveness, and gender in consumer–chatbot interactions. *Behaviour & Information Technology*, 1–15. Advance online publication. DOI: 10.1080/0144929X.2025.2605484

Chen, Y. V., Jin, X. C., & Gardiner, S. (2026). How user-generated food photos influence tourists' restaurant visits: The effect of aesthetics, familiarity, and regulatory focus. *International Journal of Hospitality Management*, *133*, 104509. DOI: 10.1016/j.ijhm.2025.104509

Chen, Y. V., Jin, X., Gardiner, S., & Wong, I. A. (2024b). How foodstagramming posts influence restaurant visit intention: The mediating role of goal relevance and mimicking desire. *International Journal of Contemporary Hospitality Management*, *36*(12), 4319–4337. DOI: 10.1108/IJCHM-12-2023-1881

Chen, Y. V., Wong, I. A., Leong, A. M. W., & Huang, G. I. (2024a). Having fun in micro-celebrity restaurants: The role of social interaction, foodstagramming, and sharing satisfaction. *International Journal of Hospitality Management*, *120*, 103768. DOI: 10.1016/j.ijhm.2024.103768

Cherukuri, B. R.Bangar Raju Cherukuri. (2024, June 30). AI-powered personalization: How machine learning is shaping the future of user experience. *International Journal of Science and Research Archive*, *12*(1), 3111–3126. Advance online publication. DOI: 10.30574/ijsra.2024.12.1.0961

Cheung, C. M. K., Lee, M. K. O., & Rabjohn, N. (2008). The impact of electronic word-of-mouth. *Internet Research*, *18*(3), 229–247. DOI: 10.1108/10662240810883290

Cheung, M. L., Pires, G. D., Rosenberger, P. J.III, & De Oliveira, M. J. (2021). Driving COBRAs: The power of social media marketing. *Marketing Intelligence & Planning*, *39*(3), 361–376. DOI: 10.1108/MIP-11-2019-0583

Choi, S., & Zhou, J. (2023). Inducing consumers' self-disclosure through the fit between chatbot's interaction styles and regulatory focus. *Journal of Business Research*, *166*, 114127. DOI: 10.1016/j.jbusres.2023.114127

Choi, Y., Hickerson, B., & Kerstetter, D. (2018). Understanding the sources of online travel information. *Journal of Travel Research*, *57*(1), 116–128. DOI: 10.1177/0047287516683833

Coelho, J. N. (2004). Waving the Flag: Football and National Identity. *International Relations*, *2*, 22. https://ipri.unl.pt/index.php/pt/publicacoes/revista-ri/arquivo-de-revista-ri/83-relacoes-internacionais-n-2

Coglianese, C., & Lehr, D. (2019). TRANSPARENCY AND ALGORITHMIC GOVERNANCE. *Administrative Law Review*, *71*(1), 1–56.

Cohen, J. E. (2019). *Between truth and power: The legal constructions of informational capitalism*. Oxford University Press. DOI: 10.1093/oso/9780190246693.001.0001

Couldry, N., & Mejias, U. A. (2019). The costs of connection: How data is colonizing human life and appropriating it for capitalism. In *The costs of connection*. Stanford University Press.

Couldry, N., & Mejias, U. A. (2019). *The costs of connection: How data is colonizing human life and appropriating it for capitalism*. Stanford University Press.

Cowls, J., & Floridi, L. (2018, June 19). Prolegomena to a white paper on an ethical framework for a good AI society. Social Science Research Network (*SSRN*). DOI: 10.2139/ssrn.3198732

Crolic, C., Thomaz, F., Hadi, R., & Stephen, A. T. (2022). Blame the bot: Anthropomorphism and anger in customer–chatbot interactions. *Journal of Marketing*, *86*(1), 132–148. DOI: 10.1177/00222429211045687

Cropanzano, R., & Mitchell, M. S. (2005). Social exchange theory: An interdisciplinary review. *Journal of Management*, *31*(6), 874–900. DOI: 10.1177/0149206305279602

Curran, D. (2023). Surveillance capitalism and systemic digital risk: The imperative to collect and connect and the risks of interconnectedness. *Big Data & Society*, *10*(1), 20539517231177620. DOI: 10.1177/20539517231177621

Cvijikj, I. P., & Michahelles, F. (2013). Online engagement factors on Facebook brand pages. *Social Network Analysis and Mining*, *3*(4), 843–861. DOI: 10.1007/s13278-013-0098-8

da Costa, G. J. C. (2022). *Digital Sports Communication in the midst of the Covid-19 pandemic: The cases of FC Paços de Ferreira and Rio Ave FC* [ISCTE - University Institute of Lisbon]. https://repositorio.iscte-iul.pt/bitstream/10071/29473/1/master_guilherme_conceicao_costa.pdf

Davenport, T. H., Guha, A., Grewal, D., & Bressgott, T. (2021). How artificial intelligence will change the future of marketing. *Journal of the Academy of Marketing Science*, *49*(1), 24–42. DOI: 10.1007/s11747-019-00696-0

Davis, N., & Jin, J. (2024). Beyond code: Consumer response to chatbots. *Current Opinion in Psychology*, *58*, 101841. DOI: 10.1016/j.copsyc.2024.101841 PMID: 38981369

Dawson, P. A., & Mäkelä, M. (2020). The Story Logic of Social Media: Co-Construction and Emergent Narrative Authority. *Style (Fayetteville)*, *54*(1), 21. https://api.semanticscholar.org/CorpusID:226735125. DOI: 10.5325/style.54.1.0021

De Bruijn, H., Warnier, M., & Janssen, M. (2022). The perils and pitfalls of explainable AI. *Ethics and Information Technology*, *24*(2), 1–10.

De Bruyn, A., Viswanathan, V., Beh, Y. S., Brock, J. K.-U., & Von Wangenheim, F. (2020). Artificial Intelligence and Marketing: Pitfalls and Opportunities. *Journal of Interactive Marketing*, *51*(1), 91–105. DOI: 10.1016/j.intmar.2020.04.007

de Oliveira, E. R., & Ferreira, P. (2014). *Research Methods: From Questioning to Scientific Discovery*. Vida Economica Editorial. https://books.google.pt/books?id=Xku7BAAAQBAJ

de Vasconcelos, B. C. (2024). *Content strategies on social media for Generation Z: TikTok and Instagram* [ISCAP - Instituto Superior de Contabilidade e Administração do Porto]. http://hdl.handle.net/10400.22/26040

De Veirman, M., Cauberghe, V., & Hudders, L. (2017). Marketing through Instagram influencers: The impact of number of followers and product divergence on brand attitude. *International Journal of Advertising*, *36*(5), 798–828. DOI: 10.1080/02650487.2017.1348035

Deloitte. (2025). *Serving up an impactful social media strategy for restaurants.* https://www.deloittedigital.com/us/en/insights/perspective/social-media-strategies-restaurants.html

DeMasters, C., Morgan, K., Schwoerer, K., & Wiley, K. (2024). Forging Connections: Nonprofits, TikTok, and Authentic Engagement – A Mixed-Methods Study. *Journal of Public and Nonprofit Affairs*, *10*(1). Advance online publication. DOI: 10.20899/jpna.dky82f18

Denzin, N. K., & Lincoln, Y. S. (2018). *The Sage handbook of qualitative research* (5th ed.). Sage.

Desai, D. (2022). Hyper-personalization: An AI-enabled personalization for customer-centric marketing. In *Customer-Centric Marketing Strategies*. IGI Global., DOI: 10.4018/978-1-7998-7959-6.ch003

Desai, P. (2021). *A strategic approach to enrich brand through artificial intelligence*. Lecture Notes in Networks and Systems., DOI: 10.1007/978-981-15-7106-0_57

Dima, T. (2015). Social Media Usage In European Clubs Football Industry. Is Digital Reach Better Correlated With Sports Or Financial Performance? *Romanian Economic Journal, 18* (55), 117–128. https://ideas.repec.org/a/rej/journl/v18y2015i55p117-128.html

Directory, S. (2025, April 16). What role does culture play in data privacy? → question. *Lifestyle → Sustainability Directory*. https://lifestyle.sustainability-directory.com/question/what-role-does-culture-play-in-data-privacy/

Dubois, E., & McKelvey, F. (2023). Algorithmic influence in platform societies. *New Media & Society*, *25*(7), 1791–1810.

Dutta, S., Ramanathan, A., Sakthi Prasath, G. B., & Edwin, T. S. (2025). AI-powered chatbots in Meta marketing (Facebook and Instagram): A game-changer for brand communication and engagement in e-commerce industries. Journal of Information Technology Teaching Cases. Advance online publication. DOI: 10.1177/20438869251338322

Dwivedi, Y. K., Balakrishnan, J., Baabdullah, A. M., & Das, R. (2023). Do chatbots establish 'humanness' in the customer purchase journey? An investigation through explanatory sequential design. *Psychology and Marketing*, *40*(11), 2244–2271. DOI: 10.1002/mar.21888

Dwivedi, Y. K., Hughes, L., Ismagilova, E., Aarts, G., Coombs, C., Crick, T., Duan, Y., Dwivedi, R., Edwards, J., Eirug, A., Galanos, V., Ilavarasan, P. V., Janssen, M., Jones, P., Kar, A. K., Kizgin, H., Kronemann, B., Lal, B., Lucini, B., & Williams, M. D. (2021). Artificial Intelligence (AI): Multidisciplinary perspectives on emerging challenges, opportunities, and agenda for research, practice and policy. *International Journal of Information Management*, *57*, 101994. DOI: 10.1016/j.ijinfomgt.2019.08.002

Eubanks, V. (2018). *Automating inequality: How high-tech tools profile, police, and punish the poor*. St. Martin's Press.

European Commission: Directorate-General for Education, Y., Sport and Culture. (2016). *Study on the contribution of sport to regional development through the structural funds – Final report* . Publications Office. DOI: 10.2766/940310

Factora, J. (2023, August 16). Target's sales fell for the first time in 6 years after backlash to pride collection. *Them*. https://www.them.us/story/target-sales-fall-pride-collection-backlash

Fairclough, N. (2013). *Critical discourse analysis: The critical study of language* (2nd ed.). Routledge. DOI: 10.4324/9781315834368

Farzan, R., Dabbish, L. A., Kraut, R. E., & Postmes, T. (2011). Increasing commitment to online communities by designing for social presence. *Proceedings of the ACM 2011 Conference on Computer Supported Cooperative Work*, 321–330. DOI: 10.1145/1958824.1958874

Félix, B. J. (2023). *Strategic communication plan for the dissemination of acrobatic gymnastics in Portugal* [ISCTE - University Institute of Lisbon]. http://hdl.handle.net/10071/30262

Filo, K., Lock, D., & Karg, A. (2014). Sport and social media research: A review. *Sport Management Review, 18*(2), 166–181. DOI: 10.1016/j.smr.2014.11.001

Fiske, S. T., Cuddy, A. J. C., Glick, P., & Xu, J. (2002). A model of (often mixed) stereotype content: Competence and warmth respectively follow from perceived status and competition. *Journal of Personality and Social Psychology, 82*(6), 878–902. DOI: 10.1037/0022-3514.82.6.878 PMID: 12051578

Floridi, L. (2014). *The ethics of information.* Oxford University Press.

Floridi, L., Cowls, J., Beltrametti, M., Chatila, R., Chazerand, P., Dignum, V., Luetge, C., Madelin, R., Pagallo, U., Rossi, F., Schafer, B., Valcke, P., & Vayena, E. (2018). AI4People—An ethical framework for a good AI society. *Minds and Machines, 28*(4), 689–707. DOI: 10.1007/s11023-018-9482-5 PMID: 30930541

Floridi, L., Holweg, M., Taddeo, M., Amaya Silva, J., Mökander, J., & Wen, Y. (2022). Responsible AI: Principles, challenges, and opportunities. *Business Ethics Quarterly, 32*(1), 1–36.

Foroudi, P., Gupta, S., Sivarajah, U., & Broderick, A. (2018). Investigating the effects of smart technology on customer dynamics and customer experience. *Computers in Human Behavior, 80*, 271–282. DOI: 10.1016/j.chb.2017.11.014

Foucault, M. (2012). *Discipline and punish: The birth of the prison.* Vintage.

Freberg, K., Graham, K., McGaughey, K., & Freberg, L. (2011). Who are the social media influencers? A study of public perceptions of personality. *Public Relations Review, 37*(1), 90–92. DOI: 10.1016/j.pubrev.2010.11.001

Fukuyama, F. (1995). *Trust: The social virtues and the creation of prosperity.* Free Press.

Funk, D. C., Filo, K., Beaton, A. A., & Pritchard, M. (2009). Measuring the motives of sport event attendance: Bridging the academic-practitioner divide to understanding behavior. *Sport Marketing Quarterly, 18*(3), 126–138. https://digitalcommons.cwu.edu/cobfac/276/. DOI: 10.1177/106169340901800302

Ganeshkumar, M., Karunakaran, S., Muzhumathi, R., & Suguna, R. (2024, October). Ai-driven marketing insights: Harnessing machine learning for enhanced consumer engagement and personalization. In *2024 First International Conference on Software, Systems and Information Technology (SSITCON)* (pp. 1-6). IEEE. DOI: 10.1109/SSITCON62437.2024.10796558

Gao, B., Wang, Y., Xie, H., Hu, Y., & Hu, Y. (2023). Artificial Intelligence in Advertising: Advancements, Challenges, and Ethical Considerations in Targeting, Personalization, Content Creation, and Ad Optimization. *SAGE Open, 13*(4), 21582440231210759. Advance online publication. DOI: 10.1177/21582440231210759

Garbarino, E., & Johnson, M. S. (1999). The different roles of satisfaction, trust, and commitment in customer relationships. *Journal of Marketing, 63*(2), 70–87. DOI: 10.1177/002224299906300205

García-Fernández, J., Grimaldi-Puyana, M., & Bravo, G. (2022). *Sport in the Iberian Peninsula*. Routledge., DOI: 10.4324/9781003197003

Gatzioufa, P., & Saprikis, V. (2022). A literature review on users' behavioral intention toward chatbots' adoption. Applied Computing and Informatics. Advance online publication. DOI: 10.1108/ACI-01-2022-0021

Gaysynsky, A., Everson, N. S., Heley, K., & Chou, W.-Y. S. (2024). Perceptions of Health Misinformation on Social Media: Cross-Sectional Survey Study. *JMIR Infodemiology, 4*, e51127. DOI: 10.2196/51127 PMID: 38687591

Gefen, D., Karahanna, E., & Straub, D. W. (2003). Trust and TAM in online shopping: An integrated model. *Management Information Systems Quarterly, 27*(1), 51–90. DOI: 10.2307/30036519

Ghalavand, H., & Nabiolahi, A. (2024). Exploring online health information quality criteria on social media: A mixed-method approach. *BMC Health Services Research, 24*(1), 1311. Advance online publication. DOI: 10.1186/s12913-024-11838-8 PMID: 39478573

Gillespie, T. (2018). Custodians of the internet: Platforms, content moderation, and the hidden decisions that shape social media. In *Custodians of the Internet: Platforms, Content Moderation, and the Hidden Decisions That Shape Social Media*. Yale University Press.

Gonçalves, R. G. (2015). *Sports organizations and new media: Trends and good practices* [University of Aveiro]. http://hdl.handle.net/10773/14627

Goncalves, M., Hu, Y., Aliagas, I., & Cerdá, L. M. (2024). Neuromarketing algorithms' consumer privacy and ethical considerations: Challenges and opportunities. *Cogent Business & Management, 11*(1), 2333063. DOI: 10.1080/23311975.2024.2333063

Gorwa, R., Binns, R., & Katzenbach, C. (2022). Algorithmic governance and platform power. *New Media & Society, 24*(9), 1961–1983.

Government of India. (2023). *The Digital Personal Data Protection Act, 2023.* Ministry of Law and Justice.

Greenhalgh, T., Robert, G., Macfarlane, F., Bate, P., Kyriakidou, O., & Peacock, R. (2005). Storylines of research in diffusion of innovation: A meta-narrative approach to systematic review. *Social Science & Medicine*, *61*(2), 417–430. DOI: 10.1016/j.socscimed.2004.12.001 PMID: 15893056

Greenleaf, G. (2018). Global data privacy laws 2017: 120 national data privacy laws. *Privacy Laws & Business International Report*, *145*, 10–13.

Green, M. C., & Brock, T. C. (2000). The role of transportation in the persuasiveness of public narratives. *Journal of Personality and Social Psychology*, *79*(5), 701–721. DOI: 10.1037/0022-3514.79.5.701 PMID: 11079236

Gretzel, U., & Yoo, K. H. (2017). Social media in hospitality and tourism. In Dixit, S. K. (Ed.), *The Routledge handbook of consumer behaviour in hospitality and tourism* (pp. 339–346). Routledge., DOI: 10.4324/9781315659657-38

Grewal, D., Hulland, J., Kopalle, P. K., & Karahanna, E. (2021). The future of technology and marketing. *Journal of the Academy of Marketing Science*, *49*(1), 1–8. DOI: 10.1007/s11747-019-00711-4

Gruss, R., Kim, E., & Abrahams, A. (2020). Engaging restaurant customers on Facebook: The power of belongingness appeals on social media. *Journal of Hospitality & Tourism Research (Washington, D.C.)*, *44*(2), 201–228. DOI: 10.1177/1096348019892071

Habibi, M. R., Laroche, M., & Richard, M.-O. (2014). The roles of brand community and community engagement in building brand trust on social media. *Computers in Human Behavior*, *37*, 152–161. DOI: 10.1016/j.chb.2014.04.016

Habib, M. D., Attri, R., Salam, M. A., & Yaqub, M. Z. (2025). Retail consumers' conundrum: An in-depth qualitative study navigating the motivations and aversion of chatbots. *Journal of Retailing and Consumer Services*, *82*, 104147. DOI: 10.1016/j.jretconser.2024.104147

Haddad, J. (2025). *Why Influencer Marketing Beats Traditional Ads in 2025.* Torro Media. https://torro.io/blog/why-influencer-marketing-beats-traditional-ads-in-2025

Hagendorff, T. (2022). The ethics of AI ethics: An evaluation of guidelines. *Minds and Machines*, *32*(1), 99–120. DOI: 10.1007/s11023-020-09517-8

Hair, J. F., Hult, G. T. M., Ringle, C. M., & Sarstedt, M. (2019). *A primer on partial least squares structural equation modeling (PLS-SEM)* (2nd ed.). Sage. DOI: 10.3926/oss.37

Hardcastle, K., Vorster, L., & Brown, D. M. (2025). Understanding Customer Responses to AI-Driven Personalized Journeys: Impacts on the Customer Experience. *Journal of Advertising*, *54*(2), 176–195. DOI: 10.1080/00913367.2025.2460985

Harsanto, P. W., Wisetrotomo, S., & Prasetya, H. B. (2025). The Declining Impact of Product Advertising Photography on Consumer Purchase Decisions. *Dirasat: Human and Social Sciences*, *52*(2), 316–327. Advance online publication. DOI: 10.35516/hum.v52i2.5203

Haugh, B., & Watkins, B. (2016). Tag Me, Tweet Me if You Want to Reach Me: An Investigation Into How Sports Fans Use Social Media. *International Journal of Sport Communication*, *9*(3), 278–293. DOI: 10.1123/ijsc.2016-0044

Havrysh, I. I., & Fen, K. S. (2022). Sports marketing: Essence, specificity and basic subjects. *Economic Sciences Series*, *66*(66), 61–68. DOI: 10.24025/2306-4420.66.2022.268591

Highfield, T., & Leaver, T. (2016). Instagrammatics and digital methods: Studying visual social media, from selfies and GIFs to memes and emoji. *Communication research and practice*, *2*(1), 47-62. https://doi.org/DOI: 10.1080/22041451.2016.1155332

Hilton. (2025). *How to use your Digital Key*. Hilton Help Center. https://www.hilton.com/en/help-center/check-in-and-check-out/how-to-use-your-digital-key/

Högberg, J., Ramberg, M. O., Gustafsson, A., & Wästlund, E. (2019). Creating brand engagement through in-store gamified customer experiences. *Journal of Retailing and Consumer Services*, *50*, 122–130. DOI: 10.1016/j.jretconser.2019.05.006

Hollebeek, L. D., Glynn, M. S., & Brodie, R. J. (2014). Consumer Brand Engagement in Social Media: Conceptualization, Scale Development and Validation. *Journal of Interactive Marketing*, *28*(2), 149–165. DOI: 10.1016/j.intmar.2013.12.002

Hollebeek, L., Srivastava, R., & Chen, T. (2019). SD logic–informed customer engagement: Integrative framework, revised fundamental propositions, and application to CRM. *Journal of the Academy of Marketing Science*, *47*(1), 161–185. Advance online publication. DOI: 10.1007/s11747-016-0494-5

Homans, G. C. (1958). Social behavior as exchange. *American Journal of Sociology*, *63*(6), 597–606. DOI: 10.1086/222355

Howard, P. N. (2020). *Lie machines: How to save democracy from troll armies, deceitful robots, junk news operations, and political operatives*. Yale University Press.

Huang, M. H., & Rust, R. T. (2021). Artificial intelligence in service. *Journal of Service Research, 24*(1), 3–18.

Huang, M.-H., & Rust, R. T. (2021). A strategic framework for artificial intelligence in marketing. *Journal of the Academy of Marketing Science, 49*(1), 30–50. DOI: 10.1007/s11747-020-00749-9

Huang, M.-H., & Rust, R. T. (2021). Engaged to a Robot? The Role of AI in Service. *Journal of Service Research, 24*(1), 30–41. DOI: 10.1177/1094670520902266

Huettermann, M., Uhrich, S., & Koenigstorfer, J. (2022). Components and Outcomes of Fan Engagement in Team Sports: The Perspective of Managers and Fans. *Journal of Global Sport Management, 7*(4), 447–478. DOI: 10.1080/24704067.2019.1576143

Huifeng, P., & Ha, H. Y. (2021). Temporal effects of online customer reviews on restaurant visit intention: The role of perceived risk. *Journal of Hospitality Marketing & Management, 30*(7), 825–844. DOI: 10.1080/19368623.2021.1897053

Hu, X., Xu, X., & Chen, C. (2025). Empowering consumers: The role of avatar choice in consumer-chatbot interaction and psychological ownership. *International Journal of Human-Computer Interaction, 41*(24), 15311–15322. DOI: 10.1080/10447318.2025.2495845

Hwang, T. (2020). *Subprime attention crisis*. FSG Originals.

IAMAI. (2023). *Digital advertising in India report*. Internet and Mobile Association of India.

Ibrahim, B., Wang, X., & Bourne, H. (2021). Exploring the effect of user engagement in online brand communities: Evidence from social media. *Sustainability, 13*(2277), 1–16. DOI: 10.3390/su13042277

Idrees, A. M., Helmy, Y., & Khedr, A. E. (2022). Credibility aspects' perceptions of social networks: A survey. *Social Network Analysis and Mining, 12*(1), 98. Advance online publication. DOI: 10.1007/s13278-022-00924-6

Ienca, M., & Andorno, R. (2017). Towards new human rights in the age of neuroscience and neurotechnology. *Life Sciences, Society and Policy, 13*(1), 1–27. DOI: 10.1186/s40504-017-0050-1 PMID: 28444626

Igarashi, M., Onishi, H., Sakai, O., & Hasegawa, S. (2026). How chatbot anthropomorphism shapes customer purchase decisions: Evidence from a field experiment on a cosmetic e-commerce retailer. *Journal of Retailing and Consumer Services*, *91*, 104721. DOI: 10.1016/j.jretconser.2025.104721

Iliadis, A., & Russo, F. (2016). Critical data studies: An introduction. *Big Data & Society*, *3*(2), 2053951716674238. Advance online publication. DOI: 10.1177/2053951716674238

Jabareen, Y. (2009). Building a Conceptual Framework: Philosophy, Definitions, and Procedure. *International Journal of Qualitative Methods*, *8*(4), 49–62. DOI: 10.1177/160940690900800406

Jain, S. P., & Posavac, S. S. (2001). Prepurchase attribute verifiability, source credibility, and persuasion. *Journal of Consumer Psychology*, *11*(3), 169–180. DOI: 10.1207/S15327663JCP1103_03

Jëol, M., Terrien, M., & Chanavat, N. (2024). Challenges, risks, and development opportunities for amateur sports clubs: The case of French handball clubs. *Managing Sport and Leisure*, •••, 1–17. DOI: 10.1080/23750472.2024.2305909

Johnson, D. G. (2023). Algorithmic accountability in automated marketing systems. *Ethics and Information Technology*, *25*(3), 1–12.

Johri, N., Rohit, , Raut, S. K., & Rana, S. (2024). Navigating cultural complexity in global markets: Insights and future directions from two decades of marketing literature. *International Journal of System Assurance Engineering and Management*, *15*(12), 5405–5419. DOI: 10.1007/s13198-024-02520-7

Jurafsky, D., & Martin, H. J. (2025). Speech and Language Processing 3rd ed. In *Stanford University*.

Jyothsna, M., Venkata Subbaiah, P., & Kryvinska, N. (2024). Exploring the chatbot usage intention: A mediating role of chatbot initial trust. *Heliyon*, *10*(12), e33028. DOI: 10.1016/j.heliyon.2024.e33028 PMID: 39027428

Kamila, M. K., & Jasrotia, S. S. (2023). Ethics and marketing responsibility: A bibliometric analysis and literature review. *Asia Pacific Management Review, 28*(4), 567–583. https://doi.org/https://doi.org/10.1016/j.apmrv.2023.04.002

Kandi, A. (2024, November 14). Personalization and customer relationship management in AI-powered business intelligence. *International Journal for Science, Technology and Engineering*. DOI: 10.22214/ijraset.2024.65159

Kang, Y., Mahendra, A., Clarke, C., Tang, L., & Mars, J. (2022). Towards Personalized Intelligence at Scale. *arXiv preprint arXiv:2203.06668.*

Karaenke, P., Schiffer, M., & Waldherr, S. (2020). The customer is always right: A value-based matching mechanism for customer-centered ride pooling. *Proceedings from INFORMS*. DOI: 10.2139/ssrn.5057432

Karami, A., Shemshaki, M., & Ghazanfar, M. A. (2025). Exploring the Ethical Implications of AI-Powered Personalization in Digital Marketing. *Data Intelligence, 7*(4), 1035–1084. DOI: 10.3724/2096-7004.di.2024.0055

Katikar, H. (n.d.). *Enhancing personalized marketing strategies and customer experiences through AI-driven personalization*. Preprint., DOI: 10.14293/PR2199.000976.v1

Keddell, E. (2018). Algorithmic justice in child protection. *Critical Social Policy, 39*(1), 116–135.

Kharmalki, G., & Raizada, S. (2020). Social Media Marketing in Sports: The Rise of Fan Engagement through Instagram. *Annals of Tropical Medicine and Public Health, 23*(17). Advance online publication. DOI: 10.36295/ASRO.2020.231721

Khera, R. (2019). Aadhaar and exclusion: A critical assessment. *Economic and Political Weekly, 54*(20), 50–57.

Kietzmann, J., Paschen, J., & Treen, E. (2022). Artificial intelligence in advertising. *Journal of Advertising Research, 62*(3), 263–270. DOI: 10.2501/JAR-2018-035

Kim, D. J., Ferrin, D. L., & Rao, H. R. (2008). A trust-based consumer decision-making model in electronic commerce: The role of trust, perceived risk, and their antecedents. *Decision Support Systems, 44*(2), 544–564. DOI: 10.1016/j.dss.2007.07.001

Kim, S. (2021). Mapping social media analytics for small business: A case study of business analytics. *International Journal of Fashion Design, Technology and Education, 14*(2), 218–231. DOI: 10.1080/17543266.2021.1915392

Kim, S., Koh, Y., Cha, J., & Lee, S. (2015). Effects of social media on firm value for US restaurant companies. *International Journal of Hospitality Management, 49*, 40–46. DOI: 10.1016/j.ijhm.2015.05.006

Kim, S., & Manoli, A. E. (2023). From horizontal to vertical relationships: How online community identification fosters sport fans' team identification and behavioral intentions. *International Journal of Sports Marketing & Sponsorship, 24*(1), 1–19. DOI: 10.1108/IJSMS-09-2021-0188

Kim, W. B., & Hur, H. J. (2024). What makes people feel empathy for AI chatbots? Assessing the role of competence and warmth. *International Journal of Human-Computer Interaction, 40*(17), 4674–4687. DOI: 10.1080/10447318.2023.2219961

Kirkpatrick, C. E., & Lawrie, L. L. (2024). TikTok as a Source of Health Information and Misinformation for Young Women in the United States: Survey Study. *JMIR Infodemiology, 4*, e54663. DOI: 10.2196/54663 PMID: 38772020

Kline, R. B. (2023). *Principles and practice of structural equation modeling.* (5th Edition). Guilford Publications. https://books.google.pt/books?hl=pt-PT&lr=&id=t2CvEAAAQBAJ&oi=fnd&pg=PP1&dq=Kline,+R.+B.+(2023).+Pri nciples+and+Practice+of+Structural+Equation+Modeling+(5%C2%AA+ed.).+Guilford+Press.&ots=sWUCS5b1fO&s ig=z6tiHh-5ux7uxlniaZw6Z_NnuJ8&redir_esc=y#v=onepage&q=Kline%2C%20R.%20B.%20(2023).%20Principles%20a nd%20Practice%20of%20Structural%20Equation%20Modeling%20(5%C2%AA%20 ed.).%20Guilford%20Press.&f=false

Krasnova, H., Veltri, N. F., & Günther, O. (2012). Self-disclosure and privacy calculus on social networking sites: The role of culture. *Business & Information Systems Engineering, 4*(3), 127–135. DOI: 10.1007/s12599-012-0216-6

Kreiss, D., & McGregor, S. C. (2019). Technology firms shape political communication. *Political Communication, 36*(2), 155–177. DOI: 10.1080/10584609.2017.1364814

Kumsawat, P., Suttikun, C., & Mahasuweerachai, P. (2025). Does credibility matter on TikTok: The influence of food content creator types on restaurants' social media engagement and purchasing intentions. *Journal of Global Marketing, 38*(3), 234–251. DOI: 10.1080/08911762.2024.2440093

Kushnarevych, A. (2024, November 19). Building loyalty programs with AI-powered online tools. *2024 IEEE 24th International Symposium on Computational Intelligence and Informatics (CINTI)*, Budapest, Hungary. DOI: 10.1109/CINTI63048.2024.10830833

Kushnarevych, A., & Kollárová, D. (2024, September 20). The possibilities of artificial intelligence usage in loyalty programs. In *Proceedings of the European Conference on Innovation and Entrepreneurship (ECIE)*. DOI: 10.34190/ecie.19.1.2533

Kusuma, T., Wicaksono, K. A. G., Sihombing, K. D., Wijaya, L., & Phungpumkaew, H. (2025). From conversations to conversions: The role of AI-enhanced chatbots in shaping satisfaction and fostering loyalty in e-commerce. In 2025 17th International Conference on Knowledge and Smart Technology (KST 2025) (pp. 284–288). IEEE. DOI: 10.1109/KST65016.2025.11003290

Lacroix, C., Rajaobelina, L., & St-Onge, A. (2020). Impact of perceived experiential advertising on customers' responses: A multi-method approach. *International Journal of Bank Marketing*, *38*(6), 1237–1258. DOI: 10.1108/IJBM-12-2019-0451

Lambrecht, A., & Tucker, C. (2011). When does Retargeting Work? Timing Information Specificity. SSRN *Electronic Journal*. DOI: 10.2139/ssrn.1795105

Lambrecht, A., & Tucker, C. (2023). Algorithmic bias? An empirical study into apparent gender-based discrimination in ad delivery. *Management Science*, *69*(2), 1129–1148.

Laurell, C., & Söderman, S. (2018). Sports, storytelling and social media: A review and conceptualization. *International Journal of Sports Marketing & Sponsorship*, *19*(3), 338–349. Advance online publication. DOI: 10.1108/IJSMS-11-2016-0084

Leão, R. R. S. (2018). *Sports Leaders in Portugal: A case study on roller hockey* [University of Évora]. https://dspace.uevora.pt/rdpc/bitstream/10174/23498/1/Mestrado%20-%20Dire%C3%A7%C3%A3o%20e%20Gest%C3%A3o%20Desportiva%20-%20Ricardo%20Rafael%20Soares%20Le%C3%A3o%20-%20Os%20dirigentes%20desportivos%20em%20Portugal...%20.pdf

Lee, K.-W., & Li, C.-Y. (2023). It is not merely a chat: Transforming chatbot affordances into dual identification and loyalty. *Journal of Retailing and Consumer Services*, *74*, 103447. DOI: 10.1016/j.jretconser.2023.103447

Lee, P. Y., Koseoglu, M. A., Qi, L., Liu, E. C., & King, B. (2021). The sway of influencer marketing: Evidence from a restaurant group. *International Journal of Hospitality Management*, *98*, 103022. DOI: 10.1016/j.ijhm.2021.103022

Lee, W.-J. (2024). Service failure by human, service recovery by AI chatbot: The impact of justice, AI efficacy on recovery effort. *Virtual Economics*, *7*(4), 48–63. DOI: 10.34021/ve.2024.07.04(3)

Le, H. T. P. M., Park, J., & Lee, S. (2023). Emotion and trust in virtual service assistant design for effective service recovery. *Journal of Retailing and Consumer Services*, *74*, 103368. DOI: 10.1016/j.jretconser.2023.103368

Lemon, K. N., & Verhoef, P. C. (2016). Understanding Customer Experience Throughout the Customer Journey. *Journal of Marketing*, *80*(6), 69–96. DOI: 10.1509/jm.15.0420

Leonard, pepsico. (n.d.). *Leonard v. Pepsico, inc., 88 F. Supp. 2d 116 (S.D.N.Y. 1999)*. Justia Law. https://law.justia.com/cases/federal/district-courts/FSupp2/88/116/2579076/

Leung, X. Y., Sun, J., & Asswailem, A. (2022). Attractive females versus trustworthy males: Explore gender effects in social media influencer marketing in Saudi restaurants. *International Journal of Hospitality Management*, *103*, 103207. DOI: 10.1016/j.ijhm.2022.103207

Levental, O. (2023). Online sports fan communities: Humor, trivial knowledge, and anti-modern tendencies. *Frontiers in Sports and Active Living*, *5*, 1280519. Advance online publication. DOI: 10.3389/fspor.2023.1280519 PMID: 37901392

Lewicki, R. J., & Bunker, B. B. (1996). Developing and maintaining trust in work relationships. In Kramer, R. M., & Tyler, T. R. (Eds.), *Trust in organizations: Frontiers of theory and research* (pp. 114–139). SAGE. DOI: 10.4135/9781452243610.n7

Libai, B., Bart, Y., Gensler, S., Hofacker, C. F., Kaplan, A., Kötterheinrich, K., & Kroll, E. B. (2020). Brave New World? On AI and the Management of Customer Relationships. *Journal of Interactive Marketing*, *51*(1), 44–56. DOI: 10.1016/j.intmar.2020.04.002

Li, F., Larimo, J., & Leonidou, L. C. (2021). Social media marketing strategy: Definition, conceptualization, taxonomy, validation, and future agenda. *Journal of the Academy of Marketing Science*, *49*(1), 51–70. DOI: 10.1007/s11747-020-00733-3

Lilly, A., Rajkumar, R., Kumar, J. V., et al. (2024, January 1). Prominence of artificial intelligence: Upholding customer loyalty via customer relationship management. *Journal of Information and Optimization Sciences*. DOI: 10.47974/JIOS-1767

Lima, M. M. D., Mainardes, E., & Cavalcanti, A. L. (2019). Influence of social media on restaurant consumers: A case study of Crab island restaurant. *Journal of Foodservice Business Research*, *22*(5), 413–432. DOI: 10.1080/15378020.2019.1631657

Lim, M. S. C., Molenaar, A., Brennan, L., Reid, M., & McCaffrey, T. (2022). Young adults' use of different social media platforms for health information: Insights from web-based conversations. *Journal of Medical Internet Research*, *24*(1), e23656. Advance online publication. DOI: 10.2196/23656 PMID: 35040796

Liu, H., Feng, S., & Hu, X. S. (2022). Process vs. outcome: Effects of food photo types in online restaurant reviews on consumers' purchase intention. *International Journal of Hospitality Management*, *102*, 103179. DOI: 10.1016/j.ijhm.2022.103179

Liu, T., Zhang, Y., Zhang, M., Chen, M., & Yu, S. (2024, December 18). Factors influencing consumer willingness to use AI-driven autonomous taxis. *Behavioral Sciences (Basel, Switzerland)*, *14*(12), 1216. DOI: 10.3390/bs14121216 PMID: 39767357

Liu-Thompkins, Y., Khoshghadam, L., Shoushtari, A. A., & Zal, S. (2022). What drives retailer loyalty? A meta-analysis of the role of cognitive, affective, and social factors across five decades. *Journal of Retailing*, *98*(1), 92–110. DOI: 10.1016/j.jretai.2022.02.005

Liu, X., Shin, H., & Burns, A. C. (2021). Examining the impact of luxury brand's social media marketing on customer engagement: Using big data analytics and natural language processing. *Journal of Business Research*, *125*, 815–826. DOI: 10.1016/j.jbusres.2019.04.042

Li, Y., Tsang, Y. P., Ho, D. C. K., Ozden, M., Lee, C. K. M., & Hu, H. (2025). Unraveling consumer resistance to innovative marketing in web 3.0: Empirical findings and large language model insights. *Enterprise Information Systems*, *19*(1–2), 2462069. DOI: 10.1080/17517575.2025.2462069

Li, Y., & Xie, Y. (2020). Is a picture worth a thousand words? An empirical study of image content and social media engagement. *JMR, Journal of Marketing Research*, *57*(1), 1–19. DOI: 10.1177/0022243719881113

Lou, C., & Yuan, S. (2019). Influencer marketing: How message value and credibility affect consumer trust of branded content on social media. *Journal of Interactive Advertising*, *19*(1), 58–73. DOI: 10.1080/15252019.2018.1533501

Lukić, S., & Petrović, J. (2023). The quality of information provided by the most popular dementia videos on TikTok. *Frontiers in Public Health*, *11*, 1266415. Advance online publication. DOI: 10.3389/fpubh.2023.1266415 PMID: 38089039

Luo, X., Tong, S., Fang, Z., & Qu, Z. (2019). Frontiers: Machines vs. humans: The impact of artificial intelligence chatbot disclosure on customer purchases. *Marketing Science*, *38*(6), 937–947. DOI: 10.1287/mksc.2019.1192

Lupton, D. (2015). *Digital sociology*. Routledge.

Luu, T. M. N., Mittal, S., & Gupta, S. (2024, November 15). Leveraging AI to tailor customer engagement with personalized marketing strategies. In *Advances in Marketing, Customer Relationship Management, and E-Services*. IGI Global. DOI: 10.4018/979-8-3373-0219-5.ch010

Lyu, T., Guo, Y., & Chen, H. (2023). Understanding the privacy protection disengagement behaviour of contactless digital service users: The roles of privacy fatigue and privacy literacy. *Behaviour & Information Technology*, *43*(10), 1–17. DOI: 10.1080/0144929X.2023.2237603

Machado, J. C., Martins, C. C., Ferreira, F. C., Silva, S. C., & Duarte, P. A. (2020). Motives to engage with sports brands on Facebook and Instagram–The case of a Portuguese football club. *International Journal of Sports Marketing & Sponsorship, 21*(2), 325–349. DOI: 10.1108/IJSMS-06-2019-0066

Mady, K., Salaheldeen, M., Refaat, H., & Battour, M. (2025). The impact of social media on consumer boycotts: Mediating roles of animosity, behavioral control, and efficacy. *Social Sciences & Humanities Open, 12*, 102041. https://doi.org/https://doi.org/10.1016/j.ssaho.2025.102041. DOI: 10.1016/j.ssaho.2025.102041

Magrizos, S., Campora, M., Lamprinakos, G., Giovanis, A., & Christofi, M. (2025). Transparency by design: The effect of privacy policies visualisation on brand trust and perceived intrusion. *Behaviour & Information Technology*, •••, 1–13. DOI: 10.1080/0144929X.2025.2520594

Malhotra, N. K., Kim, S. S., & Agarwal, J. (2004). Internet users' information privacy concerns (IUIPC): The construct, the scale, and a causal model. *Information Systems Research, 15*(4), 336–355. DOI: 10.1287/isre.1040.0032

Malik, G., Saini, P., Kumar, A., & Singh, K. (2025). Examining the impact of Instagram food vloggers on restaurant visit intentions: Structural equation modelling approach. *International Journal of Business and Systems Research, 19*(1), 71–94. DOI: 10.1504/IJBSR.2025.143556

Manigandan, L., & Sivakumar, A. (2024). Chatbot research: Unveiling evolutionary trends and collaborative pathways through bibliometric analysis. *Multidisciplinary Reviews, 7*(3), e2024045. DOI: 10.31893/multirev.2024045

Mariani, M. M., Perez-Vega, R., & Wirtz, J. (2022). AI in marketing, consumer research and psychology: A systematic literature review and research agenda. *Psychology and Marketing, 39*(4), 755–776. DOI: 10.1002/mar.21619

Markou, V., Serdaris, P., Antoniadis, I., & Spinthiropoulos, K. (2025). Personalization, Trust, and Identity in AI-Based Marketing: An Empirical Study of Consumer Acceptance in Greece. *Administrative Sciences, 15*(11), 440. Advance online publication. DOI: 10.3390/admsci15110440

Marthinus, J., Duffett, R. G., & Knott, B. (2024). Social media adoption as a marketing communication tool by non-professional sports clubs: A multiple case study approach. *International Journal of Sports Marketing & Sponsorship*. Advance online publication. DOI: 10.1108/IJSMS-04-2024-0082

Martin, K. (2022). Ethical implications and accountability of algorithms. *Journal of Business Ethics, 176*(4), 835–850. DOI: 10.1007/s10551-018-3921-3

Martin, K. D., & Murphy, P. E. (2017). The role of data privacy in marketing. *Journal of the Academy of Marketing Science*, *45*(2), 135–155. DOI: 10.1007/s11747-016-0495-4

Masternak, W. (2025, March 31). Inside the Starbucks Rewards program: A complete diagnosis. *Open Loyalty*. https://www.openloyalty.io/insider/starbucks-rewards-program

Mastromartino, B., Ross, W., Wear, H., & Naraine, M. (2020). Thinking outside the 'box': A discussion of sports fans, teams, and the environment in the context of COVID-19. *Sport in Society*, *23*(11), 1–17. DOI: 10.1080/17430437.2020.1804108

Mathai, J. (2023, August 29). Young consumers' perceptions of AI-powered in-car personalized services in a growing market for smart cars. *Journal of Promotion Management*. Advance online publication. DOI: 10.1080/10496491.2023.2251465

Mathur, A., Acar, G., Friedman, M. J., Lucherini, E., Mayer, J., Chetty, M., & Narayanan, A. (2019). Dark patterns at scale: Findings from a crawl of 11K shopping websites. *Proceedings of the ACM on human-computer interaction, 3*(CSCW), 1-32. DOI: 10.1145/3359183

Mato-Santiso, V., Rey-Garcia, M., & Sanzo, M. J. (2023). Volunteer omnichannel behavior in nonprofit organizations: Key antecedents and implications for management. *Nonprofit Management & Leadership*, *34*(2), 433–463. Advance online publication. DOI: 10.1002/nml.21579

Mayer, R. C., Davis, J. H., & Schoorman, F. D. (1995). An integrative model of organisational trust. *Academy of Management Review*, *20*(3), 709–734. DOI: 10.2307/258792

Mbare, B., Perkiö, M., & Koivusalo, M. (2024). Algorithmic management, wellbeing and platform work: Understanding the psychosocial risks and experiences of food couriers in Finland. *Labour & Industry*, *34*(4), 386–411. DOI: 10.1080/10301763.2024.2423442

McCarthy, J., Rowley, J., & Keegan, B. J. (2022). Social media marketing strategy in English football clubs. *Soccer and Society*, *23*(4–5), 513–528. DOI: 10.1080/14660970.2022.2059872

McKnight, D. H., Choudhury, V., & Kacmar, C. (2002). Developing and validating trust measures for e-commerce: An integrative typology. *Information Systems Research*, *13*(3), 334–359. DOI: 10.1287/isre.13.3.334.81

Mehrabian, A., & Russell, J. A. (1974). *An Approach to Environmental Psychology*. MIT.

Miguel, L. B. (2022). *The use of Instagram during lockdown: The case of the main Portuguese sports clubs* [ISCTE - Instituto Universitário de Lisboa]. http://hdl.handle.net/10071/26568

Mihai, A. L. (2013). The Strategic Sport Marketing Planning Process. *Manager Journal, 17* (1), 230–236. https://ideas.repec.org/a/but/manage/v17y2013i1p230-236.html

Miller, K. M., Lukic, K., & Skiera, B. (2025). The impact of the General Data Protection Regulation (GDPR) on online tracking. *International Journal of Research in Marketing*. https://doi.org/https://doi.org/10.1016/j.ijresmar.2025.03.002

Mizrak, F., Demirel, H. G., Yaşar, O., & Karakaya, T. (2025). Digital detox: Exploring the impact of cybersecurity fatigue on employee productivity and mental health. *Discover Mental Health, 5*(1), 25. DOI: 10.1007/s44192-025-00149-x PMID: 39998759

Moe, A., & Alamelu, R. (2025, January 4). Harnessing personalized emotional AI for enhanced consumer engagement in intelligent marketing. *Journal of Digital and Computational Advertising*. DOI: 10.71058/jodac.v9i1002

Mohamed, F., & Shoufan, A. (2024). Users' experience with health-related content on YouTube: An exploratory study. *BMC Public Health, 24*(1), 86. Advance online publication. DOI: 10.1186/s12889-023-17585-5 PMID: 38172765

Moir, A. (2025). Deinfluencing TikTok During the Cost-of-Living Crisis: Neoliberal Logics of (Over)Consumption Across Popular Media. *Television & New Media, 26*(8), 914–930. DOI: 10.1177/15274764251348596

Moran, G., Muzellec, L., & Johnson, D. (2020). Message content features and social media engagement: Evidence from the media industry. *Journal of Product and Brand Management, 29*(5), 533–545. DOI: 10.1108/JPBM-09-2018-2014

Morgan, R. M., & Hunt, S. D. (1994). The commitment-trust theory of relationship marketing. *Journal of Marketing, 58*(3), 20–38. DOI: 10.1177/002224299405800302

Nalivaikė, J., & Miliukaitė, G. (2024, September 25). Influence of AI-generated avatars on consumer trust in the brand. *14th International Scientific Conference „Business and Management 2024*. DOI: 10.3846/bm.2024.1191

Napoletano, E. (2024, September 30). *How to Help Build Customer Relationships and Deliver Recurring Sales*. Business Class: Trends and Insights | American Express; American Express. https://www.americanexpress.com/en-us/business/trends-and-insights/articles/using-small-business-saturday-to-build-customer-relationships-and-deliver-recurring-sales/

Naqvi, M. H. A., Jiang, Y., & Naqvi, M. (2021). Generating customer engagement in electronic-brand communities: A stimulus–organism–response perspective. *Asia Pacific Journal of Marketing and Logistics*, *33*(7), 1535–1555. DOI: 10.1108/APJML-01-2020-0053

Narayan, D. (2024). The political economy of digital platforms: Key directions. *Platforms & Society*, *1*, 29768624241263070. DOI: 10.1177/29768624241263071

Nastasoiu, A., & Vandenbosch, M. (2019). Competing with loyalty: How to design successful customer loyalty reward programs. *Business Horizons*, *62*(2), 207–214. DOI: 10.1016/j.bushor.2018.11.002

Navarro, J. G. (2025). *Influencer marketing market size worldwide from 2015 to 2025*. Statista. https://www.statista.com/statistics/1092819/global-influencer-market-size/

Nazli, M., Bulut, C., & Ozarslan, Y. (2025). Gen Z travel intentions and museum visits in the metaverse: Case of Egypt, Scotland, and Turkey. *Current Issues in Tourism*, *28*(15), 2447–2465. DOI: 10.1080/13683500.2024.2376885

Needles, A. M., & Thompson, G. M. (2013). Social media use in the restaurant industry: a work in progress. Cornell Hospitality Report 13 (7), 6–17 https://ecommons.cornell.edu/server/api/core/bitstreams/acc22f42-8dca-402b-b8e2-1c1845442272/content

Neves, A. J. G de A. (2013). *The Phenomenon of Football in Portugal—A Case Study of the Municipality of Guarda* [University of Beira Interior]. https://ubibliorum.ubi.pt/bitstream/10400.6/3512/1/relat%C3%B3rio_estagio_armandoneves_Mestr_ensinoEF.pdf

Nguyen, L., Nguyen, C., Do, Q., & Dam, K. (2026). Enhancing customer experience through AI-powered marketing: How AI-driven chatbots impact user engagement, satisfaction and purchase retention? *Concurrency and Computation*, *38*(5), e70630. DOI: 10.1002/cpe.70630

Nicoli, N., Henriksen, K., Komodromos, M., & Tsagalas, D. (2021). Investigating digital storytelling for the creation of positively engaging digital content. *EuroMed Journal of Business*. Advance online publication. DOI: 10.1108/EMJB-03-2021-0036

Nissenbaum, H. (2011). A contextual approach to privacy online. *Daedalus*, *140*(4), 32–48. DOI: 10.1162/DAED_a_00113

Nittis, F. D. (2025, June 20). *Woke culture is a trap, at least sometimes*. Human Centric Group. https://humancg.com/blog/woke-culture-is-a-trap-at-least-sometimes/#When_go_woke_leads_to_go_broke_8211_when_woke_culture_is_a_trap

Noble, S. U. (2018). *Algorithms of oppression.* NYU Press. DOI: 10.18574/nyu/9781479833641.001.0001

Nokhiz, P., & Ruwanpathirana, A. K. (2025). Consumer Autonomy or Illusion? Rethinking Consumer Agency in the Age of Algorithms. *Journal of Social Computing, 6*(3), 184–208. DOI: 10.23919/JSC.2025.0015

Nunnally, J. C., & Bernstein, I. H. (1978). *Psychometric Theory* (2nd Edition). McGraw-Hill. https://archive.org/details/dli.scoerat.1556psychometrictheorysecondedition/page/18/mode/2up

O'Neil, C. (2016). *Weapons of math destruction.* Crown.

Ojha, A. K. (2023, February 28). Navigating the algorithmic marketplace: How AI is changing consumer psychology and brand loyalty. *Journal of Psychology and Political Science*, . DOI: 10.55529/jpps.32.25.29

Okeke, N. I., Alabi, O. A., & Igwe, A. N.Nnenna Ijeoma OkekeOlufunke Anne AlabiAbbey Ngochindo IgweOnyeka Chrisanctus OfodileChikezie Paul-Mikki Ewim. (2024, October 30). AI-driven personalization framework for SMEs: Revolutionizing customer engagement and retention. *World Journal of Advanced Research and Reviews, 24*(1), 2019–2035. Advance online publication. DOI: 10.30574/wjarr.2024.24.1.3208

Okoli, C. (2015). A Guide to Conducting a Standalone Systematic Literature Review. *Communications of the Association for Information Systems, 37*(1), 43. DOI: 10.17705/1CAIS.03743

Oksüz, B., Altinay, L., & Ciftci, S. (2025). Digital or physical satisfaction? The role of social media marketing in restaurant customer satisfaction. *International Journal of Hospitality Management, 118*, 103630. DOI: 10.1016/j.ijhm.2024.104011

Olfat, M., Hedayati, M. H., Mirzaei, H., Nasir, M., Amani, M. H., & Hassanzadeh, M. (2025). "Our communications made me loyal; it's delicious now!": Commercial food influencers' interactive practices and follower retention. *British Food Journal, 127*(12), 4811–4836. DOI: 10.1108/BFJ-05-2025-0635

Oliveira, J. S., Santos de Souza Vasconcelos, M. N., & Gomes Lopes Pinheiro, A. (2024). Digital Marketing: A scientific approach to business success in the digital age. *RevistaFT, 29*(140). Advance online publication. DOI: 10.69849/revistaft/ni10202411101149

Palmatier, R. W., Dant, R. P., Grewal, D., & Evans, K. R. (2006). Factors influencing the effectiveness of relationship marketing: A meta-analysis. *Journal of Marketing, 70*(4), 136–153. DOI: 10.1509/jmkg.70.4.136

Pang, H., Hu, Z. Y., & Wang, L. (2025). How perceived motivations influence user stickiness and sustainable engagement with AI-powered chatbots: Unveiling the pivotal function of user attitude. *Journal of Theoretical and Applied Electronic Commerce Research, 20*(3), 228. DOI: 10.3390/jtaer20030228

Pansari, A., & Kumar, V. (2017). Customer engagement: The construct, antecedents, and consequences. *Journal of the Academy of Marketing Science, 45*(3), 294–311. DOI: 10.1007/s11747-016-0485-6

Pasquale, F. (2015). The black box society: The secret algorithms that control money and information. In *The black box society*. Harvard university press. DOI: 10.4159/harvard.9780674736061

Patil, D., Rane, N. L., & Rane, J. (2024, October 28). The future of customer loyalty: How ChatGPT and generative artificial intelligence are transforming customer engagement, personalization, and satisfaction. In book: The Future Impact of ChatGPT on Several Business Sectors (pp.48-106) Chapter: Publisher: Deep Science Publishing.. DOI: 10.70593/978-81-981367-8-7_2

Patil, D. (2025, January 1). Artificial intelligence for personalized marketing and consumer behavior analysis: Enhancing engagement and conversion rates. *SSRN*. DOI: 10.2139/ssrn.5057436

Patil, R. K. S., Porapur, S. M., & Kagawade, S. (2024). The role of ai-driven social media marketing in shaping consumer purchasing behaviour: An empirical analysis of personalization, predictive analytics, and engagement. In *ITM web of conferences* (Vol. 68, p. 01032). EDP Sciences. DOI: 10.1051/itmconf/20246801032

Paul, J., & Criado, A. R. (2020). The art of writing literature review: What do we know and what do we need to know? *International Business Review, 29*(4), 101717. DOI: 10.1016/j.ibusrev.2020.101717

Pavlou, P. A. (2003). Consumer acceptance of electronic commerce: Integrating trust and risk with the technology acceptance model. *International Journal of Electronic Commerce, 7*(3), 101–134. DOI: 10.1080/10864415.2003.11044275

PAYBACK. (2024a). *Score, save and win with PAYBACK on "Singles Day" and "Black Week."* Payback.De. https://www.payback.group/en/press/press-releases/detail/beim-singles-day-und-black-week-mit-payback-punkten-sparen-und-gewinnen

PAYBACK. (2024b). *Das ändert sich 2025 bei PAYBACK.* https://www.payback.group/de/presse/pressemeldungen/detail/das-aendert-sich-2025-bei-payback

Pedro, S. D. G. (2017). *Innovation and Strategic Development in Sports Organizations Aimed at Inclusion and Social Change* [Lusófona University of Humanities and Technologies]. https://recil.ulusofona.pt/server/api/core/bitstreams/e3384686-b649-4456-843e-594210d1573c/content

Peng, Y., & Lu, L. (2024). Untangling influence: The effect of follower-followee comparison on social media engagement. *Journal of Retailing and Consumer Services, 78*, 103747. DOI: 10.1016/j.jretconser.2024.103747

Pereira, J. P. H. M. M. (2024). *Sports Sponsorship of Amateur Teams in Portugal: A Study of the First Divisions of Men's Sports in Five Sports* [University of Porto]. https://repositorio-aberto.up.pt/bitstream/10216/163973/2/699921.pdf

Pereira, P., Piramanayagam, S., Mallya, J., & Patwardhan, V. (2025). How restaurant influencers' characteristics impact Gen Z's restaurant visit: An elaboration likelihood perspective. *Cogent Business & Management, 12*(1), 2532858. DOI: 10.1080/23311975.2025.2532858

Philp, M., Jacobson, J., & Pancer, E. (2022). Predicting social media engagement with computer vision: An examination of food marketing on Instagram. *Journal of Business Research, 149*, 736–747. DOI: 10.1016/j.jbusres.2022.05.078

Pires, H. (2024). *Valuing the base of the pyramid.* Liga Portugal. https://www.ligaportugal.pt/opinion/637/valorizar-a-base-da-piramide

Plassmann, H., Venkatraman, V., Huettel, S., & Yoon, C. (2015). Consumer neuroscience: Applications, challenges, and possible solutions. *Journal of Marketing Research, 52*(4), 427–435. DOI: 10.1509/jmr.14.0048

Pop, R. A., Săplăcan, Z., Dabija, D. C., & Alt, M. A. (2021). The impact of social media influencers on travel decisions: The role of trust in consumer decision journey. *Current Issues in Tourism, 25*(5), 823–843. DOI: 10.1080/13683500.2021.1895729

Portuguese Institute of Sport and Youth. (November 12, 2024). *National Sport for All Program.* Portuguese Institute of Sport and Youth. https://ipdj.gov.pt/programa-nacional-de-desporto-para-todos

Pratesi, F., Hu, L., Rialti, R., Zollo, L., & Faraoni, M. (2021). Cultural dimensions in online purchase behavior: Evidence from a cross-cultural study. *Italian Journal of Marketing, 2021*(3), 227–247. DOI: 10.1007/s43039-021-00022-z

Pretorius, C., McCashin, D., & Coyle, D. (2022). Mental health professionals as influencers on TikTok and Instagram: What role do they play in mental health literacy and help-seeking? *Internet Interventions : the Application of Information Technology in Mental and Behavioural Health*, *30*(100591), 100591. DOI: 10.1016/j.invent.2022.100591 PMID: 36458161

Pulizzi, J., & Piper, B. W. (2023). *Epic Content Marketing, Second Edition: Break through the Clutter with a Different Story, Get the Most Out of Your Content, and Build a Community in Web3* (2nd). McGraw Hill LLC. https://epiccontentmarketing.com/wp-content/uploads/2023/02/Epic-Content-Marketing-Second-Edition-WM.pdf

Puntoni, S., Reczek, R. W., Giesler, M., & Botti, S. (2021). Consumers and artificial intelligence: An experiential perspective. *Journal of Marketing*, *85*(1), 131–151. DOI: 10.1177/0022242920953847

Rahim, N. I. M., & Iahad, A., N., Yusof, A. F., & A. Al-Sharafi, M. (. (2022). AI-based chatbots adoption model for higher-education institutions: A hybrid PLS-SEM-neural network modelling approach. *Sustainability*, *14*(19), 12726. DOI: 10.3390/su141912726

Rahman, S. A. Y., Rahayu, A., & Hendrayati, H. (2025). Digital marketing evolution: Understanding the role of AI and Big Data in shaping marketing strategies. *International Journal of Financial, Accounting, and Management*, *7*(2), 197–211. DOI: 10.35912/ijfam.v7i2.2593

Rajaobelina, L., Lacroix, C., & St-Onge, A. (2019). Does experiential advertising impact credibility? *International Journal of Bank Marketing*, *37*(1), 171–191. DOI: 10.1108/IJBM-01-2017-0021

Rajaobelina, L., & Ricard, L. (2021). Classifying potential users of live chat services and chatbots. *Journal of Financial Services Marketing*, *26*(2), 81–94. DOI: 10.1057/s41264-021-00086-0

Ramadhana, M. A., & Hussein, A. S. (2022, October 1). Pengaruh penggunaan artificial intelligence terhadap customer loyalty dengan citra merek sebagai variabel mediasi. *Journal of Marketing & Public Policy*, *1*(4), 522–531. Advance online publication. DOI: 10.21776/jmppk.2022.01.4.11

Ramanathan, U. (2017). A dangerous drift: Aadhaar and privacy. *Economic and Political Weekly*, *52*(37), 61–70.

Ramos, C. M., & Hassan, A. (2021). Evaluation of the tourist experience using a framework for the analysis of the influence of social media on tourist behaviour. *International Journal of Tourism Policy*, *11*(3), 207–221. DOI: 10.1504/IJTP.2021.118663

Rather, R. A. (2024). AI-powered ChatGPT in the hospitality and tourism industry: Benefits, challenges, theoretical framework, propositions and future research directions. *Tourism Recreation Research, 50*(3), 652–662. DOI: 10.1080/02508281.2023.2287799

Ravald, A., & Grönroos, C. (1996). The value concept and relationship. *European Journal of Marketing*, *30*(2), 19–30. DOI: 10.1108/03090569610106626

Reddy, D. R. (2024, October 18). How do customers react to the integration of AI in customer experience. *International Journal for Multidisciplinary Research.* DOI: 10.36948/ijfmr.2024.v06i05.28954

Redondo, I., & Aznar, G. (2018). To use or not to use ad blockers? The roles of knowledge of ad blockers and attitude toward online advertising. *Telematics and Informatics*, *35*(6), 1607–1616. https://doi.org/https://doi.org/10.1016/j.tele.2018.04.008. DOI: 10.1016/j.tele.2018.04.008

Rehnen, L.-M., Bartsch, S., Kull, M., & Meyer, A. (2017). Exploring the impact of rewarded social media engagement in loyalty programs. *Journal of Service Management*, *28*(2), 305–328. DOI: 10.1108/JOSM-10-2015-0338

Reimer, T. (2023). Environmental factors to maximize social media engagement: A comprehensive framework. *Journal of Retailing and Consumer Services*, *75*, 103458. DOI: 10.1016/j.jretconser.2023.103458

Rein, I., Kotler, P., & Shields, B. R. (2007). *The Elusive Fan: Reinventing Sports in a Crowded Marketplace*. McGraw Hill LLC. https://books.google.pt/books?id=6Vf4gg20ZVkC

Reis, A. (2024, August 12). *Sport in Portugal: What the Portuguese need to know (in 11 points).* Community Culture and Art. https://comunidadeculturaearte.com/o-desporto-em-portugal-o-que-os-portugueses-precisam-de-saber-em-11-pontos/

Rianisa, A., Anggraini, D. S., & Sekti, B. A. (2026). Role of AI in Consumer Decision-Making Processes. In *Modern Consumer Behavior at the Intersection of AI and Social Media* (pp. 123–151). DOI: 10.4018/979-8-3373-2747-1.ch005

Rini, A. S., Wandrial, S., Lutfi, L., Jaya, I., & Satrionugroho, B. (2024). Data-driven marketing: Harnessing artificial intelligence to personalize customer experience and enhance engagement. *Join: Journal of Social Science*, *1*(6), 282–295. DOI: 10.59613/akx6j040

Roy, R., & Naidoo, V. (2021). Enhancing chatbot effectiveness: The role of anthropomorphic conversational styles and time orientation. *Journal of Business Research, 126*, 23–34. DOI: 10.1016/j.jbusres.2020.12.051

Roy, R., & Naidoo, V. (2025). The role of materialism and social judgment in human-chatbot service interactions. *Journal of Services Marketing*, *39*(4), 316–332. DOI: 10.1108/JSM-06-2024-0288

Ruvio, A. A., Khodakarami, F., Morgeson, F. V.III, & Voorhees, C. M. (2025). When rewards connect to the self: Unlocking customer engagement through experiential rewards. *Journal of Retailing*.

Sá, D., & Sá, C. (2008). *Sports marketing, the new rules of the game*. Editions of the Portuguese Institute of Marketing Administration, Marketing School for Business. https://books.google.pt/books?id=bJ4Va0aMghwC

Sabate, F., Berbegal-Mirabent, J., Cañabate, A., & Lebherz, P. R. (2014). Factors influencing popularity of branded content in Facebook fan pages. *European Management Journal*, *32*(6), 1001–1011. DOI: 10.1016/j.emj.2014.05.001

Safeer, A. A. (2024). Harnessing the power of brand social media marketing on consumer online impulse buying intentions: A stimulus-organism-response framework. *Journal of Product and Brand Management*, *33*(5), 533–544. DOI: 10.1108/JPBM-07-2023-4619

Safeer, A. A., Abrar, M., & Zhou, Y. (2025). Leveraging the potential of social media: Unveiling the influence of customer-generated photos on customer behavior. *PLoS One*, *20*(9), e0330201. DOI: 10.1371/journal.pone.0330201

Sahani, G. S., Chaudhary, M., & Ghouse, S. M. (2024, October 4). Artificial intelligence and hyper-personalization in travel platforms. In *Advances in Hospitality, Tourism and the Services Industry*. IGI Global., DOI: 10.4018/979-8-3693-5678-4.ch006

Sahut, J.-M., & Laroche, M. (2025). Using artificial intelligence (AI) to enhance customer experience and to develop strategic marketing: An integrative synthesis. *Computers in Human Behavior*, *170*, 108684. DOI: 10.1016/j.chb.2025.108684

Sarioguz, O., & Miser, E. (2024, November 30). Assessing the role of artificial intelligence in enhancing customer personalization: A study of ethical and privacy implications in digital marketing. *International Journal of Science and Research Archive*. DOI: 10.30574/ijsra.2024.13.2.2207

Schnackenberg, A. K., & Tomlinson, E. C. (2016). Organizational transparency: A new perspective on managing trust in organization-stakeholder relationships. *Journal of Management*, *42*(7), 1784–1810. DOI: 10.1177/0149206314525202

Seaton, S. S. (2010). *Measuring Return on Marketing Investment in Non-Professional Sports Event Organizations* [University of Southern Queensland]. https://research.usq.edu.au/item/q0x84/measuring-return-on-marketing-investment-in-non-professional-sports-event-organisations

Seele, P., Dierksmeier, C., Hofstetter, R., & Schultz, M. D. (2021). Mapping the Ethicality of Algorithmic Pricing: A Review of Dynamic and Personalized Pricing. *Journal of Business Ethics*, *170*(4), 697–719. DOI: 10.1007/s10551-019-04371-w

Sekti, B. A. (2025). Information Security Awareness. In *User-Centric Cybersecurity Implications for Sustainable Digital Transformation* (pp. 111–145). DOI: 10.4018/979-8-3373-3171-3.ch004

Semwal, R., Tripathi, N., Tyagi, P. K., & Nadda, V. (2024). AI-Infused Strategies for Customer Retention. In *Integrating AI-Driven Technologies Into Service Marketing* (pp. 115–134). IGI Global Scientific Publishing. DOI: 10.4018/979-8-3693-7122-0.ch007

Sen, A. (2022). Are data markets a solution to big tech market power? A competitive analysis. *Journal of Government and Economics*, *7*, 100052. https://doi.org/https://doi.org/10.1016/j.jge.2022.100052. DOI: 10.1016/j.jge.2022.100052

Shankar, V. (2018). How Artificial Intelligence (AI) is Reshaping Retailing. *Journal of Retailing*, *94*(4), vi–xi. DOI: 10.1016/S0022-4359(18)30076-9

Shin, D. (2021). The effects of explainability and transparency on trust in AI. *Computers in Human Behavior*, *113*, 106394.

Shin, Y., Noone, B. M., & Robson, S. K. (2020). An exploration of the effects of photograph content, photograph source, and price on consumers' online travel booking intentions. *Journal of Travel Research*, *59*(1), 120–139. DOI: 10.1177/0047287518817399

Shmueli, G., & Koppius, O. R. (2011). Predictive Analytics in Information Systems Research1. *Management Information Systems Quarterly*, *35*(3), 553–572. DOI: 10.2307/23042796

Silaban, P. H., Chen, W. K., Eunike, I. J., & Silalahi, A. D. K. (2023). Traditional restaurant managers' use of sensory marketing to maintain customer satisfaction: Findings from PLS-SEM and fsQCA. *Cogent Business & Management*, *10*(1), 2196788. DOI: 10.1080/23311975.2023.2196788

Silva, NDBSG e. (2023). *The Role of Social Networks in the Digital Sports Marketing of Football Clubs—The Case of Sporting Clube de Portugal* [Instituto Superior de Gestão]. https://comum.rcaap.pt/bitstream/10400.26/45829/1/Dissertacao%20MSc%20Marketing_%20Nuno%20Guerra%20e%20Silva_impressa.pdf

Simonetti, A., & Bigne, E. (2022). How visual attention to social media cues impacts visit intention and liking expectation for restaurants. *International Journal of Contemporary Hospitality Management*, *34*(6), 2049–2070. DOI: 10.1108/IJCHM-09-2021-1091

Singh, P., & Farhan, M. (2024, July 26). Personalization at scale. In *Advances in Marketing, Customer Relationship Management, and E-Services*. IGI Global. DOI: 10.4018/979-8-3693-7122-0.ch025

Smith, A. C., Stavros, C., Skinner, J., Geurin, A. N., & Burch, L. M. (2024). *Introduction to Sport Marketing* (3rd ed.). Routledge., DOI: 10.4324/9781003391319

Snyder, H. (2019). Literature review as a research methodology: An overview and guidelines. *Journal of Business Research*, *104*(1), 333–339. DOI: 10.1016/j.jbusres.2019.07.039

Soares, L. F. S. (2023). *Tribal Consumption: An Analysis of the Role of Digital Strategies in the Context of a Sports Crisis—The Case of Sporting Clube de Portugal* [ISCAP - Instituto Superior de Contabilidade e Administração do Porto]. http://hdl.handle.net/10400.22/23578

Sohaib, M., Safeer, A. A., & Majeed, A. (2025). Social media food photos and brand engagement: Role of content source, authenticity, brand stereotypes and online community influence. *Journal of Hospitality and Tourism Technology*, •••, 1–20. DOI: 10.1108/JHTT-05-2025-0388

Solove, D. J. (2021). *Understanding privacy* (2nd ed.). Harvard University Press.

Song, R., Moon, S., Chen, H., & Houston, M. B. (2017). When marketing strategy meets culture: The role of culture in product evaluations. *Journal of the Academy of Marketing Science*, *46*(3), 384–402. DOI: 10.1007/s11747-017-0525-x

Soraj Hongladarom, S., & Shoshana Zuboff. (2023). The age of surveillance capitalism: The fight for a human future at the new frontier of power. *AI & Society*, *38*(6), 2359–2361. DOI: 10.1007/s00146-020-01100-0

Spann, M., Bertini, M., Koenigsberg, O., Zeithammer, R., Aparicio, D., Chen, Y., . . . Yoo, H. (2025). Algorithmic pricing: Implications for marketing strategy and regulation. *International Journal of Research in Marketing*. https://doi.org/https://doi.org/10.1016/j.ijresmar.2025.05.001

Srnicek, N. (2017). *Platform capitalism.* Polity Press.

Srnicek, N. (2017). *Platform Capitalism.* Polity Press.

Stevens, J., Gleim, M., & Waites, S. (2024). Experience identification: Connecting online engagement to offline loyalty. *Journal of Services Marketing, 38*(8), 1012–1029. Advance online publication. DOI: 10.1108/JSM-12-2023-0466

Stokburger-Sauer, N., Bauer, H., & Wannow, S. (2008). Brand Image and Fan Loyalty in Professional Team Sport: A Refined Model and Empirical Assessment. *Journal of Sport Management, 22*(2), 205–226. DOI: 10.1123/jsm.22.2.205

Suárez, MAV, León López, LW, León López, OD, & León Vélez, RM (2023). Impact of digital communication strategies for the promotion of healthy sporting activities and integration. *RECIMUNDO, 7* (2), 171–183. https://doi.org/.(2).jun.2023.171 -183DOI: 10.26820/recimundo/7

Sui, M., Hawkins, I., & Wang, R. (2023). When falsehood wins? Varied effects of sensational elements on users' engagement with real and fake posts. *Computers in Human Behavior, 142*, 107654. DOI: 10.1016/j.chb.2023.107654

Sundar, S. M., Bopp-Bertenbreiter, V., Ziegler, D., Kosuru, R. K., Knecht, C., Pfleging, B., & Widlroither, H. (2022). PersonalAIzation-Exploring concepts and guidelines for AI-driven personalization of in-car HMIs in fully automated vehicles. *Human Factors in Transportation, 60*, 423–431.

Sun, J., & Chi, T. (2019). Investigating the adoption of apparel m-commerce in the US market. *International Journal of Clothing Science and Technology, 31*(4), 544-563.Bleier, A., & Eisenbeiss, M. (2015). The importance of trust for personalized online advertising. *Journal of Retailing, 91*(3), 390–409.

Sun, J., & Si, J. (2025). When AI chatbots ask for donations: The construal level contingency of AI persuasion effectiveness in charity human–chatbot interaction. *Journal of Theoretical and Applied Electronic Commerce Research, 20*(4), 341. DOI: 10.3390/jtaer20040341

Susser, D., Roessler, B., & Nissenbaum, H. (2019). Online manipulation: Hidden influences in a digital world. *Geo. L. Tech. Rev., 4*, 1.

Susser, D., Roessler, B., & Nissenbaum, H. (2021). Online manipulation: Hidden influences in a digital world. *Georgetown Law Technology Review, 4*(1), 1–45.

Sutton, W. A., McDonald, M. A., Milne, G. R., & Cimperman, J. (1997). Creating And Fostering Fan Identification In Professional Sports. *Sport Marketing Quarterly, 6*(1), 15–22. DOI: 10.1177/106169349700600104

Szakály, O., Pinke-Sziva, I., & Smith, M. K. (2025). The impact of digital influencers on attitude and intent to consume and travel in restaurant choice–evidences from Hungary. *British Food Journal, 127*(9), 3498–3511. DOI: 10.1108/BFJ-11-2024-1186

Talukder, M. B., Lina, F. Y., Kumar, S., & Khan, M. R. (2024). Data-Driven Personalization in the Sharing Economy. In *Building Climate Neutral Economies Through Digital Business and Green Skills* (pp. 277–300). IGI Global Scientific Publishing. DOI: 10.4018/979-8-3693-5673-9.ch012

Tam, J., Porter, E. K., & Lee, U. J. (2022). Examination of Information and Misinformation about Urinary Tract Infections on TikTok and YouTube. *Urology, 168*, 35–40. Advance online publication. DOI: 10.1016/j.urology.2022.06.030 PMID: 35809700

Teixeira, A. R. M. (2017). *Tribal Marketing: The Behavior of the Sports Consumer: The Case of Sporting Clube de Portugal* [University of Coimbra]. https://estudogeral.uc.pt/bitstream/10316/82203/1/Marketing%20Tribal%20SCP.pdf

Tellis, G. J., MacInnis, D. J., Tirunillai, S., & Zhang, Y. (2019). What drives virality (sharing) of online digital content? The critical role of information, emotion, and brand prominence. *Journal of Marketing, 83*(4), 1–20. DOI: 10.1177/0022242919841034

Tenreiro, F. (June 26, 2014). *The National Sport Model Ran Out Years Ago*. https://www.publico.pt/2014/06/26/desporto/noticia/o-modelo-do-desporto-nacional-esgotouse-ha-anos-1660460

Thandayuthapani, S., Thirumoorthi, P., Elantheraiyan, P., ... (2024, July 26). An exploration of consumer engagement strategies through the lens of artificial intelligence in marketing personalization. In *Advances in Marketing, Customer Relationship Management, and E-Services*. IGI Global. DOI: 10.4018/979-8-3693-7122-0.ch008

Theodoridis, P. K., & Gkikas, D. C. (2025). Maximizing Social Media User Engagement Through Predictive Analytics in Retail Tourism: Identifying Key Performance Indicators That Trigger User Interactions. *Applied Sciences (Basel, Switzerland), 15*(21), 11720. Advance online publication. DOI: 10.3390/app152111720

Thomas, J., & Harden, A. (2008). Methods for the thematic synthesis of qualitative research in systematic reviews. *BMC Medical Research Methodology, 8*(1), 45. DOI: 10.1186/1471-2288-8-45 PMID: 18616818

Thompson, F. M., & Chmura, T. (2015). Loyalty programs in emerging and developed markets: The impact of cultural values on loyalty program choice. *Journal of International Marketing, 23*(3), 87–103. DOI: 10.1509/jim.14.0125

Thongmak, M. (2024). Twitter content strategies to maximize engagement: The case of Thai Banks. *Computers in Human Behavior, 152*, 108081. DOI: 10.1016/j.chb.2023.108081

Ting, L., & Ahn, J. (2026). The effects of a multidimensional parasocial relationship with an influencer on customer behavioral intention in restaurants. *Journal of Hospitality and Tourism Technology*, •••, 1–20. DOI: 10.1108/JHTT-02-2025-0126

Tinkler, A. (2023, December 1). AI, marketing technology and personalization at scale. *Journal of AI Robotics & Workplace Automation*. DOI: 10.69554/CAEO7832

Toader, D.-C., Boca, G., Toader, R., Măcelaru, M., Toader, C., Ighian, D., & Rădulescu, A. T. (2020). The effect of social presence and chatbot errors on trust. *Sustainability (Basel), 12*(1), 256. DOI: 10.3390/su12010256

Torraco, R. J. (2005). Writing Integrative Literature Reviews: Guidelines and Examples. *Human Resource Development Review, 4*(3), 356–367. DOI: 10.1177/1534484305278283

Tranfield, D., Denyer, D., & Smart, P. (2003). Towards a Methodology for Developing Evidence-Informed Management Knowledge by Means of Systematic Review. *British Journal of Management, 14*(3), 207–222. DOI: 10.1111/1467-8551.00375

Trkulja, Ž. M., Primorac, D., & Martinčević, I. (2024). The Influence of Consumer Motivation on Engagement with Sports Club Social Media: An Intrinsic and Extrinsic Analysis. *Business Systems Research Journal, 15*(1), 91–109. DOI: 10.2478/bsrj-2024-0005

Truong, T. A., Piscarac, D., Kang, S., & Yoo, S. C. (2025). Virtual culinary influence: Investigating the impact of food vlogs on viewer attitudes and restaurant visit intentions. *Information (Basel), 16*(1), 44. Advance online publication. DOI: 10.3390/info16010044

Tsai, W.-H. S., & Men, L. R. (2013). Motivations and Antecedents of Consumer Engagement With Brand Pages on Social Networking Sites. *Journal of Interactive Advertising, 13*(2), 76–87. DOI: 10.1080/15252019.2013.826549

Tufekci, Z. (2015). Algorithmic harms beyond Facebook and Google: Emergent challenges of computational agency. *Colo. Tech. LJ, 13*, 203.

Turow, J. (2017). *The aisles have eyes*. Yale University Press.

Ubah, O., & Malcourant, E. (2018). *Governance within sports organizations: Exploring how non-professional sports organizations motivate and retain their volunteers*. [Louvain School of Management]. http://hdl.handle.net/2078.1/thesis:13378

Vaidhyanathan, S. (2018). *Antisocial media.* Oxford University Press.

Vakratsas, D., & Ambler, T. (1999). How Advertising Works: What Do We Really Know? *Journal of Marketing, 63*(1), 26–43. DOI: 10.1177/002224299906300103

Van Dijck, J., de Winkel, T., & Schäfer, M. T. (2023). Deplatformization and the governance of the platform ecosystem. *New Media & Society, 25*(12), 3438–3454. DOI: 10.1177/14614448211045662

Van Noort, G., Voorveld, H. A. M., & Strycharz, J. (2024). Persuasion knowledge in algorithmic environments. *Journal of Interactive Marketing, 65*, 1–15.

Vebrianti, R., Aras, M., Putri, M. S. S., & Swandewi, I. A. (2025). AI chatbots in e-commerce: Enhancing customer engagement, satisfaction and loyalty. *PaperASIA, 41*(2b), 248–260. DOI: 10.59953/paperasia.v41i2b.445

Venkateswaran, P. S., Dominic, M. L., Agarwal, S., Oberai, H., Anand, I., & Rajest, S. S. (2024). The role of artificial intelligence (AI) in enhancing marketing and customer loyalty. In *Data-driven intelligent business sustainability* (pp. 32–47). IGI Global Scientific Publishing.

Vetrivel, S. C., Arun, V. P., Saravanan, T. P., & Maheswari, R. (2024). Harnessing AI for next-generation service marketing. In *Integrating AI-driven technologies into service marketing* (pp. 265–298). IGI Global Scientific Publishing. DOI: 10.4018/979-8-3693-7122-0.ch015

Vieira, C. B. (2017). *Affectivity and consumer behavior in sports contexts: The case of football fans in Portugal.* [University of Minho]. https://repositorium.sdum.uminho.pt/bitstream/1822/49466/1/Carla%20Barbosa%20Vieira.pdf

Wang, J. J., Lalwani, A. K., & DelVecchio, D. (2022). The impact of power distance belief on consumers' brand preferences. *International Journal of Research in Marketing, 39*(3), 804–823. DOI: 10.1016/j.ijresmar.2021.11.004

Wang, R., & Chan-Olmsted, S. (2024). Brand communication through social media influencers: Trust building and trust transfer mechanisms. *International Journal of Business Communication, 23294884241255911*, 23294884241255911. Advance online publication. DOI: 10.1177/23294884241255911

Wang, X., Lin, X., & Shao, B. (2024). Security and privacy protection in developing ethical AI: A mixed-methods study from a marketing employee perspective. *Journal of Business Ethics, 200*(2), 373–392. DOI: 10.1007/s10551-024-05894-7

Wang, X., Zhu, B., Guo, Q., Wang, W., & Zhao, R. (2023). Designing mindfulness information for interaction in social media: The role of information framing, health risk perception and lay theories of health. *Frontiers in Psychology*, *13*, 1041016. DOI: 10.3389/fpsyg.2022.1041016 PMID: 36687971

Wang, Y., Sauka, K., & Situmeang, F. B. I. (2025). Anthropomorphism and transparency interplay on consumer behaviour in generative AI-driven marketing communication. *Journal of Consumer Marketing*, *42*(4), 512–536. DOI: 10.1108/JCM-04-2024-6806

Wassel, B. (2024, February 1). Starbucks to capitalize on record loyalty membership with app improvements. *Marketing Dive*. https://www.marketingdive.com/news/starbucks-rewards-loyalty-q3-personalization/706322/

Webster, J., & Watson, R. T. (2002). Analyzing the Past to Prepare for the Future: Writing a Literature Review. *Management Information Systems Quarterly*, *26*(2), xiii–xxiii. DOI: 10.2307/4132319

Wedel, M., & Kannan, P. K. (2016). Marketing Analytics for Data-Rich Environments. *Journal of Marketing*, *80*(6), 97–121. DOI: 10.1509/jm.15.0413

Wellman, M. L., Stoldt, R., Tully, M., & Ekdale, B. (2020). Ethics of Authenticity: Social Media Influencers and the Production of Sponsored Content. *Journal of Media Ethics*, *35*(2), 68–82. DOI: 10.1080/23736992.2020.1736078

Whetten, D. A. (1989). What Constitutes a Theoretical Contribution? *Academy of Management Review*, *14*(4), 490. DOI: 10.2307/258554

Whittemore, R., & Knafl, K. (2005). The integrative review: Updated methodology. *Journal of Advanced Nursing*, *52*(5), 546–553. DOI: 10.1111/j.1365-2648.2005.03621.x PMID: 16268861

Wicker, P., & Breuer, C. (2012). Understanding the importance of organizational resources to reduce organizational problems: Evidence from nonprofit sport clubs in Germany. *Voluntas, 17* (2), 24 (461-484). DOI: 10.1007/s11266-012-9272-2

Wijethilak, H. P. G. D., Singh, S. K., & Dhand, S. (2024, November 15). AI for personalizing customer interactions. In *Advances in Marketing, Customer Relationship Management, and E-Services*. IGI Global. DOI: 10.4018/979-8-3373-0219-5.ch011

Xu, H., Dinev, T., Smith, J., & Hart, P. (2011). Information privacy concerns: Linking individual perceptions with institutional privacy assurances. *Journal of the Association for Information Systems*, *12*(12), 1. DOI: 10.17705/1jais.00281

XXIV Portuguese Government. (November 22, 2024). *Sport "promotes well-being and values of life in society"*. Portuguese Republic - XXIV Government. https://www.portugal.gov.pt/pt/gc24/comunicacao/noticia?i=desporto-promove-bem-estar-e-valores-da-vida-em-sociedade

Yarış, A., & Aykol, Ş. (2021). The impact of social media use on restaurant choice. *Anatolia, 33*(3), 310–322. DOI: 10.1080/13032917.2021.1931379

Yarkin, Z., Dogan, E., & Kiliç, Ç. (2024). Content Brand Journalism Impact on Consumption and Consumer Behavior of «Big Five» Football Clubs' Digital Products. *Revista de Cercetare si Interventie Sociala, 85*(85), 15. DOI: 10.33788/rcis.85.10

Ye, H., Law, R., Fong, L. H. N., & Li, N. (2026). How do interactive online travel agencies affect customers' reuse intention? *International Journal of Hospitality Management, 133*, 104497. DOI: 10.1016/j.ijhm.2025.104497

Yin, R. K. (2018). *Case study research and applications* (6th ed.). Sage.

Young, B., Takeda, H., & Cuellar, M. (2011). Investigating the Impact of Offline Events on Group Development in an Online Sports, Proceedings of the Southern Association for Information Systems Conference Community, Atlanta, GA, USA, March 25th-26*th,* 206-211.

Youn, S., & Jin, S. V. (2021). 'In A.I. we trust?' The effects of parasocial interaction and technopian versus luddite ideological views on chatbot-based customer relationship management in the emerging 'feeling economy'. *Computers in Human Behavior, 119*, 106721. DOI: 10.1016/j.chb.2021.106721

Yousefinaghani, S., Dara, R., Wang, A., MacKay, M., Papadopoulos, A., & Sharif, S. (2023). Credibility of vaccine-related content on Twitter during the COVID-19 pandemic. *PLOS Global Public Health, 3*(7), e0001385–e0001385. DOI: 10.1371/journal.pgph.0001385 PMID: 37467276

Yu, R., Feng, J., Wang, K., Yang, L., & Feng, J. (2024). Who are you talking to? How chatbot identity disclosure affects service satisfaction. *Journal of Travel & Tourism Marketing, 41*(8), 1090–1106. DOI: 10.1080/10548408.2024.2369755

Yu, Z., Klongthong, W., Thavorn, J., & Ngamkroeckjoti, C. (2021). Understanding rural Chinese consumers' behavior: A stimulus–organism–response (SOR) perspective on Huawei's brand loyalty in China. *Cogent Business & Management, 8*(1), 1880679. DOI: 10.1080/23311975.2021.1880679

Zhang, J. N., Lu, X. Y., Zheng, W. Q., & Wang, X. L. (2024). It's better than nothing: The influence of service failures on user reusage intention in AI chatbot. *Electronic Commerce Research and Applications*, *67*, 101421. DOI: 10.1016/j.elerap.2024.101421

Zhang, R., Yu, Z., & Yao, W. (2024). Navigating the complexities of online opinion formation: An insight into consumer cognitive heuristics. *Journal of Retailing and Consumer Services*, *81*, 103966. DOI: 10.1016/j.jretconser.2024.103966

Zhang, Z., & Li, W. (2022). Customer engagement around cultural and creative products: The role of social identity. *Frontiers in Psychology*, *13*, 874851. Advance online publication. DOI: 10.3389/fpsyg.2022.874851 PMID: 35548532

Zhong, B. (2023). Going beyond fact-checking to fight health misinformation: A multi-level analysis of the Twitter response to health news stories. *International Journal of Information Management*, *70*, 102626. DOI: 10.1016/j.ijinfomgt.2023.102626

Zniva, R., Weitzl, W. J., & Lindmoser, C. (2023). Be constantly different! How to manage influencer authenticity. *Electronic Commerce Research*, *23*(3), 1485–1514. DOI: 10.1007/s10660-022-09653-6

Zuboff, S. (2019). *The age of surveillance capitalism*. PublicAffairs.

Zuboff, S. (2019). *The age of surveillance capitalism: The fight for a human future at the new frontier of power, edn*. PublicAffairs.

About the Contributors

Paula Pinheiro holds a Ph.D. in Marketing from the University of Aveiro, Portugal. She is Adjunct Professor of Marketing at the Polytechnic of Viseu (ESTGV) and Invited Professor at the University of Aveiro (ISCA-UA). Her teaching covers undergraduate and postgraduate courses in consumer behavior, marketing research, branding, negotiation, and digital marketing. Her research interests include consumer behavior, digital transformation, sustainable marketing, social innovation, and international business. She has authored and co-authored publications in peer-reviewed journals, conference proceedings, and edited volumes, and is actively engaged in international collaborations such as Collaborative Online International Learning (COIL) projects. In addition, she supervises Master's dissertations and undergraduate research projects.

Sara Santos holds a PhD in Management and Business studies by University of Porto and is currently Assistant Professor at Universidade Aberta (Portugal). Her research focuses on Digital Marketing, Social Media Marketing; Advertising; Communication; Press and Public Relations. She worked as invited professor between 2010 and 2020 at several Higher Education Institutions in Portugal, as ISCA-Universidade de Aveiro, IPC, IPB, ISPAB and IPV.

***

Ranjithkumar A is currently serving as an Assistant Professor of Political Science at the School of Law, Vel Tech University, Avadi, Chennai, Tamil Nadu. With a distinguished academic and professional career, he holds a Ph.D. in Politics and International Studies from Pondicherry University, a Master of Population Studies (MPS) from the International Institute for Population Sciences, Mumbai, and an M.A. in Development Administration from Gandhigram Rural Institute – Deemed University. He has also completed a Postgraduate Diploma in Industrial Relations and Labour Law (PGDIR & LL) from Pondicherry University and a B.P.Ed. from Vinayaka Missions University, Salem. Dr. Ranjithkumar has qualified the National Eligibility Test (NET) for Assistant Professor in Human Rights and Duties, Political Science, and Public Administration, conducted by the University Grants Commission (UGC), and was awarded the Dr. S. Radhakrishnan Postdoctoral Fellowship in Humanities and Social Sciences for the year 2014-15. His professional experience includes roles as an Assistant Professor at DLR Arts and Science College, Arcot, and Gandhigram Rural Institute, as well as research positions at Alagappa University, the National Law School of India University, and the Institute of Grassroots Governance. Dr. Ranjithkumar's research focuses on the Indian Political System, Local Government, Political Thought and Theories, Dalit Studies, and Development Administration. He has published over 35 research papers in leading journals and authored/edited 10 books on topics such as social justice, gender, and caste. He has received an International Travel Grant from the Indian Council of Social Science Research (ICSSR) to participate in the "Democratization and Autocratization: IPSA 75th Anniversary Conference" in Lisbon, Portugal, and Financial Assistance from ICSSR, Hyderabad, for organizing a National Conference on "Empowering Vulnerable Communities: Strategies for Inclusive Social Development." Dr. Ranjithkumar is an active member of professional bodies such as the International Political Science Association (IPSA) and the Indian Political Science Association, and he has organized over 10 international webinars and seminars. His areas of interest include Indian politics, local governance, Dalit studies, gender studies, and human rights.

Ayushi Agrawal is a Research Scholar at the School of Business and Management, Christ University, Bangalore. Her academic pursuits focus on marketing, consumer behaviour, service marketing, and digital marketing. She integrates multidisciplinary perspectives to deepen insights into branding and digital platforms. With a strong commitment to scholarly rigor, she is well-positioned to make significant contributions to the evolving field of digital ecosystems and marketing strategy.

Vinsens Aji Pamungkas is an emerging researcher affiliated with the Department of Computer Science, Esa Unggul University. His academic interests include Artificial Intelligence, Business Information Systems, Human-Technology Interaction, Social Networking, and Risk Management. Despite being an undergraduate student, he has actively engaged in collaborative research, academic writing, and scientific discussions in technology-related disciplines. He is passionate about bridging the gap between digital innovation and human behavior in organizational and societal contexts. His goal is to contribute to impactful, interdisciplinary knowledge through research and academic publishing.

Suzanne Amaro has a PhD in Marketing and Strategy and is a coordinating professor at the Management Department of the School of Management and Technology of the Polytechnic Institute of Viseu in Portugal. Her current research interests include consumer behaviour, e-Tourism and PLS. She has published articles on these topics in top-tier journals. She is a member of NECE-Research Centre for Business Sciences, CISED - Centre for Research in Digital Services research unit and a member of CITUR – Centre for Tourism Research, Development and Innovation.

Deepika Ameta is currently serving as an Assistant Professor at the International Institute of Management & Human Resource Development (Women). She earned her Ph.D. in Computer Science from Career Point University, Kota, in 2021. With more than five years of teaching experience, she has established herself as a committed and effective educator. Dr. Ameta has actively participated in numerous seminars, workshops, and academic conferences, reflecting her continuous engagement with professional development. She has also presented research papers at several national and international conferences, thereby contributing to the advancement of knowledge in the field of computer science.

Lara Mendes Bacalhau has a PhD in Management - specialization in Marketing and Strategy (FEP- UP), with a Master of Data Analysis and Decision Support Systems (FEP- UP) and two Bachelor's of Business Management (ISCAC- IPC) and Mathematics - Teaching branch (FCTUC- UC). She has additional training, including an MBA in Digital Marketing and a postgraduate course in Information Technology and Multimedia Communication. Professor in Marketing, Business Management, Accounting, and Taxation at ISCAC. She has also taught at ESTGV- IPV, IEFP, and ISLA Santarém. She was a member of the bachelor's degree in Marketing and International Business and is currently the director of this course and a member of the corresponding master's degree. She has coordinated workshops to prepare for the Certified Accountants' Exam. She is a researcher in Marketing (Branding, Digital Marketing, E- Commerce, and Relationship Marketing) and Business Management. She is a reviewer and co-author of scientific publications and participates in projects.

Pankaj Bhambri is an Associate Professor in the Department of Information Technology at Guru Nanak Dev Engineering College, Ludhiana, with over twenty-one years of teaching and research experience. He holds a Ph.D. in Computer Science and Engineering from I.K.G. Punjab Technical University, Jalandhar, and is currently pursuing a Post Doctorate Fellowship at Lincoln University College, Malaysia. Recognized as a Top 2% Scientist by Stanford University and Elsevier in 2025, his research focuses on areas including machine learning, AI-driven digital twins, blockchain, and sustainable technologies. He has an extensive publication record in Scopus-indexed books and journals and has guided several Ph.D. candidates to completion.

Miguel Cachulo Pereira is an Assistant Professor at the University of Aveiro (ISCA) and researcher at the CEOS.PP-Coimbra and GOVCOPP research centres, Miguel Cachulo Pereira holds the title of Specialist in Marketing from the University of Aveiro, where he also completed his Bachelor's and Master's degrees in Management, specialising in Marketing and International Business. His research focuses on MarTech and Digital Marketing, with scientific publications on Artificial Intelligence, branded apps, social media, and other marketing techniques or technologies. He combines his academic profile with over 17 years of professional experience in digital marketing, communication, and retail.

Niken Rahma Diasri is an academic and practitioner in the field of Information Systems with a strong interest in data-driven technologies for decision-making and digital transformation. Her research interests include Data Science, Artificial Intelligence (AI), Machine Learning, and Business Intelligence, with a focus on data analytics, predictive modeling, intelligent systems, and the development of business-oriented data solutions that integrate technology, data, and organizational needs.

Piali Haldar earned her MBA from the Institute of Rural Management Anand and completed her PhD at Birla Institute of Technology, Mesra. Her core areas of specialization include rural marketing, rural development, branding strategy, and consumer behaviour. With over 20 years of experience in academia and research, she has published extensively in renowned journals listed in ABDC and Scopus. She has authored one textbook on Marketing and edited three academic books. Dr. Haldar has presented her research at numerous national and international conferences and has contributed more than 50 papers to reputed journals, edited volumes, and conference proceedings.

Carla Henriques holds a PhD in Applied Mathematics and has developed research work in statistics and data modelling. She has several papers published in International scientific journals, some of them resulting from her collaboration with researchers of different areas, such as tourism, marketing, health, finance, among others. She is a professor at the Polytechnic Institute of Viseu, Portugal, and member of the Centre for Mathematics of the University of Coimbra.

Pratiksha Jagadale is a dedicated student at SaiBalaji International Institute of Management Sciences (SBIIMS), Pune, where she is pursuing her studies in management. She demonstrates a strong interest in continuous learning, professional development, and the practical application of contemporary business practices. Pratiksha is keen on developing analytical, leadership, and problem-solving skills that are essential in today's dynamic business environment, and she actively seeks opportunities to enhance her academic and professional growth.

Rishikaysh Kaakandikar boasts an exceptional academic journey, spanning over 12 years of dedicated teaching and a year of valuable industrial experience, and currently holds the esteemed position of Associate Professor at SaiBalaji Education Society's SaiBalaji International Institute of Management Sciences in Pune. His scholarly contributions shine brightly, encompassing a remarkable portfolio of over 40 research papers in prestigious journals. A sought-after intellectual resource, He has contributed substantially to academia through guest lectures, seminars, workshops, and conferences at esteemed institutions across India. His insights have enriched the academic community and stimulated engaging discussions on various facets of his field. He is a prominent finance columnist for leading newspapers in Maharashtra, including Sakal, Lokmat, Punyannagari, and Prabhat.

Rahul Khurana is an Assistant Professor at Christ University, NCR Campus, in the School of Business and Management. He holds a PhD in Management (OB & HR) from IIT Roorkee and is a recipient of the prestigious UGC Junior Research Fellowship (JRF). His teaching interests include HR Analytics, Strategic HRM, Business Analytics, and Artificial Intelligence & Machine Learning for Managers. Known for his engaging pedagogy, he incorporates case-based learning, simulations, and data tools to create impactful classroom experiences. Dr Khurana is an active researcher with publications in reputed journals and edited volumes, and has presented his work at multiple international conferences. His research explores themes such as psychological well-being, organisational fit, and digital transformation, using advanced methods like SEM and bibliometrics.

Desfara Angelita Malau is an undergraduate student in the Pharmacy Department, Faculty of Health Sciences. She has a strong interest in research, particularly in the fields of health and pharmaceuticals. She is also actively open to and interested in research collaborations that foster interdisciplinary insights. Beyond her primary field, she explores topics related to human interaction, psychology, communication, and the arts, reflecting a broad and integrative perspective in her academic pursuits.

Dev Kumar Mandal currently serves as an Assistant Professor in the Department of Management at Brainware University, Kolkata. Before this, he worked at ICRA Analytics Ltd and Shriram Finance Ltd. He holds an MBA in Finance and a

Bachelor of Commerce degree from Vidyasagar University. Additionally, he has successfully cleared the UGC NET and WB SET examinations in Management.

Sachin Pande is an Associate Professor of Marketing with over 27 years of global corporate experience. He holds an MBA in Marketing and a Diploma in Computer Science. He has also completed courses in blockchain technology and earned a Six Sigma Green Belt from Samsung India. Sachin has worked with global brands like Wizcraft, Coca-Cola, Samsung, and PAYBACK. His expertise spans consumer marketing, go-to-market strategies, and retail loyalty programs. He brings industry knowledge to academia, integrating real-world insights into the classroom. His areas of focus include marketing personalization, consumer loyalty, and startup strategies. He also explores trends in generative AI, omnichannel marketing, and personalized consumer experiences. Sachin's contributions to academia are enriched by his extensive corporate background.

Rachna Rana is an Associate Professor in the Department of Computer Science and Engineering at Ludhiana Group of Colleges, Ludhiana with over fifteen years of teaching and research experience. Her research focuses on areas including machine learning, wireless sensor networks, and network security. She has an extensive publication record in Scopus-indexed books.

Jorge Remondes holds a PhD in Communication from the University of Vigo. MBA in Commercial Management and Marketing. Professor of Marketing at ISCAP/PP. Founder and Editor-in-Chief of the International Journal of Marketing, Communication and New Media, Web of Science Journal & JCR. Author and co-author of more than two dozen books on Marketing, Communication and Management. Author and co-author of scientific articles indexed in Scopus and Web of Science in the areas of Marketing, Communication and Digital. Professor in higher education since 2005. Director of the Postgraduate Course in Digital Content Marketing & Analytics at Porto Executive Academy, Business School of the Polytechnic of Porto. Trainer in short courses, in-company training and postgraduate courses. He has experience as a trainer and marketing consultant, with a total of over 13,000 hours of consulting and executive training. He was a full-time director and manager of companies in national and multinational economic groups for 12 years. He is an honorary member of the European Higher Council for Doctorates and Honorary Doctorates.

Binastya Anggara Sekti has been a lecturer at the Faculty of Computer Science, Esa Unggul University, Jakarta, since 2016. He is actively involved in the Artificial Intelligence and Information Security Study Group. He holds a Bachelor's degree in Informatics Engineering from the Bandung Institute of Technology and a Master's degree in Information Systems Management from Trisakti University, Jakarta. Prior to entering academia, he accumulated over 25 years of professional experience as an IT practitioner in various companies across Jakarta. His work focused on developing data centers for internet service providers and delivering IT solutions for the manufacturing and oil & gas sectors. His research interests include artificial intelligence, cybersecurity, and the development of IT infrastructure.

Index

E

H

I

M

N

P

www.ingramcontent.com/pod-product-compliance
Lightning Source LLC
LaVergne TN
LVHW062325300926
849161LV00007B/1584